Challengers to Duopoly

Challengers to Duopoly

*Why Third Parties Matter
in American Two-Party Politics*

J. David Gillespie

The University of South Carolina Press

Some of the material in this book was previously included in *Politics at the Periphery: Third Parties in Two-Party America,* published by the University of South Carolina Press, 1993
This revised edition published by the University of South Carolina Press
Columbia, South Carolina 29208

www.sc.edu/uscpress

Manufactured in the United States of America

21 20 19 18 17 16 15 14 13 12   10 9 8 7 6 5 4 3 2 1

Library of Congress Cataloging-in-Publication Data

Gillespie, J. David, 1944–
    Challengers to duopoly : why third parties matter in American two-party politics /
J. David Gillespie. — 1st ed.
        p. cm.
    Includes bibliographical references and index.
    ISBN 978-1-61117-013-9 (hardback) — ISBN 978-1-61117-014-6 (pbk)
    1. Third parties (United States politics)—History. 2. Political participation—
United States—History. 3. United States—Politics and government. I. Title.
    JK2261G55 2012
    324.273—dc23
                                                                    2011046340

Contents

Illustrations

Figures

Tables

Preface

Two roads diverged in a wood, and I—
I took the one less traveled by.

Robert Frost, "The Road Not Taken"

You are entitled to know something about my approach to the topic of this book. Paraphrasing words from a chilling query from the McCarthy era, I am not now, nor have I ever been, a member of any third political party. I am interested in them all. I have been since 1967, when, as a young graduate student at Wake Forest University, I attended a university-sponsored symposium on alternative politics. Two of the speakers there were unforgettable.

Norman Thomas, then eighty-two, had carried the presidential standard of his Socialist Party in six consecutive elections from 1928 through 1948. Thomas had served as a kind of "left-wing conscience" during the Great Depression. Several of his party's platform planks—Social Security among them—had found their way into public policy during the New Deal era.

George Lincoln Rockwell, the founder and commander of the American Nazi Party, provoked a hostile Wake Forest audience with his racist views. Standing in front of him in silent protest was an African American football player waving a large American flag. Months later Rockwell lay dead at age forty-nine, the victim of an assassin's bullet fired by a renegade former member of Rockwell's party.

One of those symposium speeches I found instructive. The other astounded me by its bare-knuckled viciousness. I came away from them both more convinced than ever that a free marketplace of ideas is the surest approach to truth.

Hopes can inspire, but people with the impulse to step beyond major-party bounds, to craft or support third parties, should also be fortified by stiff resolve and a devotion to cause. Those taking this less-traveled road need to know the barriers they will face along the way.

Far more than a naturally evolved two-party system, the American polity has become a *duopoly:* a system in which the electoral route to power has been jointly engineered by Democrats and Republicans to underwrite their hegemony. They have done it by gravely disadvantaging outside challengers.

It is unsurprising that minor-party and independent candidates normally do not win elections. Given the cards that are stacked against them, what is remarkable is that they ever win them at all.

Defenders of the American party system often insist that it facilitates consensus building and promotes stable government. A look at the relationship between the Republican and Democratic parties in government during the Clinton, George W. Bush, and early Obama years may very well lead the examiner to the opposite conclusion: interparty hostility, zero-sum assumptions (save in the common project of keeping the ladder pulled up against those outsiders), and paralysis in the policy process.

Despite the infirmities they bear, third parties do matter. They have mattered over nearly two centuries in the public life of the United States. Many of the nation's most important policies and institutional innovations were third-party ideas—sometimes they were the common currency of many third parties—before either major party dared to embrace them. Among these were abolition, women's suffrage, transparency in government, popular election of senators, and child labor and wages and hours legislation. Third parties were the first to break every single de facto gender, race, and sexual orientation bar on nomination for the highest offices in the land.

Purpose and Organization

I have aimed to provide in one accessible volume a reasonably comprehensive look at third-party movements—from the earliest ones growing up just decades after the nation's birth to those now working as current or incipient challengers to the Republicans and Democrats. Woven into the accounts are stories of some of the men and women who took the initiative to found and lead these minor parties.

Chapter 1 establishes the core premise about duopoly and its impact upon American politics. It also offers poll and electoral data suggesting that some opportunities have opened for third-party and independent challengers over the last twenty-five years.

The many barriers third parties face are presented in chapter 2. Some of these are existential: they are because they are. Others are the invidious arrangements Republicans and Democrats have made for closure and their mutual self-protection. Minor parties are certainly among the losers; so too are the voters and their democratic freedom to choose.

Chapter 3 focuses upon a variety of themes: the nation's party systems and their transformation over time; third-party types; and why third parties matter. The chapter carries the story of the Prohibition Party, the nation's most ancient living minor party.

The Constitution, Green, and Libertarian parties—the leading contemporary national third-party challengers—are featured in chapter 4.

Chapters 5 through 8 present histories of America's national short-lived parties—one of the most important third-party types. Chapter 9 covers a related theme: the "independent" movements launched and led by John Anderson and Ross Perot, and the later initiatives by Perot and others to institutionalize their movement.

Chapter 10 examines the involvement of women, African Americans, and Latinos in third-party movements. It also bears historical case studies of their party-building activities: the National Woman's, Black Panther, and Raza Unida parties.

Continuing doctrinal parties—the Socialists and Communists and the Neo-Nazis—are featured in chapters 11 and 12.

Chapter 13 glimpses state/local significant others: third parties important within the domain of their communities or states but unwilling or unable to extend beyond those territorial bounds.

The concluding chapter 14 provides a brief retrospective of the third-party past, along with some commentary and projection about present and future.

What you read may prod your interest in exploring the topic further. If so, you will find many worthwhile reading choices in the "Suggestions for Further Reading" section at the close of this book.

Acknowledgments

Over many years I have sat and talked with leaders and activists of third parties covering the ideological gamut. Many of these encounters occurred at party headquarters or convention gatherings. I have met Libertarians, Greens, Reform Party folks, and independents outside federal courtrooms where they were gathered to challenge ballot-access or other duopolistic barriers.

Some of my interviewees invited me home to talk. I spent a summer morning in Elmer Benson's rustic Lake Superior cabin listening as the ex-governor told fascinating tales of Depression-era Minnesota farmer-labor politics. The leader of a party revering the memory of Mao Zedong met me in a New York coffee shop. He said he was very sorry we could not go to his home, but his wife had come down with the flu!

Had I been answering instead of questioning, I might well have doubted the questioner's motives and fairness. It amazed me how open and forthcoming most of these people were. Some of the interviews were exciting and challenging. With one exception, maybe two, they all were informative, worthwhile encounters. None of my interviewees asked for editorial oversight of what I would write about them or their parties. I appreciate the willingness of these people, some of them positioned far outside the mainstream, to trust that I would give an honest account.

I am the beneficiary of new relationships of respect, indeed friendship, forged with scores of third-party leaders and candidates countrywide. Among those leaders, let me single out Eugene Platt, Erin McKee, Gregg Jocoy, Mac McCullough, Rob Groce, and Scott West in South Carolina for special thanks.

I treasure the insights of my many university students over the years. I occasionally teach or lead a seminar on third-party politics at the College of Charleston. The students' best thoughts and observations inform and inspire me each time we meet for class. I thank them and the students who have preceded them.

Judi Gillespie, a proficient writer who happens to be my spouse, maintained unending patience and provided priceless support and assistance as I tried out sections of the narrative on her, and together we tediously searched many times for the perfect word. I appreciate her interest and am deeply grateful for all she has done.

Technology has opened a new and widening circle of third-party information sharing and advocacy. *Independent Political Report* (independentpoliticalreport .com), a daily blog, is one of its most fruitful components. I thank Trent Hill, Paulie Cannoli, and others who manage *Independent Political Report* and maintain its quality and value.

Sooner or later any scholar or advocate of third parties will come to know, or know of, Richard Winger. Winger has devoted his professional life to opening electoral processes to third-party and independent candidates and widening the choices available to voters. Winger is an expert on third-party history. No one knows more about ballot access law. Winger has an uncanny knack for sniffing out new duopolistic bills as soon as they appear in legislative hoppers anywhere. Lawyers representing clients seeking ballot access—or fairness in campaign funding or redress of other inequities produced on behalf of the established parties—routinely contact him to enlist his help. Winger maintains an informative blog (ballot-access.org) and produces the monthly *Ballot Access News*. He and his work are cited throughout this book.

The University of South Carolina Press is fortunate to have Karen Beidel, Jonathan Haupt, and Linda Fogle on staff. These very competent, supportive professionals know my gratitude and debt to them in the production and showcasing of this book.

Something new and glittering has recently appeared on the third-party scene. Americans Elect, a resolute, well-financed new movement, is flying high in 2011. Ignored at first, Americans Elect now has captured the notice of influential bloggers and even some elements of more conventional media: an endorsement from Thomas Friedman of the *New York Times* and features on NPR and on *The Colbert Report*. Americans Elect will use new digital technologies to empower citizens to select issues and choose a presidential candidate. It has set out to nominate in 2012 a compelling alternative to the presidential standard-bearers of the ideologically polarized, seemingly gridlocked major parties.

Americans Elect is hard at work cracking ballots. By the end of August 2011, its Web site (americanselect.org) was reporting nearly 2 million petition signatures already collected toward gaining presidential ballot access everywhere for 2012. And breaking new ground, Americans Elect is laying plans for an online convention. The invitation has gone out for any registered American voter to become an online delegate, with a vote in selecting the Americans Elect presidential nominee. Third-party history lives on, and despite the constraints they have to endure, alternative parties continue to offer items of value in the marketplace of ideas.

1

★ ★ ★

Duopoly and Its Challengers

> When the variety and number of political parties increases, the chance
> of oppression, factionalism, and non-critical acceptance of ideas
> decreases.
>
> *James Madison*

> One of the best-kept secrets in American politics is that the two-party
> system has long been brain dead—kept alive by . . . state electoral laws
> that protect the established parties from rivals and federal subsidies and
> so-called campaign reform. The two-party system would collapse in an
> instant if the tubes were pulled and the IV's were cut.
>
> *Political scientist Theodore Lowi*

The American party system is a duopoly, an *enforced* two-party system. For a century and a half, the Democrats and Republicans have dominated and shared the coveted center ring of American party politics. These two major parties fight over many things, but they have long been aware of their shared interest in mutual self-protection, in taking steps to shut out challengers to their exclusive places inside that center ring.

Over the last century, state and federal decision makers—Democrats and Republicans—have enacted and enforced duopolistic measures that stymie, disadvantage, or shut out the electoral initiatives of third parties and independents. The American political system has assumed many characteristics of a party state as a result.

Most Americans speak of their nation's party system as a two-party system. They might be surprised to know that this term was not even coined until 1911. Richard Winger, an expert on election law and a leading advocate for opening the election system to participation by minor parties and independent candidates, points out that the term *two-party system* was devised to mean "a system in which two parties are much larger than all the other parties. It doesn't mean a system in which there are just two parties."[1]

Two-party systems are more compatible with democratic values than are one-party systems. Defenders of two-party systems also contend that they are better than multiparty systems at providing for stable government. If confirmed in fact, that might provide a plausible argument for the legitimacy of a two-party system, provided that the system develops and is sustained by the cultural characteristics of a nation or by institutional practices devised without the intention to discriminate. America's two-party system does not stand on its own, although there are many who contend that it would be capable of doing so.

At a conference held in Copenhagen at the close of the Cold War, the United States, Canada, and thirty-three European nations enunciated and committed themselves to a set of human rights, rule of law, and democratic principles.[2] Among these Copenhagen benchmarks there are obligations to "respect the rights of citizens to seek political or public office . . . without discrimination" (Article 7.5), and to "respect the right of individuals and groups to establish, in full freedom, their own political parties . . . and provide them with legal guarantees to enable them to compete on the basis of equal treatment" (Article 7.6).

In party terms *duopoly* is a two-party system that is undergirded by discriminatory systemic measures designed to burden, disadvantage, or entirely shut out challenges to the major parties' lock on electoral politics. Democratic principles may receive better service from a duopoly than from a one-party regime; but the case cannot be made that duopoly meets, or that it even aspires to, such internationally recognized benchmarks of best democratic practices as those registered in articles 7.5 and 7.6 of the Copenhagen agreement. This should be seen as a real dilemma for the nation that considers itself—and sometimes is regarded by others—to be the world's leading democracy.

The American party system is often identified with those of Great Britain and Canada. The British and Canadian systems, like that of the United States, feature two prevailing national parties along with various regional and national third, or minor, parties. But there are important differences between the American party system and its Canadian and British counterparts.

Third parties are always present in British and Canadian parliamentary life. Britain's third parties won 86 of 650 parliamentary seats in 2010. One of them, the Liberal Democrats, then joined the major-party Conservatives in forming a coalition government. The leftist New Democrats captured 102 of 308 seats in the 2011 Canadian House of Commons elections. Though historically a third party, the NDP thereby actually replaced the Liberals as the official major-party opposition to Canada's ruling Conservatives.

British and Canadian laws on ballot access do not discriminate. Parliamentary candidates receive ballot placement in their districts by complying with reasonable and undifferentiated requirements: submission of a petition with a very modest specified number of signatures and payment of a filing fee. Britain and Canada set a standard for political stability, doing so without duopolistic rules for the protection of the major parties.[3] Much the same could have been said a century ago about the nondiscriminatory nature of interparty relationships in the United States. That is not the case today.

Ballot-access requirements that American major-party decision makers legislate and enforce are so difficult, bewilderingly diverse from state to state, and costly to surmount that they stop many would-be third-party challengers in their tracks. Antifusion and sore-loser policies in force in most states protect the primacy of Democrats and Republicans. The federal program of public (taxpayer-supported) funding of presidential campaigns distinctly favors the major parties and their candidates. The same is true of the policies of some of the states that have instituted public funding of their statewide and legislative elections.

It is not unusual for many candidates, even some fringy ones, to participate in televised Democratic or Republican debates before or early in the period during which the major parties are holding primaries and caucuses leading toward the selection of the nominee for president. But for the general election, the bipartisan Commission on Presidential Debates sets the access bar so forbiddingly high that a minor-party or independent candidate almost never gets invited to take part.

Reforms have been proposed that could broaden representation and inject some democratic vigor into the election process. But some of these reforms pose a threat to the protected status of the two major parties, and many governing bodies dominated by Democratic and Republican decision makers have routinely ignored or refused to enact them.

The Fruit of Duopoly: Stability or Paralysis?

Apologists for the current American party system present grim scenarios of instability, even chaos, in selected cases involving multiparty politics: in Germany during the Depression, for example, or Italy after World War II. By contrast, they say, the American system has proven to be a paragon of consensus building and stability.

The historical record of interparty relationships during the Clinton, George W. Bush, and early Obama years suggest otherwise: zero-sum thinking and the filibuster threat, intractability on health care and other issues, a policy process swerving sharply away from bipartisan comity (except in preserving duopoly), paralysis and virtual gridlock. Though pork builds up cholesterol in the human body, members of Congress appear to assume that "pork" is a vital nutriment sustaining the body politic. Congressional business requiring bipartisan support routinely comes heavily larded.

A month and a half before congressional Democrats passed health-care reform without a single Republican vote, Tim Rutten of the *Los Angeles Times* observed that

> it has been more than four decades since the Congress . . . has been able to muster the will to pass a major piece of social legislation. Not since 1965, when

Medicare and the Voting Rights Act both overcame decades of opposition to become law, has Congress proved itself up to the task.

[Now] the chances of substantively addressing the regulatory breakdown that allowed Wall Street's irresponsible speculation to precipitate the worst financial crisis since the Depression seem to recede every day.

Dissatisfaction with both political parties runs deep.[4]

Indeed Americans have lost affection for their party system, if affection they ever had. Millions of voters now reject major-party labels, opting instead to identify as independents or even to document their affiliation with a minor party.[5] Opinion polls conducted over the last two decades consistently reveal a loss of popular faith in the legitimacy of the party system. Consider, for example,

- a 1992 *Washington Post* poll, 82 percent of the respondents to which concurred that "both American political parties are pretty much out of touch with the American people";[6]
- a 2006 Princeton Survey Research poll in which 82 percent declared that the nation's problems are beyond the capacity of the divergent, quarreling major parties to resolve and 73 percent expressed a desire for electoral options beyond those provided by the Democrats and Republicans;[7]
- a Zogby poll, taken in the summer of 2009, in which 58 percent of the respondents said that they believe the United States needs more than two major political parties.[8]

Many citizens understand the condition of the parties, and they realize that the party system falls far short of best democratic practices. Public opinion may be motivating and mobilizing those who want to construct a more inclusive and vigorously democratic political process by demolishing the duopolistic underpinnings that were designed to protect the major parties from challenges coming from outside the center ring.

Breakthroughs at the Polls

Early in the 1990s, a window of opportunity—the most significant since the Great Depression—opened for those who might challenge the lock held by the major parties on elections in America. The indications that this was coming already were surfacing by November 6, 1990. On that day two third-party gubernatorial candidates, Lowell Weicker of Connecticut and Alaska's Walter Hickel, were elected, and Bernard Sanders, running as an independent, won the lone Vermont seat in the U.S. House of Representatives. In victory all three had overcome both Democratic and Republican adversaries.

Weicker took the governor's office under a makeshift label: A Connecticut Party. (That *A* would give Weicker's party first place on the ballot two years later.) In three U.S. Senate terms, Weicker had been clearly identified with the progressive wing of the Republican Party. One of the accomplishments of his four years as Connecticut's independent governor was the establishment of a needed state income tax system.

Hickel ran as the nominee of the Alaskan Independence Party, but that party and its candidate were a mismatch from the start. He formally left the party near the end of his four-year term. Hickel had been an early champion of Alaskan statehood, and in Alaska and Washington, D.C., he had come to be known for his progressive environmentalist views. The Alaskan Independence Party's conservative positions on gun rights, home schooling, and other issues mirror the rugged individualism of Alaska's frontier. Founded in the 1970s, the party has long been identified with a secessionist vision of an independent Alaska. Its platform pushes the goal of a statewide referendum on the future status of America's largest state.

News of the Alaskan Independence Party again reached the lower forty-eight late in 2008, accompanied by a good bit of election-year chatter. It was reported that Todd Palin—Alaska's "First Dude," the husband of Governor Sarah Palin, who was running for vice president with Arizona senator John McCain on a "Country First" theme—twice had registered with election officials as a member of the Alaskan Independence Party.

Sanders won Vermont's House seat in 1990 with a 56 percent share of the vote. Reelected seven times, he served Vermonters as their congressman from 1991 through 2006. In November 2006 Sanders won an open seat and a six-year term in the U.S. Senate, racking up more than 65 percent of the votes. Though running as an independent, he found allies among House and Senate Democrats, and he has affiliated with the Democratic conferences in the chambers where he has served.

As a public figure, Sanders clearly resides on the left. He is the only current member of Congress declaring himself to be a socialist.[9] Late in the 2008 campaign, McCain and Palin began brandishing the *s*-word to drub Senator Barack Obama, their Democratic presidential opponent. Their charge usually was indirect, either quoting some remark made by "Joe the Plumber" or declaring that Senator Obama's voting record was even more liberal than the senator's who called himself a socialist.

Vermonters of course know of their independent senator's socialist claim. They also understand his connection to their state's Progressive Party. Before going to Congress, Sanders had served four terms (1981–89) as the mayor of Burlington, his rural state's largest city. In the early 1980s, Burlington progressives established their city's Progressive Coalition. They made Sanders its lead nominee and de facto leader.

A major party in city politics, Burlington's PC eventually went statewide, recasting itself as the Vermont Progressive Party. Progressive Anthony Pollina won a quarter of all votes cast for lieutenant governor in 2002 and 22 percent in his 2008 independent campaign for governor. Vermont's Progressives won thirteen state legislative elections in the 1990s and seventeen from 2000 through 2008.[10] Theirs may be the most remarkable nonnational third-party success story of the last three decades.

Before the 1990 gubernatorial victories of Hickel and Weicker, just one candidate not running as a Democrat or Republican had won a state governorship in the years since the end of World War II. Three other such victories followed Weicker's and Hickel's in the 1990s. Running as an independent, Angus King, a well-known businessman and on-screen host on Maine public television, was elected governor of Maine in 1994 and won reelection in 1998.

Jesse Ventura was elected governor of Minnesota in 1998. Flamboyant in style, Ventura was a former professional wrestler and the past mayor of the Minneapolis suburb of Brooklyn Park. He had run as the nominee of the Reform Party, which Texas billionaire businessman Ross Perot had launched just three years before Ventura's Minnesota election victory.

Table 1.1 Victorious 1990s Third-Party and Independent Governors

State and Year	Candidate	Designation	Vote and Percent of Total Cast
Alaska 1990	Walter Hickel	Alaskan Independence	75,721 (38.9)
Connecticut 1990	Lowell Weicker	A Connecticut Party	460,576 (40.4)
Maine 1994	Angus King	Independent	180,829 (35.4)
Maine 1998	Angus King	Independent	246,772 (58.6)
Minnesota 1998	Jesse Ventura	Reform	773,403 (37.0)

Ross Perot and His Movement: The Center, with an Attitude

Few would have predicted it, but it was Perot who devoted his quirky appeal, immense wealth, and sheer grit to fostering and leading one of the most powerful twentieth-century assaults on the nation's duopoly. Remarkably Perot and his supporters—some called them Perotistas—defied the conventional wisdom that the brightest potential for a third-party movement lies either to the left or the right of both major parties. They built their movement squarely at the ideological middle.

Centrist though it was, this was a movement with an attitude, and it enlisted the support of millions who were "mad as hell" at all those inside-the-Beltway people who held the power. Micah Sifry, the author of an engaging book on recent third-party politics, dubbed Perot and his movement "the angry middle."[11]

One very angry private citizen had in fact generated the wave on which the movement would ride. In 1990 retired businessman Jack Gargan drew up a mad-as-hell diatribe he titled "Throw the Hypocritical Rascals Out!" and then devoted his own money to getting it published as a full-page ad in six newspapers nationwide.[12] Although Perot and Gargan often differed and eventually split, Gargan was the movement's original spark and an important factor in building it up.

Perot grasped the visceral feeling of millions of Americans that they were not being served by the two-choice menu of conservative Republicans and liberal

Democrats. Perot was a centrist, but a militant one. Despite his wealth and connections, he carved out for himself the image of the archetypal Washington outsider. Given to populist speech and earthy sound bites, he vowed that he was going to "clean out the barn."

Perot wanted balanced budgets, term limits, and a fundamental change in the way elections and campaigns are run in America. A trade-policy protectionist, he predicted that NAFTA—the North American Free Trade Agreement—would produce a "giant sucking sound" of American jobs being outsourced to Mexico. Perot's views on the global economy are reflected in some of the positions taken by today's antiglobalization activists on both right and left.

The accomplishments of Perot's 1992 bid for the presidency as an independent were spectacular by nonmajor-party standards. Spending more than sixty-eight million dollars—the bulk of it from his own wealth—on the campaign,[13] Perot made his name a household word nationwide. Opinion polls in May and June 1992 actually had him leading both the incumbent president and his Democratic challenger, Arkansas governor Bill Clinton. Perot's movement surmounted, state by state, the burdensome requirements to get its candidate's name placed on every ballot in the nation.

Perot participated in all three of the fall general election debates with Clinton and President George H. W. Bush. Through 2008 not a single other nonmajor-party presidential candidate since—not even Perot himself—has been invited to join the major-party nominees in even one fall debate. Perot's 19 percent general election tally was the second highest since the Civil War for a presidential candidate not running as a Democrat or Republican. Only ex-president Teddy Roosevelt, running in 1912 as a Bull Moose Progressive, had done better than Perot.

The movement was institutionalized in 1993 as United We Stand America, a grassroots citizens organization with 1.5 million dues-paying members. Then, in 1995, the Reform Party was born. In 1996 Perot made a second presidential run, this time as the Reform Party nominee.

Perot was entitled by virtue of his 1992 vote tally to public general election funds, and he decided to take them even though they were less than half the size of the grants the major-party nominees received. His decision burdened his campaign in several ways. In taking the money, he undoubtedly stained his image as the outsider demanding radical reform of the way American campaigns are run. And with the money there came the requirement that he accept a legal cap on what he could spend on the campaign.[14]

Perot's 1996 tally was 8.4 percent. His vote plus the smaller totals for other 1996 third-party and independent presidential campaigns added up to just over 10 percent. The 1992 and 1996 presidential elections were the first two consecutive ones since the Civil War in which the combined votes for the Democratic and Republican nominees failed both times to total at least 90 percent of all votes cast.

Like important third-party movements of the past, Perot's challenge to the Democratic and Republican electoral lock reverberated in the public policy arena. Term limits and other themes of the 1992 Perot campaign plainly influenced some of the planks in the 1994 Republican "Contract with America," a set of legislative promises that proved to be the driving force bringing the GOP to majority status in the U.S. House for the first time in forty years. The Perot movement's pressure for balanced budgets was probably decisive in pushing President Clinton and the Congress toward the budget surpluses they achieved in the late Clinton years.

Many Republicans blamed Perot for spoiling Bush's 1992 reelection bid by siphoning away millions of votes. Their charge may be credible, but there are reasons to doubt it. As a centrist Perot was in a position to draw support from base voters of both major parties. Among Perot voters responding to 1992 exit polls, 38 percent said that, in the absence of Perot, they would have voted for Bush; but another 38 percent declared that their votes would have gone to Clinton.[15] Turnout was high in 1992, and millions of Perot's votes came from independent first-time voters, many of whom would have stayed home if the Perot option had been unavailable.

The Reform Party, the partisan house that Perot built, turned out to be ephemeral, short lived, and an unvarnished disappointment for those hoping to institutionalize the fight against duopoly. Jesse Ventura achieved his 1998 Minnesota gubernatorial victory without financial support either from Perot or the national party.[16]

Reform endured a nasty fight for its 2000 presidential nomination and for the $12.5 million in federal funds to which the party's 2000 presidential campaign was entitled due to Perot's 8.4 percent vote share in 1996. Pat Buchanan, the ultraconservative who won that fight, went on to take just 0.4 percent of the vote in the general election. Four years later the diminished, irresolute party devoted what energy it had left to supporting the independent presidential candidacy of Ralph Nader, the left-progressive lawyer, writer, and consumer advocate.

Some Reform Party veterans seek now to recast their movement as the Independence Party of America and to anchor it in its original centrist ideological moorings. Led by Frank MacKay, New York's Independence Party is one of several minor parties enjoying influence and some power in the politics of that state. The Independence Party also has a well-established presence in Minnesota. Dean Barkley, the Minnesota party's 2008 U.S. Senate candidate, took more than 15 percent of the votes, even though the national media spotlight was almost entirely upon the two-party horse race between Republican incumbent Norm Coleman and Democratic challenger Al Franken.

Ralph Nader and the Nader Movement

While many Americans longing for a permanent new major party had focused their hopes on Perot's movement at the middle, others looked to the left to Ralph Nader

Ralph Nader signing books at Barnes & Noble Union Square, New York City, January 30, 2007. By permission of David Shankbone, photographer. Obtained through Creative Commons.

as the possible catalyst for that new alternative. Nader was a candidate for the presidency in four consecutive elections. The nominee of the nation's Greens in 1996 and 2000, he competed as an independent in 2004 and 2008.

Nader brought to his campaigns his remarkable forty-year record of public-interest activism and wide public recognition as the nation's leading consumer advocate. Taking on the nation's largest automobile manufacturer, Nader exposed shoddy craftsmanship and serious safety defects in GM cars. He launched a small army of idealistic young reformers. Public Citizen, his organized consumer advocacy group, had gotten under way in 1971. Nader's influence underlay the birth of the Occupational Safety and Health Administration, the Environmental Protection Agency, and the Consumer Product Safety Administration.[17]

Lacking Perot's financial base, Nader won less than 1 percent of the votes in three of the four campaigns he waged. His share of the 2000 vote was a more substantial 2.7 percent. Controversy and rancor surrounded the 2000 presidential election, the first since 1888 in which the candidate with the largest popular vote lost the election. Although Vice President Al Gore won nearly 550,000 more votes nationwide than Texas governor George W. Bush, his Republican rival, Bush took the presidency with 271 of the 538 electoral votes.

The epicenter of the 2000 partisan storm was Florida, where nearly six million votes were cast and where, according to official tallies—bitterly disputed to this day—Bush won a razor-thin 537-vote plurality over Gore. Bush took Florida's twenty-five electoral votes and the election. The outcome left a residue of bitterness following weeks of acrimonious partisan conflict over voter intent and pregnant chads and a split U.S. Supreme Court decision ending the recount of Florida votes.[18]

Nader's Florida tally—97,477—far exceeded Bush's tiny Florida margin of victory over Gore. Democrats were quick to declare that most of those 97,477 would, without Nader, have been Gore's, and to brand Nader the spoiler who put Bush in the White House. If that is what happened, it had not come without warning. Pre-election television and radio commentaries and scores of newspaper articles had raised the prospect that Nader might spoil things for Gore. Some others speculated, to the contrary, that Pat Buchanan's Reform Party candidacy might deny Bush the election.

Throughout the fall campaign, Democratic leaders found ways to warn Nader fans not to waste their votes on a candidate who was destined to lose. Prudent voters, they were saying in effect, must concentrate on the two-party horse race, choosing their preferred *electable* candidate. Worried about a possible Bush victory, some progressives entered into unenforceable online agreements to trade votes for Gore in in-play swing states for Nader votes in states the Gore campaign had written off as hopeless.

Although the 2000 Nader-as-spoiler claim still is hotly debated, there is evidence supporting it. In Voter News Service exit polls, 45 percent of Nader's voters said that if he had not run, they would have voted for Gore. Just 27 percent said they would have chosen Bush.[19]

Even if the claim is true, the Nader scenario is just one of several, any one of which accounts for Bush's victory. Gore would have won if he had taken his home state of Tennessee or one other Bush state anywhere in the country. He would have won if the election system awarded the presidency to the popular vote winner rather than the candidate with an electoral vote majority. Gore *might* have won if Florida's Democrats and Republicans had come to terms about how to count disputed votes and the U.S. Supreme Court had not ended the recount.[20]

To those who said he was the spoiler whose supporters had wasted their votes, Nader's response was unequivocal and defiant; and although his reply has evolved,[21] Nader has held firmly to the heart of it in the face of critics' withering words blaming him even for the mistakes and failures of the George W. Bush era. What Nader has to say about this deserves earnest consideration by anyone whose faith in the two major parties has been shaken or lost, and by all who seek a more vigorous, robust democratic politics.

It would matter, Nader says, which major-party candidate wins if what separates the major parties really counted for more. There *are* some important issue differences between Republicans and Democrats, and the relationship between the two parties may have become dysfunctional, even poisonous. But in the grand scheme of things, what matters most is the corporatization of politics—of both major parties—and whether the powerful business interests served by one of these parties would really feel disserved by victory for the other. For Nader the answer is obvious. Pushing back against corporate power has been at the core of every Nader presidential campaign.

Elections featuring more real voter choices are good for democracy, Nader insists. Hobbled though it was by limited resources, unfriendly media, and the disabling rules for ballot access, his candidacy had energized the contest. It mobilized nearly three million voters, many of whom, alienated from both major parties, would not have voted if he had not run.

Votes belong to the candidate who receives them, and it is arrogant and presumptuous for anyone else to claim them by right. By urging voters not to "waste their votes," a major party campaign like Gore's is far better positioned to take votes away from a minor-party candidate than the other way around. A recurrent theme of American voter complaint is about elections that reduce the practical choice to choosing "the lesser of two evils." A wasted vote, Nader contends, is one that bypasses the voter's true preference in favor of the lesser of two evils.[22]

2006 and 2008

Two New England candidates won election to the U.S. Senate by running as independents in 2006. There was Bernie Sanders of Vermont, already a veteran in the House. In Connecticut it was Joe Lieberman, for whom this was really a reelection. Lieberman had won three previous senatorial campaigns as a Democrat. On November 6, 2006, he appeared on the ballot as the nominee of the Connecticut for Lieberman Party.

A well-known national figure, Lieberman had run for the vice presidency with Al Gore in 2000. Due largely to Lieberman's hawkish views on the Iraq War, he lost to challenger Ned Lamont in Connecticut's 2006 Democratic senatorial primary. In a state possessing a sore loser law, that defeat would have ended Lieberman's reelection bid; but because Connecticut has no such law, Lieberman was in a position to continue his campaign under a different label. In victory he took 50 percent of the vote against Lamont and a weak Republican challenger.

Like Sanders, Lieberman affiliated with the Democratic senatorial conference in the 110th and 111th Congresses (2007–11). But he reasserted his independence in 2008 by endorsing and actively campaigning for Republican presidential nominee John McCain.

Although he had founded the Connecticut for Lieberman Party and had run successfully as its nominee, Lieberman never showed any interest in it as an organization. Remarkably opponents of Lieberman have become its leaders. The party nominated anti-Lieberman activist John Mertens for the seat Christopher Dodd announced he would be vacating after 2010, and a most ironic scenario began to surface: if Lieberman should decide to seek reelection in 2012, one of his election adversaries could very well be the nominee of the Connecticut party carrying his name![23]

During the two-year lead-up to 2008, anyone seeking them could find signs—false, as it turned out—that 2008 might be a breakthrough year in building a movement really capable and vigorous enough to take on the entrenched duopoly. Unity 08, a third-party joint venture launched in 2006 to offer voters an attractive centrist alternative to the major parties' presidential campaigns, faltered and failed long before election day 2008.

There also were the widely circulated rumors that Michael Bloomberg, the effective, respected New York City mayor who in 2007 declared that he was an independent, intended, or could be persuaded, to make an independent run for the presidency in 2008. Many who pushed this scenario assumed that Bloomberg, one of America's wealthiest citizens, would be generous in the manner of Perot in bankrolling his own campaign, and that a Bloomberg candidacy would combine center-right positions on the economy with liberal perspectives on social issues.

New books appeared during the early stages of the 2008 campaign, some with the cachet of prominent authorship.[24] Critical of politics as practiced in the United States, they either predicted or called for a new, transformed politics. Each in its own way confirmed that the window of opportunity opened in the early 1990s is open still to those who would use it.

The Revolution: A Manifesto was released in April 2008, and it quickly rose to the top of the *New York Times* list of nonfiction best sellers.[25] Ron Paul, its author, is a Texas physician and Republican congressman—a most unorthodox one—who had been elected ten times to the U.S. House of Representatives. Paul ran in 1988 as the Libertarian Party presidential nominee. He has kept close ties since then with people who want to build and sustain a substantial third-party movement. Many of them hoped that their then seventy-three-year-old friend would take up the charge again, running in 2008 as a third-party standard-bearer. To this day minor parties of various ideological stripes feature "End the Two-Party Monopoly!" on their Web sites. Paul had written that statement in 2004 to condemn the actions of major-party turf guardians to keep Nader off election ballots.

The Revolution skewers the "false choices" the major parties feature in each round of elections and much else that stands as current policy and political practice. Its pitch to Americans is to return their country to its libertarian roots. When *The Revolution* went on sale, Paul was running for the GOP nomination for president, and the book served to rally support for his campaign.

The mainstream media and some of his Republican competitors treated Paul as a quixotic candidate from out on the radical fringe, but his major-party candidacy did afford some opportunities for him to introduce to voters his minimalist view of government's role, his hostility to the Federal Reserve, and his isolationist foreign policy views. Media searches into his past uncovered some demeaning remarks about blacks, Jews, and gays in newsletters published under Paul's name back in the 1980s and 1990s. Paul responded that the offending articles had been ghostwritten without his editorial oversight or review and that the remarks they bore did not reflect his personal views.[26]

Paul won the support of scores of people, many of them young and many who embraced him as an inspiring movement leader—even a prophet—rather than a run-of-the-mill candidate for office. Through his voice and congressional votes, even in the aftermath of September 11, 2001, he had plainly taken the side of those who opposed preemptive war and governmental invasions of liberty and privacy.

On September 10, 2002, Paul had inserted into the *Congressional Record* a statement he titled "Questions That Won't Be Asked about Iraq." Another six months passed before the launch of the invasion of Iraq, and Paul's warning was barely noticed at the time. Years later many have read it as a statement possessing remarkable prophetic power.

Paul's distinctly techno-savvy Republican presidential campaign broke all previous records for single-day Internet fund-raising with a December 16, 2007, take of more than six million dollars.[27] By early January he had taken in twenty-eight million dollars, mostly collected over the Internet from small donors. Paul videos circulated widely on YouTube, and his 2008 campaign rivaled the early stages of Obama's in skillful, effective online social networking.

Paul finished fourth in the Republican race, behind Senator McCain and former governors Mitt Romney and Mike Huckabee. He then invited Libertarian nominee Bob Barr, the Green Party's Cynthia McKinney, Chuck Baldwin of the Constitution Party, and independent candidate Ralph Nader to join him at a September 10, 2008, news conference in Washington, D.C. Announcing at the news conference that he would not be supporting McCain, he endorsed and recommended to voters the four alternative candidates he had invited to attend.

Nader, Baldwin, and McKinney attended Paul's news conference, but Barr did not show up. His campaign spokesman said that it was because he did not want to appear to be sanctioning McKinney and her controversial stands on issues;[28] but many in the third-party blogosphere declared Barr's absence to be a snub of Paul. Twelve days after the news conference, Paul gave his specific endorsement to Chuck Baldwin, the Baptist minister and political activist who was running as the nominee of the Constitution Party. Paul was in a sense returning a favor. Very early in the major-party contests back in 2007, Baldwin had strongly endorsed Paul for the GOP presidential nomination.

The 2008 election confounded the hopes of those seeking viable third-party and independent candidacies and disappointed anyone really wanting to take on the American duopoly. Only a handful of nonmajor-party contenders for state legislative seats won in 2008: a half dozen Vermont Progressives, a Green in Arkansas, and seven independents scattered through six states in New England and the Midwest.

Although Nader was the best-known national figure among nonmajor-party presidential contenders in 2008, two of the other third-party presidential nominees entered the race possessing some name recognition for their past service as members of the Georgia delegation in the U.S. House. Green Party nominee McKinney had been a magnet for controversy during her twelve years of congressional service as a Democrat. Barr, a former Republican, had played an important part in the impeachment of Bill Clinton. As the Libertarian presidential candidate, he recanted his previous support of George W. Bush administration policies that flew in the face of libertarian philosophy; but he was kept on the defensive by some Libertarian Party purists, who spoke out against the pragmatic considerations that had led their party to nominate him.

As in many past years, the outreach initiatives of the minor-party and independent campaigns in 2008 were crippled by meager funds and by the need to devote scarce human and money resources to the goal of cracking as many states' ballots as possible.

No 2008 candidate other than Obama and McCain appeared on the ballot of every jurisdiction with electoral votes to cast. Nader and Barr came the closest, each making the ballots of forty-five states. Nader, but not Barr, also made it on in the District of Columbia. Just four nonmajor-party candidates—Nader, Barr, McKinney, and Baldwin—made the ballots of states with electoral votes totaling to at least 270, the number required for even a theoretical chance of winning the presidency. Three other parties placed their candidates on the ballots of from eight to twelve states. Five minor-party and independent candidates appeared on two or three states' ballots, and nine others appeared on a ballot line in a single state. Some candidates applied successfully for write-in status in various jurisdictions where they had failed to qualify for ballot access.[29]

Nader won nearly 750,000 general election votes in 2008. Barr took more than 500,000, Baldwin almost 200,000, and McKinney just over 160,000. Voters gave only 1.4 percent of their votes to these four and all other 2008 minor-party and independent campaigns. Obama and McCain took almost all the rest.

Many factors explain the failure to launch a vital, vigorous third-party movement in 2008. Still in effect were ballot access and other barriers that turf-protecting Republican and Democratic decision makers had built up over many years, and no third-party leader or group arose with the commitment, following, and financial clout to assault that formidable duopolistic fortress. Even if it had, popular obsession with the history-making 2008 two-party contest and the worst financial meltdown since the Great Depression might have combined to snuff out even the most dedicated third-party-building impulse.

By 2008 eighteen years had passed since the victories of Hickel, Weicker, and Sanders had provided the first indications of shifting ground, of vulnerability for the major parties and new opportunities to take them on. The money dilemma and the continuing power of duopolistic rules to limit and disable were clear to all those on the outside looking in. Opportunities had opened for third-party and independent campaigns, but no one thought this meant a level playing field for challengers to the duopoly and its beneficiaries.

2010 and Looking to 2012

GOP resurgence and Democratic defeats at all levels were the principal fruit of the 2010 elections. A lot of this was due to voter mobilization by the Tea Party, a new movement that placed itself not entirely inside but not quite outside Republican ranks. But there was a subtext, clear though not widely recognized: 2010 was a very good year for many candidates running contrary to the prevailing winds of either major party. It was much better than 2008 had been for independents and minor-party nominees.

In Rhode Island, Lincoln Chafee, the nation's first victorious independent gubernatorial candidate since 1998, defeated both his major-party adversaries. Meanwhile Maine independent Eliot Cutler and Tom Tancredo, the nominee of Colorado's Constitution Party, were finishing in strong second places in their campaigns for governor. Running as a write-in candidate, Alaska U.S. senator Lisa Murkowski won reelection, beating both her Republican and Democratic foes. Joe Miller, her Tea Party–endorsed opponent, had earlier beaten Murkowski in the GOP senatorial primary.[30]

Following the 2010 elections, ballot-access blogger Richard Winger announced that voters in eleven states, the largest number of states since 1922, had elected to state and federal offices candidates who were not major-party nominees. Most of these were independents running for state legislative seats. Seven were Progressives elected or reelected to the Vermont Senate and House. One or more minor parties held recognized ballot status in thirty-five states at year's end. And in those states where voters can register by party, only 73.5 percent—quite likely the smallest percentage ever recorded—were registered as Democrats and Republicans.

In December 2010 a core of prominent Americans came together to launch No Labels, a centrist movement they dedicated to cutting through the "hyperpartisanship" and gridlock now seen as paralyzing the nation's electoral and policy processes.[31] Opinion pieces published in America's leading newspapers late that year called for or predicted the advent of a major third party at the "radical center" in time to wage a formidable presidential campaign in 2012.[32] Trial balloons also went up for both Bloomberg and Donald Trump, each as a potential independent presidential candidate. Either would be rich enough to finance an end-run around both the disabling state-imposed ballot-access obstacles and the wildly discriminatory money provisions in current federal law. By 2011 Americans Elect, an energized new electoral movement, was challenging the duopoly and vying to provide a third option for the 2012 presidential election.

2

★ ★ ★

Protecting Major-Party Turf

> Our democracy is but a name. We vote. What does that mean? . . . We choose between two . . . bodies of autocrats. We choose between Tweedledum and Tweedledee.
>
> *Helen Keller*

> The necessity for [strict scrutiny] becomes evident when we consider that major parties, which by definition are ordinarily in control of legislative institutions, may seek to perpetuate themselves at the expense of developing minor parties.
>
> *Justice Thurgood Marshall, dissenting*
> *in Munro v. Socialist Workers Party (1986)*

Over the years some of the most vocal critics of America's party system have declared that there really are not two major national parties. They contend that there are just two branches of one party—two brands in effect, one Democratic, the other Republican, both offering nearly identical products to the voting consumer.

Helen Keller believed this. Remembered for her bravery, perseverance, and the remarkable life she lived in the face of her deafness and blindness, Keller was an activist in the left-wing politics of her day. She belonged to the Socialist Party, campaigned for Socialist candidates, and took part in the National Woman's Party, the militant wing of the suffragist movement. According to Keller the Republican and Democratic parties are like Tweedledum and Tweedledee, those two look-alike, think-alike curmudgeonly characters in Lewis Carroll's *Through the Looking Glass, and What Alice Found* (1871).

George Wallace, the segregationist Alabama politician who took nearly 14 percent of the presidential vote in 1968 running on his American Independent Party ticket, believed it too. "There's not a dime's worth of difference between the Democrat [*sic*] and Republican parties," Wallace charged in the heat of his third-party campaign.

Even some prominent Democrats and Republicans have lamented the sameness of the products their parties have sometimes offered voters. Harry Truman thought

Helen Keller, 1905. Courtesy of the U.S. Library of Congress Prints and Photographs Division. Obtained through Wikimedia Commons.

that Democratic candidates defeat themselves when they talk and act like Republicans, because when they do, "people will vote for the real Republican all the time." In selecting "A Choice, Not an Echo" as his campaign theme or mantra, Barry Goldwater, the GOP's conservative 1964 presidential nominee, was in effect criticizing his own party for three decades of following at the heels of its Democratic rival.

Those whose frame of political reference has been the 1990s and since may want to dispute the notion of Tweedledum and Tweedledee as characters representing the two major parties. In President Clinton's impeachment and trial for lying under oath about his sexual affair with Monica Lewinsky, and then in the high-stakes 2000 struggle over Florida's disputed presidential votes, the two parties' behavior was more like armies at war than similar brands.

Toxic became the adjective of choice in media reporting of the unfriendly, even dysfunctional, relationship between congressional Republicans and Democrats during the Bill Clinton and George W. Bush presidencies; and partisan rancor and strife continued after President Obama's inauguration in spite of the new president's resolve to reach across the aisle and to set in Washington a "postpartisan" tone.

There are those who see all this as little more than smoke and mirrors. Whatever the truth about a breach between Republicans and Democrats, nothing indicates any erosion or weakening of the two parties' shared interest in and commitment to protecting their exclusive places in the center ring of American politics. Micah Sifry has described the system as "a one-party system shared by two parties."[1] That may be the most accurate designation of America's duopoly as its exists today.

Politics as Hardball

"Politics ain't beanbag. Tis a man's game, and women, children, an' pro-hybitionists'd do well to keep out iv it." So said Mr. Dooley, the fictional very Irish saloonkeeper and homespun philosopher in Finley Peter Dunne's *Mr. Dooley in Peace and War* (1898).[2] Dunne meant to convey that politics bears no resemblance to a gentle children's game. Politics is hardball, and it is the very tough and committed who have the chance to survive and thrive in it.

Dunne provides a useful insight as one looks at the cards that have been stacked against third parties. There are measures—the very teeth of duopoly—that flagrantly discriminate and were designed for the purpose of making the major parties a protected class and to disadvantage or shut out all challengers. It might be very hard not to conclude that these are at odds with and unworthy of the democratic values and practices to which the United States claims to adhere.

On the other hand, there are factors that work to marginalize third parties but that do not seem particularly unjust, given the hardball nature of politics. These include

- the co-opting effect of Democratic and Republican primaries, with their nominating procedures that are accessible to the candidacies of outsiders and mavericks and to participation by disaffected voters, people who otherwise might lead or support a third party;[3]
- Democratic and Republican appropriation—theft—of third-party positions on issues when these are seen to be popular with voters;
- voters' rejection of particular minor-party or independent candidates because they are politically inexperienced (most are), fringy or doctrinaire (many are), or mediocre, unattractive persons;
- inequalities, even vast ones, between major and minor parties in organization and finance, insofar as these do not result from discriminatory public policies;
- and cultural characteristics of the nation that are said to favor a system of just two major parties.

Particular elements of the nation's institutional framework—the single-member district plurality system for electing legislators and the Electoral College for presidential elections—also serve in effect to protect the interests and privilege of two major parties. Although policy makers—Democrats and Republicans for the most part—have been disinclined to reform or abolish them, it cannot be said that these processes were originally designed and deployed for the duopolistic purpose of two-party turf-guarding.

Finally there is a factor that derives from everything else. This is the mainstream media's flagrant neglect of third-party and independent campaigns and its clear preference for covering the two-party contest.

Cultural Characteristics and Political Socialization

According to culture theory, the United States in its history avoided any sustained experience with feudalism, monarchy, or a state church. As a result the sharp ideological divisions and class consciousness found elsewhere never really sprouted on American soil. What developed instead, and in consequence, is a broad cultural consensus about core values, particularly liberty, individualism, and equal rights. These central values define and delineate the political mainstream. Major parties are said to defer routinely to this cultural consensus. Any other group or (third) party unable to verify its faithful devotion to the core cultural values is consigned—actually it consigns itself—to the periphery.[4]

Sharing as they do in this consensus about core values, mainstream Americans also manifest a cultural duality that they most likely inherited from the British. There is an old saying—hyperbole to be sure—that in France the number of opinions, and of political parties to express them, precisely equals the number of French citizens. In America issues have more frequently divided opinion into two main camps: among others, federalists versus antifederalists, North versus South, urban versus rural, labor versus owners and managers, and pro-life versus pro-choice. This duality is said to undergird and support a system of just two major parties.[5]

Political socialization is the process whereby people, particularly nonadults, acquire knowledge, feelings, and evaluations about the political system and their relation to it. Responses to recent polls consistently reveal that Americans are dissatisfied with the condition of their party system. Even so, political socialization continues to evoke some anxiety about the possible effects of a multiparty deviation from the national two-party pattern, and it usually encourages either loyalty to one or the other major party or an independent outlook ("vote for the person, not the party"). More children would be learning to devote themselves to the Libertarians or Greens if there were more Greens or Libertarians to teach them.

Media Attitudes and Practice

Mainstream media concentrate on the two-party horse race, notoriously ignoring outside challengers. A study of presidential coverage by the *New York Times* and the *Washington Post* revealed that between August 5 and November 5, 2008, these two newspapers devoted a combined total of 6,781 news stories, opinion pieces, letters, and photographs to Obama, McCain, and their campaigns but just 66 to the four leading nonmajor-party candidates and campaigns—a remarkable hundred-to-one ratio.[6]

Such media neglect is nothing new. Researchers studying three prominent national newspapers and three weekly newsmagazines found that in 1980 these media gave Jimmy Carter and Ronald Reagan ten times the coverage received by the other eleven candidates combined.[7] Given the significance that year of John Anderson's independent bid, a campaign that drew nearly 7 percent of the November vote, a gap this large or larger is bound to be a regular occurrence in presidential rounds.

Mainstream electronic media are no more demonstrably inclusive than print with regard to third-party and independent campaigns, despite the proliferation of cable options and the need to fill the time in twenty-four-hour news cycles. Television becomes duopoly's partner by bringing into American living rooms general election debates from which nonmajor-party candidates are regularly and routinely excluded. Viewers wanting to tune in to the nominating stage of Libertarian, Green, and Constitution party national conventions need to locate C-SPAN with their television remotes.

Media watchers point out that, as with so much about Ross Perot's 1992 campaign, it was a marked exception to the generalization about media neglect of general election campaigns not run under major-party labels. The February 20, 1992, edition of CNN's *Larry King Live* was in effect Perot's nominating convention, the venue he chose to launch the campaign. He made his announcement following King's persistent query, "Is there any scenario on which you would run?" King later recalled that he had felt "like Mark Antony, offering Caesar the crown three times."[8]

If in the rest of his 1992 campaign the media accorded Perot treatment more favorable than what other third-party candidates can expect to receive, this was due mainly to Perot's personality and to his wealth and willingness to spend. Political scientist Jonathan Laurence reports that Perot's "candidacy was aimed over the heads of the parties and traditional media, directly at 'the people.' Perot shunned the campaign trail (and the boys and girls on the bus), invigorated the talk show circuit as a locus of campaign communication, and spent forty-five million dollars on unprecedented half-hour and hour-long television advertising spots."[9]

Although far from leveling the playing field, the Internet has come to be a remarkable benefit to minor parties and independent campaigns, both for internal networking and for reaching out. Irrespective of a third party's nearness to or distance from the mainstream and its values, the party is likely to recognize the significance of a well-maintained, attractive, and informative Web site.

There are numerous third-party bloggers and important information and advocacy sites, notably Ballot-access.org and Independentpoliticalreport.com. Twitter and Facebook—common stock and valuable social networking resources in society at large—are inexpensive and accessible media now widely used by people on the third-party periphery.

The Single-Member District Plurality System

Election systems do matter, and their particular design may have a decisive, even if unintended, effect upon the character of the democracy in a particular nation. This point was very well illustrated by the distinguished French social scientist Maurice Duverger in his *Political Parties* (1954).[10] Duverger's central premise has had such influence that political scientists have come to refer to it as **Duverger's law.** According to Duverger's law, there is a strong tendency for a two-party system to evolve in nations that use the single-member district plurality system for election to their legislative assemblies.

A lot can be said on behalf of Duverger's premise. It is neither surprising nor coincidental that Britain and Canada, like the United States, employ the single-member district plurality system for electing national legislators and that Britain, Canada, and the United States all possess systems of two nationally prevailing parties. And it stands to reason that in elections in which, district by district, just one candidate wins, most voters will settle eventually into a routine of *strategic voting*—avoiding "wasted votes" by bypassing a candidate who, however appealing to the voter's heart, seems destined to lose and voting instead for the voter-preferred electable candidate. Most voters have never heard the term *strategic voting*. They are more likely to describe their act as "voting for the lesser of two evils."

Duverger presented a corollary, referred to by some as **Duverger's hypothesis,** that multiparty systems are likely to evolve in countries using proportional representation (PR), an alternative to the single-member district plurality system.[11] PR is a newer system than single-member district plurality. Although the oldest PR systems date only from the late nineteenth century, today most democratic nations use PR or a combination of PR and single-member districts in electing their legislators.

There are several forms of proportional representation,[12] but in all of them "the principle . . . is that blocs of like-minded voters should win seats in legislative assemblies in proportion to their share of the popular vote."[13] Proportional representation elections are multimember elections, taking place either within districts or countrywide. The 120 members of the Israeli Knesset are elected nationwide, and each party's share of the Knesset seats is in proportion to the share of votes the party receives from Israeli voters. It is no wonder that Israel, like many nations adopting the various PR forms, has a developed multiparty system.

PR is not unknown in the United States, and it has been used in the past in some big-city elections. Cincinnati used it for a third of a century, and New York City's voters adopted a form of it in 1936. During its PR days, the Big Apple sent Communist Party members Peter Cacchione and Benjamin Davis and allied leftists of the American Labor Party to its city council. In 1947 New York abandoned PR as an early casualty of the Cold War.[14]

Some people prefer "first past the post," with its allusion to winning a horse race, as the name for the single-member district plurality system. In most American jurisdictions, a plurality, not an absolute majority, is all that is needed to take the legislative seat in a single-member district race.

Single-member district has been the most prominent form for congressional elections since the American nation's earliest days. Although some states, especially smaller ones, used at-large elections to choose their members of the U.S. House in the early years of the Republic, Congress legislated a single-member districting requirement in 1842, resurrected that mandate in 1862, and sustained it in legislation passed every ten years from 1862 through 1911. A congressional statute now in force and requiring single-member House districts dates from 1967.

U.S. senators have been popularly elected since adoption of the Seventeenth Amendment in 1913. Although the two senators of every state represent their state at large, the method of their election replicates in every way the single-member district system. Single-member district is also the predominant system for electing American state senators and representatives.

Due to America's size and diversity, a nationwide PR system like Israel's probably would not be feasible for the United States. But PR might work very well in state legislative elections or in choosing U.S. House delegations from the large states. Third parties and their candidates would likely benefit if policy decisions were made to institute PR. The more general beneficiaries would be the voters, whose preferences could be more fully and vigorously represented in elections and policy making.

Insofar as the two major parties control the process of reform, the prospect for instituting PR is very dim. The future appears much brighter for **instant runoff voting (IRV)**, a reform that can deepen democracy within any election in which just one candidate wins.[15] By the beginning of 2009, IRV had been used in mayoralty or council elections in San Francisco; Burlington, Vermont; and a handful of other locations, and it had been approved for use in nearly fifty American cities and counties.

IRV gives voters the power to order by rank their voter choices. Voters can if they wish vote with their heads but also their hearts; if the election is partisan, they can cast a ballot for a major-party candidate but also give a first- or second-choice vote to a minor-party nominee or an independent. If none of the candidates takes a majority of first-choice votes, the candidate with the fewest first-choice votes is eliminated, and the other votes on the loser's ballots are redistributed to the candidates who remain. This process continues until a winner emerges with a majority of the votes received by the remaining candidates.

IRV is not likely to increase substantially the number of third-party elected officials; but adopted for use in any single-member district, it could eliminate problems of wasted votes, spoiling, and elections won by small pluralities. It is said that candidates treat each other more civilly in IRV, because each candidate wants the lower-choice votes of voters who select someone else as their first choice. Many IRV advocates claim that it may even improve voter turnout over time.

If IRV were adopted for use in U.S. presidential elections, Americans would accomplish in one cost-effective stage something similar to what the French achieve in their two-stage presidential elections. Under IRV Al Gore probably would have won the 2000 presidential election. IRV would have enabled Ralph Nader supporters to vote strategically for Gore but also to cast a first- or second-choice vote for Nader. By the same token, under IRV George H. W. Bush would have been reelected in 1992 if enough Perot voters had also cast strategic votes for Bush.[16]

One reality of America's single-member district election system is the very large number of uncompetitive, safe districts. Just 7 percent of the U.S. House seats shifted from one party to another in 2008, a year that has been chronicled by some as one of those rare election years in which partisan realignment was taking place.

Voters in elections for state legislatures often find not even two choices, but just one candidate standing for the seat in the general election. In the 2008 elections for South Carolina's lower house, only 40 of the 124 districts featured any general election contest. In 36 of these, a Republican faced a Democrat. In 4 others the incumbent of a major party defended against a third-party challenger or a "petition" (independent) candidate. Voters in the other 84 districts had no choices at all.

Many factors work to reduce or eliminate competition in America's single-member districts. An important one is the wide use of the partisan gerrymander in drawing up legislative district lines. Because the power to gerrymander rests with the majority party in the state legislature when the time comes to redistrict, there is reason to blame the majority party for the gerrymander's effect in stifling and suppressing democratic competition. What is often overlooked is the two major parties' overlapping interests, even in the practice of gerrymandering. The majority party seeks benefit for itself in as many districts as possible; but an effect of its design may be to make other districts safe, or safer, for the nonmajority major party.

The Electoral College

The Electoral College is a complex institution, and many aspects involved in assessing it have little or nothing to do with its impact upon independents and minor parties.[17] The effect it does have upon nonmajor-party presidential candidacies derives almost entirely from the longstanding practice of electing party-chosen slates of electors and the tradition, embodied even in statute in some states, that the members of the elected slate are to vote as a bloc, awarding all of the state's electoral votes to the presidential and vice-presidential nominees who won the popular plurality in the state.

In twenty-six of the forty-three presidential elections from 1836 through 2004, not a single elector in any state violated the winner-takes-all understanding, and in ten others only a single elector in just one state gave his or her vote to a presidential candidate other than the one who received the state's other electoral votes. Some, though not all, of these single dissenters were the so-called **faithless electors**—electors who vote their personal preference, violating their commitment to the nominee of their party.

Nebraska split in 2008, giving four electoral votes to McCain and one to Obama; but the outcome there had nothing to do with a faithless elector. In 1969 Maine revamped its policy, moving away from winner takes all. The new policy in Maine has been to award two electoral votes to the statewide winner and one to the winner in each congressional district. Nebraska followed suit in 1991, but it was not until 2008 that a congressional district in either state voted for a presidential candidate who was not the statewide choice. It happened in Nebraska's Second District, metropolitan Omaha.

The winner-takes-all principle still is firmly entrenched in forty-eight states and the District of Columbia; and because under it no party receives electoral votes without coming in first in some jurisdiction with electoral votes to cast, this means that even those third parties with substantial popular backing are unlikely to receive any share of electoral votes. In 1992 Perot received not even 1 of the 538 electoral votes, despite his having taken nearly one in every five popular votes cast. Only when, as with the Dixiecrats in 1948, the strength of an important minor party is heavily concentrated in a single region or in particular states can the party hope to take a share of electoral votes as large as or larger than its popular share.

Winner takes all underlies the recurrent charge in mainstream media that popular votes for a third-party presidential campaign are likely to accomplish nothing more than to spoil the election for one major-party candidate by tipping to the other major nominee the electoral votes of one or more crucial states. This charge was laid in particular at Nader's doorstep, both before and after the 2000 election. The spoiler claim certainly influenced and restrained the votes of many who might otherwise have voted for Nader, and it may have altered the decisions of potential third-party voters in later campaigns.

This is partly counterweighted by the fact that winner takes all in presidential elections has produced a large number of safe Republican or Democratic states. Some voters in these safe states come to understand that they can vote for a third-party candidate without worrying about election spoiling. Hundreds of thousands of Nader's votes in 2000 were cast in states that were so reliably Republican that it would have been futile to cast a strategic vote for Gore.[18]

Amending the Constitution is difficult, and over the years the Electoral College has survived many attempts to abolish it. A new initiative that now aims to reform by interstate agreement may actually bear some fruit. This is the movement for the **National Popular Vote compact.** The states would retain their shares of electoral votes, but those states entering into this interstate compact would commit to casting all of their electoral votes for the candidate who wins the nationwide popular vote. This commitment would not take effect until the electoral votes of states entering the compact totaled 270, the majority that is required for electing the president.

California, eight other states, and the District of Columbia had committed to NPV by August 2011. Collectively they account for nearly half the electoral votes needed to implement the compact. If this initiative does succeed, it will accomplish the goal of popular election of the nation's chief executive. It also would liberate third-party candidates and supporters from the 2000 scenario—from the possibility, however remote, that third-party votes might contribute to the election of a major candidate not popular enough to win the votes of even a plurality of his or her fellow citizens.

The Teeth of America's Duopoly

Of all American political parties, the Democrats and Republicans are the only ones powerful enough not to need to be a protected class. Yet there are the rules and regulations that were designed precisely to preserve their duopolistic control. These include restrictive ballot-access requirements, policies that sharply discriminate in access to debates and to public campaign funds, and sore loser and antifusion laws. Their defenders may seek to justify them by alluding to the hardball nature of politics or to the role the duopolistic rules are said to play in providing for stable government. To try to defend them on democratic grounds is likely to prove a futile gesture. These are rules designed by the duopoly's beneficiaries to protect the major parties at the expense of the American voter by reducing the range of voter choices and diminishing the power of the voting act.

Restrictive Ballot-Access Requirements

Through most of the nineteenth century, there were no restrictions on parties' access to the ballot. Before the adoption state by state of the "Australian" secret ballot in the 1880s, the parties had printed their own ballots ("tickets" they called them) and distributed them to voters. Because voting was a public act and it was hard or impossible to vote a split ticket, there were some powerful incentives for a voter to turn down the offer of a minor party's ticket. But in principle at least, this older system had given all parties equal access to voters on election day.[19]

With the adoption of the secret ballot, the states took both the responsibility to produce the ballot and the prerogative to set the conditions for access to it. They began to enact petition requirements to appear on the ballot. The stringency of those requirements substantially increased over the years, as the states came to use their place as ballot gatekeeper to protect major-party primacy by disadvantaging or excluding others. States also designed their conditions for retaining ballot certification—usually a specified minimum vote percentage received in a designated recent past election held in the state—to serve duopolistic purposes.

This did not happen all at once. Ballot-access requirements imposed by the states during the period 1892–1930 were remarkably lenient and reasonable as compared with those that came later. At no time during the 1892–1930 period did the valid signatures required for a new party to make the presidential ballots of all the states total as many as one hundred thousand; and because many states did not keep statewide registration lists, election officials often may not have done a lot of checking before declaring that the signatures on the submitted petitions were valid. No state required petition circulators to await a particular date before beginning to collect signatures, and most states imposed an October deadline for submitting the petition. This compares with deadline medians in September during the years 1932–56 and in August for 1960 and since.[20]

During the 1892–1930 period, there were third-party presidential campaigns that made the ballot in every jurisdiction with electoral votes to cast. The People's Party—its leaders and followers were known as Populists—did that in 1892. Presidential nominees of the Socialist Party made every ballot in 1904, 1912, and 1916. Robert M. La Follette did not declare his 1924 Progressive campaign for the presidency until July, but his name appeared on every November ballot except Louisiana's.

States toughened their ballot-access laws after 1930, but it was in the 1960s and 1970s that the most disabling barriers to third-party and independent campaigns were in place. To make every presidential ballot in 1964, the campaign of a new party would have had to submit 920,505 valid signatures nationwide. Between 1931 and 1964, individual states enacted provisions

> requiring a petition to be circulated within a two-week or 24-day period; forcing the circulators to pay to print a list of all the signers in one newspaper in each county in the state; forcing groups to pay to have their petitions checked by elections officials; subjecting petition signers to a subpoena to investigate whether they had actually signed the petition; jailing circulators who allegedly misled the signers about the contents of the petition; banning "subversive" parties from the ballot; forbidding circulators from working outside their home precincts or their home magisterial districts; forbidding anyone to circulate a petition without first getting "credentials" to do so from the county elections office; making it illegal to submit a surplus of 20 percent of the needed signatures; or simply eliminating all procedures for new parties or their nominees, or independent candidates, to get on the ballot.[21]

In all the elections of the 1930s through the 1970s, not a single third-party or independent presidential candidate made the ballot of every jurisdiction with electoral votes to cast. George Wallace, the 1968 American Independent Party standard-bearer, came close. The Wallace campaign appeared on the ballots of all fifty states but not that of the District of Columbia.

Wallace's team of ballot-crackers had discovered that in Ohio they faced an impossibility. Their campaign would have had to produce a petition signed by some 433,000 Ohioans, and they would have had to file it by February before the November election. In a Wallace challenge that went all the way to the U.S. Supreme Court, Ohio admitted that the motivation for its statute had been to preserve the two major parties' lock on elections in Ohio. A six-judge Supreme Court majority struck down the Ohio law but left many other states' less draconian ones in place.[22]

Ballot-access barriers have eased somewhat in the 1980s, the 1990s, and since. Evidence of this may be seen in the success of some nonmajor-party presidential candidates in getting on all fifty-one ballots. Two did that in 1980, one in 1988, two in 1992, and two in 1996.

This does not mean that the barriers really have been effectively taken down. A new party seeking ballot-access everywhere for its presidential candidate would have needed 634,727 validated signatures in 2004, and that number was higher in 2008.[23] Formidable restrictions remain in many states, and ballot-access laws are so bewilderingly diverse from state to state that a third party serious about challenging the Republicans and Democrats still would be well advised to employ on its staff experts in election law.

Disparate practices apply to write-in votes. Sustained by a 1992 Supreme Court decision,[24] Hawaii and some other states prohibit them. A very few permit write-ins for most elections but forbid voters to cast them for the presidency. Most states allow write-ins, but some of these fail in their commitment to count and report the results.

Oklahoma maintains the toughest, most impenetrable barriers to access to the presidential ballot today. The threshold requirements for making Oklahoma's ballot are high, and the state does not allow write-in votes. In both the 2004 and the 2008 presidential elections, Oklahomans were the nation's only voters who could choose only the Republican or Democratic nominee and no one else, not even on write-in.

The Colorado and Florida ballots have been, by comparison, commendably accessible. Colorado voters could find the names of sixteen presidential candidates on their 2008 ballot. In the history of ballot-access laws, no state had ever offered its citizens that many presidential choices. Florida's 2008 presidential ballot carried thirteen names.[25]

For those campaigns that do surmount the ballot-access barriers, the personnel and financial costs laid out for that achievement can be devastating. John Anderson's 1980 independent presidential campaign made all fifty-one ballots, but it spent more than half of the $7.3 million it collected between March and September on petition drives and legal fees.[26] Lenora Fulani's 1988 New Alliance Party presidential candidacy also made every ballot, but the drive for ballot access drained it of 70 percent of the $2 million it took in.[27] Meanwhile Anderson's and Fulani's Democratic and Republican opponents were using their far more substantial human and financial resources to reach voters and solicit their votes.

Sore Loser Provisions

Along with their imposed burdens on ballot access, American states have enacted "sore loser" policies. Today forty-six states—all except Connecticut, New York, Vermont, and Iowa—have and enforce either sore loser statutes or early filing deadlines that accomplish the same purpose.[28] Whatever its form and wording, the practical effect of sore loser policy is to banish from the general election ballot candidates seeking to run for an office for which earlier in the year they tried but failed to win the nomination of a political party. Sore loser laws serve to protect the primacy of the major parties, and they are defended because sometimes they eliminate fringe candidates. But they are an additional barrier to third-party and independent challenges, and they come at some cost to voters, whose general election choices are reduced when a candidate is excluded. In 1974 the U.S. Supreme Court upheld, 6–3, a stringent California sore loser law.[29]

Dr. Ron Paul, the maverick Texas congressman, failed in his campaign for the GOP presidential nomination in 2008. Hanging on to hope, many of his supporters then tried to draft him to run for the presidency on the Libertarian Party ticket. There were some, even among those devoted to Paul, who offered the opinion that because of enforceable Republican Party pledges he had taken as the condition for being admitted to the primary ballot in several states—sore loser provisions in a different form—he was prohibited from accepting a third-party general election candidacy.[30]

But a consensus may be developing that sore loser provisions cannot be enforced against candidates for the presidency. John Anderson made his 1980 run for the presidency as an independent after failing to take the Republican nomination. Anderson had entered some two-thirds of the GOP's 1980 presidential primaries. He thereafter made the ballots of the fifty states and the District of Columbia. Four states still claim that their sore loser laws apply to presidential candidates. But precedent apparently was set by Anderson's ballot-cracking success, and it is unlikely that the courts would uphold a state seeking to apply sore loser law to banish a presidential candidate from its general election ballot.[31]

Antifusion Laws

Fusion occurs when two or more political parties coalesce in support of a candidate and sometimes in embrace of a common program. Fusion was readily available and widely practiced when the parties themselves printed and distributed ballots to voters, and it continued to be used frequently during the period (1892–1930) of lenient ballot-access laws. Fusion tickets connecting minor parties with major ones were particularly widespread during the last thirty years of the nineteenth century.

For third parties fusion undeniably carries some hazards. On rare occasions a major party has devoured its minor fusion partner by co-optation—by appropriating its issues, raiding its support base, and taking away its reason to exist.

But fusion has far more frequently benefited than burdened third parties. Verification of this can be found in the current duopolistic laws banning fusion in most of the states. Fusion heightens the opportunity for a minor party to affect the political process by electing its own or allied candidates and by influencing the policy agenda of the major partner.

Following the states' assumption of responsibility for ballot production, fusion came to be identified with a practice called cross-endorsement. **Cross-endorsement** occurs when two or more parties nominate the same candidate and indicate their endorsements on the general election ballot. Cross-endorsement may imply a quid pro quo; typically a minor party endorses the nominee of a major party—though sometimes it is the other way round—in return for the prospect of sympathetic attention to policy concerns and sometimes the patronage demands of the minor party.

In most fusion states, the cross-endorsed candidate's name appears on the line of every party whose nomination the candidate received, and the candidate's vote tallies from the ballot lines are summed and totaled. On the ballots of Vermont and Oregon, the candidate's name appears on just one ballot line, but alongside it a list indicating the names of the endorsing parties.

Statutes in most of the states now prohibit this ballot-level fusion. Clearly the motive of legislators has been a defense of the primacy of the major parties—the parties to which they themselves belong. There are, by most counts, just eight fusion states now: New York, Connecticut, Vermont, Delaware, South Carolina, Mississippi, Idaho, and (since 2009) Oregon. Fusion is technically legal in two others, but the conditions imposed on its use are very difficult, and fusion is rare in those states.[32]

Fusion has been widely practiced in New York for many years, and it is there that its benefits, not only for minor parties but for democracy itself, have been on best display. Due mainly to fusion, third parties arise and come to exert important tertiary roles and powers in the New York political system. New Yorkers have encountered the American Labor, Liberal, and Right to Life parties in the past, and today the Conservative, Independence, and Working Families parties.

Each of New York's third parties has had its strategic objective. The Conservatives, for instance, have sought to be a moderating influence upon the generally liberal nature of politics in their state. These Conservatives usually cross-endorse Republican nominees; but Republicans know that if the GOP candidate is deemed too liberal or is at odds with nonnegotiable Conservative policy positions, the Conservatives may run their own candidate instead. New York Conservatives' most important win as an independent party came in 1970 with the victorious campaign of James L Buckley, the brother of conservative literary icon William F. Buckley Jr., for a six-year term in the U.S. Senate. In that race Buckley took on and defeated both Democratic and Republican foes.

Born in New York in 1998, the movement of state Working Families parties is the direct descendent of the New Party, a short-lived party of the 1990s. Like their progenitor, these Working Families parties have embraced fusion as their principal electoral strategy. Working Families parties are active now in New York and in other states where fusion is allowed.

The New Party was a social democratic party with links to labor and connections to low-income community organizations affiliated with ACORN—the Association of Community Organizations for Reform Now. The New Party endorsed Democratic candidates who committed themselves to key positions it put forward on behalf of its labor and low-income constituents. Where fusion was permitted, the party cross-endorsed. Where it was not, the New Party put out the word about candidates it was endorsing. Barack Obama was a New Party member during his 1996 Democratic campaign for the Illinois state senate, and NP gave Obama its endorsement.[33]

The New Party and fusion were the immediate losers in *Timmons v. Twin Cities Area New Party* (1997), one of the most important third-party cases the Supreme Court has ever taken up.[34] The 6–3 *Timmons* majority rejected the NP's argument that when states forbid fusion they are violating the Constitution. All third parties really lost in *Timmons,* along with hopes of opening up and democratizing American elections. The winners were duopoly and the two large parties it serves.

Writing for the Court, William Rehnquist affirmed for states the right to "decide that political stability is best served through a healthy two-party system." "Unreasonably exclusionary restrictions" are unjustified, the Chief Justice declared, but "states need not remove all of the many hurdles third parties face in the American political arena today."[35]

Duopoly in Debates

Televised debates have become essential rituals of presidential politics. Though often criticized, and rightly so, for the forms they take, these debates may provide pivotal glimpses of the candidates—of their backgrounds, values, and goals and of their wit and wisdom (or lack thereof)—leaving impressions that many voters will take with them all the way to the voting booth. Candidates understand that their participation in these debates can establish their bona fides as serious aspirants for the presidency.

Intraparty presidential debate stages often are crowded places. In 2007 ten Republican hopefuls took part in their party's three earliest debates. Eight candidates participated in Democratic debates before the winnowing that eventually brought the nomination to Obama.

Not so the general election debates; for these the rules are stacked so heavily that normally third-party and independent candidates cannot beg their way onto the debate stage. Over the nearly half century from 1960—the year of the first televised presidential debates—to 2008, the Democratic and Republican presidential nominees faced off against each other in twenty-six debates. Just one nonmajor-party presidential candidate won the invitation to participate against both of his two major-party foes: Ross Perot in 1992. By almost every account, Perot's performance and indeed his very presence in the three 1992 debates substantially bolstered his stature as a presidential candidate.

On only one other occasion has a nonmajor candidate faced the nominee of even one major party. In the first fall debate of 1980, independent John Anderson debated Ronald Reagan, the Republican nominee. Incumbent President Jimmy Carter refused to take part in a debate to which Anderson was invited. Carter and Reagan then confronted each other with Anderson excluded in a last debate a week before the election.

For twelve years the League of Women Voters, a nonpartisan group, oversaw the debates, but it divorced itself from the operation in October 1988. The separation was anything but amicable. The league let it be known that it would not be a partner in what it said was the major parties' goal of transforming the debates into fraudulent, stage-managed charades.[36]

Overseeing things since then has been the Commission on Presidential Debates. The commission is a bipartisan body, always headed by former chairs of the Democratic and Republican national committees. Although nongovernmental, the commission exercises a quasi-governmental power, and its rulings have survived numerous third-party and independent challenges.

In 2000 the commission adopted the rule that candidates seeking to take part in a general election presidential debate must have the support of at least 15 percent of the respondents in five recent national opinion polls. Given that since the Civil War only three presidential candidates not running in the general election as Democrats or Republicans have ever received as much as 15 percent of the votes cast, the commission's rule is remarkably prohibitive. It provides unvarnished illustration of the major parties' penchant for joining together to protect their duopoly, and it confirms the truth of the colloquial saying that "them that has, gets."

Some access criterion is needed to prevent vanity candidates from using the presidential debates to take their fifteen minutes of fame. Many advocates of freer access contend that general elections debates—*at least* one in every election round—should be open to all candidates who have surmounted the ballot-access barriers of states with electoral votes totaling to 270: in other words to all candidates who theoretically could win the presidency by taking the required majority of electoral votes. In the fall of 2008, that would have meant at least one debate with four minor candidates joining the two major-party nominees on stage. That did not happen, of course.

Discriminatory Public Campaign Funding Policies

Congress passed the **Federal Election Campaign Act** in 1971, with important amendments added in 1974. Campaign reform clearly was a motive underlying FECA and especially its post-Watergate 1974 amendments. But FECA's provision for public (taxpayer-supported) funding of presidential campaigns is so discriminatory that the legislation has come to be seen as a "major-party protection act."[37]

Under FECA's provisions major-party presidential nominees may forgo the use of private contributions and accept instead federal funds, adjusted for inflation in each election round, to finance the costs of the general election campaign. Both McCain and Obama were eligible in 2008 for FECA general election funds of slightly more than eighty-four million dollars.[38]

Presidential nominees of other parties that in the most recent presidential election received 5 percent or more of the vote do qualify for general election funds. The size of these grants, far from equal to those of the major-party candidates, is computed as the ratio of the party's vote in the last presidential election to the average vote for the major candidates in that election. Ross Perot, the 1996 Reform Party nominee, received slightly more than twenty-nine million dollars in federal general election funds based upon the 19 percent vote share he had taken in his 1992 presidential quest. By comparison Perot's 1996 major-party opponents each received general election funds of nearly sixty-two million dollars.[39]

It is true that certain elements of current federal campaign policy may in some ways mitigate the impact of this discrimination. FECA provides for the grant of federal funds to match private contributions during the nominating season, and the qualifications for receipt of these matching funds do not differentiate between minor- and major-party candidates. Some minor candidates have received matching funds over the years. Ralph Nader received $881,494 in matching funds in 2008.[40]

In its 1976 *Buckley v. Valeo* decision, the Supreme Court ruled that the FECA limits on spending by a candidate from the candidate's personal funds were "constitutionally infirm" because of their intrusion upon First Amendment rights. Perot was a practical beneficiary of this ruling, and in 1992 he spent millions of dollars of his own money in a campaign against the FECA-funded major-party nominees. *Buckley* also modified the FECA requirement that parties report to the administering Federal Election Commission (FEC) the names of all donors of two hundred dollars or more. The decision recognized the claim of exemption from such forced disclosures by parties able to demonstrate "reasonable probability" that the disclosures would subject the identified givers to "threats, harassment, or reprisals."[41]

Based on *Buckley* the FEC exempted from required disclosure the Communist and the Socialist Workers parties.

Five of the states have put in place public funding policies that cover gubernatorial, statewide, and state legislative campaigns. At least seven others have instituted public funding of campaigns on a more limited scale. The programs in Arizona and Maine are commendably nondiscriminatory in their treatment of major- and minor-party candidacies. Some other states have implemented public funding programs that are more blatantly discriminatory than that provided by FECA as modified by *Buckley*.[42]

Sanctions against Left-Radical Parties

Americans old enough to remember the events of September 11, 2001, know something about fear. Fear can grip. Fear can overpower reason. Benjamin Franklin understood this. One of Franklin's most enduring maxims may have been intended as a warning to his fellow countrymen in generations to come. "Those who give up essential liberty to obtain a little safety," Franklin wrote, "deserve neither liberty nor safety."

On two occasions in the twentieth century, the nation's reason gave way to a crippling fear of the Left—a fear of domestic leftists, of their real and assumed external allies, and of the danger these leftists were said to pose to public safety and the nation's security. Freedom suffered on both occasions, not at the hands of those accused of wanting to destroy it but by the actions of freedom's self-proclaimed defenders.

The First Red Scare

In April 1917 the United States entered World War I. In November the Bolsheviks seized power in Russia's capital. A fear, approaching hysteria in some quarters, simultaneously gripped Americans. This was to be the nation's first Red Scare, a terror, lasting from 1917 into 1921, during which authorities sought to root out the danger and disloyalty they suspected were lurking among anarchists, in the leadership and ranks of the radical Industrial Workers of the World and also in the words and actions of people in both the Socialist and the emerging Communist parties.

With the nation at war, Congress sharply curtailed freedoms of expression and association. Taking the word *espionage* far beyond what it had always meant, the 1917 Espionage Act made it a crime to interfere with the operation and success of the military. The Sedition Act in 1918 criminalized the use of "disloyal, profane, scurrilous, or abusive" speech to criticize America's government, military, or flag. States followed suit with their own "criminal syndicalism" statutes.

Socialists and other radicals were tried and imprisoned for their antiwar, antidraft advocacy and agitation. In 1919 and again in 1920, the U.S. House refused to seat duly elected Wisconsin Socialist Victor L. Berger, who had been convicted of violating the Espionage Act. In 1920 five elected Socialists were expelled from the lower house of the New York state legislature.

One of the era's most famed American political prisoners was Socialist Party leader Eugene V. Debs. In 1920 Debs ran the last of his five campaigns for the presidency as an inmate of the federal prison in Atlanta.[43] Almost a million of his fellow citizens voted for Debs that year.

Supreme Court decisions of this period sustained the federal and state strictures on liberty.[44] The Palmer Raids of 1919–21, a roundup that was overseen by Attorney General A. Mitchell Palmer and conducted by a young J. Edgar Hoover, produced thousands of arrests and the deportation of many immigrant radicals. Federal, state, and local authorities arrested scores of Communists—some five hundred in California alone—for advocating violent revolution. Hundreds of these went to prison.[45]

McCarthyism / The Second Red Scare

"Are you now, or have you ever been, a member of the Communist Party?" That question helped shape and define a decade. Interrogating subpoenaed Hollywood witnesses, the House Committee on Un-American Activities (HCUA, often seen as HUAC) first raised this query in 1947. The second Red Scare, the era of McCarthyism, was on. The icon of the era was Joseph R. McCarthy of Wisconsin. During his decade in the Senate (1947–57), McCarthy achieved national fame for his red-baiting demagoguery.

HUAC's question was itself ironic. Though under attack—the official assault on the party, its members, and its alleged "fellow travelers" grew in ferocity in the ensuing years—the Communist Party was a legal party, and one that, along with the Soviet Union, had been allied with the United States from the beginning of America's entry into World War II. The Cold War, however, had changed everything.

Older Americans may recall the perjury trial of former State Department official Alger Hiss as well as the trial and executions of Julius and Ethel Rosenberg for passing atomic secrets to the Russians. Millions of schoolchildren in the early 1950s participated in air raid drills that were supposed to prepare them in case of atomic attack. Popular culture was filled with red menace drama. *I Led Three Lives,* a television series that ran for more than three years, offered the wildly fictionalized escapades of an American who had infiltrated the Communist Party as an FBI spy in the 1940s. An incessant theme of the period's science fiction films was invasion by outside evil others and the carnage, mayhem, and death to come.

Personal and civil liberties were seriously infringed upon during the McCarthy era. In 1951 the Supreme Court sustained the conviction under a 1940 act of eleven Communist Party leaders who had been charged not with any revolutionary act or even advocacy, but only with the conspiracy to organize and the conspiracy to teach and advocate the forcible overthrow of American government.[46] Congress passed the McCarron Act in 1950. McCarron declared that the members of the Communist Party had to register with the attorney general, and it imposed other draconian limits on Communists' rights of association.

Communists were not the only ones targeted. The witch hunt's reach also extended to those deemed or suspected to be fellow travelers and even to some other leftist groups that were bitter rivals of the Communist Party. Senator McCarthy and others used the term "Fifth Amendment Communists" to berate witnesses who invoked their freedom from self-incrimination. Government workers lost crucial security clearances. Professors were fired. Hundreds of Hollywood actors, directors, and screenwriters were blacklisted.

The Communist Party had supported, and had come to influence or control, parts of America's labor movement, particularly among some affiliates of the Congress of Industrial Organizations. During the second Red Scare, organized labor found itself on the defensive. Union leaders were purged for refusing to declare, often as a matter of principle, that they were not Communists.

The spirit of McCarthyism was waning by 1954. On March 9 of that year, Edward R. Murrow, the era's most respected American television journalist, devoted the full half hour of his *See It Now* program on CBS to a report critical of McCarthy for his reckless, contradictory, unsubstantiated, and damaging charges.

The final act of the McCarthy drama began a week later, as a Senate committee launched a public inquiry into the charges that were being lobbed back and forth between the U.S. Army and Wisconsin's red-baiting senator. Millions of homemakers who tuned in and watched ABC's live coverage of the Army-McCarthy hearings that spring saw, unfiltered, the irresponsibility and demagoguery of the man whose name was beginning to identify the era. Near the end of 1954, the Senate passed a resolution censuring McCarthy.

By 1957 the Supreme Court under Chief Justice Earl Warren began dismantling, case by case, the constitutional benchmarks under which the red witch hunt had occurred.[47] In the ensuing years, Congress and the states rescinded many of the anti-red statutes they had legislated during the second Red Scare.

Some of the McCarthyist impulse continued on in the form of COINTELPRO—the Counter Intelligence Program—a covert FBI program of surveillance and destabilization that was overseen by FBI director Hoover from 1956 until just before his death in 1972. COINTELPRO did reach into the radical Right, including various Ku Klux Klan groups. But the program's principal trajectory entailed Old Left and New Left movements, notably the Black Panther, Communist, and Socialist Workers parties.

Under COINTELPRO the FBI sent agents and paid informants to infiltrate groups. It used dirty tricks to sow intergroup hatred and violence. The bureau manufactured prosecution evidence and suppressed documents supporting the defense in some trials of targeted activists. It sometimes even arranged for and carried out the assassinations of group leaders. When some of these activities came to light, COINTELPRO's defenders invoked public safety and national security to justify what had been done.[48]

Freedom and safety do conflict at times, a fact etched in the American psyche by the 1995 Oklahoma City bombing and the national calamity of September 11, 2001. Yet Americans assume that freedom is their nation's core value, the platform upon which the national identity rests.

Although today they would almost certainly be unenforceable, McCarthy-era statutes barring Communists from running for public office remain on the books in six U.S. states.[49] The McCarthy era's more general legacy may be that it produced a suspicion by many voters that *all* third parties—and all candidates other than the Democrats and Republicans—are fringy, dangerous, and unworthy of support.

If anything positive grew out of McCarthyism, it is that in reacting to it, many Americans came to realize that curtailing freedom is no way to defend it and that protecting everyone's rights require protecting the rights even of those who may be suspected of wanting to deny them to others.

3

★ ★ ★

On the Outside, Looking In

If I could not go to heaven but with a party, I would not go there at all.

Thomas Jefferson

I'd rather be right than president.

Line from Prohibition Party song

It was undeniably historic, that 2008 presidential election, and the excitement it generated both in and outside the United States had little to do with the third-party and independent candidates vying far beyond the media spotlights. The historic milestones set in 2008 were being set in the two-party center ring.

Senator Barack Obama prevailed to become the first African American ever elected to the U.S. presidency. He surpassed on his way the campaign of Senator Hillary Rodham Clinton, whose supporters left a glass ceiling with eighteen million cracks and their standard-bearer closer to a major-party presidential nomination than any other woman in history. Senator John McCain, Obama's general election adversary, chose as his vice-presidential running mate Alaska governor Sarah Palin. Palin was the first Republican woman ever to take the second slot on her party's ticket.

Almost completely beyond media or public gaze in 2008, the Green Party nominated Cynthia McKinney and Rosa Clemente, two African American women, for the presidency and vice presidency. Remarkable though that was, it really broke little new historical ground. This was not the first time that a third party had selected two minority women to run together for the nation's top offices. If there is a lesson this illustrates, it is that whatever your definition of *there* is, one third party or another almost always gets there long before either major party arrives.

Years before slavery ended, Frederick Douglass and other free black men joined whites in leading the 1840s abolitionist Liberty Party. Thousands of southern blacks and whites participated in the politics and fusion campaigns of the Greenback and People's (Populist) parties in the last quarter of the nineteenth century.[1]

The Prohibition Party, founded in 1869, is the nation's oldest minor party. From its earliest days, Prohibition women took leadership positions in their party. In 1872

Victoria Woodhull stood as the presidential candidate of the Equal Rights Party. That was forty-eight years before the achievement of women's suffrage nationwide.

Nominated by the Socialist Party for the presidency in 1980 and again in 2000, David McReynolds was the first openly gay person ever to run for America's top political office.[2] During the twentieth century, many minor parties broke down gender or racial barriers in selecting candidates for the presidency or vice presidency.

Third parties also have been on the front lines of policy innovation and democratic structural reform. The Liberty and Free Soil parties staked out positions sharply at odds with the defenders of slavery; likewise the Republicans, who began as a third party before arriving in the ranks of the majors. Neither major party endorsed women's suffrage until 1916, a scant four years before the women's suffrage Nineteenth Amendment entered the Constitution. Long before that, a half-dozen minor parties had embraced and worked toward that goal.

The direct election of U.S. senators, initiative and referendum, the progressive income tax, minimum wage and anti–child labor legislation, Social Security—all these and others appeared as planks in third-party platforms before either major party took up their cause. It was from the third-party periphery that the heinous costs and dangers of the emerging Cold War were raised, term limits pushed, and economic globalization challenged.

Minor-party representatives rarely sit in decision-making bodies in numbers large enough to put their own imprimatur on policy enactments and structural changes. Third parties' impact more often comes when, having demonstrated the popularity of ideas they push, these parties find their ideas appropriated—taken up or stolen—by one or both major parties.

One should not infer from any of this that the visions, goals, methods, and accomplishments of all third parties are useful, good—or even safe. Nativism and virulent anti-Catholicism were central themes of the Know Nothings—the American Party—an ephemeral group that once seemed positioned to achieve major-party status. Relatively few outside the thinning ranks of today's Prohibition Party share that party's nostalgia for the fourteen-year federal ban on the manufacture and sale of beverage alcohol. There are, and have been, third-party groups pursuing racist agendas or advocating change by force and violence. This chapter explores the good, but also the bad and the ugly, in the histories of this nation's third parties.

America's Two-Party Systems

Contrary to what some may believe, the Constitution's most influential framers were downright hostile to the notion of parties, and a party system—two-party or otherwise—was not a part of their grand design, their vision of "a more perfect Union." In his famed *Federalist* no. 10, James Madison laid out the theoretical indictment of parties and also interest groups—"factions," he called them. Factions divide, and they bear seeds of potential tyranny. Even after the nation's first parties were launched, George Washington still warned in his 1796 Farewell Address about the "baneful effects of the spirit of party."

Some of the founders of new third-world nations have harbored an antipathy toward parties that is reminiscent of the attitudes of America's first leaders. But the American prescription—remedy, some would say—was extraordinary and, by comparison, remarkable in its liberality. Associational freedoms were enshrined in the First Amendment, though the Constitution nowhere specifically mentions parties or groups.

Separation of powers, with checks and balances, and federalism were embodied as central features of the new political structure, partly due to the framers' hope that these would serve as barriers blocking the potential for partisan mischief.[3] The historical effect of this prescription as safeguard is debatable; but unquestionably separation of powers and federalism have made of American parties creatures different in role and function from the parties that operate within parliamentary systems.

Federalists versus Democratic-Republicans (early 1790s–1816)

Realists they were, and in spite of their own well-documented antiparty views, it was America's nation builders who also created its first organized national parties.[4] Elite rule was a feature of earliest U.S. political life. These first parties—Federalist and Democratic-Republican—began as elite parties-in-government during the first Washington administration, later developing the organizations needed to reach out to voters in the restricted electorate. Alexander Hamilton, Washington's Treasury secretary, was the Federalist founder. Secretary of State Thomas Jefferson, along with Congressman Madison, then launched the Democratic-Republicans.

The life span of the Federalist Party—the party of Hamilton and of John Adams (Washington too was considered a Federalist)—was actually quite short. Though a remnant of their party lasted into the early 1820s, Federalists ran their last presidential candidate in 1816. The 1820 presidential election took place in the context of one-party rule. Then in the 1820s the Democratic-Republicans broke into factions—National Republicans and Democrats—giving rise in the early 1830s to a new party system.

Democrats versus Whigs (1833–1854)

By 1832 one branch of the party of Jefferson had transformed itself into a new party—the party of Andrew Jackson—and by 1833 another new party, opposed to Jacksonian democracy, was coming to life. Thus were born the modern Democratic Party and also its first major-party adversary, the Whig Party.

Two third parties challenged the primacy both of Democrats and Whigs in the 1850s. The nativist, anti-Catholic appeal of the Know Nothings first captured the allegiance of millions of American-born Protestants who opposed the massive immigration of Irish and German Catholics occurring at the time. Then just as Know Nothings seemed poised to join the national major-party ranks, the issue on which their appeal was based was preempted by other, more pressing and corrosive issues—issues of sectionalism. These deeply divided the Democrats, and they utterly destroyed the Whigs.

The Republican Party was born in 1854. Though this new party gathered many interests and its earliest views on slavery lay in the direction of antiextension rather than abolition, proslavery interests understood and feared the Republicans' widening appeal.

In 1856, for the first time in history, a Republican, John C. Fremont, faced a Democratic nominee in the election for president. Fremont lost to Democrat James Buchanan. A third candidate, former president Millard Fillmore, ran as a Know Nothing. Fillmore also received Whig endorsement, but that support lacked substantial value, given the near-death state by 1856 of the once-vigorous party. Republicans took 38 percent of the U.S. House seats in 1856, though the majority went to the Democrats. All indicators showed a party system in flux. By the end of 1856, the two-year-old Republican Party was already far along on its path toward major-party status.

Birthplace of the Republican Party as a third party, Ripon, Wisconsin, 1854. Photograph by Ripon Historical Society president William Wooley. Courtesy of Little White Schoolhouse, Inc.

Republicans versus Democrats (ca. 1860–)

As civil war threatened, Republican Abraham Lincoln won the 1860 presidential election. Democrats and Republicans have prevailed since then in retaining possession of the center ring of American presidential contests, though there have been occasions when outside challengers briefly entered the ring or came very close.[5]

The relative positions of strength of Democrats and Republicans—the two major parties—have ebbed and flowed over the past century and a half. The historical record suggests in fact that at least four party systems have emerged in sequence over the years since Lincoln's 1860 victory.

Realignment, a rare electoral event, has preceded and determined the advent of each of these systems. Realignment may occur during a single election cycle or during a lengthier but brief critical period. Voter turnout rates are uncharacteristically high during realignment. Realignment may alter the relative strengths of the major parties or bring a new party into the company of the majors. Parties during realignment often define or redefine themselves ideologically, programmatically, or even geographically, and both the size and demographic makeup of their electoral coalitions are recast, sometimes radically.[6]

Barack Obama's 2008 vote percentage was the second highest any Democratic presidential nominee had received since World War II. His victory and those of other Democrats in 2006 and 2008 brought forth a spate of articles either declaring or raising the premise that realignment had occurred or that the nation had entered a new critical period of electoral realignment favorable to the Democratic Party.[7]

If ever there has been a third-party golden age in the United States, that was in the nineteenth century. Third-party members of the U.S. House numbered thirty-four in 1833, some fifty-one in 1855, and twenty-six in 1897. The Great Depression brought the largest number of twentieth-century third partisans to the House: thirteen in the 1936 elections. Though always exceptional, elections won by third-party and independent gubernatorial candidates occurred far more often in the nineteenth century than since.

No minor party since the nineteenth century has achieved what the Republicans did in becoming a major party. The most serious threats to the century-and-a-half dominance by Democrats and Republicans to date came from the Populists in the 1890s and the Bull Moose Progressives in and around 1912. Other windows of opportunity have opened on occasion, most recently in the 1990s.

Third Parties: Coming to Terms

One of the things distinguishing major parties from minor ones is the success of major parties in building "big tent" coalitions. The goal of election motivates and drives both major parties. Seeking victory at the polls, the Democratic and the Republican parties both coalesce a range of diverse, sometimes conflicting, interests.

Many business executives, evangelicals, Mormons, pro-lifers, southern whites, Cuban Americans, Plains states residents, college graduates, veterans, physicians, and gun-rights advocates are among those associated with the GOP. The Democratic camp includes millions of African Americans, Latinos, union households, northeasterners and Pacific state residents, Jews, unmarried people, environmentalists, feminists, professors, trial lawyers, and young voters.

Some minor parties also want to erect big tents, but few achieve that goal, and of those that do, not one arising since the Civil War has sustained what it has built. Many do not even try. Third-party activists often envy the achievements and power of the major parties, but they also hold a disdain for their expediency. Purists dominate the ranks of many minor parties, and even when leavened by the presence and influence of some pragmatists, a party may hold that its commitment to creed or devotion to defining issues is more important than winning elections. Some minor parties are very narrow in the range of their primary interests. It was its devotion to the anti-abortion cause that sustained New York's Right to Life Party for more than twenty years.

Third parties include all those that prove unable either to transform the national party system into a multiparty arrangement or to replace one of the existing major parties within the national two-party system. Though many third parties have sought national major-party status, only one—the Republican Party, early in its history—ever achieved it. Given the central positions occupied by the Republicans and Democrats since the Civil War, the third-party designation applies to all post-1865 parties other than the Democrats and Republicans.

A **third party** is an organized aggregate of leaders, members, and supporters that

- designates itself a party,
- articulates interests of its devotees,
- presses these interests using electoral and/or other political methods, and
- either never attains or is unable to sustain the primary or secondary share of loyalties of people making up the national electorate.

Third parties are not all of one type. Years ago the political scientist V. O. Key identified two kinds of nationally or regionally organized third parties: the **continuing doctrinal and issue parties** and the **short-lived parties**—in Key's words, "the recurring, short-lived . . . party eruptions."[8] Some writers apply the designation *minor party* to the doctrinal and issue parties, reserving for the short-lived parties the term *third party*. I make no such distinction, and throughout this book *third party* and *minor party* are used as synonymous, interchangeable terms. To Key's two third-party types—the continuing doctrinal and issue parties and the short-lived parties—I add a third. These are the parties I designate the **state/local significant others.**

Continuing doctrinal and issue parties sustain themselves for several decades at least. Some of these parties have long records of running candidates, and on rare occasions they have won local, state, or even congressional office. But these parties' stability and continuity—their remarkable longevity—are better explained by their devotees' faithful commitment to their party creed or issue goal than by genuine hope of election victory.

A student once told me that these parties reminded her of asteroids, those bits of rock and dust that orbit the sun in the general vicinity of much larger planets. Though far from perfect, her analogy is instructive. Sometimes a party of this kind has influenced the mainstream. The Prohibition Party played a part in the enactment of the Eighteenth Amendment. Socialist Party platforms influenced the development of Social Security and other New Deal programs, and Socialists governed the city of Milwaukee as recently as 1960. The Communist Party exerted some clout in the labor, minority, and academic communities in the 1930s and 1940s. Even so, parties of this type never seriously threaten the national electoral dominance of the major parties. As Key observed, these doctrinal and issue parties are "in a sense outside the system."[9]

Many mainstream Americans may perceive a doctrinal party to be too radical, distant from their own values, or even dangerous. Voters may find the issue position motivating an issue party to be obscure, not compelling, or simply wrong. No presidential candidate running solely as the nominee of a continuing doctrinal or issue party ever has won more than 6 percent of the popular vote. Some of these parties offer token election campaigns, seeking to reach the public through whatever media coverage may come their way. Others regard the whole election process as a sham and do not run candidates.

Short-lived parties often originate either as movements of economic protest or as splinters from one of the major parties. Many of them have been tied to and identified with the powerful personality, agenda, and will of a single founder or standard-bearer.

Anti-Masons and Know Nothings, Libertymen and Free Soilers, Greenbackers, Populists, and Progressives, Dixiecrats and American Independents, Reform Party leaders and followers—these and others were unable to sustain their place as significant actors in American politics. Short-lived parties sometimes do score impressive electoral tallies, even determining which major-party candidate wins.

The early demise of a minor party cannot be taken as proof that its life was in vain. One reason for these parties' failure to dig in for the long term is the major parties' remarkable ability to soak things up like a sponge.[10] The Republicans and Democrats both carry a history of appropriating—lifting for themselves—third parties' most appealing ideas, taking along with them the challenging party's reason to exist. The strength of a third party's threat to the primacy of the major parties may be a very real factor in shortening that party's life expectancy.

State/local significant others find an influential place for themselves in the politics of their community or state. Some even become major-party actors there. They are not disinterested in national politics. Some have sent nominees to Congress. A very few have managed to supplant in power the state branch of a national party or to develop in effect a satellite relationship with the national Democrats or Republicans. But in their electoral base, the state/local significant others remain primarily confined to the boundaries of their state or community.

Examples are plentiful. The Virginia Readjusters were a late-nineteenth-century party with a biracial outreach and ambitious goals for public education. At their peak around 1883, Readjusters held the Virginia governor's office and six seats in the U.S. Senate and House. The Minnesota Farmer-Labor Party and the Wisconsin Progressive Party were statewide governing parties during the Great Depression. Burlington, the largest city in Vermont, has maintained a genuine three-party system since the early 1980s. In 2011 the Vermont Progressive Party held the Burlington mayoralty, several seats on the Burlington city council, and seven in the Vermont state legislature.

Prohibition: The Oldest Living Minor Party

Birmingham, Alabama, June 18–19, 1979.[11] Delegates from various states have gathered here. This is the first time the Prohibition Party has ever selected a Deep South site for its national convention. The party was born in 1869. It is the third oldest living American party. The GOP was just fifteen years old at the time of this party's birth.

What these delegates will do—nominate candidates for president and vice president, adopt a platform, and rally to capture whatever free media attention may come their way—is pretty standard stuff for American national parties. But the setting and scene may surprise a mainstream observer. This convention is not being held in one of the mega-arenas the Democrats and Republicans select. The location, the Motel Birmingham, has been deliberately chosen to reward this city's only "dry" (no alcohol allowed) lodging facility.

These delegates number less than one hundred, not the four thousand who attended Prohibition's 1892 Cincinnati convention or the thousands selected to attend Republican or Democratic national conventions today. A few, who also belong to the Woman's Christian Temperance Union, still nostalgically recall what it was like in their youth, when prohibition was national law. Almost all the delegates are old. Before adjourning, they will eulogize Prohibition saints who have died in the four years since their party last met.

Their platform bears planks embracing an array of conservative issues like those on which Republican Ronald Reagan also will run next year. But the centerpiece of this Prohibition document is, as always, alcohol: "We . . . favor the prohibition of the manufacture, distribution, and sale of all alcoholic beverages." To prepare the way, the Reverend Charles Ewing delivers a stirring keynote, "Liberty and the Liquor Traffic."

Local media watchers will not hear of this speech. The media, in fact, will be quite inattentive to these events at the Motel Birmingham: a few humorous clips on

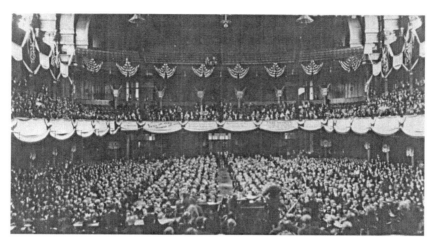

Prohibition National Convention, 1892. Original copyright by Barnum and Cumback, Indianapolis. Courtesy of the U.S. Library of Congress Prints and Photographs Division. Obtained through Wikimedia Commons.

local television news, a newspaper article or two. One, on the front page, will tell of the eccentricities of these Prohibition windmill tilters.

This party harbors no illusions about its chances in the upcoming election. The delegate presenting the party's presidential nominee will publicly declare him to be "the "man who *should be* the next president." Before leaving for home, these Prohibitionists will sing their party's beloved old song, "I'd Rather Be Right Than President":

> I'd rather be right than President, I want my conscience clear;
> I'll firmly stand for the truth and right, I have a God to fear.
> I'll work and vote the way I pray—no matter that the scoffers say—
> I'd rather be right than President, I want my conscience clear.

Nominated in that 1979 Birmingham gathering, Benjamin Bubar managed in 1980 to make it to the ballots of just eight states and to bag a disappointing 7,212 votes. Party fortunes have been even more meager in the decades since that Birmingham meeting.

Beginning in 1984, Earl F. Dodge many times bore Prohibition's standard as its presidential candidate. Dodge had enlisted in the cause as a nineteen-year-old in 1952. He came to be acknowledged, even by intraparty critics, for holding things together during some of the party's leanest years. But over these years, jarring controversy arose over the style and course of his leadership.

In 2003, four years before Dodge's death, the old party formally split into pro- and anti-Dodge factions. These two factions—legally they were separate parties—vied for control of their party's brand, and in 2004 each nominated its own presidential candidate.

Dodge's critics pointed to two confounding defects in his party stewardship. He was, they said, very authoritarian in dominating the party organization and control of its money. And, dividing his attention among an array of conservative, religious, and other causes, he did not attend as he should to Prohibition party-building activities.[12]

By early 2008 devoted partisans were picking up the pieces and reconfiguring their party. The 2008 ticket of Gene Amondson and Leroy Pletten served public notice that the party lived and still had the will to kick. In June 2009 a small but determined cadre from around the country gathered in a Memphis church for a two-day session devoted to charting out a future for the nation's longest-lasting minor political party. Their party turned 140 years old that year.[13]

The sting that today's Prohibitionists surely feel over their party's condition may be lessened by reflecting upon its glory days. Prohibitionists' crowning achievement was the Eighteenth Amendment. This provision, which went into the Constitution in 1919, banned the manufacture, sale, transportation, importation, or exportation of "intoxicating liquors." The Prohibition Party was an important part of the coalition pushing for the amendment, though the Anti-Saloon League was the primary locomotive for this ban on beverage alcohol.

The Twenty-first Amendment repealed the Eighteenth in 1933. Prohibitionists often refer to the Eighteenth Amendment as an "experiment" in prohibition. They blame the experiment's failure on paltry law enforcement and attitudes of the major parties.

By its own account, the Prohibition Party has traversed three stages in its history. During its prophetic phase (1869–96), the party foresaw for itself the role of catalyst for an "evangelistic transformation" to a higher social order in America. Party leaders during the pragmatic period (1896–1932) held no such grandiose designs or illusions. Accepting that they were not going to supplant either of the major parties, they joined in coalition with other temperance, women's suffrage, and progressive associations. In the fundamentalist era (1932–), the party departed from its traditional attachments to progressive causes and was born again as a conservative, small, and peripheral group.[14]

Through all these periods, one fault line has divided the perspectives of the party's faithful. There have been the "narrow-gauge Prohibitionists," for whom prohibition is the single important and unifying issue, and the "broad-gauge Prohibitionists," who want to participate in a multifaceted reform of American society.[15]

Although it was in 1892 that Prohibition scored its most impressive presidential result—270,889 votes, 1 of every 45 cast that year—the evidence suggests that the party really enjoyed its heyday during its pragmatic phase. That was when the Eighteenth Amendment became the law of the land. It was the time when, in 1916, Prohibition's Sidney J. Catts won 47.7 percent of the votes and the governorship of Florida,[16] and when Los Angeles–area voters sent Prohibitionist Charles H. Randall to three consecutive terms (1915–21) in the U.S. House of Representatives.[17]

Prohibition Party members during their party's best years tended to be a good bit better educated than the public at large and more likely to live in cities and towns.[18] Throughout their party's history, evangelical Protestants, including many clergy, have dominated the Prohibition Party's membership rosters.

Those unimpressed by Prohibition's longevity, its occasional electoral victories in the past, or by the quixotic fidelity and devotion of its partisans today may decide that one other fact provides the most compelling testimony to this party's historical significance. Through both its prophetic and pragmatic phases, Prohibition was strongly devoted to the equality of women.

In 1869 more than a half century before women's suffrage became the law of the land, Prohibition granted full participating delegate rights to the women attending the party's first national convention. The women who took their seats at that Chicago meeting were the first ever accorded that prerogative by any American political party.

The Woman's Christian Temperance Union (WCTU) first organized itself as the women's arm of the Prohibition Party. During the two decades in which Prohibitionist Frances Willard—the first woman ever honored by a likeness in Statuary Hall of the U.S. Capitol—led it, the WCTU far outstripped in importance even the Prohibition Party itself. It became the largest women's organization of the nineteenth century and the heart of the organized demand for prohibition and women's rights as well as for prison and labor reform, for public support for neglected children, and for peace—in short for a transformed society dedicated to social justice.

Prohibition placed a women's suffrage plank in its 1872 platform, and by 1892 the party platform was demanding equal pay for equal work.[19] Other late-nineteenth-century minor parties took up the call for women's suffrage, but votes for women planks did not appear in national Democratic and Republican platforms until 1916.

With nationwide women's suffrage finally in place in 1920, Prohibition broke new ground by nominating women for seats in the U.S. Senate. Prohibition's Ella A. Boole took 159,623 votes (5.8 percent) in New York, and in Pennsylvania Leah Cobb Marion won 132,610 (7.5 percent).[20] Marie Brehm, Prohibition's vice-presidential nominee in 1924, became the first female nominee of any party for one of America's top two public offices since women won the franchise nationwide.

Why Third Parties Matter

The value of some of America's minor parties is esoteric at best. There are, to be blunt, many stories of weird, eccentric parties. For four days in July 1960, for example, bohemian delegates of the American Beat Party gathered at a café on West Tenth Street in New York. These delegates, representing (among other places) New York's Washington Square Park, Valle de Bravo in Mexico, and the mythical state of Utopia, are said to have written a platform and nominated a candidate for president. If these Beats were the partisan precursor of anything, it was the Youth International

Party—the Yippies—a New Left counterculture group that facetiously nominated a pig named Pigasus for the presidency in 1968.[21]

The Minnesota Twin Cities–based Archonist Party may no longer exist; but when it did, its members embraced what they called the Klinger Plan as a response to preparations for war. In the event of the resurrection of the draft, party members intended to counsel young men to follow the lead of Corporal Klinger of the television series *M*A*S*H* and dress in drag to render themselves undraftable. And there is the Libertarian National Socialist Green Party, its name a brilliantly crafted oxymoron, conveying as it does a commitment to ideologies—Nazism on the one hand, libertarianism and green politics on the other—that are so divergent as to be irreconcilable. There are those who believe this party is imaginary; but even if it is, someone has created an interesting Web site in its name.

Florida's Thomas J. Kelly founded the British Reformed Sectarian Party in 2003 to protest a ruling by a three-judge panel of the federal Eleventh Circuit in a case that Kelly lost. He chose a name for his party so that its acronym, BRS, would correspond to the first letters of the surnames of his three offending judges. Running as the BRS nominee in 2008, Kelly won nearly a third of the votes in his two-way race with the Republican incumbent for the Thirty-fifth District (Winter Park) in the Florida house.[22]

Eligible though these particular parties may be for the marquee at the Theater of the Absurd, that should not obscure the fact that as a general phenomenon third parties do matter. Third parties have mattered ever since they appeared on the scene early in the nineteenth century. They are role players in the political system. They fulfill certain needs of those who participate in them. Third parties also are social utilities, especially in presenting as policy proposals important reforms that are eventually transferred into the mainstream and passed by governmental decision makers, most of them Democrats and Republicans.

Third-Party Roles

In dealing with political phenomena, scholars often use role analysis. They write about roles that presidents play, such as chief executive, head of state, and commander in chief. Party specialists also employ role analysis. Just about any book on the subject points out that the main role of political parties—usually the writer is thinking about the major ones—is to link people with their political system. In so doing they carry out related roles or functions:

- helping organize the political selection process, especially elections;
- mobilizing citizen participation;
- contributing to the popular understanding of politics;
- channeling and reducing conflict, thereby helping to build the consensus that democracy needs; and
- organizing and running the government and/or opposition.

Steven Rosenstone and his political science colleagues rightly observe that the roles major parties play also are performed by third parties.[23] Small parties do differ, from each other and from the major parties, in the ways in which they may discharge these roles and in the impact of the roles they play. Some minor parties participate regularly in elections. Others never take part or do so infrequently. Rarely do parties other than the Republicans and Democrats find themselves in a position either to organize and run the government or to establish a significant presence in governing bodies as parts of the loyal opposition.

Third parties may also perform two other roles. They are vehicles for presenting, channeling, and pursuing views of the disaffected. By expending and dissipating the energies of dissident challengers, they may serve in effect to maintain the political system, including the pattern of just two major parties. And some third parties contribute, by the example of their own popular appeal, to altering or correcting the policy positions, even the ideological course, of a major party.

There are built-in limits to the value of role analysis in assessing why minor parties matter. Role analysis carries with it conservative baggage, conservative in the system-maintaining sense. It imagines the political process—the system—to be like a scripted play. The roles are what the script assigns to the actors for the success of the play. Minor-party activists of every ideological stripe are likely to disagree with its conclusions about their parties and those who take part in them.

Some of the spirit of insurgency exists in almost all minor parties. Even Ross Perot's centrist movement was centrism with a mad-as-hell attitude. There are some third parties dedicated to the goal of revolution. The Revolutionary Communist Party advertises it in its name.[24] Most third parties do seek redress for their grievances through reform, not revolution. But the notion of system-maintaining role playing may be alien to almost every third party's conception of what it is and what it is to do.

Third Parties and Their Participants

Some people who associate with a third party have personal needs that the party can assist in fulfilling.

There are those—a minority—who are attracted to lost causes and find reality and significance in a vision that stands little or no chance of achievement. It is easy to find lost causes, attractive visions, and impossible dreams in the myriad of minor parties.

An elderly man, now deceased, once told me that he had voted in every presidential election since he turned twenty-one. Only once had he voted for a major-party candidate: his 1972 ballot went to George McGovern, the Democrat who won only Massachusetts and Washington, D.C. He came to regret even that one major-party vote. In every other election, he voted for someone on the third-party left, usually the Socialist Party nominee. When his candidate did not make the ballot, he would write in the name. He spurned the notion that "politics is the art of the possible"

Do Minor Parties Attract "Political Agitator" Types?

Harold Lasswell, in a classic psychoanalytical work, revealed that among political figures there are two distinct personality types: **political agitators** and **political administrators**. Political administrators are pragmatic, goal-centered people who are most successful, and gratified personally, in positions of governmental leadership and influence. Political agitators are more rigid people who invest their psychic energies in a mission or cause. They frame their political appeals in emotional and exhortative language, and they vilify their adversaries as enemies of the good. Gratification for political agitators comes in the heat of the political contest, the struggle, rather than in the daily routines of governing.

In 1968 Alabama governor George Wallace ran one of the twentieth century's most influential third-party presidential campaigns. Wallace's biographers present a character profile of him that is the epitome of the political agitator. Given the consignment of third parties to the political margins and the devotion of so many of them to a mission or cause, it is a reasonable hypothesis that third parties attract relatively large numbers of political agitators to their positions of leadership.

A previously published study I conducted of leaders of twelve minor parties provides some evidence supporting this hypothesis, especially for parties with values most distant from the political mainstream. More research is needed on this and on a related question: is there a personality type associated with the tendency to join a third party's rank and file?

Sources: Harold Lasswell, *Psychopathology and Politics* (Chicago: University of Chicago Press, 1930); J. David Gillespie, *Politics at the Periphery: Third Parties in Two-Party America.* (Columbia: University of South Carolina Press, 1993), 267–82, 306–10.

and the charge that votes like his had spoiled elections for liberal candidates and put conservatives in the White House. His vision was very different from that conveyed by either major party. He believed, like the Prohibitionists, that being right—or what he thought was right—was far more important than winning elections.

Of course many principled people who come to a third party because of its vision or program would be gratified if the party succeeded. These people follow a cause because they believe it is right, not because it is lost. They may be convinced of a wrong that cannot or will not be remedied by the major parties, at least not without minor-party pressure.

Minor parties, like other groups, also attract some people who have particular emotional wants or needs for affiliation. They may be seeking community, solidarity, friendship, or other, deeper forms of intimacy.

And there are those looking to satisfy ego needs. Think how much easier it might be to attain a position of third-party leadership—membership on the national committee or even the positions of chair or executive director—than to win a major party's nomination for an important office or to be selected as a delegate to the Democratic or Republican national convention.

This point was driven home to me years ago, when I interviewed the chair of a Manhattan-based minor party. His party possessed a grandiose global vision: supranational unification with most of the English-speaking world and with Western Europe under the leadership of the United States and the authority of the U.S. Constitution. Although he claimed 450 party members, no evidence surfaced that party membership numbered many more than the chair himself. Much of our conversation was devoted to clippings that the chair readily showed me from Canadian newspaper reports about his party's design for American-Canadian political consolidation.

Third Parties as Social Utilities

Third parties' most important social value may lie in what they contribute to America's marketplace of ideas. Many of the noblest and most far-reaching advances in freedom appeared as minor-party proposals years before either major party would touch them. Twenty years before the Civil War, the Liberty Party was already fighting the good fight for the abolition of slavery. Many third parties preceded the Democrats and Republicans in pushing for women's suffrage.

Table 3.1 Some Important Issues Presented and Advanced by Third Parties

Issue	Third Parties[a]	Adoption
Public transparency; opposition to secrecy	Anti-Masonic Party	Evolutionary adoption; underlying rationale for modern sunshine legislation
Slavery	Liberty Party: abolition; Free Soil Party, Republican Party (1854): antiextension and opposition to federal protection	Emancipation Proclamation (1863) and Thirteenth Amendment (1865)
Women's suffrage	Prohibition Party, Equal Rights Party, Greenback Party, Socialist Party, National Woman's Party, Progressive Party (1912)	Nineteenth Amendment (1920); earlier statutes in some states
Free coinage of silver	People's Party, Democratic Party (in a fusion ticket with People's Party, 1896)	Defeated by Gold Standard Act (1900); gold standard ended (1933)
Initiative and Referendum	People's Party, Socialist Party, Progressive Party (1912)	Enacted in some states; not at national level
Direct election of U.S. senators	Prohibition Party, Greenback Party, People's Party, Progressive Party (1912)	Seventeenth Amendment (1913)

Table 3.1 continued

Issue	Third Parties[a]	Adoption
Graduated/progressive income tax	Greenback Party, People's Party, Socialist Party, Progressive Party (1912)	Sixteenth Amendment (1916)
Prohibition (alcohol)	Prohibition Party	Eighteenth Amendment (1919); repealed by Twenty-first Amendment (1933)
Wages and Hours	Greenback Party, People's Party, Socialist Party, Progressive Party (1912)	Fair Labor Standards Act (1938) and earlier laws in many states
Government/public ownership of railroads	People's Party, Socialist Party, Progressive Party (1924)	Amtrak (1971)
Abolition of child labor	Greenback Party, Socialist Party, Progressive Party (1912)	Keating-Owen Act (1916) and state statutes
Unemployment and disability insurance; old age pensions	Socialist Party	Social Security Act (1935); later federal legislation
Public works for the unemployed	Socialist Party	Various federal enactments (1932–35)
Nonracial polity; full participation by African Americans	Greenback Party, People's Party, Communist Party, others	*Brown v. Board of Education* (1954); Civil Rights Act (1964); Voting Rights Act (1965); others
Toughness on crime	American Independent Party (1968)	Omnibus Crime and Safe Streets Act (1968); later legislation

a. Other minor parties also participated in presenting and advocating some of these issues.

SOURCES: Arthur M. Schlesinger, ed., *History of U.S. Political Parties,* 4 vols. (New York: Chelsea House, 1973); and *National Party Conventions, 1831–1980* (Washington, D.C.: Congressional Quarterly, 1983).

It is true, of course, that most of the ideas that minor parties present never become public policy. For example, the ink had barely dried on the amendment for women's suffrage when the National Woman's Party began to pressure for an Equal Rights Amendment. Congress finally got around to proposing it a half century later, and thirty-five states then went on to ratify it. But the amendment never mustered the thirty-eight states it needed to become part of the Constitution. And mainstream policy makers did not seriously consider the demands of former vice president Henry Wallace and his 1948 Progressive Party that the Cold War be stopped and an American-Soviet relationship like that which had existed in World War II be restored.

On many issues—issue positions that eventually make their way into the mainstream and win enactment as public policy—it is a minor party, and sometimes more than one, that provides the early test of the waters. But the connection between presentation and fruition normally is complex and multifaceted, and interest groups may be more powerful vehicles than third parties for mainstreaming an issue.

The civil rights issue may illustrate the point. Groups such as the Southern Christian Leadership Conference, the National Association for the Advancement of Colored People, and the Student Nonviolent Coordinating Committee were the organizational core of the modern civil rights movement. No third party either fostered or led that movement, despite some claims by opponents that it was the offspring of the radical Left.

Yet decades before the 1955 Montgomery bus boycott, American radicals were speaking out strongly on behalf of the rights of African Americans. In the 1930s Communists led in organizing many of Alabama's black and poorest farmers as the Alabama Sharecroppers Union.[25] James W. Ford was the first African American ever to win popular votes in a campaign for one of America's top two offices. Ford was the Communist Party's vice-presidential nominee in 1932, 1936, and 1940.[26]

It is undoubtedly true that political motivations, and even some duplicity, were a part of what underlay Communists' support of African Americans during the Jim Crow era. But political calculations also motivated the unconscionable silence, inactivity, or even hostility of so many major-party politicians on the rights of Americans of color.

America's remarkable array of minor parties offers the marketplace a virtually unlimited range of perspectives, from radical to reactionary, rational to eccentric, and soberly serious to playful. This is a positive thing, and not just for the good ideas that some third parties have been able to present and to point toward the mainstream. The very presence of such partisan diversity testifies to the nation's respect for its pluralism and its deference to the associational rights guaranteed by its Constitution.

Sadly the record on this matter is far from unblemished. Twice in the twentieth century, fear drove Americans to the paradoxical and self-defeating conclusion that preserving freedom may require that it be limited or even destroyed for those who were deemed not to believe in it.

And there are the props, developed over the last century and still being constructed today, to build up and sustain duopoly—the two major parties' protected and exclusive place in the center ring of American politics. Duopoly limits what third parties can contribute to the marketplace of ideas, and it calls into question just how free that marketplace really is.

4

★ ★ ★

Constitutionalists, Greens, and Libertarians

> Throughout the centuries there were men who took first steps down
> new roads armed with nothing but their own vision.
>
> *Ayn Rand, The Fountainhead*

> Always vote for principle, though you may vote alone, and you may
> cherish the sweetest reflection that your vote is never lost.
>
> *John Quincy Adams, quoted by 2008 Constitution Party
> presidential candidate Chuck Baldwin*

Hobbled by duopolistic regulations and other structural and cultural infirmities, people wanting today to build a third-party movement with the strength really to take on the major parties also face a conundrum: where on the ideological spectrum is there sufficient and attractive space for constructing such a movement? Put another way, at what point might the oxygen be found to breathe life into this new party?

To Ross Perot it appeared that the two major parties had moved far apart on policy and ideology, leaving millions of middle-of-the-road voters feeling alienated and disenfranchised. Perot invested his energies and a substantial portion of his wealth on the supposition that a well-nurtured centrist movement could succeed provided it was a movement with an attitude—a movement hostile to insiders and professional politicians and dedicated to a handful of issues that, though important to many voters, were being ignored by the major parties.

Perot's 1992 presidential showing was the second best that anyone other than a Democrat or Republican has mustered since the Civil War. His organized movement—United We Stand America and then the Reform Party—turned out to be disappointingly ephemeral and short lived; but there are those outside that major-party realm who still are betting on Perot's hunch about a movement at the center.

Some of these people, in Minnesota, New York, and elsewhere, are trying now to build the Independence Party of America. Another movement was attempting in 2009 to launch the American Moderate Party of the United States. The Moderate Party has fielded candidates in Illinois. It achieved state recognition and ballot status in Rhode Island in 2009 and has been at work to crack the California ballot.

Other builders, real and potential, reject this assumption about room at the center. For them talk about the major parties moving far apart may seem to be just idle chatter. They are laying their bets on what Helen Keller declared and many have long considered to be conventional wisdom: the Democrats and Republicans are as alike as Tweedledum and Tweedledee, and if a third-party is to succeed, it will be built to the left or the right of both major parties.

Table 4.1 Presidential Campaigns of the Constitution and Green Parties

	Constitution Party[a]		Green Party	
Year	*Presidential Candidate*	*Votes (Number of Ballots)* [b, c]	*Presidential Candidate*	*Votes (Number of Ballots)* [b, c]
1992	Howard Phillips	43,369 (21)	——	——
1996	Howard Phillips	184,820 (39)	Ralph Nader	685,297 (22)
2000	Howard Phillips	98,022 (41)	Ralph Nader	2,883,105 (44)
2004	Michael Peroutka	144,499 (36)	David Cobb	119,859 (28)
2008	Chuck Baldwin	199,750 (39)	Cynthia McKinney	161,797 (32)

a. Until 1999, the party's name was the U.S. Taxpayers Party.

b. Given minor discrepancies in reporting popular votes, the table presents the highest vote reported by the sources.

c. The maximum number of ballots is fifty-one (fifty states and the District of Columbia). The popular vote totals include tallies in states where candidate had ballot access but also reported write-ins in states where the candidate's name did not appear.

Sources: Federal Election Commission reports; *Ballot Access News;* and Dave Leip, Atlas of U.S. Presidential Elections, http:\\uselectionatlas.org (accessed August 1, 2011).

On the Right: The Constitution Party

To the right of the right flank of the GOP, the major party that declares its devotion to conservative principles and to conservatives' interests, there resides the Constitution Party. Its partisans contend that most of what the Republican Party has for sale ideologically is a neoconservative sham. The truth—conservative truth as they see it—lies largely outside the mainstream parameters set by the parties of the duopoly.

Howard Phillips, the Constitution Party's principal founder and three-time presidential candidate, has long been a recognized leader of the New Right movement. Phillips directed the Office of Economic Opportunity in the Nixon administration. He parted ways with Nixon because of the president's decision to continue some Great Society programs inherited from the Johnson administration. When Phillips and others launched their new party in 1992, they chose to name it the U.S. Taxpayers Party.[1]

Although renamed the Constitution Party in 1999, this party has retained radical tax and fiscal reform as one of its crucial domestic themes. The Constitution Party seeks to abolish the graduated income tax, and it opposes any move to replace it with a federal flat tax or a value-added (sales) tax. Funding for the federal government would come from tariffs, excise taxes, and (if needed) revenue levies placed upon states and based entirely upon the relative populations of the states.

If empowered to do so, this party would phase out Social Security and eliminate many other domestic social programs. Except for payments to veterans, Washington would play no role in education; and although the party platform has a distinct states' rights flavor, even the states would be denied any authority to limit parents' rights to educate their children as they see fit. Constitutionalists—this party's leaders and activists[2]—welcome into their ranks conservative Christian homeschoolers, along with gun rights advocates, gay marriage opponents, and other constituents on the right.

Constitution Party members seek and occasionally win local offices. In Utah elections on November 3, 2009, Constitutionalists won council seats in two small towns, and a party member won the mayoralty in a third.[3] Party members won offices in three Nevada counties in 2010.

Constitutionalists' self-designation as a party is expressly Christian. Their platform's preamble acknowledges "the blessing of our Lord and Savior Jesus Christ" and declares that the nation was founded by Christians. Their party's antiabortion stance is the one domestic issue outranking taxes in importance. The "sanctity of life" plank, the first in the platform, carries a clause that allows no exception even in cases of rape or incest.

The national party is a confederation of virtually independent state parties, and not all of them have adopted the Constitution Party name.[4] For example Nevadans can find the Constitution Party's presidential and vice-presidential nominees on ballot lines as the Independent American Party. In Alaska it is the Alaskan Independence Party that serves that role. The American Independent Party, founded during George Wallace's 1968 run for the presidency, has served as the California affiliate of the Constitution Party.

The "no exceptions" clause in the party's sanctity of life plank and a comment from the party's Nevada branch contradicting it prompted a breach that has damaged the party ever since 2006. Christopher Hansen, the Nevada chair and gubernatorial candidate in 2006, declared that he thought exceptions could be warranted in cases of rape or incest or to save the mother's life. In reaction party purists—their adversaries called them extremists—undertook a campaign to excommunicate the Nevada party. They failed, but party branches in several states came to the defense of the "no exceptions" position by severing their own connections with the national party.

Revealed in this is a deep religious fissure running through a party that takes its religious values seriously. Many of the voices expressing the will to consider some exceptions belong to practicing Mormons in the Constitution Party. Independent Baptists and other self-proclaimed traditional Christians in the party have tended on the other hand to embrace the "no exceptions" hard line.

Alan L. Keyes and America's Independent Party

For reasons at least partly related to the exceptions controversy, California's American Independent Party gave its 2008 presidential line to Alan Keyes, and Chuck Baldwin's name did not appear anywhere on the California ballot.

Keyes, an African American, earned a Ph.D. at Harvard. He held several important diplomatic posts during the Reagan era. He has been a perennial candidate for various offices, usually running as a conservative Republican. In 2004 Barack Obama defeated Keyes, who had been nominated by Illinois Republicans for a seat in the U.S. Senate. A Roman Catholic, Keyes allied himself with those in the "no exceptions" wing of the Constitution Party. He has vocally supported the war in Iraq and is identified with other "globalist" positions at odds with official positions of the party.

Failing in his bid for the Constitution Party's presidential nomination in 2008, Keyes launched America's Independent Party as a new alternative on the third-party right. In addition to his placement on the California ballot by the American Independent Party, Keyes appeared on the Colorado and Florida ballots as the candidate of America's Independent Party.

Running on the Constitution Party line in 2006, Rick Jore won a seat in the Montana legislature. He thus became the party's highest-ranking elected public official ever. The national party chronicled this breakthrough, though its celebration was understandably subdued. The Montana party was one that had disaffiliated over the exceptions controversy.

Some but not all of the seceding parties have since returned. In 2008 Montana's party declined to put party nominee Chuck Baldwin on the ballot. It offered Ron Paul instead, even though Paul had declined to run and had endorsed Baldwin.[5]

On foreign and defense policies, the Constitution Party position is unabashedly noninterventionist. A steady opponent of the war in Iraq, the party demands a declaration of war before any commitment of American troops to foreign combat. It calls for trade protection, termination of foreign aid, and a crackdown on illegal immigrants. And it seeks U.S. withdrawal from the UN and NATO, from NAFTA and the World Bank, and from the nation's other "globalist" commitments.

There is a subtext here. Although it may not immediately register in the eye of an outsider, it is something that bonds the party ideologically with other right-wing antiglobalist groups and even overlaps with some of the ideas presented by antiglobalists on the left. From top to bottom in their party, many Constitutionalists are convinced that there are powerful people, worldwide and in the United States, who are dedicated to the goal of a New World Order—an authoritarian world governmental entity that would eradicate America's sovereignty and abrogate the Constitution.

Chuck Baldwin has recurrently sounded this theme, warning his audiences that many in America's elite—Republicans and Democrats, presidents and vice presidents, key members of the national security establishment, judges and congressmen, media influentials and neoconservative intellectuals—have a global strategic agenda, and that what they appear to be may be very different from what they really are.[6]

On the Left: The Greens

To the left of the New York Democratic Party, the Working Families Party of that state has become a powerful force in the politics of the nation's largest city. The WFP has forged intimate connections with public- and private-sector unions there. It is a practitioner and distinct beneficiary of the ballot-level fusion through cross-endorsement that has long been permitted and used in New York. State Working Families parties also are at work in Connecticut, Delaware, Vermont, South Carolina, and Oregon—all of them among that small group of states that permit cross-endorsement on their ballots.[7]

But it is the Greens who have organized themselves nationally as well as locally and have sought traction for themselves throughout the country as an independent partisan movement to the left of the Democrats. America's Greens have run candidates for the presidency ever since 1996. Even before that they were seeking local and state offices in some of the states.

As their name implies, Greens are devoted to environmentalism and to building sustainable systems. But their movement does not have a single-issue focus, and it would be a mistake even to assume that Greens in general would identify ecological concerns as the principal bond connecting them with their movement. According to political scientist David Reynolds, the Green movement developed as "the electoral expression of the New Left," uniting in one partisan household the environmental, women's, and peace movements.[8]

America's Greens belong to a worldwide Green politics movement that began in the Australian state of Tasmania in 1972. The Green Party of the United States is the American member of Global Greens, the network linking nearly seventy-five national Green parties throughout the developed and developing worlds. Greens in the United States must envy many of their counterparts in Europe, where the returns from running in proportional representation election systems have taken the Greens into, or very near, the political mainstream. In Germany, for instance, Greens held ministerial seats in the national government led by the Social Democrats during the years 1998–2005.

Unsurprisingly for a party seeking space for itself to the left of the Democrats, the platform of the Green Party of the United States embraces abortion rights, gay marriage, the graduated income tax, a single-payer universal health-care system, an end to the death penalty, and immediate withdrawal from the Iraq War. But it is from ten fundamental principles that the Green movement really derives its self-identity. Originally drafted at the first national gathering of Greens in St. Paul, Minnesota, in 1984, these still are featured in platforms as the "Ten Key Values of the Green Party": grassroots democracy; social justice and equal opportunity; ecological wisdom; nonviolence; decentralization; community-based economics; feminism and gender equality; respect for diversity; personal and global responsibility; and future focus and sustainability.

There is within the Green Party none of the rigid and authoritarian centralism that is found among the many small Leninist parties lying to the left of the Greens. The Green Party has in fact drawn some of its leadership and support from refugees from such Far Left parties. The late Peter Camejo is a case in point. Camejo ran in 1976 as the Socialist Workers Party (SWP) presidential nominee; but his Trotskyist comrades later expelled him from the SWP because of his rising devotion to *democratic* socialism. Camejo ran three times as a Green for governor of California.[9] In 2002 he took nearly four hundred thousand votes—5.3 percent. Joining Ralph Nader's independent ticket, Camejo ran for the vice presidency in 2004.

For years Camejo spoke of the watermelon—"green on the outside, red on the inside"—to explain his political views. By 2004 he had changed the metaphor, referencing instead the avocado. He had been transformed to "green on the outside, green on the inside"; and he was urging his sister and brother Greens to be the same, inoculating themselves against the Democratic Party's power to co-opt.

Like Camejo, many joining the Green movement have brought diverse, unusual backgrounds with them. There was, for example, Roberto A. Mondragon, who took 10.4 percent of the votes as Green nominee for governor of New Mexico. Mondragon, a former lieutenant governor, was a well-known member of his state's large Latino community. His 1994 gubernatorial tally established New Mexico as an early trailblazer state for the Greens.[10]

Cynthia McKinney, the Greens' 2008 presidential candidate, had been a six-term Democratic U.S. House member from Georgia. McKinney made headlines for her controversial claims that the Bush administration may have known in advance of the September 11, 2001, attack, and for her persistent calls for Bush's impeachment.

McKinney was back in the news the year after her presidential campaign. On June 30, 2009, the Israeli navy seized the freighter *Spirit of Humanity* eighteen miles off the coast of the Gaza Strip and arrested McKinney and twenty other Free Gaza Movement activists from eleven nations who were the ship's passengers. Their mission had been to elude the Israeli blockade of Gaza and deliver tons of medical supplies for Gaza's Palestinian inhabitants.[11] After a week spent in an Israeli prison, McKinney was deported by Israel on July 7, 2009.

McKinney's 2008 running mate, Rosa Clemente, is an interpreter and spokesperson for hip hop culture. Winona LaDuke, who ran with Nader in 1996 and 2000, is

Cynthia McKinney, prior to the
Green Party presidential debate, San
Francisco, January 13, 2008. Photo
released into public domain by
photographer Robert B. Livingston.
Obtained through Wikimedia
Commons.

a Native American activist. Elaine Brown, an early candidate for the 2008 Green
Party presidential nomination, had served from 1974 to 1977 as chair of the Black
Panther Party.

Matt Gonzalez is a Mexican American lawyer who was elected to the board of
supervisors in San Francisco and served there from 2001 to 2005. In 2003 Gonzalez
took more than 47 percent of the votes in his losing run for San Francisco mayor.
Gonzalez was Nader's running mate in their 2008 quest for the presidency and vice
presidency.

An issue over which Greens have divided and quarreled is how much of the
movement's energies should be devoted to electoral politics. There are the Greens
who concentrate on the party's full deployment as the electoral instrument of the
progressive Left, but others who insist that it is far more important to build at the
grassroots and to influence public policy on green issues. Some in the movement
have wanted Greens to run only in potentially winnable local elections. Greens regularly assembled in national gatherings from 1984 on, and by 1991 their movement
was ready to express itself in party form. The name they chose—Greens / Green
Party USA—reflected the movement's continued ambivalence about this move into
the electoral arena.

The Green movement sanctioned and launched Nader's 1996 bid for the presidency. Having tasted the campaign, Greens who wanted to push the electoral role
then developed the Association of State Green Parties, renaming it the Green Party
of the United States in 2001. There was a good bit of internal carping after the 2000
election and the onus the mainstream media placed on Nader and the Greens for

allegedly spoiling the election for Gore and putting Bush in the White House. Even so, the election-focused Green Party of the United States has surpassed and replaced Greens / Green Party USA as the Green movement's pivotal national organization.

Greens have reason for pride in what they have achieved already as a minor party. As of October 2008, 255,019 voters were registered as Greens in those states (and Washington, D.C.)—a minority of all states—where it was possible to declare a Green affiliation when registering to vote.[12] Three Green nominees have won state legislative elections: Audie Elizabeth Bock in California in 1999, Maine's John Eder in 2002 and 2004, and Richard Carroll in Arkansas in 2008.

By their party's own count, in December 2008 there were 193 elected Green officeholders in twenty-eight states and Washington, D.C. Most had won their offices in local nonpartisan elections. Greens held five of twenty council seats in Madison, Wisconsin, and were serving on the city councils of Boston; Cleveland; Minneapolis; Portland, Maine; and San Francisco. Richmond, California, mayor Gayle McLaughlin was a Green, and there were Green mayors of four smaller municipalities in California, Kansas, and New York.[13]

Table 4.2 Libertarian Party Presidential Campaigns

Year	Presidential Candidate	Votes (Number of Ballots) [a, b]
1972	John Hospers	3,674 (4)
1976	Roger MacBride	173,019 (32)
1980	Ed Clark	921,128 (51)
1984	David Bergland	228,111 (40)
1988	Ron Paul	432,179 (47)
1992	Andre Marrou	291,627 (51)
1996	Harry Browne	485,798 (51)
2000	Harry Browne	386,064 (50)
2004	Michael Badnarik	397,367 (49)
2008	Bob Barr	523,715 (45)

a. Due to minor discrepancies in reporting popular votes, the table presents the highest popular vote reported by the sources.

b. The maximum number of ballots is fifty-one (fifty states and the District of Columbia). The popular vote totals include tallies in states where the candidate had ballot access but also reported write-ins in states where the candidate's name did not appear.

SOURCES: Federal Election Commission reports; *Ballot Access News;* and Dave Leip, Atlas of U.S. Presidential Elections, http://uselectionatlas.org (accessed August 1, 2011).

The Libertarian Response

David F. Nolan and others who shared his views launched the Libertarian Party in Nolan's living room in 1971. The spark for them to become party architects was the Nixon administration's decision to impose wage and price controls to fight inflation.

Partisan Libertarians—the people who lead, join and support, or register and vote for the Libertarian Party—claim no stake in that dispute as to where on the spectrum the oxygen may lie for new-party life. Libertarians insist that the ideological spectrum is itself a faulty, defective way of thinking about political beliefs; and it is true that libertarian thought cannot be pinpointed along that spectrum.[14]

Libertarianism is the philosophy of individual freedom, radically defined and applied. Libertarians extend economic freedom beyond where most mainstream conservative "free traders" take it, and personal freedom a good bit further than most of today's liberals are willing to go.[15] Adam Smith, Thomas Jefferson, and John Stuart Mill are venerated heroes and intellectual forebears of today's Libertarian Party. So are Ayn Rand and Friedrich Hayek. Many of the party's policy positions have been incubated at the Cato Institute, a Washington, D.C.–based "independent" libertarian think tank.

Libertarian perspectives, borne in the party's platforms, attest to the fact that freedom remains a radical idea even deep into the third century of the American polity. Throwing down the gauntlet to the "cult of the omnipotent state," Libertarians in their 2008 platform declared their goal to be "nothing more or less than a world set free in our lifetime." This platform devoted the party to

- unfettered freedom of expression and freedom both of and from religion;
- equal rights irrespective of "sexual orientation, preference, gender or gender identity" in marriage, adoption and child custody, immigration, and military service;
- marriage to be recast as a private contract between consenting partners;
- freedom to choose with regard to abortion, but without government subsidies;
- the individual right to keep and bear arms;
- government serving to protect private property and adjudicate disputes, but without power to redistribute wealth, subsidize businesses, or impose any restriction on "wages, prices, rents, profits, production, . . . (or) interest rates";
- repeal of the income tax, passage of a balanced budget amendment, and abolition of "all federal programs and services not required under the U.S. Constitution";
- privatization and free enterprise in education, health care, and Social Security;
- elimination of entangling alliances and of America's role as "world policeman";
- military nonintervention, restriction of the military role to defending the nation from aggression, and no abridgement of the Bill of Rights, even in times of war;
- virtually open borders, except for entry controls on "foreign nationals who pose a threat to security, health, or property";
- no denial or abridgement by government of individual rights based on "sex, wealth, race, color, creed, age, national origin, personal habits, political preference or sexual orientation"; and

- abrogation of imposed limits on free, representative elections, including repeal of laws that "effectively exclude alternative candidates and parties (and) deny ballot access."[16]

Other, more radical, provisions—on matters ranging from legalizing hard drugs to the eventual elimination of all taxes—had appeared in earlier Libertarian platforms. Like many minor parties, the party is the stage for a fight between party purists and pragmatists. For purists fidelity to principle is a far more significant party cachet than winning elections. Some Libertarian purists are outright anarchists; in a 2007 survey of 677 party members, 6 percent of the respondents chose "anarchist" rather than "libertarian" or some other word as the best characterization of their political perspective.[17]

The pragmatists too are devoted to principles, but they also want to bolster the party's outreach and broaden its voter appeal. In 2006 pragmatists of the Libertarian Reform Caucus succeeded in sacking much of the language in the party platform but then failed to achieve their goal of inserting softer wording with the potential to reach mainstream voters.

Libertarian Party pragmatists scored another victory in 2008 with the nomination of former Congressman Bob Barr. Leaving the GOP in 2006, Barr had enlisted in the Libertarian Party as a "lifetime member." His 2008 vote tally was the second highest achieved to date by any Libertarian presidential nominee. Only Ed Clark, the party's 1980 nominee, did better.

It was Barr's record during four terms in Congress that left many purists cold. Barr himself would come to recant several nonlibertarian positions he had taken in the House. But for some the baggage he carried placed him beyond redemption. He had been a leader in passing the anti-gay-marriage Defense of Marriage Act in 1996. He had voted for the first PATRIOT Act and for the 2002 resolution authorizing war in Iraq. And for years he was a powerful voice opposing the legalization of marijuana even for medical use. By election day 2008, many Libertarian purists were determined to reclaim the party leadership before the next election round.

The Boston Tea Party

Reacting to the fight, a group of the purists left the Libertarian Party in 2006 and founded another. They chose a name calculated to warm any libertarian heart: the Boston Tea Party. Although the national Tea Party movement born in 2009 carries some of the libertarian ideas dear to people in the Boston Tea Party, the two movements are distinct from each other. Reporting an active membership roster of 1,656 in early 2010, the Boston Tea Party announced that it was planning an online national convention for May 26–June 2, 2010.

Libertarian conventions feature exotic things that are missing from the major parties' convention fluff. In meetings during party's infant years, tie-dye hippie lifestyle radicals rubbed elbows with people dressed and coiffed like they had just walked off Wall Street. The hottest items the vendors could sell at the 1983 Libertarian convention were T-shirts with slogans honoring the memories of the left-anarchist Emma Goldman and of Gordon Kahl, a martyred leader of the right-radical tax resistance Posse Comitatus group.[18] When the time comes to nominate presidential and vice-presidential candidates, "None of the above" can count on warm applause. This party is antistatist, after all, and there are some anarchists on the convention floor who clearly prefer "None of the above."

The Libertarians have offered a candidate in every presidential round since 1972. John Hospers, the party's first presidential nominee, was a philosophy professor. Hospers received the one and only electoral vote cast so far for a Libertarian presidential candidate. Theodora B. "Tonie" Nathan, Hospers's running mate, was the first woman of *any* party ever to receive an electoral vote. Roger MacBride, a Virginia Republican who was committed to Nixon, voted for Hospers and Nathan instead. Libertarians chose MacBride as their own presidential nominee in 1976. It was in part MacBride's reward for his act as a faithless elector four years earlier.

Six Libertarian presidential nominees have had careers in the business world, three of these as corporate lawyers. Barr served as a federal prosecutor. Ron Paul is a physician. As Republican congressmen, Paul and Barr have been the highest-ranking elected public servants. In 1984 voters in Alaska elected Libertarian nominee Andre Marrou to a term in their state legislature. Marrou won the party's presidential nomination in 1992.

Libertarians say that their party is *the* third party of the United States. That claim is not without some justification. Whatever the future holds, the Libertarian Party already carries an achievement record that is remarkable in the realm of U.S. minor parties. It runs far more candidates for public offices than any other minor party. In 2008, 127 Libertarians ran for the U.S. House and 279 for seats in state legislatures.[19] State legislative candidates have won on Libertarian ballot lines in Alaska in 1978, 1980, and 1984 and in New Hampshire in 2000, and Libertarians have won seven other legislative races running in fusion campaigns linking the party with a major party. By the Libertarians' count, in early 2009 there were 207 elected Libertarian officeholders, many having won their posts in nonpartisan local elections. There were Libertarian mayors and county executives, county council and school board members, and even a Libertarian sheriff: Bill Masters, the long-serving sheriff of Colorado's San Miguel County.[20]

5

★ ★ ★

The Early Years
Short-Lived Parties before 1860

> The country is divided into two great parties, and ninety-five out of every hundred voters are under the control of the wire-pullers of said parties. . . . Few are prepared to act independently.
>
> *Liberty Party leader Gerrit Smith*

If ever there were a golden age of third-party politics, it was in the nineteenth century. Party lines and divisions would harden later on—some say they are downright ossified today—but over the first 125 years of American nationhood they remained reasonably soft and subject to change.

An array of national issues each possessed at some point during the nineteenth century the power to mobilize people and alter party loyalties. Among these there were demands for openness or transparency in the evolving American democracy; slavery and the array of moral, economic, and sectional issues surrounding it; new waves of immigration that were altering the nation's demographics in ways traditionalists found disturbing; and, late in the nineteenth century, industrialized America, government support of business, and the counterclaims of toiling and vulnerable farmers and urban workers.

Moreover until states adopted the secret ballot late in the century and then later used their new ballot-access prerogative to assist the two major parties in pulling up the ladder against challenges from outside, there had been at least the form of equal access to voters for minor as well as major parties.

Third parties of all three types described in chapter 3 abounded in the nineteenth century. The short-lived Anti-Masonic Party is regarded by most American historians as having been the first nationally significant minor party. But the Anti-Masons had their nonnational minor-party contemporaries: workingmen's and labor parties in Boston, New York, Philadelphia, and other cities.[1] The nation's first continuing doctrinal and issue parties—the Prohibition and then the Socialist Labor parties—made their appearance late in the century.

And there was a fourth third-party type: the third party that came in from the cold. Born in 1854, the Republican Party rose like a shooting star. In much less than a decade, the party system would be transformed, and this new party would emerge as one of America's two major political parties.[2]

Short-Lived National Parties: Some Generalizations

A song that made its way to the top of the country music charts many years ago bore this evocative line: "I want to live fast, love hard, die young, and leave a beautiful memory."[3] Third parties were far from the mind of Joe Allison, the songwriter, but his line seems to say something about some of them anyway. Most of America's most significant minor parties have indeed died young. Their brief lives may be hard ones, endured on the political periphery, even if just beyond the mainstream in some cases. But many of them leave behind substantial and potent legacies.

Short-lived national parties often are the self-appointed agents of reform or change. Their demands may be in support of the underdog, for reconstruction of the party system and other revisions in the political process, for reordering the priorities and substance of public policy, or for many or all these things. Exceptions arise, it is true. Constitutional Union, an ephemeral party on the eve of the Civil War, was made up of what the British call "yesterday's men." Their wish was for quiet and stability at a time when the old order was unraveling. But protest and insurgency underlie the spirit of many short-lived parties, and their revisionism and agitation may momentarily capture the mood and enlist the support of large, disaffected segments of the electorate. People happy with the status quo are likely to greet them with hostility, suspicion, and scorn and to demand a return to "legitimacy and civility."

Transient parties sometimes are born to institutionalize economic protest. Others have arisen due to a galvanizing issue such as immigration or slavery. Inspired

---

★ ★

Were the Quids America's First Minor Party?

Their name was derived from *tertium quid,* Latin for "a third something." In *Others,* his important work on minor-party history, Darcy Richardson makes a plausible argument that that history may have begun with the Quids, more than two decades before the birth of the Anti-Masonic Party. Led by John Randolph of Virginia, the Quids were at the least a very distinct and separate faction of the majority Democratic-Republican Party. During their movement's short life—circa 1805–12—the Quids drew support in Virginia, Pennsylvania, and, to a lesser degree, the other states. Six Quids served in the Eleventh Congress (1809–11). The Quids opposed many of the policies put forward by the Jefferson and Madison administrations, and they held strongly to the states' rights position that had been a Democratic-Republican article of faith before that party's federal election sweep in 1800.

★ ★

---

by the vision, charisma, and grit or resolve of a founding leader, some parties live their short lives largely as agents in quest of their leader's goals.

Some of the short-lived parties arise as breakaway movements, leaving—seceding from—one or the other major party. A breakaway party may seek by its withdrawal to punish the major party and to force it to reformulate itself or change its position on crucial issues. Alternatively its leaders may intend to leave for good and to work to alter the party system itself. Among the breakaway parties, there were in the nineteenth century the Southern Democrats (1860), Liberal Republicans (early 1870s), and, less consequentially, the Silver Republicans near the century's end.

The record of accomplishment of the most successful nineteenth-century transient parties clearly trumps that of most of their twentieth-century counterparts. Between 1831 and 1898, standard-bearers of short-lived national parties won at least thirty-two gubernatorial elections in twenty-one states.[4] Sizable numbers of Anti-Masons, Free Soilers, Know Nothings, Greenbackers, and Populists served in Congress at various times during the century. Many historians rank the late-nineteenth-century Populists as first among all third parties in policy impact and legacy. Some of the issues raised and presented by their People's Party substantially contributed to the agenda of progressives during the early-twentieth-century Progressive Era.

The Anti-Masonic Party

Freemasonry is the world's largest secret fraternal society. Its adherents, the Masons, can trace their rather obscure origins back to the workers of medieval stonemasons' and builders' guilds. But modern Freemasonry has attracted to its ranks many professional and high-status men.

The guarded secrecy with which Masons discharge their rituals and carry out their fraternal life has over the centuries fed charges from outside that Freemasonry is a worldwide conspiracy against Christianity, national sovereignty, or democracy. Freemasonry long ago was condemned by the Roman Catholic Church, and in the twentieth century many Communist and third world countries imposed bans upon it.

The lines of the attack and counterattack between Freemasonry and its nineteenth-century adversaries resembled in tone today's American culture wars and, within it, the conservative Christian invective against "secular humanism." Masons were associated in the public mind with the Enlightenment and its secular spirit. The circle of Freemasonry had included Washington, Franklin, Patrick Henry, and other American nation builders. Some of these men had been secular deists, with religious views distant from the orthodoxy of traditional Christians. Opponents saw them as "humanists." It was claimed that Masons used the cross for perverse and sacrilegious rites. Presbyterians and Methodists passed resolutions condemning the order.[5]

Many nineteenth-century Americans believed there was a Masonic conspiracy to deprive ordinary citizens of their liberty and share of power in the Republic. The fraternal order's English connections and its secret titles of nobility were constant grist for the propaganda mill. And nothing surfaced to hold out hope for Freemasonry's foes that Masonic strength might be dissipating. James Monroe, Henry Clay, and Andrew Jackson were Masons. So were others who were prominent in politics and public life during the nation's second and third generations.

"We have met the enemy, and he is us." Although that phrase was not turned until the twentieth century,[6] it could very well be applied retroactively to Masons of the century before. By an action they took on September 12, 1826, some western New York Masons did substantial damage to the Masonic order. Their act unintentionally triggered the party that dedicated itself to exposing Masonic secrets and to revealing and then eradicating the society's alleged elite, monopolistic hold on power in America. If, as most historians contend, the Anti-Masonic Party was the first national minor party, then America's third-party history really begins in upstate New York on that late summer day in 1826.

William Morgan, an ex-Mason with an ax to grind, wrote a book exposing Masonic secrets and oaths. Morgan was far from the wealth and power that Anti-Masons attributed to men of the Masonic order. He was a down-on-his-luck stonecutter living in the small town of Batavia, New York. It was news of the impending publication of Morgan's exposé, *Illustrations of Masonry,* that apparently pushed New York Masons over the edge.

As Morgan's book neared release and those standing to profit began their publicity hype, local authorities with Masonic connections arrested him for petty theft, released him, then retook him for a $2.69 debt. A donor, probably a Mason, made good the debt. As Morgan left jail, some revenge-minded Masons kidnapped him. Morgan's corpse ended up in the Niagara River, tied down with weights.[7]

Morgan's murder could not stop the presses. Incensed both by the book's revelations and the failure of Masonic judges and juries to indict his kidnappers (and likely killers), the Anti-Masons spread like wildfire. Or, it could be said, like a weed: Thurlow Weed, a New Yorker, founded and edited the *Anti-Masonic Enquirer.* The *Enquirer* gave voice to the movement and became its most effective propaganda agent.

In their prime the Anti-Masons were a powerful force in several northeastern states, where, before the rise of the Whig Party, they served as the opposition to Jackson and his party movement. In New York Anti-Masons held seventeen seats in the assembly and four in the state senate in 1828. The New York Anti-Masonic gubernatorial candidate in 1830 narrowly lost, but he took a 48 percent share of the vote. Anti-Masons won the 1835 Pennsylvania gubernatorial race, and Vermont's Anti-Masons took and then held their state's governorship in four consecutive annual election contests (1831 through 1834). The Anti-Masonic bloc in the U.S. House numbered twenty-five at the opening of the Twenty-third Congress in 1833. These Anti-Masonic lawmakers came to Washington from Pennsylvania and New York, from Vermont, Massachusetts, and Rhode Island, and from Ohio.[8]

The Anti-Masonic message—notably its opposition to secrecy, elitism, and secularism—drew revival-minded Protestants and many people of humble birth and limited means. But the party also attracted people of ambition and accomplishment, men such as William Henry Seward, Frederick Whittlesey, Francis Granger, and Thaddeus Stevens.

Considering its available talent pool, it is surprising that the Anti-Masons nominated William Wirt for their one and only presidential race. In that 1832 contest, Wirt proved to be an ineffective campaigner who carried an ironic and most damaging load: he was a Mason who had not renounced his connection to the enemy order! Even so, he took 7.8 percent of the nation's popular vote and the seven electors of Vermont. Wirt received almost no popular votes in any state south of the Mason-Dixon Line.

The life of this national transient party was a scant ten years. By the end of 1836, Anti-Masonry was a memory but also a legacy. The Whig Party was firmly established within the ranks of the major parties by the middle of the 1830s. Although some former Anti-Masons joined Democratic ranks, most of partisan Anti-Masonry was absorbed into this new Whig Party. The dying party thus passed into the ascendant Whigs a spirit of egalitarianism and evangelism and at least a residue of agitation for political reform.[9]

Anti-Masonic was the first party ever to use a national convention to nominate presidential and vice-presidential candidates and to adopt a platform. It was in fact the first to present its program in a written platform.[10] America's premier national convention, the Anti-Masonic, met in Baltimore late in September 1831. This innovation was a sizable democratic step away from the closed-caucus nominating procedures used by earlier political parties. The Democrats, following suit, have convened every four years since 1832. The Whigs did likewise until their own demise in the 1850s, and the GOP has conducted its affairs through quadrennial conventions ever since that then-two-year-old party first convened nationally in 1856.

Although Freemasonry was scarred by the Anti-Masonic assault, the wounds were not terminal. At least eleven of those who succeeded Jackson to the U.S. presidency have been Masons. But Anti-Masonic suspicion of secrecy did leave permanent marks on the national landscape. The Phi Beta Kappa honor society and other secret orders unveiled themselves in response to Anti-Masonic agitation. Today many universities take initiatives against the secrecy and elitism that historically underlay their fraternity and sorority Greek systems.

Federal and state freedom of information acts now provide some access to agency records and files (though segments are often redacted prior to receipt). Sunshine laws have opened governmental deliberations to the scrutiny of press and public. Cause-and-effect relationships tend to be complex, and it would not be possible to confirm a linear connection between Anti-Masonic agitation and current policies like these. But that the Anti-Masons contributed substantially to the nation's understanding that transparency and openness are among democracy's prerequisites can scarcely be denied.

Whether it was credible or fantastic, the bill of particulars against Freemasonry was not the issue that most vexed and divided Americans during the third of a century leading up to the Civil War. As events came to show, sectionalism and slavery were the most pressing public business the nation faced.

As slavery was abolished or gradually died in states above the Mason-Dixon Line and as the nation expanded westward, interregional conflict arose over the balance of power in setting federal policies. Tariffs became one of the difficult policy issues that separated North from South.

Tariffs were an important revenue source for federal programs; but it was another purpose that led congressional majorities from the industrializing North to set tariffs very high. The northerners acted to protect vulnerable new industries from product and price competition from imported goods, particularly manufactured items coming from industrialized Britain. Southerners opposed high tariffs because these would increase product prices, retard foreign textile manufacture and the demand for exported southern cotton, and prompt Britain and other nations to impose retaliatory tariffs on cotton and other agricultural products.

Congress passed high tariff acts in 1828 and again (with more restraint) in 1832. Though southern born, President Jackson gave his nod to the northern position. South Carolinian John C. Calhoun, Jackson's first vice president, resigned that post in 1832, primarily because of his differences with Jackson and northern congressmen over tariffs. South Carolina, acting on Calhoun's contention that it is a state's right to nullify federal acts, then declared the 1828 and 1832 tariff acts null and void. Although this Nullification Crisis was resolved by compromise in 1833, tariffs remained a nettlesome issue in the years leading up to the Civil War.

Slavery, with its acute moral as well as economic ramifications, was never far from the surface in the sectional conflict—Calhoun himself was among slavery's most prominent defenders—and in the 1850s slavery and the prospect of its expansion surpassed other dimensions of the sectional divide. But there was a time when optimists believed the issue resolved—resolved politically, the moral blight notwithstanding.

Their hope grew out of passage of the Compromise of 1850, a series of acts intended to settle sectional issues arising from the 1846–48 Mexican War. The compromise admitted California as a free state, organized the New Mexico and Utah territories, and authorized these territories' citizens to settle the issue of slavery within their boundaries by popular sovereignty. It forbade the slave trade, but not slavery

★ ★

The Nullifiers

The Nullifier Party, a short-lived third party, was born in 1828 in support of the southern position on tariffs and in embrace of Calhoun's nullification premise. Nullifiers served in the U.S. Senate from 1831 to 1837 and in the House from 1831 to 1839. South Carolina–based, the Nullifiers also found some support elsewhere in the South. An Alabama Nullifier sat in the House with seven or eight Nullifiers from South Carolina during the Twenty-third and Twenty-fourth congresses (1833–37).

★ ★

itself, in the District of Columbia. The Fugitive Slave Law, the most troubling element of the compromise, promised federal action to stop the practice of assisting runaway slaves.

The Know Nothings

During the first half of the 1850s, a new issue challenged the place of sectionalism and slavery on the nation's agenda. In a very early wave of new immigration, millions of Irish and German Catholics came to America in the 1830s, 1840s, and 1850s. Calamitous natural and political events back home sometimes sparked their leaving, but they also came because of the American promise. These new immigrants inevitably competed with American-born poor and working-class people for jobs and wages. The established parties, particularly the Democrats, recognized the importance of wooing new citizens' support and votes, and Irish American politicians rose to positions of Democratic Party leadership in northern cities.

Fear and hatred of the new immigrants and of their Roman Catholic religion spread like a pandemic among millions of the nation's poor, and a third-party mass movement—ephemeral, as it turned out, but remarkable in the support it was able to rally while it lasted—arose to give voice to nativism. Born in New York in 1843, the party went national two years later. This anti-Catholic, anti-immigrant party went by various names. In 1855, at the height of its grip on national power and influence, it declared itself to be the American Party. In its day it came to be known—and it has been remembered since—as the Know Nothing Party.

So self-evident, it has become a cliché that America has for long been a land of immigrants and their descendants. As a truism that may register with bitter poignancy in communities of Native Americans. *E pluribus unum*, the nation's motto, evokes thoughts of the melting pot but also pride in its ethnic, racial, and religious diversity. The inscription on the Statue of Liberty eloquently welcomes new immigrants. Americans observed the global reach of its symbolism when in 1989 Chinese students demanding freedom erected a statue in its image in Tiananmen Square.

The pre–Civil War immigration wave was followed by others, and the Know Nothing movement was far from the last nativist reaction. An 1879 modification of California's constitution abolished Chinese contract labor,[11] and in 1882 Congress legislated the Chinese Exclusion Act. During World War II, Japanese Americans were rounded up and sent to internment camps for no other offense than their ancestry in the nation that had carried out the Pearl Harbor attack. Today a handful of politicians and media talking heads build their careers inveighing against "illegals" and the growing number of Latinos living in the United States.

Private vigilantes patrolling along the Mexican border, threats or acts of violence targeting Muslims or Vietnamese refugees—incidents such as these attest to the sustained emotion and power of American nativism. So, in its own way, does the organized movement to make English the nation's official language. A term has entered the political lexicon for nativists of all generations. They may hear themselves called "know nothings."

Horace Greeley, the founder and editor of the *New York Tribune*, coined that term and applied it pejoratively to the anti-Catholic, anti-immigrant party of the late 1840s and the1850s. There were fundamental differences between the nativist party and the party of the Anti-Masons, even though both were born in Greeley's Empire State. The Anti-Masons hated secrecy and the mischief they believed secrecy inspires. The nativists, recognizing that there were many who found their message to be ugly, reprehensible, even dangerous, were secretive themselves.

In much of the country, membership in the American Party—said to have reached a million in the party's prime—came by entry into the Order of the Star Spangled Banner, a clandestine, oath-bound, Protestant-only society. To queries about their order, party, and related activities, members replied that they knew nothing. There was the term, ready and waiting for Greeley to appropriate, and the nickname stuck and spread through the land.[12] Many Know Nothings embraced Greeley's disdainful expression like a badge of honor.

Know Nothing secrecy largely accounts for some disparity in the reports about the number of its members in Congress at the party's peak, the Thirty-fourth Congress (1855–57). The party's share of the seats in the House was certainly huge. Most counts of American Party House members in 1855 place their number at fifty-one (21.8 percent).

Nathaniel Banks, a Know Nothing, was the only minor-party U.S. House member ever elected to the position of Speaker. But despite its congressional presence and possession of the House presiding gavel, the party failed in the policy arena. Notably Congress failed to pass nativist proposals for a twenty-one-year waiting period for naturalized citizenship and for an immigration ban on "foreign paupers, criminals, idiots, lunatics, insane, and blind persons."[13]

Know Nothing victories in state and local elections were nothing short of phenomenal. The party came to control the legislatures of Rhode Island, New Hampshire, Connecticut, Maryland, and Kentucky, and it was the principal opposition in nearly a dozen more. It swept across northern cities, winning mayoralty elections in Boston, Philadelphia, Washington, Chicago, and San Francisco. Between 1854 and 1857, Know Nothings won governorships in Massachusetts, California, Connecticut, Kentucky, New Hampshire, and Maryland.

In the South too the party emerged as a factor of some strength and political importance. Many historians contend that nativist anti-Catholicism was less apparent in southern branches of the party and a good bit less crucial to the birth, care, and feeding of the southern party. Remarkably in 1855 Louisiana Know Nothings nominated a Catholic for governor, and he came very close to winning the election. The Know Nothing appeal in the southern states may have been due in part to voters' belief that the party and its candidates were more interested than the region's Democratic candidates in preserving the Union.

After the Whig collapse around 1854, southern Know Nothings stepped in to assume the conventional role of loyal opposition to the usually dominant Democrats. Outside the South it was the Republicans, not the Know Nothings, who succeeded the Whigs as the Democrats' counterpoint. Southern Know Nothings thus held on to much of their organizational vitality even as they watched their party die in the North. As late as 1859, Texas Know Nothings' endorsement and support contributed substantially to the victory of Sam Houston, an iconic figure in Texas history, as governor of the Lone Star State.[14]

In 1854 the passion surrounding the issues of sectionalism and slavery was rekindled by the Kansas-Nebraska Act, legislation that voided the 1820 Missouri Compromise. For over a third of a century, that carefully crafted compromise had provided a workable balance between proslavery and antislavery interests in the most northerly regions of the vast Louisiana Purchase tract.

Illinois Democratic senator Stephen A. Douglas, the Kansas-Nebraska Act's chief sponsor, capitulated to southern demands to secure its passage. It was a decision for which he would never earn the forgiveness of many northerners who were opposed to the territorial expansion of slavery. The legislation he pushed through organized the Kansas and Nebraska territories and empowered these territories' citizens to decide whether slavery would be allowed within their boundaries.[15]

In Kansas the fruits of this act were bloody violence and a nasty, bitter, and protracted political struggle. "Bleeding Kansas" was a bounty for the Republican Party, as news of it bled voter support away from other parties. The damage the Kansas-Nebraska Act and the prospect of a new territorial opening for slavery did to the divided Democrats was substantial, but unlike for the Whigs, it was not death-dealing. Never able to resolve this corrosive issue, the hopelessly divided Whig Party was destroyed by the act and its aftermath.

The Whig demise brought some short-term benefit to the American Party, which achieved many of its most spectacular election victories in 1854 and 1855. But what damaged the Democrats and destroyed the Whigs also split the Know Nothings. The Republican Party was born the year the Kansas-Nebraska Act was legislated, and only the Republicans were the long-term beneficiaries of the outraged reaction to the act and to events in Kansas. Many northern Know Nothings demanded that their own party take a stand against the extension of slavery, and they eventually faded away to take part in the Republican Party. The northern Know Nothing base would shrink further following the proslavery 1857 Dred Scott decision.[16]

The American Party waged just one significant campaign for the presidency, in 1856.[17] Many northern delegates to their party's convention that year worked fruitlessly to nominate someone known for his opposition to extending the slavery option to territories in the North. The convention nod went instead to former president Millard Fillmore. Fillmore's presidential tenure had been short, a thirty-two-month interim following the death of Whig Zachary Taylor.

As Whig president and later even as Know Nothing nominee, Fillmore showed no passion for the nativist cause. Just before his 1856 nomination, in fact, he learned that he had been granted a request he had made for an audience with the Pope.[18] His Know Nothing campaign muted and largely ignored the nativist theme, avoided the issue of slavery, and concentrated upon "preserving the Union." Fillmore also ran on the Whig ticket, but the contribution of the dead Whig label to his election total was inconsequential.[19]

Fillmore took nearly 22 percent of the popular votes, an impressive result though it landed him in third place. His state-by-state vote totals bore testimony to the degree to which the party strength was both diminishing and shifting southward, as northern Know Nothings deserted in droves to join the Republican cause. Fillmore took nearly 42 percent of the popular votes in the South. Border states' voters gave Fillmore 48.5 percent of their votes. Maryland's eight electoral votes went to him. His popular showing was low by comparison throughout the North. He took 21 percent of the votes in New York and 18 percent in Pennsylvania, but fewer than 6 percent of New England's voters voted for the American Party nominee.

The Know Nothings, like many other third parties, failed in their goal of finding a sustained place in national major-party ranks; but of all these failed ventures, theirs was the one that came closest to doing just that. The Republican Party did make the meteoric rise from third to major party, but the Whigs were not one of the two partisan forces standing in its way. It was through the Democrats and Know Nothings that the Republicans had to clear their path.

Challenging Slavery: The Liberty, Free Soil, and Republican Parties

By the time of the firing on Fort Sumter—the second "shot heard around the world"—on April 12–13, 1861, the antislavery Republican Party was already a major actor in the nation's politics. Two years after the birth of his party in 1854, Republican John C. Fremont had taken a third of the votes for president, and his party won 38 percent of the seats in the U.S. House. By 1860 the Republican position was powerful enough to put Abraham Lincoln in the White House.

Neither the Liberty Party nor the Free Soil Party, two earlier antislavery parties, had successfully projected itself into national major-party ranks. It was in part a matter of timing, the electorate not yet being ready to embrace the antislavery messages Liberty and then Free Soil presented. But Liberty and Free Soil were important for their antislavery agitation and for laying the foundation upon which the Republicans later built.

Sharply contrasting perspectives beset the antislavery movement in the decades leading up to the Civil War. As new territories and states appeared on the map, the antiextensionists insisted that they be closed to slavery. Antiextensionists also opposed the 1850 Fugitive Slave Law, and many of them agitated against the continued commerce in slaves from state to state and in support of banning slavery in the nation's capital. Despised they certainly were by proslavery interests; but the antiextensionists were the relative moderates in the antislavery cause. The abolitionists were the radicals.

Among abolitionists there were deep divisions as to both means and ends. Some demanded immediate emancipation. Others were gradualists. "Moral suasion" was seen by some as the vehicle to promote their abolitionist cause. Others chose to use the political process but divided over whether to work with individual antislavery Whigs and Democrats or to lunge headlong into building a new antislavery third-party alternative. Some abolitionists envisaged full citizenship for the emancipated slaves. Others labored in the nineteenth-century movement to resettle former slaves in West Africa.[20]

The abolitionists' public image was heavy baggage to carry. There were people around the country who believed or claimed that abolitionists were terrorists who wanted to replay murderous events such as Nat Turner's 1831 slave rebellion.

The Liberty Party

Born in 1839–40, the Liberty Party lasted only until 1848. Its soul and philosophy were abolitionist, though Liberty's leaders and program conceded that the federal government lacked the authority to abolish slavery by fiat. The Liberty Party's principled stand for abolition and its refusal to speak with conviction and force to the broad array of other issues that counted with Americans in the 1840s sharply curtailed its appeal.

The Liberty Party scored miserably in its 1840 bid for the presidency. Nominee James G. Birney, a Kentucky abolitionist who had owned slaves in his early life, took only one in every four hundred votes in the nation. Birney won 2.3 percent nationally four years later. His 1844 tallies in Massachusetts, New Hampshire, and Vermont exceeded 8 percent of the votes cast in each.

Birney took 15,812 votes in New York in 1844. Democrat James K. Polk's New York tally surpassed Whig Henry Clay's by just 5,106 votes. Since Clay would have won the presidency if he had received New York's electoral votes, Libertymen probably were justified in their claim that they had spoiled the election for Clay and put Polk in the White House.[21]

Liberty was the first third party to recruit and attract African American leadership and support. Black church parishioners attending a conference in Albany, New York, threw their support to the party. So did the *Colored American*, the most important New York black newspaper of the time. Among African American abolitionists who became leading Libertymen were Samuel Ringgold Ward, Henry Highland Garnet, and eventually the eminent Frederick Douglass.[22]

The Free Soil Party

Free Soil was the immediate descendent of the Liberty Party and the Republicans' forebear in the antislavery struggle. Born in 1848, the party adopted "Free Soil, Free Speech, Free Labor, and Free Men" as its slogan. Free Soil's spirit was far more pragmatic than Liberty's, and Free Soil was a good bit more inclined to seek to build

Free Soil campaign poster, 1848, featuring Free Soil candidates Martin Van Buren and Charles Francis Adams. Created by Nathaniel Currier Firm. Courtesy of U.S. Library of Congress Prints and Photographs Division. Obtained through Wikimedia Commons.

coalitions. To purists' charges that all this spelled expediency, many Free Soilers answered that to be right and fail is no victory for what is right.

In its formation Free Soil brought together three groups: Libertymen from the older party, Massachusetts-centered Conscience Whigs, and New York Barnburner Democrats. In the bifactional politics within the New York Democratic Party, the Barnburners had been the reformers who, it was said, were ready to burn down the barn to destroy the rats. Many of the Barnburners and the Conscience Whigs were much closer to the antiextensionist perspective than to abolition.[23]

Free Soil pragmatism was evident in the party's eclectic interest in issues in addition to slavery. The 1848 platform called for a homestead act—an important initiative later echoed by the Republicans and passed in 1862 by the Republican-controlled Congress. It also demanded federal support for internal improvements and a moderate policy of tariffs sufficient only to provide funding for federal operations.

In selecting its first presidential candidate, this party went for someone with all the name recognition of an ex-president. That was Martin Van Buren, who had won the presidency as a Democrat in 1836 but lost his 1840 bid for reelection. Charles Francis Adams, Van Buren's 1848 running mate, was the son of another former president, John Quincy Adams. Free Soil's selection of Van Buren in 1848 came at some cost. The candidate was an antiextensionist but no abolitionist, and his public record bore some embarrassing early remarks in which he seemed to defend slavery. And there were some antislavery Whigs for whom it was not easy to consider a candidate whose past party connections had been with the Democrats.

Van Buren took more than a quarter of the vote in Vermont, Massachusetts, Wisconsin, and New York, and it is likely that he spoiled the election for Democrat Lewis Cass and put Zachary Taylor, the Whig, in the White House. But his national total—10.1 percent—disappointed many Free Soilers. Van Buren earned not a single electoral vote anywhere, though his popular vote tally did place him in second place in New York, Massachusetts, and Vermont.

Devotion to antislavery led Free Soilers into alliances with like-minded Democrats in the North. This substantially aided the selection of Charles Sumner, Salmon P. Chase,[24] and of other strong foes of slavery for the U.S. Senate as well as the election of Free Soilers to the House. At the peak of its congressional presence, from 1849 to 1851, Free Soil's House caucus numbered nine, and there were others—major-party opponents of slavery—who won election on fusion tickets with Free Soil participation and support.

This Free Soil penchant for coalition building undoubtedly strengthened the antislavery voice in Washington. But it is likely that it also diminished the party's ability to sustain itself as an independent, long-term partisan force. Free Soil's fiercest loyalists in seeking to preserve the party as a separate entity turned out to be its purists rather than its pragmatists.

Control of Free Soil Party affairs eventually fell by default to the doctrinaire abolitionists, and the party became both purer and less widely appealing. John P. Hale from Free Soil's Libertymen branch was the party's last presidential candidate in 1852. Hale won just under 5 percent of the vote.

From 1854 on the brand-new Republican Party easily absorbed Free Soil's surviving remnants. It was the Republicans' achievement to organize the antislavery movement, together with other interests, into a partisan force capable, by 1860, of winning the presidency.

6

★ ★ ★

Union, Reform, and Class
Short-Lived Parties, 1860–1908

You shall not crucify mankind upon a cross of gold.
Democratic/Populist presidential nominee
William Jennings Bryan, 1896

A remarkable 81 percent of those eligible turned out for the November 6, 1860, presidential election. The two leading candidates were Illinois politicians who had faced off against each other before. In that contest Abraham Lincoln, the Republican, had thrown down the gauntlet to the Democratic incumbent. "I believe," Lincoln had said, "this government cannot endure permanently half slave and half free." Lincoln lost that 1858 race—the Democratic legislative majority in Springfield returned Stephen Douglas to the U.S. Senate—but 1860 belonged to Lincoln and the Republicans.

Lincoln won almost 1.9 million presidential votes in 1860, a half million more than Douglas. Except in Virginia the Republicans received not a single popular vote for president in any of the states that left the Union after Lincoln's election. That may have resulted from shrewd projections about the meager benefits and high costs (including probable physical danger) of distributing the antislavery party's ballots in the South. But Lincoln ended with 180 of the 303 electoral votes, 28 more than was required to take the White House in 1860.

Douglas won popular votes in every one of the thirty-two states in which a popular contest for the presidency was held. But he had managed to alienate important interests everywhere. He had antagonized Democratic incumbent president James Buchanan and his administration. Antislavery voters nursed a bitter grudge, blaming him for Bleeding Kansas. Southerners were angry because Douglas had helped lead the opposition to Kansas's admission to statehood under its proslavery Lecompton Constitution. Slavery interests had stacked the deck, winning approval in Kansas for a constitution that did not come close to having the blessing of most of the territory's citizens. Even so, southerners saw Lecompton's defeat in Congress as a violation of a gentleman's agreement in the Kansas-Nebraska Act.[1] Douglas's share of southerners' votes was an anemic 8.4 percent.

Table 6.1 Presidential Election Results, 1860

Lincoln (Republican) Plurality States

	Lincoln (R)	Douglas (D)	Breckinridge (SD)	Bell (CU)	Electoral Votes[a]
California	38,733 (32.3%)	37,999 (31.7%)	33,969 (28.4%)	9,111 (7.6%)	4
Connecticut	43,488 (58.1)	15,431 (20.6)	14,372 (19.2)	1,528 (2.0)	6
Illinois	172,171 (50.7)	160,215 (47.2)	2,331 (0.7)	4,914 (1.5)	11
Indiana	139,033 (51.1)	115,509 (42.4)	12,295 (4.5)	5,306 (2.0)	13
Iowa	70,302 (54.6)	55,639 (43.2)	1,035 (0.8)	1,763 (1.4)	4
Maine	62,811 (62.2)	29,693 (29.4)	6,368 (6.3)	2,046 (2.0)	8
Massachusetts	106,684 (62.8)	34,370 (20.2)	6,163 (3.6)	22,331 (13.2)	13
Michigan	88,481 (57.2)	65,057 (42.0)	805 (0.5)	415 (0.3)	6
Minnesota	22,069 (63.4)	11,920 (34.3)	748 (2.2)	50 (0.1)	4
New Hampshire	37,519 (56.9)	25,887 (39.3)	2,125 (3.2)	412 (0.6)	5
New York	362,646 (53.7)	312,510 (46.3)	—	—	35
Ohio	231,709 (52.3)	187,421 (42.3)	11,406 (2.6)	12,194 (2.8)	23
Oregon	5,329 (36.1)	4,136 (28.0)	5,075 (34.4)	218 (1.5)	3
Pennsylvania	268,030 (56.3)	16,765 (3.5)	178,871 (37.5)	12,776 (2.7)	27
Rhode Island	12,244 (61.4)	7,707 (38.6)	—	—	4
Vermont	33,808 (75.7)	8,649 (19.4)	218 (0.5)	1,969 (4.4)	5
Wisconsin	86,110 (56.6)	65,021 (42.7)	887 (0.6)	161 (0.1)	5

Douglas (Democratic) Plurality States

	Lincoln (R)	Douglas (D)	Breckinridge (SD)	Bell (CU)	Electoral Votes[a]
Missouri	17,028 (10.3)	58,801 (35.5)	31,362 (18.9)	58,372 (35.3)	9
New Jersey	58,346 (48.1)	62,869 (51.9)	—	—	4 Lincoln; 3 Douglas

Breckinridge (Southern Democratic) Plurality States

	Lincoln (R)	Douglas (D)	Breckinridge (SD)	Bell (CU)	Electoral Votes[a]
Alabama	—	13,618 (15.1)	48,669 (54.0)	27,835 (30.9)	9
Arkansas	—	5,357 (9.9)	28,732 (53.1)	20,063 (37.1)	4
Delaware	3,822 (23.7)	1,066 (6.6)	7,339 (45.5)	3,888 (24.1)	3
Florida	—	223 (1.7)	8,277 (62.2)	4,801 (36.1)	3
Georgia	—	11,581 (10.9)	52,176 (48.9)	42,960 (40.3)	10
Louisiana	—	7,625 (15.1)	22,681 (44.9)	20,204 (40.0)	6
Maryland	2,294 (2.5)	5,966 (6.5)	42,482 (45.9)	41,760 (45.1)	8
Mississippi	—	3,282 (4.8)	40,768 (59.0)	25,045 (36.4)	7
North Carolina	—	2,737 (2.8)	48,846 (50.5)	45,129 (46.7)	10
South Carolina[b]	—	—	—	—	8
Texas	—	18 (0.0)	47,754 (75.5)	15,383 (24.5)	4

Bell (Constitutional Union) Plurality States

	Lincoln (R)	Douglas (D)	Breckinridge (SD)	Bell (CU)	Electoral Votes[a]
Kentucky	1,364 (0.9)	25,651 (17.5)	53,143 (36.3)	66,058 (45.2)	12
Tennessee	—	11,281 (7.7)	65,097 (44.6)	69,728 (47.7)	12
Virginia	1,887 (1.1)	16,198 (9.7)	74,325 (44.5)	74,481 (44.6)	15

Table 6.1 continued

Vote Totals

	Popular Votes	Electoral Votes
Lincoln, Republican	1,865,908	180
Douglas, Democratic	1,380,202	12
Breckinridge, Southern Democratic	848,019	72
Bell, Constitutional Union	590,901	39

a. In New Jersey the electoral votes were split, as indicated in the table, between Lincoln and Douglas. In every other state except South Carolina all the states' electoral votes went to the winner of the popular plurality in the state.

b. South Carolina did not adopt the system of voter election of electors until after the Civil War, so there was no popular vote for president in South Carolina in 1860. The state's electoral votes all were cast for Breckinridge.

SOURCE: *Presidential Elections since 1789* (Washington, D.C.: Congressional Quarterly, 1975), 32 and 71.

Eighteen sixty really featured a four-candidate race, one in which Douglas finished last in electoral votes and Lincoln won the presidency with one of history's most tepid popular pluralities. Only 39.8 percent of the nation's voters cast ballots for the Lincoln ticket.

The Constitutional Union and Southern Democratic Parties

The real contest in the South as well as in several border states pitted two ephemeral, flash-in-the-pan parties. Tennessean John Bell, a former U.S. senator, took his home state plus Kentucky and Virginia as the choice of the Constitutional Union Party. The rest of the South plus Maryland and Delaware went to the candidate of the Southern Democratic Party, incumbent vice president John C. Breckinridge of Kentucky. Outside the South Breckinridge ran second only to Lincoln in both Pennsylvania and Oregon.

As a party the Constitutional Unionists were reactionaries linked to a world already lost. Embracing the Constitution, they dedicated themselves to the futile hope of saving a Union that was about to be split, then ultimately restored, by the bloodiest war in the nation's history. Their platform, all two hundred words of it, skirted or ignored slavery and every other issue except union. Constitutional Union drew its leadership from ex-Whigs and ex–Know Nothings. Bell, the party's sixty-three-year-old presidential candidate, had left the Senate the year before still wearing the label of the extinct Whig party. Delegates attending the party's convention "were or appeared to be venerable gentlemen representing a generation of almost forgotten politicians, [most of whom] had retired from public life involuntarily."[2]

Of the two third parties, Constitutional Union had the more aristocratic ambiance. Southern Democrats' voter base was of a grittier, earthy character. Southern Democrats ran best in rural counties where there were relatively few slaves. Constitutional Unionists found their support among large landowners and in the commercial interests of the cities.[3]

The Southern Democratic Party was the only nationally significant U.S. party ever to speak unequivocally in defense of slavery. Historians sometimes refer to the party as Secessionist Democrat. That label carries a double meaning. Depending upon one's view of events in 1860, the Southern Democrats either seceded or were expelled from the national Democratic Party. And many of this new party's leaders and supporters were willing, even eager, to think the unthinkable: withdrawal of slave states from the United States. Breckinridge himself became a Confederate major general. As the Civil War drew to a close, he was serving as the Confederate secretary of war.

The Southern Democratic Party came to life at two 1860 conventions of the national Democratic Party: the first in Charleston, South Carolina, in April, the other in Baltimore two months later. In Charleston southern delegates demanded that the platform include some measures for the defense of slavery interests. When the convention refused and instead invoked the Supreme Court as the agent to set-tle the issue of slavery, delegations from the Deep South and some delegates from Arkansas and Delaware withdrew in protest.[4]

Failing in Charleston even to settle upon a presidential nominee—the rule at the time required support for a candidate by two-thirds of the convention—the national Democrats reconvened in Baltimore in June. There the forces supporting Douglas manipulated the process to secure his selection. Most crucially they denied reinstatement to many of the delegates who had walked out in Charleston, replac-ing them instead. When that happened, delegations from the rest of the South and also from distant California and Oregon headed for the doors of the convention hall. Delegates who were denied reinstatement and those who had just walked out then reconvened in rump session and nominated Breckinridge. Another group of southerners, many of them veterans of the Charleston convention, met in Rich-mond and endorsed Breckinridge. Their Southern Democratic Party was born. Its short life as an American party ended upon the election of Abraham Lincoln.[5] The same was true of the Constitutional Union Party.

South Carolina seceded on December 20, 1860. Six other southern states left the Union before Lincoln's inauguration on March 4, 1861, and four more followed suit in the days and weeks immediately following the firing on Fort Sumter. The exigen-cies of war over the next four years constricted even two-party competition, leaving no space at all for third parties to grow up and thrive.

The Republicans emerged from the Civil War as the more powerful of the two major parties. Late-nineteenth-century America underwent rapid business and in-dustrial growth and westward expansion. Corporate interests rallied to the banner of the probusiness Republican Party. The party coalition also encompassed non-southern farmers, emancipated former slaves in the South, western homesteaders, and Union veterans.

The Liberal Republican Party

The Liberal Republican Party was the first transient party to appear on the national scene after the Civil War. Its electoral life lasted only from 1870 through 1872. Although it was an insurgency targeting the GOP, the party was far from anything resembling revolution from below. Some of the early Republican Party's most prominent figures—men like Salmon P. Chase, Charles Sumner, and Charles Fran-cis Adams—went on to take part in the Liberal Republican Party. The party won warm endorsements from influential Republican newspapers in Springfield, Mass-achusetts, and in Cincinnati, Chicago, Louisville, and New York City.[6]

Three issues breathed life into Liberal Republican Party and provided what inter-nal coherence the new party was able to muster. First, Liberal Republicans recoiled at the deep-seated corruption in the Republican administration of Ulysses S. Grant, and they wanted to replace the spoils system in Washington with a federal civil service. Second, they opposed Republican high-tariff policies. Finally, the Liberal Republican Party declared that with new constitutional amendments bestowing civil and political rights upon former slaves, the goals of Reconstruction had already been achieved. They thus opposed the Republican "radicals" (who were dominant in Congress) and their program of Reconstruction in the southern states. Finding common ground in this with the major-party opponent of the GOP, the Liberal Republicans readily entered into electoral alliances with the Democrats.

The Liberal Republican movement began in Missouri in 1870, the brainchild of Republican U.S. senator Carl Schurz. Liberal Republican–Democratic fusion tickets threw out the Republican establishment in Missouri and won the governor's office for Liberal Republican B. Gratz Brown in 1870. Two Liberal Republicans represented House districts in Missouri during the Forty-second Congress (1871–73).

Two years later Missouri voters again delivered the governor's office to a candidate of the two parties in fusion, and Liberal Republicans contributed to the election of Democratic nominees for governor in Louisiana and elsewhere. Liberal Republican U.S. House candidates in 1872 won election in Alabama, Ohio, Louisiana, and Arkansas.

At its May 1872 convention, the Liberal Republican Party nominated the sixty-nine-year-old Horace Greeley. Greeley's running mate was B. Gratz Brown, the well-known Missouri fusionist. Desperate to unseat President Grant, Democrats at their July convention then nominated Greeley and Brown and adopted the Liberal Republican Party platform verbatim.

This 1872 Liberal Republican–Democratic presidential joint venture certainly was one of the signal events in the history of fusion politics. But Greeley's selection was, for both parties, an egregious mistake. A reformer he certainly was, but he was also tactless, alienating, and eccentric. He had an uncanny knack for outrageous remarks.

> Soon after Ft. Sumter he had urged Lincoln to make peace with the Confederacy on their own terms. Then he became an enthusiastic champion of military conquest. [Even while he was seeking] Democratic support for his candidacy, he said he would not endorse any Democratic nominee for office. Most Democrats [and Liberal Republicans] opposed high tariffs. But Greeley was a protectionist. . . .
>
> The campaign was a disaster. Greeley made a series of blunders. He denounced a Union soldier's convention as "rekindling the bitterness and hatred . . . of civil war." He called Negroes "ignorant, deceived, and misguided" for voting against him. He even said he would accept secession if the southerners voted for it in a fair and open election.[7]

President Grant won thirty-one of the thirty-seven states on his way to reelection in 1872. The Greeley-Brown fusion ticket did take 43.8 percent nationally and popular majorities in Missouri, Kentucky, Maryland, Texas, Georgia, and Tennessee.

———————————————— ★ ★ ————————————————

The First Women Presidential Nominees

Victoria C. Woodhull was the first woman ever nominated for the presidency. Belva Ann Lockwood is said to have been the first to wage an active campaign for the office. Both were nominated by the Equal Rights Party, Woodhull in 1872 and Lockwood in 1884 and 1888. Woodhull did what she did forty-eight years before national women's suffrage.

According to political scientist Jo Freeman, a well-known feminist scholar, Woodhull won the enthusiastic endorsement of several hundred people attending her new party's 1872 convention even though she was younger than thirty-five, the minimum age for service as president. Freeman describes Woodhull as a "notorious woman," one who supported herself as a "clairvoyant healer, a stockbroker, and a newspaper publisher" and who "both charmed and frightened many men." Known for her advocacy of free love, Woodhull was in jail on the day of the 1872 election. She had been picked up on a charge of "distributing an obscene publication." There is no record that Woodhull's party printed and distributed ballots or that she received any popular votes anywhere.

Belva Lockwood was a person of remarkable accomplishment, the first woman lawyer ever admitted to practice before the U.S. Supreme Court. She claimed that for her 1884 presidential bid her party had named presidential electors in nine states, and that 4,711 voters (all of them men) in seven states had voted for her.

Sources: Jo Freeman, *We Will Be Heard: Women's Struggles for Political Power in the United States* (Lanham, Md.: Rowman & Littlefield, 2008), 86–87; Julia Davis, "A Feisty Schoolmarm Made the Lawyers Take Notice," *Smithsonian Magazine,* March 1981, 133+; and Richard Winger, "2008, the Year the Major Parties Started to Catch up with Minor Parties in Candidate Diversity," *Ballot Access News,* August 30, 2008, http://www.ballot-access.org/2008/08/30/2008-the-year-the-major-parties-started-to-catch-up-with-minor-parties-on-candidate-diversity/.

———————————————— ★ ★ ————————————————

But many thousands of the nation's Republicans who might have cast for some other Liberal Republican–Democratic presidential candidate voted for Grant and reset their long-term devotion to the party of Lincoln.

As a national movement, the Liberal Republican Party died in effect on election day 1872, in the aftermath of Greeley's disastrous campaign. A core of its leaders did hold on to their devotion for some years longer, and in 1876 they gathered to consider, but then did not launch, a new Liberal Republican bid for the presidency.[8]

"Get Thee Behind Me, (Mrs.) Satan." Biting caricature by Thomas Nast depicting Victoria Woodhull as "Mrs. Satan" with a scroll reading, "Be saved by free love." The wife in the background, carrying children and a drunken husband, says, "I'd rather travel the hardest path of matrimony than follow your footsteps." Originally in *Harper's Weekly,* February 7, 1872, 140. Courtesy of U.S. Library of Congress Prints and Photographs Division. Obtained through Wikimedia Commons.

Greeley himself died on November 29, 1872, weeks before the electors cast their votes. Of the sixty-six electors committed to him, eighteen gave their presidential electoral votes to B. Gratz Brown. Forty-five voted for one of three other politicians. Three Georgia electors faithfully (or stubbornly) voted for Greeley, but Congress refused to certify their votes for a dead man.

Many of Liberal Republicans' prime movers remained in politics after the collapse of their third-party movement, and some of them still were active when two cherished party goals became public policy. In 1877 Republican president Rutherford B. Hayes announced the withdrawal of the last federal occupying troops from Louisiana and South Carolina and closed the book on Reconstruction. Congress in 1883 adopted the Pendleton Act, a major early step toward replacing the old federal spoils system with a merit-based civil service. Both of these policy changes would have been warmly applauded within the Liberal Republican Party if they had passed while the party still lived; but the historical evidence does not suggest that Liberal Republican agitation on their behalf caused their eventual enactment.[9]

Greenbackers and Populists: Pushing Back on Wealth and Power

The nineteenth century's last three decades provided fertile ground for aspiring third parties. The Prohibition Party, today still possessing a beating heart, was born in 1869. The Socialist Labor Party, the nation's oldest nationally organized Socialist party, marked its 132nd birthday in 2008. Important, though temporary, state-level parties grew up in various parts of the country. Campaigning on a third-party ticket for mayor of New York City in 1886, the radical economist Henry George ran a strong second to the candidate of the powerful Tammany machine despite widespread electoral fraud.[10]

The Greenbackers

The Greenback Party, also known as the Greenback-Labor Party, was an important early venture into class-based politics. It was the first nationally organized party to enlist the support of hundreds of thousands of farmers and workers in opposition to the power and policies of capital and on behalf of a program of progressive reform. Originating in Indiana around 1873, the party developed as an organized national movement in 1875–76.[11] Though Greenback strength peaked in 1878, the movement lived on until around 1886.

The Greenback experience documented that grievances shared by farmers and workers were a sufficient foundation for farm-and-labor coalition politics. It was a lesson learned by the end-of-the-century Populists as well as by farmer-labor movements in the twentieth century.

Greenback's earliest organizers responded to a litany of grievances, many of them borne by farmers. The monopolistic and heavily subsidized railroads charged exorbitant rates for shipping farm products to market. Farmers demanded federal and state railroad regulation, and by 1875 nearly a million of them were taking part in granges, the local units of the progressive National Grange. State-level antimonopoly parties grew up in nearly a dozen states in the West and Midwest in the early 1870s. Their policy goals soon influenced the agenda and platforms of the Greenback movement.

The new movement's name came from the label people used for the paper money, unbacked by silver or gold, that the Union floated during the Civil War. Nearly a half billion dollars in greenbacks had gone into circulation during the war. By contrast the bulk of government-issued currency before the war had been coins minted in gold, silver, or copper. Federal law had prescribed the number of grains of gold or silver to go into a coin, and it had set the ratio of value of silver grains to grains of gold.

After the war conservative hard-money advocates began pushing policy toward constriction of the money supply and renewal of a specie-based currency system. In sharp contrast Greenbackers and their constituency—farmers, many with accumulated debt burdens, and wage workers—favored the greenbacks, soft money, and expansion of the money supply.

A sharp downturn in the industrial cycle brought suffering to scores of industrial workers in the 1870s and, for many, a loss of trust in the capitalist system. The darkest depression the nation had ever known hit in 1873, and it took nearly six years to run its course. The stock market was deeply affected, banks failed, plants and businesses shut down, and many workers found themselves in breadlines.

The Specie Resumption Act, passed in 1875, prescribed the phaseout of greenbacks and the resurrection by 1879 of a specie currency system, one based not on silver and gold bimetallism but on gold alone. Although an unambiguous victory for the monetary conservatives and a clear defeat for Greenback money goals, the law provided valuable service, enlisting farmer and worker support for the Greenback cause. It was a bitter setback for silver interests too. As such it helped set the stage for the Populist movement as the century drew to a close.

Internal disputes over both policy and strategy—especially differences between Greenback's farmer and labor wings—were a fact of party life. Many labor leaders were far less convinced than their agrarian counterparts that the electoral benefits of fusion with the Democrats or Republicans outweighed the dangers of co-optation and possible absorption of the third-party movement.

But the party was not paralyzed by such intramural disagreements. Planks appearing in Greenback's national and state platforms written during the years 1878–80 reveal a maturing party unified around its currency theme but also devoted to progressive positions on a wide range of policy issues. Greenback platform planks called for legislation prescribing an eight-hour workday, banning child labor, and regulating labor conditions; railroad regulation and antimonopoly legislation; women's suffrage and the direct election of U.S. senators and presidents; and a graduated income tax.[12]

In 1878 the Greenbacks ran candidates in all thirty-eight states. The party's most substantial returns that year came in Iowa and Maine. Outside the South the party most often entered into fusion campaigns with the Democrats. Greenback won at least thirteen seats in the U.S. House: two each in Maine, Pennsylvania, and Iowa and one each in Vermont, Indiana, Illinois, Missouri, North Carolina, Alabama, and Texas.

In the South, where 90 percent of all African Americans lived, the Greenback movement enlisted blacks and whites in a common cause. African Americans from the South were delegates to Greenback's 1876 founding national convention. Texas was the party's strongest southern state. Delegates to the 1878 Texas Greenback convention came from 482 local chapters, 70 of which were all-black. Twelve Green-backers won election to the Texas legislature in 1878, more than the number of elected Republicans.[13]

Southern Greenbackers were fusionists. In Virginia they coalesced with the Read-justers, a state-level reformist party. In Mississippi, Alabama, and other southern states, Greenback was the agency through which white and black independents could join with Republicans in challenging the Democrats. J. J. Spellman, a promi-nent black Mississippian, ran unsuccessfully for secretary of state on a Greenback-Republican statewide ticket in 1881.[14]

Depression was ending by 1879, and the return of good times was not good for the Greenback movement. Fusion politics did produce some Greenback points of light in the 1880s. Democratic-Greenback gubernatorial tickets in 1882 won the Massachusetts governorship for Benjamin F. Butler and Michigan for Josiah Begole. But Greenback history in the 1880s was mainly a record of precipitous decline. Vot-ers in 1880 elected ten Greenback candidates to the U.S. House, but only three in 1882 and just one in 1884 and 1886.

It was Greenback's misfortune that the movement's best year, 1878, was not a presidential election year. The party's 1876 returns in its first bid for the presidency were very feeble, with nominee Peter Cooper taking less than 1 percent of the votes. In its last presidential campaign in 1884, Benjamin Butler ran as nominee of both the Anti-Monopoly and Greenback parties. Butler's vote share fell just under 2 percent.

The party's best presidential showing was for the 1880 candidacy of Iowa Green-back congressman James B. Weaver. Weaver was the first nominee of any party to take his campaign to every corner of the nation. But the depression had ended, and the vitality of Greenback's farmer-labor coalition was already waning. Whether jus-tified or not, the Republicans were declaring that it was their hard money policy that had brought the economic recovery. And both major parties warned voters about election spoiling and wasted third-party votes.

Weaver ended with just 3.3 percent of the votes nationwide, though his numbers broke into the double digits in Texas and Iowa. It would not be the candidate's last presidential campaign. The People's Party nominated Weaver to run in 1892.

In 1887, as Greenback's light flickered out, Congress fulfilled what had been one of the party's most cherished goals: an Interstate Commerce Commission with the authority to regulate the railroads. Greenback passed most of its other eventually enacted proposals on to its third-party heir, the far more influential People's Party. Populism's calls in turn helped set the agenda for the Progressive Era, the twentieth century's first two decades.

Greenback had given itself a formal name in 1878: the National Party. Ten years later Edward Bellamy published *Looking Backward: 2000–1887,* his renowned utopian novel. That manifesto for humanizing the industrial system was to become one of the most influential American literary works ever. *Nationalism* was the word Bellamy used for the good society he forecast and wanted to see. He borrowed that term from the National Party. Borrowing in turn from Bellamy, Theodore Roosevelt in 1912 chose the New Nationalism as the theme under which he sought to regain the presidency as a Bull Moose Progressive. Many later presidents also have found brands—the New Deal, the New Frontier, and others—for their vision and goals. Greenbackers must have had some hand in all that.

The Union Labor Party was a coalition linking elements of the Knights of Labor with some radical farm groups in the late 1880s. Partly filling a void left by Greenback's demise, it soon yielded up that space to the rising People's Party. Alson J. Streeter, Union Labor's presidential nominee, took nearly 1.5 percent of the national votes in 1888. Despite his party's name, Streeter scored his best results in rural midwestern and southern states. He took more than 11 percent of the votes in Kansas and 7–8 percent in Texas and Arkansas.

Populism and the People's Party

Like dozens of other parties, Populism—the People's Party and the Populists, the party's leaders and rank and file—never quite succeeded in scaling the wall between periphery and mainstream. But Populism may well have been the most important of all these parties in influencing public policy and affecting the course of the nation's history.

In 1879 the federal government had extended gold backing to greenbacks, enabling people wishing to do so to redeem those treasury notes for gold. Easy-money veterans of the old Greenback movement then moved on to bimetallism, demanding silver coinage along with gold. The "free and unlimited coinage of silver and gold" would be the rallying cry of Populism and of its People's Party. That won wide support for the new party in the silver-mining western states.

Domestic overproduction and competition from agricultural imports combined to produce a serious decline in farm commodity prices late in the nineteenth century. And there was farmers' continued rancor toward the railroads. Their grievances led white farmers to set up two regional reformist interest groups, the Northern Alliance and the Southern Alliance. African American farmers, residing mainly in the South, organized themselves as the National Colored Farmers Alliance.[15]

Populism's center of gravity always was in agrarian states of the Midwest plains and, to a lesser degree, in the rural South and silver West. But like its Greenback forebear, the People's Party incorporated labor interests into its electoral coalition and actively appealed for the support of working-class voters. When the People's Party appeared as a national organization, it was launched as the initiative and common venture of the three farmers alliances and of the Knights of Labor.

The People's Party was radical in its hostility toward capitalism and its ownership class. This was the Gilded Age, the era of robber barons. Americans perceived the People's Party as radical, and conservative mainstream newspapers subjected it to scathing attack. But there also was something reactionary in the Populist vision. Many Populists looked back nostalgically at an agrarian participatory democracy they believed was being devoured by industrialization, urbanization, and big-business plutocracy.[16]

By 1890 state People's parties already were growing up in the midwestern farming heartland. One of the first, in Kansas, already had developed the organizational strength and popular support by 1890–91 to sweep state legislative elections and five of the seven Kansas seats in the U.S. House and to send a Populist to the Senate. The 1891–93 Populist bloc in Congress also included a senator from South Dakota and three other House members, two from Nebraska and one from Montana.

In the South thousands of agrarians, white and black, constructed truly biracial state Populist parties, first in Texas and then in Louisiana, Georgia, and North Carolina. Southern Populism produced a leader of national stature, Georgia's Thomas E. Watson. One of the founders of the national People's Party movement, Watson spoke out courageously on behalf of poor African Americans as well as whites. Victories in a biracial North Carolina fusion campaign in 1894 produced Republican-Populist state legislative majorities and sent Populist Marion Butler to the U.S. Senate and four Tarheel Populists to the House.

The challenge for Populism in the South was in confronting the racial chauvinism that for many in the region trumped class solidarity as a motivating force. Scores of poor southern whites were devoted to the Democrats, the party with "populist" leaders, such as South Carolina's "Pitchfork Ben" Tillman, who claimed to champion the (white) common man. The southern Democrats were engaged in a virulent, mounting, and ultimately successful campaign for racial segregation, black disenfranchisement, and white supremacy. Populism's southern problem delayed the advent of the national People's Party.

The birth of the national party finally came at a St. Louis convention in February 1892.[17] Given the times, it was a remarkable event. Some eight hundred delegates showed up, sent by the three farmers alliances, the Knights of Labor, and various other reformist and radical associations. Nearly one hundred were African Americans from the Colored Alliance. Women delegates were there representing suffrage or prohibition causes.[18]

The Populists reconvened, this time in Omaha, in early July to adopt a platform and nominate the first People's Party presidential ticket. The 1,300–1,400 Omaha delegates reportedly stood and cheered wildly as Ignatius Donnelly, the convention's keynote speaker, delivered his radical address: "We meet in the midst of a nation brought to the verge of moral, political, and material ruin. Corruption dominates the ballot box, the legislatures, the Congress, and touches even ... the bench. ... The newspapers are subsidized or muzzled, business prostrated, our homes covered with mortgages, labor impoverished, and the land concentrated in the hands of capitalists. ... The fruits of the toil of millions are boldly stolen to build up colossal fortunes, unprecedented in history, while their possessors despise the Republic and endanger liberty. ... We charge that the controlling influences dominating the old parties allowed the existing dreadful conditions to develop." Donnelly spoke of "a vast conspiracy against mankind" that, if not overcome, "forebodes terrible social convulsions, the destruction of civilization, or the establishment of an absolute despotism."[19]

In its preamble, planks, or "expressions of sentiment," the Omaha platform demanded "the free and unlimited coinage of silver and gold at the present legal ratio of 16 to 1," expansion of the money supply, and a graduated income tax and called for government ownership and operation of the railroads and telephone and telegraph services; the secret ballot, initiative and referendum and direct election of U.S. senators; equal rights for men and women;[20] and the eight-hour workday and ending the practice of importing contract labor.

Iowa's James B. Weaver, the veteran of Greenback's 1880 presidential campaign, was selected at Omaha to carry the People's Party standard for president. Weaver took 8.5 percent of the votes Americans cast in 1892. He won the popular vote in Nevada, Colorado, Idaho, Kansas, and North Dakota and received twenty-two electoral votes. In three-way popular vote contests, Weaver came in second in Oregon, Nebraska, South Dakota, Alabama, Mississippi, and Texas.

Judged by its electoral appeal, the People's Party was at its peak from 1894 through 1896. During those years Populists, Democrats elected on Democratic-People's fusion tickets, and candidates of allied third parties won governors' races in Nebraska, Nevada, Idaho, Kansas, Montana, South Dakota, and Idaho. Reflecting the 1896 election results, twenty-two Populists, three Silver Republicans, and a Nevada Silverite served in the House during the Fifty-fifth Congress. A dozen members of these parties belonged to the Senate. Hundreds of Populist daily and weekly newspapers were operating in the 1890s. Kansas alone had at least 182, and there were around 100 in Texas.[21]

But for partisan Populism, two serious dilemmas were already at hand by 1896. Both turned out to be unsolvable factors that sent the movement, as an independent partisan force, down a slippery slope to extinction. The Democratic Party was complicit in both. Imagery of a big, hungry fish swimming at the tail of a smaller fish comes to mind.

In the South the biracial Populist movement suffered unrelenting, merciless race-baiting from a conservative establishment desperate to defend its interests against Populist radicalism. Southern newspapers editorialized that Populism stood for rule by "ignorant Negroes and unscrupulous whites" and that Democrats represented southern white dignity, autonomy, and—most important—supremacy. The message was that race was what mattered, not class—not what white common folk might have thought they shared with poor people of color. It was the classic, and successful, game of divide and conquer.[22]

Populists were already hemorrhaging from this southern race-baiting when, in 1896, the national Democrats offered the People's Party a presidential fusion deal. Some Populists warned that it was a siren song, but others thought it too good to pass up.

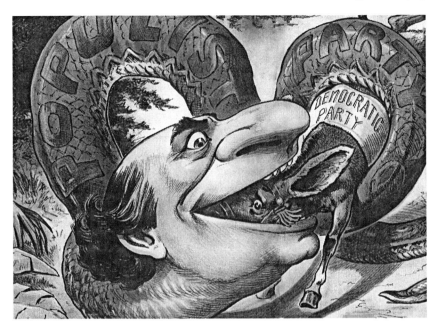

Populism swallows the Democratic Party. Cartoon from *Judge* magazine, 1896, showing the Populist Party with the face of William Jennings Bryan and the body of a snake, devouring the Democratic Party. Obtained through Wikimedia Commons.

Long before this deal was struck, Populists had become deeply divided over the matter of fusion. There were party purists who, suspecting that the Democrats' goal was to snuff out the life of the independent People's Party, adamantly opposed fusion. Outside the South many People's-Democratic fusion campaigns had already occurred, with undeniably beneficial election outcomes for Populists and their allies. Among Populism's pro-fusion pragmatists, there were some who were ready to accept—even to advocate—a full merger between the People's and Democratic parties.

Southern Populists had also played fusion politics, building alliances with the Republicans. Southern Populism's bitter adversary was the Democratic Party. Given the hostile relationship between the Democratic and People's parties in the South, the very notion of a presidential campaign partnership between them carried a distinctly foul odor for many southern Populists.

Delegates attending the 1896 Democratic National Convention embraced the Populists' silver coinage position and gave their nomination, on the fifth ballot, to William Jennings Bryan of Nebraska. This was the first of three quests for the presidency by Bryan as the Democratic nominee.

The charismatic thirty-six-year-old Bryan had brought down the house with his "Cross of Gold" speech, an address still regarded as a masterpiece in the annals of political oratory. Bryan had scores of friends in the People's Party. His commitment to their "free silver" position was genuine, and he may have been sincere in his expressed devotion to other Populist progressive positions.[23] Bryan did clearly reveal an expedient streak by selecting Arthur Sewall, an antilabor conservative, to run with him. Even Populist fusionists had wanted him to choose antifusionist Tom Watson of Georgia.

As their convention closed on July 11, the Democrats proclaimed to the nation's Populists that it was time to unify around Bryan and his campaign, that the Populists must give up "selfish" devotion to party and dedicate themselves to "principle."[24] That was the dilemma—or opportunity—facing Populists when their own People's Party convened on July 24.

Despite dire warnings from party purists about Democrats' untrustworthiness, Populism's fusionists carried the day. North Carolina Populist Marion Butler, his party's national chair, endorsed the proposed joint venture. Embracing his candidacy, the People's Party nominated Bryan. It did repudiate Sewall, offering Watson instead for the vice presidency.

The Republicans had held their convention nearly a month before the Democrats. The 1896 GOP nominee was Ohio former governor William McKinley. When the Republicans adopted a platform strongly backing the gold standard, a group of prosilver dissidents from western states walked out. They went on to found the National Silver Republican Party. Like the Populists the Silver Republicans gave their nomination to the Democrat Bryan.[25] Bryan also won endorsement by the Silver Party, Nevada's governing party at the time.

McKinley, promising "a full dinner pail," wildly outspent Bryan's campaign. He drove home his claim that Bryan was a dangerous populist radical who was intent on destroying the free enterprise system. McKinley took 51 percent of the national popular vote against Bryan's 46.7 percent.[26] Bryan took 63–64 percent of the votes in the South and West. McKinley swept the Northeast and two-thirds of the states in the Midwest. Realignments in 1896 cast the GOP even more clearly into the position of the nation's majority party

The antifusionists had been right in declaring that the 1896 Democratic-Populist partnership for Bryan portended a bleak, short future for the independent People's Party. Populist representation in Congress fell precipitously after the 1898 elections, and it tumbled again in 1900. By 1903 there were no Populists left on Capitol Hill.

In 1900 the People's Party "fusion faction"—by then virtually absorbed into the Democratic Party—went through the motions of endorsing Bryan. Antifusionists attending to the remnant that the independent People's Party had become nominated Wharton Barker, a former Republican. Barker picked up just one of every three hundred votes cast.

Watson then bore what was left to the People's standard. Many years later scholar V. O. Key declared that Watson may well have been "the nation's ablest Populist leader."[27] But by the time Watson took the baton, it was entirely too late. He

★ ★

The People's Party and the Wizard of Oz

The Populist cause had an impact on literature and popular culture. Although usually observed and enjoyed only as superb children's entertainment, the 1939 movie *The Wizard of Oz* and L. Frank Baum's 1900 *The Wonderful Wizard of Oz,* on which the movie was based, really present an allegory of the Populist movement. As a South Dakota rural newspaper editor at the beginning of the 1890s, Baum had observed the birth and early development of the Populist movement.

Baum's Scarecrow stands for the farmer, the Tin Woodsman for the industrial worker. The Cowardly Lion is 1896 Democratic-Populist nominee Bryan, known for his roar but not much else. They are carried down the yellow brick road—the gold standard—which goes nowhere. Arriving in Emerald City, they seek favors from the Wizard of Oz—the president (*oz* was an abbreviation for ounce, the standard measure for gold). Dorothy, the Kansas farm girl who symbolizes Everyman, goes along with them. Dorothy is so naively innocent that she sees truth before the others.

The Wicked Witch of the West—the banks—had kept the little Munchkins "in bondage for many years, making them work for her night and day" (Baum's words). The Wicked Witch of the East was Baum's symbol for large industrial corporations.

Baum's message was that "the powers that be survive by deception. Only people's ignorance allows the powerful to manipulate and control them."

Sources: Peter Dreier, "The Way it wOz and iz," *In These Times,* September 27–October 3, 1989; and Henry M. Littlefield, "The Wizard of Oz: Parable on Populism," *American Quarterly* 16 (1964): 47–58.

★ ★

campaigned actively in 1904 in a vain attempt to revive the party ghost. Watson took less than 1 percent in 1904 and a pitiful 0.2 percent in 1908.

As their party withered and died, Populist leaders and activists struck out in various political directions. Newspaper editor J. A. Wayland aligned with the Socialist Party. From his base in tiny Girard, Kansas, he edited the *Appeal to Reason* and distributed thousands of copies nationwide. The *Appeal* became American Socialism's most influential newspaper ever.[28] Ex-senator Marion Butler joined the Republicans and faded into political obscurity with a North Carolina GOP relegated evermore to the margins by the march of the Democratic Solid South.

Figuratively holding his nose, Watson joined the Democrats, the party against which he had for so long waged war. He won election to the U.S. Senate in 1920. Years before his death in 1922, he was garnering notoriety as a latter-day convert to vicious Negro-baiting and anti-Semitism.[29] Watson's bitterness, demoralization, and demise seemed in a way to replay that of the Populist movement he had worked to build and tried to sustain.

But if you seek its legacy, look around. According to historian Richard Hofstadter, Populism was America's first significant movement "to attack seriously the problems caused by industrialization," the first "to insist that the federal government had some responsibility for the common weal."[30]

Free silver coinage—Populism's signature issue—went down to defeat along with Bryan in 1896. The nation maintained its gold standard until 1933.

But many of the movement's other stands—direct election of U.S. senators, initiative and referendum, a graduated income tax, improvements in the condition of labor, and others—long ago were institutionalized nationally, at the state and local levels or throughout the nation. Populists worked to hold back the rising wave of official disenfranchisement of African Americans in the South. And Populism would, even more than its Greenback forebear, inspire twentieth-century builders of farmer-and-labor movements.

Populists and their People's Party were a significant spark for good-government groups and single-issue reformers, for Socialists and muckraking writers, for third-party Progressives and progressives in both major parties—in short for those who set the reform agenda of the Progressive Era.

7

★ ★ ★

Thunder Left and Right
Short-Lived Parties, 1912–1960s

> The old parties are husks with no real soul within either, divided by
> artificial lines, boss-ridden and privilege-controlled, each a jumble of
> incongruous elements, and neither daring to speak out wisely and fear-
> lessly on what should be said on the vital issues of the day.
>
> *Theodore Roosevelt, speaking at national convention*
> *of the Progressive Party (Bull Moose), 1912*

> The elephant lives in the Northland, the donkey resides in the South. But
> don't let either one fool you. They've got the same bit in their mouth.
>
> *Ditty sung during 1948 Progressive Party campaign*

Duopoly has prevailed for more than a century now. Twentieth-century third parties found no opening wedge, no rupture or tear in the hegemony shared by two
particular major parties like those which in the nineteenth century fueled Anti-
Masonic, Know Nothing, Republican, and Populist hopes of breaking for the long
term into national major-party ranks.

Twentieth-century Democratic and Republican policy makers used their power
to erect a duopolistic wall of protection for the two major parties, going to great
lengths to neutralize challengers. Above all there have been notoriously onerous
state ballot-access laws, especially legislation passed since 1930. In all presidential
elections from 1920 through 1976, not a single nonmajor-party presidential campaign cracked the ballots of every jurisdiction, and only seven have ever been able
to do so since.

But transient national parties as well as independent electoral campaigns did
arise in the twentieth century. Some of these influenced the making and substance
of public policy, and there were those with vote tallies that affected election outcomes and occasionally even secured election victory. Four of them ran presidential
candidates who racked up higher vote percentages than did any nonmajor-party
candidate in the last third of the nineteenth century:

Theodore Roosevelt, Progressive (Bull Moose) (1912)   27.4
Ross Perot, independent (1992)   18.9

| Robert La Follette, Progressive, other (1924) | 16.6 |
| George Wallace, American Independent (1968) | 13.5 |

Transient nonmajor-party electoral movements in the twentieth century were unlike their nineteenth-century predecessors in several respects. Many in the twentieth century organized around the will, objectives, and personality of a founder, existed as the agency for the founder's goals, and withered and died when the founder's interest and commitment were withdrawn. The third-party and independent stories involving Teddy Roosevelt and La Follette, Wallace and Perot, have few if any parallels in the century before.

Unlike their predecessors, many of these transient movements organized from the top down, not the grass roots up, and they focused upon presidential election politics. This was due in part to opportunities opened by new electronic media to communicate directly with voters and potential contributors. And it is one reason why few candidates running as national transient parties' nominees won twentieth-century elections to congressional and state offices. The nine Progressives elected in 1912 made up the largest twentieth-century short-lived national party bloc in the U.S. House, and just two candidates from parties of this type won twentieth-century gubernatorial elections. Some state-level third parties were more successful than that in winning governor's races.

There were in the twentieth century, especially in its later years, some electoral challenges to the major parties that organized and presented themselves as independent candidacies rather than as the offerings of new or established parties. At play in this were the intricacies of ballot-access laws, some of which make access easier for independents than for minor-party candidates. There also has been the popular disaffection for parties that led so many voters themselves to declare that they were independents.

The major parties in the twentieth century used poll results to fortify their argument that votes for outside challengers would be "wasted" on campaigns doomed to fail. Partly because of this, the most significant of the third-party and independent challengers suffered an average drop-off in support of about 34 percent from peak to just before election day.

As table 7.1 indicates, there also was the intractable problem of money—the "mother's milk" of politics. Except for Perot in 1992, no challenging presidential candidate came anywhere close to the bankroll available to and used by the major-party campaigns.

The Progressive Era

According to the historian Arthur Schlesinger, American history unfolds in cycles.[1] Periods of agitation, change, and reform and years of ascendant conservative values and cautious policies succeed each other. The twentieth century's earliest years are remembered as the Progressive Era—a period of reform and change that clearly had

Table 7.1 Expenditures by Campaigns of Short-Lived Parties and Independents
Receiving More Than Two Percent of the Popular Vote for President, 1912–96 [a]

Year and Party	Third-Party Campaign Expenditures (in dollars)	Average of Major Parties' Campaign Expenditures (in dollars)	Third-Party Campaign Expenditures as Percent of Major Parties' Campaign Average	Third-Party Vote as Percent of Major Parties' Voter Average
1912 Progressive (Bull Moose)	665,420	1,103,199	60.3	84.2
1924 Progressive (and Socialist, Farmer-Labor)	236,963	2,564,659	9.2	40.0
1948 Progressive	1,133,863	2,431,815	46.6	5.0
1948 States' Rights (Dixiecrat)	163,443	2,431,815	6.7	5.1
1968 American Independent	7,223,000	18,498,000	39.0	31.4
1980 National Unity (Independent)	15,040,669	29,040,183	51.8	14.4
1992 Ross Perot (Independent)	68,314,358	55,200,000[b]	123.8[b]	47.0
1996 Ross Perot (Reform)	30,100,000[c]	61,800,000[c]	46.7[c]	18.7

a. The Socialist Party, a continuing doctrinal party, also surpassed the 2 percent threshold in votes for president. It did so six times: in every election from 1904 through 1920 and in 1932. These Socialist campaigns were even more critically underfunded than most of the transient party and independent campaigns presented in table 7.1.

b. Major-party averages include 1992 Federal Election Campaign Act grants to the major-party candidates ($55.2 million each for Bill Clinton and George H. W. Bush). They do not include soft-money funds disbursed by the major parties or other permitted supportive spending either coordinated by or independent of the major-party campaigns. If these had been included, reported expenditure by each major party would exceed that of the Perot campaign.

c. Includes FECA grants ($61.8 million each for Clinton and Bob Dole, $29.1 million for Perot, plus $1 million in private funds spent by Perot campaign).

SOURCES: Steven J. Rosenstone, Roy L. Behr, and Edward H. Lazarus, *Third Parties in America: Citizen Response to Major Party Failure,* 2nd ed. (Princeton, N.J.: Princeton University Press, 1996); *Historical Statistics of the United States* (White Plains, N.Y.: Kraus International, 1989); Alexander Heard, *The Costs of Democracy* (Chapel Hill: University of North Carolina Press, 1960); Herbert E. Alexander and Anthony Carrado, *Financing the*

1992 Election (Armonk, N.Y.: M. E. Sharpe, 1995); John C. Green, ed., *Financing the 1996 Election* (Armonk, N.Y.: M. E. Sharpe, 1999); and Federal Election Commission expenditure reports for 1980, 1992, and 1996.

run its course by 1920, when Republican Warren Harding won the presidency on the promise of returning the country to "normalcy."

The movement of progressives in the Progressive Era drew from the Populists and other late-nineteenth-century radical wells. There also were radical strains in the movement itself: socialists of various stripes and muckraking writers and reporters exposing America's seamy side in a range from filthy food processing to the destitution of the lives of the nation's poor. But a substantial portion of the movement's soul was undeniably middle class and liberal, with energies devoted to extending the participatory power of ordinary citizens, eradicating corruption, and building good government.

Sometimes it is said that the advantage of a federal system is that states can serve as experimental laboratories for policies that, if proven successful, may be enacted in other states or by the nation as a whole. Wisconsin progressives may give a little too much credit to their state when they claim that progressivism was "the Wisconsin Idea" and that Wisconsin was *the* important incubator for the liberal programs of the Progressive and New Deal eras;[2] but it is scarcely deniable that Wisconsin and its native son Robert "Fighting Bob" La Follette strongly influenced the nationwide progressive agenda and accomplishment during the earliest years of the twentieth century.

Elected governor in 1901, La Follette revamped his state's GOP into the progressive agency it was to be over the ensuing third of a century. From the state university in Madison, La Follette gathered a core of natural and social scientists into what today would be termed a think tank. The professors did research and wrote treatises on progressive reforms and their likely results. La Follette thereby brought the techniques of science to his program of change. Wisconsin under La Follette's influence pioneered the use of primaries, initiatives and referenda, and advanced conservation measures. In 1906 he went to the U.S. Senate, where he remained until his death in 1925. From his Senate position, La Follette devoted himself to sharing the "Wisconsin Idea" with the nation at large.[3]

American progressives accomplished a lot during the twentieth century's earliest years, with legislation against child labor and on behalf of workers' rights, the consumer, and the environment. Constitutional amendments adopted during the Progressive Era provided for the graduated income tax, direct election of U.S. senators, and women's suffrage. In their campaign to democratize politics and to cleanse it of its seemingly endemic corruption, progressive policy makers initiated direct primaries; nonpartisanship in local elections; at-large arrangements for municipal councils; and initiatives, referenda, and recalls in various parts of the nation. They brought democratic reform to the operation of the U.S. House. And they launched the commission and council-manager systems as alternatives to mayor-council city governments.[4]

Electoral support for progressive candidates and their reforms may have peaked on November 5, 1912. On that day, unique in American electoral history, just 23 percent voted to reelect conservative Republican William Howard Taft. Woodrow Wilson, the victorious Democrat, took 42 percent. Remarkably a third of the electorate deserted their major-party commitments and habits and voted instead for left-of-center third-party candidates. Six percent cast for Socialist standard-bearer Eugene V. Debs; 27.4 percent voted for the Bull Moose Progressive nominee, former president Theodore Roosevelt.

It took some doing to push cautious and, for the most part, liberal people into breaking out of the major parties' protective cocoon and into the more radical course of building up a third party. But TR persuaded his most faithful devotees to do just that in 1912. His Progressive loyalists seceded from the GOP, splitting it and assuring its defeat that year. In the early 1920s, after the Progressive Era had run its course, La Follette gathered up what was left of the movement. He again offered American voters a Progressive option when he ran for the presidency in 1924.

Teddy Roosevelt and the Bull Moose Progressive Party

Without Teddy Roosevelt the Bull Moose Party would never have been. Its creation was due to the appeal and ambition of Roosevelt himself. The party was from the beginning a vulnerable house built upon foundations laid in sand, and when it lost his interest and support, it seemed doomed to wash away.

Roosevelt had won the vice presidency as a Republican in 1900. When President McKinley succumbed to an assassin's bullet on September 14, 1901, Teddy Roosevelt became, at forty-two, the youngest man ever inaugurated as president. After serving three and a half years of the second McKinley term, Roosevelt won the 1904 presidential election. Following customary practice, he then stood down in 1908 and supported the successful campaign of Republican William Howard Taft.

Roosevelt and Taft drew apart ideologically during the Taft years, and each blamed the other for the drift. Roosevelt eventually decided to seek, even at Taft's expense, a third presidential term in 1912.[5]

A lot of the Roosevelt vigor and macho remained in 1912, and the man and his policies were enormously popular. Fathers still told their sons about the charge of TR and his Rough Riders up San Juan Hill during the bloodiest battle of the Spanish-American War. Millions of voters admired the presidential "bully pulpiteer" for his trust-busting, his big-stick diplomacy, and his remarkable achievements in conservation and in expanding the national park system.[6]

After an African big-game hunting safari and a European trip, Roosevelt returned to the United States to prepare for the contest. In a 1910 speech, he adopted

"The New Nationalism" as his campaign theme. In February 1912 he threw his hat into the Republican ring. In ten primary battles with the incumbent Taft, Roosevelt won nine states. With popular appeal like that, today a candidate would be well on the way to nomination. But in 1912—and as recently as 1968—the selection of most delegates and thus control of the nomination remained in the hands of major-party establishments. In 1912 most of the GOP establishment stuck with Taft.

Meeting on June 18–22, the 1912 Republican convention turned into a raucous affair, one marked by the secession of many in the party's progressive wing. It was there that the Bull Moose Progressives really were born as a party. When the GOP nomination went to Taft, Roosevelt's loyalists bolted and unanimously selected him for a third-party bid.

The Progressives convened in Chicago two months later to launch the new party, nominate their man, and adopt a platform. The two thousand assembled delegates covered a range of "social workers, reformers, intellectuals, feminists, Republican insurgents, disgruntled politicians, and businessmen who favored the New Nationalism."[7] Many women attended. African American delegates were there, attending from some northern states. But deferring to southern white supremacist sentiments, the convention refused to seat black delegates from the South, and it did not approve a proposed antidiscrimination platform plank written by W. E. B. Du Bois.[8]

Singing "Onward Christian Soldiers," the convention nominated Roosevelt for the presidency and California governor Hiram Johnson as his running mate. Jane Addams, the well-known founder of Hull House, gave one of the seconding speeches for the presidential nominee.[9] To a reporter's insolent suggestion that he might now be past his prime, Roosevelt declared that he felt "as fit as a bull moose." From this came the party's nickname as well as its symbol or logo.

The new party's platform demanded federal assistance to farmers, better working conditions, the prohibition of child labor, women's suffrage, minimum wages for female employees, direct election of senators, an income tax, conservation of natural resources, a federal agency for the regulation of trusts, and a range of other progressive reforms.

One platform plank raised an issue that would remain unresolved, controversial, and still under discussion nearly a century later. Roosevelt was the first American presidential candidate ever to campaign on a platform calling for an employer-based insurance program to provide health care for all Americans.

Although years would pass before scientific polling came into being, it was apparent from the beginning of the general election campaign that Taft would not win reelection. Thus 1912 was unique in that the two major parties both aimed their sharpest barbs at a third-party campaign. The bad blood between Roosevelt and Taft and Taft's deep resentment at Roosevelt's splitting the GOP led Taft to particularly acerbic attacks on his third-party adversary. He must have found some solace in watching the election trend toward Democrat Woodrow Wilson rather than Roosevelt.

In Milwaukee on October 14, 1912, a fanatic named John Shrank, raising a cry against a third-term presidency, brandished a gun and shot Roosevelt in the chest. Seriously wounded, his shirt soaked in blood, Roosevelt insisted on going on with his speech.[10]

Roosevelt was the third and so far the last ex-president to seek reelection on a third-party ticket. His showing was better than either of the two preceding him. He finished with 88 electoral votes, Wilson with 435, and Taft a paltry 8. Roosevelt took Pennsylvania, Michigan, Minnesota, South Dakota, and Washington state. Helen Scott, a Progressive elector in Washington, became the first woman ever to cast electoral votes for president and vice president. Roosevelt and his California running mate also won a plurality and 11 of 13 electors in the Golden State. The Progressive ticket ran ahead of Taft in twenty-two of the other forty-two states.

Still at the party's peak in 1913, a senator and nine elected representatives took their seats as Progressives in the U.S. Congress. Six Progressives won U.S. House elections in 1914, and California governor Hiram Johnson won reelection as a Progressive.

During its brief life, the party broke down barriers and influenced policy in some states.[11] Credit for enacting women's suffrage in Illinois in 1913 largely belonged to the determined Progressive bloc in the state legislature. Colorado Progressives nominated a woman, Agnes L. Riddle, for secretary of state in 1914, Also in 1914 a coalition of seventy-nine Democrats and nineteen Progressives in the New York state legislature elected Progressive Homer C. Call to an unexpired term as state treasurer.

In Louisiana, a state in which Republicans were unelectable, Progressives served for a time as the party in opposition to the dominant Democrats. Even in 1918 the seventeen Louisiana Progressive state legislators were holding 11 percent of the seats in Baton Rouge.

But for viability and maintenance over the long term, the fragile Bull Moose organization needed what it did not receive: Theodore Roosevelt's nurture and devotion. When the party approached him about a 1916 rerun for the presidency, his answer was no. That really was to be the party's death knell as a national movement.

La Follette and His 1924 Progressive Campaign

The 1912 returns from Wisconsin surely disappointed Teddy Roosevelt. In that progressive heartland, the Bull Moose nominee had finished a poor third, twelve points below his national share of the vote. Wisconsin voters deferred to their own "Mr. Progressive," Robert La Follette. Vying for the 1912 GOP presidential nomination, La Follette had ended behind both Taft and Roosevelt. He tried again, without success, over each of the next three election rounds.

Theodore Roosevelt as an opera singer who wins the favor of "Miss Insurgency" while Robert La Follette watches in disgust. Cartoon by Clifford K. Berryman. Obtained through U.S. National Archives and Records Administration.

La Follette was far from subtle in his sentiments about Roosevelt. Roosevelt, he said, was an opportunist who manipulated and used the progressive program to further his own political ambitions. There was not much in the Bull Moose platform with which La Follette disagreed in principle. He had in fact helped usher many of its policy proposals into the political mainstream. But when Roosevelt entered the third-party track, La Follette did not endorse him or give any support.

La Follette would also become deeply disenchanted with Woodrow Wilson and his administration. The Wisconsinite regarded America's 1917 entry into Word War I as an act of deep presidential cynicism. Wilson, after all, had won reelection in 1916 reminding voters that "he kept us out of war."

By the close of the century's second decade, La Follette's views were shifting further to the left. Through his *La Follette's Magazine,* he produced and disseminated a comprehensive, radical perspective on events of the time:

Big Business, operating through the "System," . . . permeated government in the United States. The people, operating through the progressives and . . . insurgents, had been on the verge of restoring government to the people. Skillfully, the managers of Big Business and the "System" . . . backed Theodore Roosevelt to crush progressivism and elect Wilson. Then, partly to secure profits and partly to suppress progressive criticism, the forces of monopoly . . . combined with militarists and jingoes and corrupt politicians to bring American participation in the war. Wilson went to Paris, abandoned the idealism he had voiced in his Fourteen Points at the beginning of the war, and came back with a "League of Damnations"—a victor's vengeful peace which would make the world safe for American monopolists, imperialists, and militarists but not for democracy.[12]

News of the Bolshevik Revolution and the early years of the developing Soviet regime interested La Follette as it did many progressives. On a three-month European tour in 1923, La Follette, his wife, and their son Robert Jr. traveled to Moscow. Though never an uncritical apologist for every action taken in the name of Soviet power, La Follette was convinced that Russia's peasants loved Lenin, and he predicted that the Soviet Union would eventually develop a genuine socialist democracy. After his visit, he called on other American progressives to go and observe for themselves the Soviet experiment in building a new society.[13]

In February 1922 representatives of union, farm, liberal Christian, and third-party groups and a handful of independent progressives gathered in Chicago and launched the Conference for Progressive Political Action (CPPA). Some of these "La Follette radicals" already were thinking about the CPPA as a foundation upon which a new mass party might be constructed; but as the name they chose suggested, they were not ready to take that step.

Voters in several states that November elected or reelected a group of La Follette radicals running for Congress. Official records listed these members of Congress by their affiliation with major or minor parties. Yet when the new Sixty-eighth Congress got under way in 1923, they joined together as a voting bloc, virtually operating as a small cohesive party in government.

La Follette made a final, unsuccessful bid for the Republican nomination in 1924. Meeting in Cleveland, the CPPA then tapped him to run for the presidency. La Follette chose as his running mate Senator Burton Wheeler, a Montana Democrat with a reputation as a stalwart prolabor progressive.

The campaign platform, which La Follette himself wrote, condemned monopolies, imperialism, militarism, and war. Platform planks demanded

- fundamental reform of the executive branch,
- the election of federal judges and direct election of the president,
- policies for freer international trade,
- government ownership and operation of the railroads, and
- development of the federal power plant at Muscle Shoals, Alabama (a precursor of the Tennessee Valley Authority launched in 1933).

★ ★

Toward a National Farmer-Labor Party

From 1919 and into 1924, various unions and local and state-level labor or farmer-labor parties coalesced around the objective of building a significant national Farmer-Labor Party. Farmer-Labor candidate Parley P. Christiansen received 265,398 votes (nearly 1 percent of all votes cast) in the 1920 presidential election.

Anticipating that the Conference for Progressive Political Action might eventually serve as a framework for building a major national labor party, the Socialist Party of America gave its support to the CPPA and to La Follette's 1924 presidential campaign.

On the other hand, the Workers Party (a name American Communists used during the 1920s) became a participant in and eventually dominated the national Farmer-Labor movement. The national Farmer-Labor Party named a presidential candidate in 1924 but later withdrew his candidacy, supporting instead William Z. Foster, the Workers Party nominee. Five state Farmer-Labor parties endorsed La Follette and placed his name on their ballot lines.

Although it had largely dissolved as a national movement by 1925, Farmer-Labor lived on for years as a third-party movement in some of the states. As ensuing events confirmed, the most important of these state-level parties was the one in Minnesota.

★ ★

In 1924, for the first—and only—time in what would be its very long history, the continuing doctrinal Socialist Party of America joined in a fusion presidential campaign, giving its endorsement to La Follette. For the La Follette campaign, the blessing of Socialist support was not unmixed. Memories of the first Red Scare still were fresh, and La Follette was vulnerable to his adversaries' overblown claims about Far Left allies. But the Socialists' presidential campaign experience and their savvy in the quest for ballot access also brought some undeniable benefits. November 1924 ballots in at least eight states carried La Follette's name as the nominee of the Socialist Party.[14]

The Socialist contribution proved particularly important to La Follette in cracking the California ballot. After submitting a petition with more than fifty thousand signatures—nearly twice the number then required by law—the La Follette campaign suffered an adverse ruling (allegedly politically motivated) from the California Supreme Court. Thereafter appearing on the Golden State ballot solely as the Socialist nominee, La Follette took 424,649 votes. That was 33.1 percent of the California total, behind Republican incumbent Calvin Coolidge but far ahead of John W. Davis, the Democratic nominee.[15]

Farmer-Labor parties in Colorado, Montana, Oklahoma, Pennsylvania, and West Virginia also selected La Follette. Of the 510,785 votes he received in these states, 294,435 were given on Farmer-Labor ballot lines.

Although embracing the Progressive label and receiving Socialist and some Farmer-Labor support, La Follette really ran in 1924 as an independent. He and his followers might have used their CPPA foundation to build a real party, but they never did. The La Follette campaign was poorly managed and underfinanced, and it suffered the aura of quixotic hopelessness.

Coolidge, who had succeeded to the presidency upon the death of Warren Harding in 1923, was a popular incumbent who had rebuilt the public confidence lost by his scandal-drenched predecessor. Of the three-million-dollar war chest promised to La Follette by organized labor, less than 1 percent of the money ever materialized. Many of the CPPA's other affiliated groups, realizing that the chance of victory was extremely slim, failed to provide organizational or financial support. La Follette's sons, Robert Jr. and Philip, were among his most enduring, faithful hands in the 1924 campaign.

Despite the problems he had faced, La Follette took 4,831,706 votes—16.6 percent against Coolidge's 54.1 percent and 28.8 percent for Davis. Only in Louisiana did he not appear on any ballot line. In his home state, he won a popular majority and Wisconsin's thirteen electoral votes. In North Dakota, where he received strong backing from the leftist Nonpartisan League, he took 45.2 percent. La Follette's Minnesota share was 41.3 percent. He also placed second—ahead of Davis—in California, Idaho, Montana, Nevada, Oregon, Washington, Wyoming, Iowa, and South Dakota.

The Congress for Progressive Political Action died the next year. Its demise could be attributed to La Follette's own death on June 18, 1925, but also to the temper of the times. Progressivism had been relegated to the periphery in a conservative decade more devoted to prohibition and bathtub gin, speculation and growth, profit and prosperity. Nationally the third-party impulse lay largely dormant in the late 1920s.

Depression was the stick to prod its reawakening. The Farmer-Labor Party came to equal or surpass the strength of the long-dominant state GOP in Depression-era Minnesota. In neighboring Wisconsin, Robert Jr. and Philip La Follette, the sons and political heirs of "Fighting Bob," recast their movement as the powerful Wisconsin Progressive Party in 1934.

Given the radical impact of the Great Depression in Germany and other industrial nations, what seems surprising is that the reinvigoration of the third-party impulse in the 1930s was no stronger than it was in the United States. President Franklin Roosevelt succeeded in rekindling the confidence of distraught, desperate citizens. He also appropriated and adopted some important ideas put forward by minor parties.

The Depression Years and the Union Party

Miseries fostered by the Depression left some seeking radical solutions to the nation's dilemma and their own personal problems. The 103,307 votes taken in

1932 by William Z. Foster and by James W. Ford, his African American running mate, were the best returns ever by a Communist presidential campaign. The Socialist Party rebounded that year. Norman Thomas received 884,885 votes in 1932. Those were more votes than Eugene V. Debs, Thomas's venerable Socialist predecessor, had received in three of the five campaigns in which Debs had competed.

The Communist and Socialist votes dropped precipitously in 1936, and just one new 1930s short-lived national party was ever to bag a significant share of a presidential vote. That was the Union Party of 1936.

As its presidential candidate, the Union Party named North Dakota congressman William Lemke, a nominal Republican who had helped to found and was still linked to the leftist Nonpartisan League. Lemke managed to take nearly 2 percent of the national vote—and 13.4 percent in North Dakota—despite the partial success of a concerted Democratic effort to keep his name off as many ballots as possible.

The Union Party ethos defied easy placement on the political spectrum. It was in fact an uneasy amalgam of left and right values that some observers found to be a bitter blend. Lemke himself must have appeared more than a little weird to many voters. When his fans dubbed him "Liberty Bill," foes quipped that "the Liberty Bill has cracked."

The Union Party coalesced Francis E. Townsend's "Share Our Wealth" campaign with the surviving remnants of the "Share the Wealth" movement of Louisiana's late Huey P. Long. Townsend, a physician, had garnered fame for his movement to force Washington to provide a two-hundred-dollar monthly stipend to all citizens over the age of sixty. Public pressure from the Townsend forces had contributed to passage of the Social Security Act of 1935.

Long's political star had risen when he was elected as Louisiana governor, then U.S. senator. People everywhere came to know him as the Kingfish. "Every Man a King" was Long's slogan and the title of his 1933 autobiography. To his foes Long was the epitome of the charismatic authoritarian populist demagogue. He had developed a sharply redistributive "soak the rich" platform on which he may have intended to wage a third-party electoral campaign against Roosevelt in 1936. Whatever his national designs, they ended in 1935 when, at age forty-two, he was shot and killed at the state capitol in Baton Rouge.[16]

The ideological perspective of the Union Party was the brainchild not of Lemke, Townsend, or Long but of the party's founder, Father Charles Coughlin, a Roman Catholic priest. Coughlin certainly was among the most powerful of the demagogues swept into national prominence by the Great Depression. The principal source of his influence was his nationally broadcast weekly radio message, which at times reached a listening audience of forty-one million—one in every three Americans. Coughlin also spread his message through his magazine, *Social Justice,* and activities of his National Union for Social Justice. One of his most ambitious moves to capture the nation's allegiance began on June 19, 1936, when he announced on radio the birth of the Union Party.[17]

Coughlin fed his listeners a steady diet of vitriol spewed out against designated ogres. Although anticommunist in tone from the start ("choose God or Communism," he told his audience), he seemed at first an apostle of the Left. Coughlin inveighed against capitalism ("the enemy of civilization") as passionately as against Marxism. In 1932 he lent his support to FDR ("Roosevelt or ruin"). During the early years of the first Roosevelt term, an appreciative president sometimes dined with Coughlin at the White House.

But long before 1936, Coughlin broke with the New Deal and its "anti-God" president. He also veered to the hard right. By 1936 Coughlin was proclaiming that "I take the road of fascism." His anti-Semitism was to become virulent and vulgar from 1936 on. Participants in late-1930s pro-Nazi rallies roared their enthusiasm when Coughlin's name was invoked. The Union Party died after the November 1936 election, and in the late 1930s Coughlin's appeal in mainstream America plummeted as well. He eventually was silenced by a combination of popular demand, orders from his church, and the wartime censorship authorities of the federal government.[18]

Dixiecrats and Progressives, 1948 and Beyond

One of the most iconic photographs of the Harry Truman era was snapped on November 3, 1948. That was the day after the nation's voters gave their presidential incumbent a plurality (49.5 percent) returning him to the presidency, which he had occupied since the death of Franklin Roosevelt in 1945. The picture showed Truman grinning ear to ear as he held up the early morning edition of the *Chicago Daily Tribune* with its famously false headline, "Dewey Defeats Truman." Truman ended up with 303 electoral votes, 37 more than he had to have to win.

Thomas Dewey, the Republican, must have felt deep disappointment as the incoming late-night returns indicated that the election was going to Truman. So did two third-party insurgent candidates—one to Truman's left, the other on his right—both of whom had clearly aimed to trip up the incumbent in his bid for victory that November.

Henry Wallace, the Progressive nominee, had apparently entered the race really hoping to win, though as the campaign developed he could not have escaped the reality that that was not going to happen. His 1948 Progressive campaign was the first minor-party electoral movement ever organized to protest foreign policy. These Progressives' core objective was to stop the U.S.-Soviet Cold War and American Cold War policies before they could go any further.[19]

The States' Rights Democrats—better-known as Dixiecrats—who made Strom Thurmond their standard-bearer had aimed unsuccessfully to deny Truman his necessary majority of electors. They wanted to open up the possibility of a quid pro quo, compelling Truman Democrats to forsake their civil rights commitments as the price for receiving the needed votes from Dixiecrat electors. Dixiecrats complained about the national Democrats' liberal constituencies and pro-union bent. But the Dixiecrat movement had really come to life to protest the Democrats' developing devotion to civil rights for African Americans. They proclaimed themselves to be the true Democrats, the mechanism in effect to correct the national party's errant course. The essence of their insurgency—segregation, white supremacy, and states' rights—confined their party's appeal almost entirely to the South.

Wallace garnered 2.4 percent of the national vote even though, due largely to Democratic efforts to block ballot access, it was not possible to vote for Wallace in Illinois, Oklahoma, or Nebraska. Forty-four percent of all votes he took were cast in New York, where he ran on the line of the influential state-level American Labor Party.

In addition to their presidential returns, the Progressives could lay claim to a congressional victory. Vito Marcantonio of the American Labor Party won reelection to a seventh term in the House in 1948. Marcantonio was serving an East Harlem working-class district heavily populated by Italians and Puerto Ricans.

The Dixiecrats took their 2.4 percent national share in just seventeen states. Nearly 99 percent of Thurmond's votes came in the eleven states that had left the Union in 1860 and 1861. Because their appeal was concentrated in a single region, the Dixiecrats (unlike their Progressive counterparts) took electoral votes: the thirty-eight belonging to Alabama, Louisiana, Mississippi, and South Carolina plus the vote of one Tennessee Democratic faithless elector. In much of the Deep South, sympathetic Democratic establishments arranged to have Thurmond and Mississippi governor Fielding Wright, Thurmond's running mate, appear on the ballot as the Democratic nominees.[20]

Despite the efforts of Alabama Democratic governor Jim Folsom, a populist with markedly progressive racial views, Alabama voters did not have even a Truman option in 1948. As their alternatives to Thurmond-Wright, Alabamians could vote Republican or Progressive or Prohibition, but there was no slate of Alabama electors running committed to the sitting president who won election that year.

Henry Wallace and the Progressives

As some older Americans still recall, the 1948–52 Progressives were one of the most controversial transient parties ever to surface in American politics. Like its Dixiecrat counterpart, this Progressive movement had deep roots within the Democratic Party. Henry Wallace had been a prominent New Dealer. He had served as secretary of agriculture during Roosevelt's first and second terms and as vice president during his third. Roosevelt replaced him with Truman on the 1944 ticket but then appointed Wallace as secretary of commerce. Wallace broke with President Truman, who fired him as commerce secretary in 1946. That December, Wallace and others who were interested in building a third-party movement set up the Progressive Citizens of America.

Progressives met in Chicago in January 1948 to plot strategy, then formally convened in Philadelphia in July to launch the new Progressive Party. The party tapped liberal Idaho Democratic senator Glen Taylor to stand as Wallace's running mate on the Progressive ticket.

But there was another feature—the grist for constant controversy—of this Progressive Party's character and essence. This was a last hurrah for the Popular Front, a strategy developed by Moscow in the mid-1930s and faithfully followed by the Communist Party USA and the other client parties that were linked together and connected to the Soviet Union through membership in the Communist International (the Comintern).[21]

Launched in response to the rise of the fascist powers and the Nazi suppression of the German Communists, the Popular Front sent Communists to build antifascist coalitions with liberals, socialists, and other progressives worldwide. Although it was shelved when the Soviet Union entered into a nonaggression pact with Germany on August 23, 1939, this strategy was resurrected when Germany invaded the Soviet Union in June 1941. In the late 1930s, then again after crucial events (especially the Pearl Harbor attack) in 1941, American Communists billed themselves as Roosevelt's staunchest allies on the domestic radical left.

During World War II, many people came to see the Grand Alliance—the coalition linking the Americans, Soviets, British, Chinese, Free French, Australians, Canadians, and others at war with the Axis powers—as the embodiment of the Popular Front. Henry Wallace and other non-Communist progressives in the Roosevelt administration admired the Soviets for their strong, decisive role in the war in Europe.

Hopes for sustained postwar American-Soviet cooperation may have been naive, but they were certainly understandable. Truman's Cold War policies—containment, the Marshall Plan, and others—are credited with stabilizing and rebuilding Europe, but many progressives at the time saw them as provocative moves for capitalism and American hegemony. The Soviet Union's American friends—and even its foes— were less aware than they would eventually come to be of Stalin's tyranny and crimes.[22]

Not offering a presidential candidate under its own label in 1948, the Communist Party sent its members and supporters to work in the Progressive campaign. The degree to which the Stalinists were able to dominate the movement—to turn the Progressive Party into a Communist front—is still debated. Wallace himself expressed deep resentment over heavy-handed Communist attempts to control the party. In his speech accepting the Progressive presidential nomination, Wallace spoke of his own vision of "progressive capitalism."

Communists did strongly influence the process of Progressive platform writing. The 1948 platform demanded friendly relations between the United States and the

Soviet Union. It condemned "Big Business control of our economy and government," the two major parties ("both represent a . . . program of monopoly profits through war preparation, lower living standards, and suppression of dissent"), the activities of the House Committee on Un-American Activities, and the moves to outlaw the Communist Party. The platform also denounced Jim Crow racial policies and the antilabor Taft-Hartley Act, and it called for "a true American Commonwealth" and public ownership of basic industries.[23]

The 1948 Progressive campaign failed in its objective of uniting the disparate, far-flung elements of the American Left. With few exceptions African American civil rights leaders stuck with the Truman Democrats. The Socialist and Socialist Workers parties distanced themselves from the Progressives, each offering its own presidential campaign instead.

Organized labor was beginning to root out its internal Communist influences. In 1944 many anticommunist New York union leaders, finding Communist power growing within the American Labor Party, had left the party and gone on to help found the New York Liberal Party. Other labor leaders later withdrew from the American Labor Party when it endorsed Wallace for the presidency. In 1948 the Congress of Industrial Organizations undertook a bitter, far-reaching purge of its Communist-led unions.

Some leftists who gave early support to the Wallace campaign later withdrew, usually in favor of Truman, as Communist strength in the 1948 Progressive movement became more evident. Through its own outreach to progressives, the Democratic Party was able to co-opt much of the support that might have gone to the Wallace campaign.

It is likely that the Wallace tally in New York—8.3 percent of all votes cast in the Empire State for president—delivered that state and its forty-seven electoral votes to Dewey rather than Truman. The Wallace factor may also have contributed to Dewey's victories in Michigan and Maryland.

As the nation descended in the late 1940s into the vituperative red-baiting of the Joseph McCarthy era, a leftist's political compass in 1948 ("Were you for Truman or for Wallace?") became a litmus test for determining whether he or she would be left untouched or denounced as a Communist or "fellow traveler" with Communists.

Although a remnant of the Progressive Party hung on for one more presidential election round, the pro-Communist position the party took on the Korean War cost it most of what was left of its already depleted non-Communist wing. Wallace had left the party, and in 1952 he published *Where I Went Wrong*. In this mea culpa, he confesses his ignorance about Stalin and admits that he had been naive in his dealings with Stalin's American minions.

Vincent Hallinan and Charlotta Bass, the 1952 Progressive Party presidential and vice-presidential candidates, won 140,416 votes. That was just under 1 in every 400 cast. New York voters gave Hallinan and Bass 45 percent of the votes they received.

Bass's place on the ticket broke new historical ground. She was the first African American woman ever nominated for one of the nation's two highest offices.

Thurmond and the Dixiecrats

Strom Thurmond of South Carolina was Wallace's counterweight on the right in 1948. During the course of his long life, Thurmond traveled to about as many places on the party spectrum as it is possible for a successful politician to go. Born, like so many other twentieth-century southerners, into a Democratic home, Thurmond won the South Carolina gubernatorial election in 1946. In 1948 he momentarily left the Democrats to bear the Dixiecrat presidential standard. Though returning to the Democrats, he publicly backed Eisenhower's Republican candidacy in 1952.

Thurmond went on to become the nation's first write-in candidate ever to win a U.S. Senate seat against a balloted foe; 143,444 South Carolinians—nearly two-thirds of all who turned out in 1954—voted for Thurmond, whose name was not even on the ballot.[24] In 1956 Thurmond resigned his Senate seat and then ran successfully as a Democrat to fill the vacancy. He served continuously in the Senate for the next forty-six years, finally stepping down at age one hundred in January 2003.

During the 1964 presidential campaign of Republican Barry Goldwater, Thurmond left the Democratic Party and affiliated with the increasingly conservative GOP. He remained forever after a loyal and powerful Republican. In 1968 every Deep South state except Thurmond's voted for American Independent Party nominee George Wallace. Though Wallace was Thurmond's ideological heir, he failed to get the South Carolinian's support. Thurmond managed to hold the Palmetto State for Republican Richard Nixon.

Thurmond's trek through parties became a kind of road map that most southern whites came to follow. Between 1964 and 1980, millions of white southerners deserted the Democrats and realigned with the Republicans, and the GOP firmly rooted itself in the once-hostile South.

During his political career, Thurmond embarked on two political courses, either of which might in theory have taken him to the presidency. As the Dixiecrat presidential nominee in 1948, he took 39 electoral votes and would have become president with just 227 more. Thurmond later served for a dozen years in the ceremonial post of Senate president pro tempore, a position from which he would have inherited the presidency if bubonic plague or some other catastrophe had befallen the president, vice president, and speaker of the House. It is hard to say at which of these times Thurmond came closer to the presidency. He was not very close either time.

Warmhearted humor often circulated in South Carolina about Thurmond. In 1968, years after his first wife's death, Thurmond, then sixty-six, took a twenty-two-year-old former Miss South Carolina as his bride. Eyebrows raised, many in his Bible Belt state declaring that his attractive new wife was "young enough to be that man's granddaughter!" Jaws dropped further as the new couple began to produce a family of four children. In 1991 the senator, at age eighty-eight, announced that he and his wife were separating. One of the popular down-home jokes featured a lead-in to the local late-night news: "Thurmond's Third Wife Born Yesterday! (Offspring at 11:00)."

Soon after Thurmond's death, his family confirmed what had long been a whispered rumor throughout South Carolina. As a young man, Thurmond had fathered a mixed-race daughter in 1925. Her name was Essie Mae Washington-Williams, and her mother had been a sixteen-year-old maid working in the Thurmond home. Thurmond gave financial support, and when he was governor he visited his daughter privately when he went to speak at her college, South Carolina State. Washington-Williams and the Thurmond family reached out to each other, and on the Thurmond monument on the state capitol grounds her name was added to the list of Thurmond's children.

Thurmond's public face was never that of a vicious demagogue like Mississippi's Theodore Bilbo. In the years before his 1948 run for the presidency, he had even found the national media sometimes describing him as a southern progressive. Yet despite being the father of a mixed-race child, Thurmond's early devotion to segregation and white supremacy was beyond dispute. Seeking defeat of a civil rights bill, he filibustered for twenty-four hours and eighteen minutes on one occasion in 1957. But both black and white South Carolinians came to appreciate Thurmond's office for its dedicated, effective constituent service. He was one of the first Deep South senators to desegregate his congressional staff, and some of his votes in later years—to extend the Voting Rights Act and to establish the Martin Luther King holiday—led many to decide that the old man really had mellowed and moderated his racial views.[25]

There was nothing moderate about the Dixiecrat insurgency that collared Thurmond for a presidential run. Many historians have described the 1948 Thurmond- and Wallace-led movements as ideological opposite bookends, each as far out as the other from the national mainstream. That was not the stance the Dixiecrats took in defending their movement. They insisted that it was the national Democrats who had stepped out of bounds and that the Dixiecrats were duty bound to bring them back.

It is likely that if the Progressives had not materialized as a third-party force in 1948, the Dixiecrats would not have seceded from the national Democrats. At the outset of the campaign, Truman proposed a glittering array of liberal measures: national health insurance, slum clearance and low-income housing, federal assistance to education, and substantial increases in Social Security benefits and the minimum wage. On civil rights the president called for a federal antilynching law, the abolition of poll taxes and other barriers to black voting rights, and the elimination of discrimination in jobs and interstate travel. Truman's moves grew in part out of the need to stop the hemorrhaging of his own campaign by co-opting as much of the potential support for Wallace and the Progressives as possible.

The Democrats met in national convention on July 12–14. Backed by the Truman administration—newly cautious after rumors floated of a southern revolt awaiting any attack on "the southern way of life"—the platform committee offered a bland civil rights plank designed to offend nobody except anyone wanting real change. A progressive floor fight ensued, out of which the convention voted to replace the proposed plank with a "minority plank." Radical for its time, this new incarnation devoted the party to bringing to an end lynching, school segregation, and job discrimination. Leading the fight was Hubert Humphrey, the young Minneapolis mayor, who both worked the floor and gave a rousing speech persuading many to insert the more radical plank into the 1948 platform.

Thereupon the entire Mississippi delegation and half of the delegates from Alabama headed for the doors, signaling by their secessionist act of leaving that a new party was coming to be. The States' Rights Democratic Party took shape a week later at a hastily convened conference in Birmingham. Attending were "the big brass of the Democratic Party in Mississippi, . . . conservative leaders of Alabama, . . . Governor Thurmond of South Carolina and his entourage, and a miscellaneous assortment of persons of no particular importance from other states."[26]

This new issues-oriented southern party was never the exclusive property of Thurmond or of anyone else. Evidence suggests that he was the party's third choice for the presidency, the first two having declined the honor of being nominated.[27]

In their short platform, the Dixiecrats repudiated "selfish appeals" by minorities and praised the Constitution as a defending bulwark against the "chains of slavery" forged by "tyrannical majorities." The platform denounced the Democrats' minority plank and strongly implied that both major parties, but especially the Truman Democrats, were acting to create in America a "totalitarian police state." It demanded that the Democrats return to their party's states' rights traditions. The platform called for "home rule, local self-government, and a minimum of interference with individual rights"; and it put the new party on record as standing "for the segregation of the races . . . and the right to choose one's associates, to accept private employment without governmental interference, and to earn one's living in any lawful way."[28]

The Dixiecrats failed to surmount an array of problems they faced. Although Truman lost the electoral votes of most of the Deep South when his party adopted the minority plank, that platform provision may have won him and the Democrats some nonsouthern electoral votes by mobilizing the support of millions of northern African American voters. In the Upper South, most Democratic establishments remained loyal to Truman. In Virginia, Tennessee, North Carolina, Florida, Arkansas, and Texas, Thurmond finished third, behind Truman and behind even Dewey, in popular votes.

The States' Rights Democrats expired as a party in 1951, when South Carolina governor James F. Byrnes declined an offer to lead it; but the party's ethos prevailed in parts of the South for some years to come. In 1960 all of Mississippi's electoral votes and over half of Alabama's went to conservative Virginian Harry F. Byrd rather than to Democratic candidate John F. Kennedy. Until 1965 the Democratic column on the Alabama ballot bore the defiant motto "White Supremacy." A federal court order removed it.

By the mid-1960s progressive winds from the region's newly mobilized and empowered African American citizens brought southern wings of the Democratic Party more in tandem with the national party. Sometimes it took outside pressure from black-led biracial state third parties—the Mississippi Freedom Democratic Party (1964) and the National Democratic Party of Alabama (1968)[29]—to stimulate biracial inclusiveness inside the regular southern Democratic parties. The United Citizens Party, founded for that purpose in South Carolina in 1969, still operates today as a minor actor in Palmetto State politics.

8

★ ★ ★

George Wallace and Beyond
Short-Lived Parties, 1968 and After

> There's not a dime's worth of difference between the Democrat and
> Republican parties.
>
> *George Wallace, 1968*

> Saying we should keep the two-party system simply because it is work-
> ing is like saying the *Titanic* was a success because a few people survived
> on life rafts.
>
> *Eugene McCarthy*

Some years are as bland as dry toast. Others spark excitement even long after they
have passed. Nineteen sixty-eight excites the memory of those who lived through it,
though there are many who recall its torment far more than its triumphs.[1] It was the
year of the Tet Offensive, a military setback but morale victory for Vietnamese
Communists because it revealed to Americans that no light could be seen at the end
of the tunnel; the year of My Lai, the most infamous mass atrocity that American
forces ever committed in Vietnam. In China the Cultural Revolution was raging.
France went to the brink of revolution. Czechoslovakia's Prague Spring tragically
was ended by Soviet force of arms.

In the United States, attitudes bristled during the long, hot summer when
African Americans, recoiling from years of racial injustice, burned down huge sections of America's northern ghettos. The social contract appeared to be breaking
down as Martin Luther King Jr. and then Robert Kennedy were gunned down and
killed, Black Power and separatism replaced integration and reconciliation as core
values of many victims of white racism, and millions of young whites deserted liberal idealism ("Ask not what your country can do for you; ask what you can do for
your country") to enlist in the New Left or the counterculture. In 1968 a young man
could be drafted and kill and die in Vietnam. But if he was under twenty-one, most
states deemed him too young to be trusted with something as important as the vote.

The National Organization for Women celebrated its second birthday in 1968.
Another four years passed before Congress proposed the Equal Rights Amendment,

and five before the Supreme Court found a constitutional right to an abortion. The birth of the gay and lesbian rights movement was still a year away.

Nineteen sixty-eight was Ronald Reagan's second year of eight as California governor—a dress rehearsal, as it turned out, for the presidency. It was the year when a wartime president, Lyndon Johnson, withdrew from his race for reelection after a poor showing in the New Hampshire primary against a peace candidate of his own party, Eugene McCarthy.

Antiwar demonstrators during the Democrats' August convention acted provocatively in Chicago streets, and the brutal ferocity of city police amounted to what some investigators came to call the "Chicago Police Riot."[2] On the convention floor, a young network reporter named Dan Rather was roughed up on camera, and CBS anchor Walter Cronkite declared that "we've got a bunch of thugs here, Dan!"

Nineteen sixty-eight was the last year when an establishment candidate, Vice President Hubert Humphrey, could avoid submitting through primaries to the voters' will and still take his party's nomination. It was the year Richard Nixon first won the presidency. Nineteen sixty-eight was the kind of year that breathes life into third parties.

Wallace, the American Independent Party, and Their Legacy

Americans who experienced 1968 may never forget the lightning bolt first illuminating southern skies as a signal of an impending national storm. That year former governor George Wallace of Alabama launched and led a coast-to-coast movement of conservative whites who were eager to "send Washington a message" that African Americans had pushed too far too fast, that wars worth fighting are worth winning, that it was time to get tough on crime and to suppress ghetto riots and antiwar militancy. Wallace's movement became a crusade of people wanting to shout to all those in power that they were mad as hell about what was happening in the 1960s.

By then Wallace had been a nationally recognized political figure for more than five years. In 1963, at his first inauguration as Alabama governor, he had sounded the theme of his new administration: "Segregation now! Segregation tomorrow! Segregation forever!" That was also the year when the new governor had "stood in the schoolhouse door," symbolically defying the commitment of federal power to desegregating the University of Alabama.

Although by 1964 Wallace was thinking of making a third-party run for president, he decided first to seek the Democratic nomination. He ran well in the Wisconsin, Indiana, and Maryland primaries; but Johnson, the incumbent president, was not to be denied his party's nomination. By their nomination of conservative Barry Goldwater, the Republicans took away much of Wallace's potential support and also emptied his campaign war chest. He decided to sit out 1964.

Alabama governor George C. Wallace "standing in the schoolhouse door," symbolically defying the federal desegregation mandate, at Foster Auditorium, the University of Alabama, June 11, 1963. Photograph by Warren K. Leffler for *U.S. News & World Report.* Courtesy of the U.S. Library of Congress Print and Photographs Division. Obtained through Wikimedia Commons.

Although Wallace committed in the ensuing four years to wage a campaign from outside the bounds of the major parties, it took some time to come up with a suitable name for his impending movement. He at first thought of the Free American Party, but then decided that the acronym FAP sounded very unappealing. Finally he and people close to him came up with the name. Wallace would run as the candidate of the American Independent Party.[3]

Wallace came very close in 1968 to cracking ballots everywhere. Recruiting a team of four young lawyers—three Alabamians and a South Carolinian—to work full-time on ballot access, the campaign got Wallace onto the ballots of all fifty states. Ohio law had stacked the cards impossibly high against any nonmajor-party campaign. Wallace's entry onto the Buckeye State ballot required his campaign to play the one trump it had: an appeal to the U.S. Supreme Court.[4] Wallace's name did not appear on the ballot of the nation's capital. Given the hostility to Wallace among the largely African American constituency there, that probably brought very little pain to the AIP and its presidential candidate.

There was a curious irony to the devotion of Wallace's ballot crackers in a year when it was people on the left who were chanting "all power to the people." As the authors of a work on the 1968 election point out, "the drive to get Wallace's name placed on the ballot of all fifty states . . . was perhaps the most remarkable triumph of participatory democracy at the grassroots in the campaign of 1968."[5]

The ballot achievement was extraordinary because it was accomplished for a party that was little more than a name. In 1968 the American Independent Party established no national headquarters, held no national convention, selected no national officers, set up no national bank account. Wallace was in essence an independent candidate bearing the AIP label,[6] and even the label could not be applied everywhere. Wallace's name appeared under different affiliations—the American Independent Party, the American Party, the George Wallace Party, and three others—on various ballots around the country. The party, such as it was, was to be found in its various state-level branches and in the Wallace campaign.

The essence of Wallace's 1968 movement really lay in the personal connection—built up and sustained through sentiment (critics called it prejudice), the campaign's use of media, and the campaign itself—between the candidate and his millions of followers. Speaking as a populist, Wallace declared that this campaign would speak for and empower the nation's cops, dime-store clerks, hard hats, and people who love God, pay their taxes, and obey the law.

Surveys revealed that the person most likely to vote for Wallace in 1968 was a white, unskilled worker under thirty years old who lacked a high school diploma and had little if any self-identity as a Democrat or Republican. People in the Wallace camp were most likely to oppose school integration, want to use all necessary force to suppress urban violence, and believe that the federal government was too powerful.[7]

Beyond the rank and file in Wallace's coalition, there were those able and determined ballot crackers: the lawyers but also a small army of people who collected signatures on state petitions. Some local notables also joined in the Wallace movement. A few candidates around the country ran for various offices on the ticket he headed. But not many people who had tasted real political power enlisted in the AIP insurgency. Some who did were southern segregationists—men such as Georgia governor Lester Maddox, Louisiana congressman John Rarick, and Leander Perez, the longtime boss of Louisiana's Plaquemines Parish. Maddox was famous for choosing the Bible and an ax handle as symbols of his undying opposition to desegregation. Maddox and then Rarick eventually made presidential runs as nominees of a surviving remnant of the AIP.

Senator Thurmond did not join the Wallace movement. That may have been in part payback on a twenty-year grudge. Back in 1948 Wallace, then a twenty-eight-year-old Alabama delegate to the Democratic National Convention, had declined to join Thurmond's Dixiecrats, sticking instead with Truman. In 1968 Thurmond worked to deliver South Carolina for Nixon. Seeking to co-opt potential Wallace support, the Nixon campaign developed its "southern strategy." Nixon signaled that his administration would ease up on pressures for school desegregation, clamp down hard on crime and welfare cheats, and appoint southern "strict construction-ists" to the Supreme Court. South Carolina's Harry Dent, a longtime Thurmond aide, was the architect and point man of the southern strategy during the campaign and then in the Nixon administration.[8]

The 1968 movement produced a lengthy AIP platform filled with the invective its candidate was using to appeal to voters. It denounced a national establishment unwilling or unable to deal with "riots, minority group rebellions, domestic dis-orders, student protests, spiraling living costs, soaring interest rates, a frightening increase in the crime rate, war abroad and a loss of personal liberty at home." It gave a dire prognosis of the state of the union, citing "cities . . . in decay and turmoil; . . . local schools and other institutions . . . stripped of their rightful authority; law enforcement agencies and officers . . . hampered by arbitrary and unreasonable restrictions imposed by a beguiled judiciary; crime [running] rampant through the nation; . . . unreasonable government [farm] subsidies; welfare rolls and costs [soar-ing] to astronomical heights; our great American institutions of learning in chaos; living costs [and taxes] [rising] ever higher; interest rates . . . reaching new heights; [and] disciples of dissent and disorder [being] rewarded for their disruptive actions at the expense of our law-abiding, God-fearing, hard-working citizenry."[9]

Given its litany of grievances and woe, the platform's policy prescriptions were surprisingly vague and filled with glittering generalities. It called for law and order, states' rights, a cutoff of aid to nations that criticized U.S. actions in Vietnam, and "freedom from interference and harassment from and by the government at all lev-els." One of the document's most specific proposals was for periodic elections of or referenda on federal district judges and "reconfirmation" of higher judges at "rea-sonable intervals."[10]

More influential than the platform and far more emblematic as trademarks of this third-party insurgency were the Wallacisms—those memorable sound bites that the candidate used and reused in speeches he made on the campaign trail. Though some were borrowed, most were Wallace originals. There were those, like *law and order* and *there's not a dime's worth of difference,* that captured themes of the campaign. Some praised the virtuous, *the cops and hard hats.* Others called out the villains: *briefcase-toting bureaucrats* and *(pointy-headed) pseudo-intellectuals* and *welfare queens.*

Wallace's voter appeal, like that of other independents and candidates of tran-sient parties, peaked too soon. Although nearly a quarter of the electorate backed him in mid-September, that number had seriously eroded as November approached. Mainstream media were unrelentingly and almost unanimously hostile to the Wal-lace campaign. Each major party warned that he could not win and that a vote for him could only contribute to victory for the major-party candidate less palatable to the voter. Retired U.S. Air Force general Curtis LeMay, the slash-and-burn hawk who was Wallace's running mate, may have burdened the AIP ticket. LeMay had seemed to say he wanted "to bomb [the Vietnamese] back into the stone age." The major-party campaigns each spent two or three times as much as the Wallace campaign, and much of the AIP funds had to go to cracking ballots.

Considering these problems Wallace faced, his election day accomplishments were remarkable. He failed to achieve his goal of denying an electoral vote majority to either Nixon or Humphrey, which might have opened the way to striking a deal beneficial to the AIP candidate and his supporters. But his 13.5 percent share of the national vote was the third-highest return any post–Civil War nonmajor-party candidate had received up to that time. Wallace received nearly ten million votes. That was more than double the tally of any previous nonmajor-party candidate ever, and it has since been surpassed only once, by Perot in 1992.

The popular tallies for Wallace reached double digits in Michigan, Ohio, and twenty-one other states. His share of the vote ranged from 65.8 percent in his home state, Alabama, and 63.5 percent in Mississippi down to 1.5 percent in distant Hawaii. The forty-five electors in Alabama, Mississippi, Arkansas, Georgia, and Mississippi and one North Carolina Republican faithless elector cast their electoral votes for Wallace and LeMay.

The 1968 Wallace factor put a majority mandate from America's voters out of reach for either Nixon or Humphrey. Nixon won in a photo finish, taking 43.52 percent, compared to Humphrey's 42.75 percent. The disparity in electoral votes was larger: 301 for Nixon, 191 for Humphrey.

It is far from clear even today whether support for Wallace deprived Humphrey of victory and put Nixon in the White House. Absent Wallace, most Wallace supporters might well have decided that Nixon, not Humphrey, was the lesser of two evils. On the other hand, without the Wallace option, many white southerners might still have clung to the party of their birth, joining with millions of newly empowered southern blacks in voting for Humphrey.[11]

Wallace's Legacy

The legacy—the long-term impact—of the movement Wallace led in 1968 should be clear to anyone earnestly looking for it. The influence of Wallace and his American Independent Party on the direction of the GOP and on the fate of both the Republicans and Democrats was substantial. Because of this impact upon the two major parties, the 1968 Wallace-led insurgency was the most significant third-party movement to be born in the last half of the twentieth century.

The strength of Wallace's appeal in 1968 went beyond white backlash: "Wallace defined a new right-wing populism, capitalizing on voter reaction to the emergence of racial, cultural, and moral liberalism. Wallace demonized an elite Democratic establishment, providing a desperately sought-after moral justification to those whites who saw themselves as victimized and displaced by the black struggle for civil rights and by broader social change."[12]

As journalists Thomas and Mary Edsall point out, the 1968 Wallace factor was decisive in producing a "sea change" in American politics, "the replacement of a liberal majority with a conservative majority. . . . [It] involved the conversion of a rather small proportion of voters: the roughly five to ten percent of the electorate, made up primarily of white working class voters, empowered to give majority status to either political party. Alabama Governor George C. Wallace was the politician who showed the Republicans how to seize lower income white voters. . . . Wallace capitalized [in 1968] on the huge defection of white Democrats, particularly in the South, as the Democratic Party formally repudiated segregation. . . . Wallace and Nixon together that year won 57 percent of the vote, establishing what would become the conservative presidential majority."[13]

Driven by the need to take for themselves as much of Wallace's soft potential support as possible, the Nixon Republicans had deployed their strategy of reaching out to southern whites and to conservative working-class whites nationwide. Achieving success, Republicans glimpsed their future and found it bright. Over the years that followed, the Republican Party, trending to the right, built a strong base in the South, the region the party had once regarded as hostile and forbidding.[14] Taking their cue from Wallace's "us against them" politics, Republican tacticians began the practice of driving wedges between various constituencies of what since the 1930s had been the Democratic majority coalition. Race and then abortion and gay rights became key wedge issues.

Though it was perceived by Nixon Republicans to be a dangerous rival, the Wallace insurgency turned out to be a valuable gift to the GOP. Republicans controlled the presidency for all but twelve of the next forty years following Nixon's election in 1968. Ten of the twelve who joined the Supreme Court during those forty years were selected by Republican presidents. Republicans won House and Senate majorities in 1994. They held the House continuously and the Senate almost continuously for the next twelve years. Not until 2006–8 did political currents shift, indicating that for Democrats there was a reason to hope that the conservative majority that emerged in 1968 and the years that followed might at last be fading away.

The American Independent Party after 1968

Though keeping open his third-party option, George Wallace undertook a serious race to win the 1972 Democratic presidential nomination. Clearly the antiestablishment man, Wallace hoped to win through enlisting the support of ordinary voters in Democratic primaries. A big victory in Florida on March 14 bought him some begrudging respect even from the hostile national Democratic Party elite.

George C. Wallace

Wallace biographers have described their man as "the most influential loser" in twentieth-century politics. He was certainly one of the most enigmatic of American politicians. Observers at various times described him as a liberal, progressive, or populist, as a conservative, traditionalist, or states' righter, and as a racist demagogue or even a fascist. Episodes from his career could be brought to bear in support of any of these claims.

Born in tiny Clio, Alabama, Wallace grew up poor in the rural southeastern region of the state. Physically strong but short in height—detractors sometimes called him a Napoleonic bantam rooster—he won the Alabama bantamweight boxing championship in 1936 and again in 1937. In 1942 Wallace received his law degree at the University of Alabama. He then joined the U.S. Army Air Corps and flew combat missions. During World War II, Wallace married the former Lurleen Burns. The couple had three daughters and a son.

Launching his political career, Wallace twice won election to the legislature and then was elected as an Alabama circuit judge. In the legislature, especially during his first term, when Jim Folsom was governor, Wallace became a legislative leader of Folsom populism and interracialism. At the 1948 Democratic National Convention, he was one of the Alabama delegates who did *not* walk out of the convention hall to enlist in the Dixiecrat insurgency.

In his first bid for governor, in 1958, Wallace denounced the Ku Klux Klan and won endorsements from the NAACP and from his state's small but significant Jewish community. He lost in the all-important Democratic primaries to John Patterson, a Klan-backed segregationist. In defeat the disappointed Wallace told someone that he had been "outsegged" by Patterson—one account, later denied by Wallace, had him saying "out-niggered"—and that no one would ever "outseg" him again.

Wallace won the governor's office by a landslide in 1962. His first gubernatorial term (1963–67) was in some respects one of the most progressive in his state's history. The governor undertook ambitious programs for industrial growth, creating jobs beneficial to both to black and white Alabamians. A new system of vocational and postsecondary technical education took shape. Conservation measures were passed, and nursing homes and medical clinics built.

But Wallace remembered his vow not to be outsegged. During the 1962 campaign and then his first term as governor, he came to be known nationally as an agitator who used racial invective and "us against them" politics. In his critics' view, Wallace was—or became—a racist demagogue. In his 1963 inaugural address, he declared, "This nation was never meant to be a unit of one, but a unit of the many . . . and so it is in our racial lives. . . . If we amalgamate into the one unit . . . we become . . . a mongrel unit of one under a single all-powerful government. . . . Today I have stood where Jefferson Davis stood, and took an oath to my people. It is very appropriate then that from this Cradle of the Confederacy, this very heart of the Anglo-Saxon Southland, that today we sound the drum of freedom. . . . In the name of the greatest people that ever trod this earth, I draw the line in the dust and toss the gauntlet before the feet of tyranny. And I say 'Segregation now! Segregation tomorrow! Segregation forever!'"

Five months later Wallace stood blocking a Foster Auditorium door at the University of Alabama and gave a states' rights speech verbally defying federal power. Symbolism completed, he then stepped aside, in effect allowing the admission to the university of African American students Vivian Malone and James Hood.

The Alabama constitution forbade a governor to succeed himself, and Wallace's determined and heavy-handed attempt to amend it failed. So in 1966 he ran his wife. During Lurleen Wallace's gubernatorial tenure, her husband was governor in every way except name. He served, it was said, as prime minister, with Lurleen attending the ceremonial role of chief of state.

Lurleen Wallace died of cancer in 1968, the year her husband ran for the presidency as a third-party candidate. He eventually married twice again, his second and third marriages ending in divorce.

Alabama eventually changed its basic law to Wallace's benefit. Waging a racially charged campaign, as he had also done in 1962, Wallace retook the governorship in 1970. He won again in 1974 and one final time in 1982. No other Alabamian has come close to the Wallace tenure in the governor's mansion.

Non-Alabamians are most likely to remember him as the man who in 1968 claimed the podium to speak for the nation's hard hats, police, and other "decent, God-fearing, tax-paying, law-abiding" Americans and who waged rhetorical war on black militants and "welfare cheats," hippies and antiwar demonstrators, "pointy-headed pseudo-intellectuals" and "briefcase-toting bureaucrats." But Wallace was laying the groundwork for his national movement years before 1968. By 1963 he was on the speakers' circuit. University students on northern campuses often greeted him with boos and heckles.

With just seven hundred dollars to spend, Wallace filed in the 1964 Democratic primary in Wisconsin, progressivism's old heartland. Over opposition from the Catholic Church, mainline Protestant denominations, and the Wisconsin Democratic Party, Wallace took more than a third of the Wisconsin primary vote. He won 30 percent in Indiana and nearly 45 percent in Maryland.

In 1972, after his momentary venture into third-party politics, Wallace made another bid for the Democratic presidential nomination. Campaigning in a suburban shopping center in Laurel, Maryland, on May 15 Wallace was shot four times by a fame seeker named Arthur Bremer. The next day Wallace won the Democratic primaries in Michigan and Maryland, but the would-be assassin's gun ended forever his quest for the presidency. Wallace lived his last twenty-six years as a paraplegic, and he reportedly endured chronic pain.

In the early 1970s, even before the shooting, Wallace shelved his racist appeal, and the remaining years of his public service in Alabama apparently were grounded in the progressive values of his early career. During his third and fourth administrations,

Governor Wallace channeled large infusions of state and federal funds to Tuskegee and other black belt towns where African American candidates were winning elections to mayoralties and councils. Black voter support played a substantial role in Wallace's fourth gubernatorial election in 1982. He went on to appoint two African Americans to major cabinet posts in his last administration.

A drama of reconciliation unfolded in March 1995, when the wheelchair-bound ex-governor and African American marchers who had finished retracing the steps of the famed 1965 march from Selma to Montgomery greeted each other with open arms. In 1996 James Hood and Vivian Malone, the targets of Wallace's 1963 schoolhouse door stand, met with their erstwhile foe. The three were, after all, University of Alabama alumni, and they had experienced a remarkable transformation in the state. Accepting Wallace's apology, Hood invited him to the university commencement at which Hood was about to receive his doctorate. Wallace gratefully agreed to attend.

Peggy Wallace Kennedy, a daughter of George and Lurleen Wallace, gave her support to Barack Obama in 2008. In an article she wrote, Kennedy conjectured that had her father lived, he well might have joined her in supporting Obama.

Many people believe to this day that the "real George Wallace" was seen in the racist words and deeds of his 1962 campaign and first gubernatorial term. Others remember him as a political opportunist willing to say and do whatever it took to achieve his goals.

Wallace himself presented a different picture in reflecting on his past. Though admitting to serious errors, he contended that he had been misunderstood. His real objective, he said, had been to defend states' rights far more than segregation. And he insisted that by his symbolic defiance he had tried to deflect—and did deflect—what might otherwise have been violent resistance from the good old boy types.

Taming physical violence may have been one of Wallace's objectives. But the effect of his racist rhetoric may actually have stimulated some violent acts. Of the twenty-nine people known to have been killed in the modern civil rights struggle, ten were slain in Alabama during Wallace's first term as governor.

Whatever conclusions one draws about the essential George Wallace, the man's impact was beyond dispute. The Wallace factor motivated the law-and-order provisions in the 1968 Republican platform, and it set the southern strategy that has charted the GOP course ever since. Wallace demonstrated to Nixon and his Republican successors that millions of white southerners could be persuaded to abandon a Democratic Party in which African Americans were playing leading roles. Wallace also helped pave the way for the presidencies of Jimmy Carter and Bill Clinton and for a new generation of southern governors shorn of their region's racial stain.

Sources: Marshall Frady, *Wallace* (New York: World, 1968); Stephan Lesher, *George Wallace: American Populist* (Reading, Mass.: Addison-Wesley, 1994); Dan T. Carter, *The Politics of Rage: George Wallace, the Origins of the New Conservatism, and the Transformation of American Politics,* 2nd ed. (Baton Rouge: Louisiana State University Press,

2000); J. David Gillespie, "George C. Wallace," in *The Encyclopedia of Third Parties in America,* 3 vols., ed. Immanuel Ness and James Ciment (Armonk, N.Y.: Sharpe Reference, 2000), 727–31; Jack Bass, "How History Will See Wallace," *The State* (Columbia, S.C.), April 9, 1989; and Peggy Wallace Kennedy, "Commentary: My Father, George Wallace, and Barack Obama," available online at http://articles.cnn.com/2008-11 -03/politics/wallace.kennedy.obama_1_george-wallace-graves-desecrating?_s= PM:POLITICS (accessed September 3, 2011).

———————————————— ★ ★ ————————————————

Wallace's wins in Michigan and Maryland on May 16 were large but also anticlimactic. On the day before, Arthur Bremer, a man with assassination in mind, had hit the governor with four shots. One of Bremer's bullets had reached Wallace's spinal column, leaving him permanently paralyzed from the waist down. Those split seconds in a suburban shopping center outside Washington, D.C., ended forever Wallace's quest for the presidency.

That was hard for Wallace's most devoted AIP loyalists to accept. Many of them had set out in 1969 to build and institutionalize the party, and they settled on the American Party as its name. In a conference call to their fallen standard-bearer in his Birmingham hospital room, they offered him their 1972 nomination. Wallace said no.

Meeting in convention at Louisville, the American Party then nominated John Schmitz, a first-term congressman from conservative Orange County, California. Schmitz was a well-known member of the ultra-right John Birch Society, and he peppered his 1972 campaign oratory with Birchite themes about conspiracy and the new world order.[15]

Though Schmitz's November returns were far below what Wallace's had been, they were not unimpressive. Schmitz took 1,100,868 votes—1.4 percent of the national total—in the thirty-seven states where it was possible to vote for him. His best returns were outside the South. Schmitz won 9.3 percent of the Idaho votes. Around the nation most of those who in 1968 had supported Wallace voted for Nixon, not Schmitz, in 1972.

Soon after the November 1972 election, the party split in two. One faction kept the American Party name. The other renamed itself the American Independent Party. In most elections between 1976 and 1988, both offered presidential candidates. The votes they received were always small.

California's American Independent Party, the state branch of the party of Wallace, remained intact until 2008. A ballot-qualified party, the AIP served as the California affiliate of the national Constitution Party from 1992 until 2008. The AIP split into two factions in 2008. Because of this break, Chuck Baldwin, the 2008 Constitution Party presidential nominee, did not appear on the California ballot. Alan Keyes ran instead on the California AIP ballot line.

★ ★

A New "Populist Party"

Around 1984 veterans of what had been the Wallace AIP movement took the lead in creating a far right party they named the Populist Party. Bill Shearer, for example, with his wife, Eileen, had joined George Wallace himself in establishing the AIP back in the late 1960s. The new Populist Party was the brainchild of Willis Carto. Carto was known for his anti-Semitic views and vituperative rants about conspiracy, corruption, and dictatorial design at the highest levels of American government. Another founding member was Mississippi Ku Klux Klan activist Robert Weems, the Populist Party's first national chairman. The party reached out to whites holding traditionalist racial attitudes and a deep-seated hostility toward the federal government and to those who held power within it.

Candidates ran for the presidency under this Populist label in 1984, 1988, and 1992. Their tallies ranged from 47,000 to 106,000. Bob Richards, the party's first presidential candidate, had won two Olympic gold medals in pole vaulting in the 1950s. David Duke, the 1988 nominee, was well-known for having been a leader and spokesman for the Klan and other extreme right groups. James "Bo" Gritz, a Vietnam-era Special Forces officer, was tapped by the Populists for the 1992 presidential contest. It was not the first charge Gritz had taken up, and it was not his most glamorous. In 1982 Gritz had led a Rambo-style raid into Laos in a failed mission to seek and liberate U.S. prisoners of war.

If allegations by Hillary and Bill Clinton about a "vast right-wing conspiracy" are valid, that conspiracy may well have hatched in venues such as those of this Populist Party.

Source: James Ridgeway, *Blood in the Face: The Ku Klux Klan, Aryan Nations, Nazi Skinheads, and the Rise of a New White Culture* (New York: Thunder's Mouth, 1990).

On the Left, 1968–1984
The Peace and Freedom Party

Judged by its impact upon mainstream politics, the movement Wallace led in 1968 was unequaled by any other third party running that year. But another electoral insurgency, far to the left of Wallace and of the Republicans and clearly left even of the liberal Democrats, surfaced in 1968. In 1967 people experienced in a range of radical movements—new leftists, old leftists, black nationalists, farmworker unionists—had joined in organizing the Peace and Freedom Party.

Rejecting as unrealistic the approach of those whose goal was to transform the Democrats into a peace party, Peace and Freedom partisans set out to peel away from the Democratic constituency people who had been radicalized by Vietnam, the civil rights struggle, and other elements of 1960s storm and stress. The PFP's first platform demanded immediate withdrawal from Vietnam, community control of schools and police, abortion rights, and environmental protection.[16]

Eldridge Cleaver was the Peace and Freedom Party nominee in 1968. The minister of information in the militant Black Panther Party, Cleaver published that year *Soul on Ice,* his raw, gritty autobiographical polemic on African American life in racist America. At the time of his campaign, he was a felon on parole and also awaiting trial on an attempted murder charge.[17] At just thirty-three years old, Cleaver was two years too young to meet the constitutional age requirement for the presidency.

Cleaver's age and troubles with the law brought the PFP even more than the usual ballot-access difficulties faced by a new party. The party had made the California ballot by persuading far more than the necessary 66,059 voters to register or re-register as members of the party; but in California and also Utah no name appeared on the lines intended to designate the PFP nominee.

Dick Gregory, a well-known African American humorist and social critic who had made a failed bid for the PFP nomination, stood in on the ballots of some states that had declined to list Cleaver. In its Cleaver, Gregory, and no-name manifestations, the movement took 111,607 votes (many of them cast as write-ins) in some fifteen states where it was possible to vote for the party.[18]

Eldridge Cleaver, 1968. Photograph by Marion S. Trikosko, a staffer for *U.S. News & World Report.* Courtesy of U.S. Library of Congress Prints and Photographs Division. Obtained through Wikimedia Commons.

After 1968 most of the ephemeral state Peace and Freedom Party organizations simply dissolved. California was the exception. There the PFP established itself as a permanent if minor partisan force on the left. Except for a four-year hiatus beginning in 1999, the PFP has retained its lines on the California ballot. It has run many candidates for state and national offices. In its state platform and pronouncements, the party declares its devotion to socialism, feminism, and environmentalism.

Ralph Nader and Matt Gonzalez (of San Francisco) appeared on the California ballot in 2008 as the presidential and vice-presidential nominees of the PFP. Supporting the resolve of many party activists to begin rebuilding the national party, Nader and Gonzalez used the Peace and Freedom Party label in securing access to the ballots in Iowa and Utah.[19]

The People's Party

Founded in 1971, the People's Party was the creation jointly of the Peace and Freedom Party, the Liberty Union Party of Vermont, and other leftist groups and radical organizers. Dr. Benjamin Spock, the famous "spare the rod" author of *Baby and Child Care* (1946), was the People's Party nominee in 1972. Spock ran on a platform calling for withdrawal of all U.S. forces from abroad, universal free health care, and the legalization of abortion, homosexuality, and marijuana. Seventy percent of Spock's 78,759 votes were cast in California, where the nominee ran on the Peace and Freedom Party line.

The party ran again in 1976, but in this, its last presidential bid, nominee Margaret Wright found herself overshadowed by another challenger on the left. That was former senator Eugene J. McCarthy of Minnesota.

The McCarthy Campaign

Progressives in the 1970s remembered and venerated Eugene McCarthy for having been the first peace candidate to enter the Democratic race in 1968. McCarthy's 42 percent vote share in the New Hampshire primary had brought to Lyndon Johnson the persuasive message that he should not seek reelection that year.

Forgoing the 1976 Democratic primaries, McCarthy set out to run for the presidency as an independent. Though the war had ended by the time of his 1976 independent bid, the candidate remained a sharp and persistent critic of U.S. national security policy. McCarthy called for diplomatic ties with Cuba and Vietnam and for slashing $20–30 billion from the Pentagon budget. On the home front, he proposed a thirty-five-hour workweek and radical new measures to curb energy consumption.[20]

McCarthy in 1976 appealed to voters to desert the two-party system. Three-quarters of a million did that for at least the time it took to give him their votes. The McCarthy campaign's remarkable penchant for going to court—there were at least eighteen lawsuits—helped place him on ballots in three-fifths of the states. It also eased the ballot-access burdens other third-party and independent campaigns faced late in the twentieth century.[21]

The Citizens Party

Nineteen seventy-nine may not have been the worst of times for the American Left, but it was far from the best. Double-digit inflation, nightmare scenarios growing out of a near meltdown at the Three Mile Island nuclear power plant in Pennsylvania, conflict with OPEC, and the demoralizing issue of U.S. hostages held in Iran all weighed down the nation's soul and devoured the political capital of its Democratic incumbent, Jimmy Carter. The New Right was strong, growing stronger, and in 1980 American conservatism took its next great leap forward with Ronald Reagan's election to the presidency.

Many liberals and other leftists believed that the man from Plains, Georgia, was the most conservative Democrat who had won the presidency in the twentieth century. That assessment may have been untrue; but it was such frustrations, coupled with leftist idealism and hopes, that fueled the birth of the Citizens Party in the summer of 1979.

Writers for *Newsweek* called the new Citizens Party "an anti-business amalgam of environmentalists, consumerists, anti-nuclear activists, and minority rights advocates."[22] It was from the beginning a party flush with well-known leftist talent. "Among those present at the creation were Adam Hochschild, publisher of *Mother Jones* the Gray Panthers' Maggie Kuhn; author Studs Terkel; consumer advocate Ralph Nader; (and) Mario Savio, a leader of the Berkeley Free Speech Movement."[23]

Barry Commoner was the Citizens Party's early driving force and first presidential nominee. The 275 delegates who attended their party's inaugural convention in Cleveland in April 1980 nominated Commoner and chose LaDonna Harris to run with him. Harris was a Comanche activist in the Native American movement.[24]

Commoner contributed the most to whatever gravitas this new party was able to muster. Trained as a biologist, he had long been known in environmentalist circles as "Dr. Ecology." *The Closing Circle,* his best-selling book, was famous as one of the manifestos of the modern movement for ecology and sustainable living.

The Citizens Party ethos blended environmentalism, feminism, social democracy, and other values dear to people on the left. Adopting as its emblem the evergreen tree, the party called for terminating nuclear power plants and a radical shift to solar power. It developed ties with the rising international Green movement and won recognition from prominent European Greens as America's Green party.[25] Attributing many of the nation's woes to big business greed, the Citizens Party demanded citizen representation on corporate boards, public control of energy and other key industries, and policies for revitalizing small businesses and family farms. It wanted local grassroots initiatives for citizens to reclaim power, massive military cutbacks, price controls, and firm new commitments to human rights.

The party's devotion to feminism and its outreach to minorities produced affirmative action rules under which 48 percent of the delegates attending the 1980 founding convention were women and 14 percent were from racial and ethnic minorities. Sonia Johnson, the 1984 Citizens Party presidential nominee, was a self-described radical feminist who had been excommunicated by the Mormon Church in 1979 because of her activism on behalf of the proposed Equal Rights Amendment and other objectives of the women's movement.[26]

Many twentieth-century short-lived parties concentrated their limited resources and energies upon the presidential campaign, leaving themselves fragile and underdeveloped at the grass roots. The Citizens Party reversed this pattern. Though never amounting to much nationally, the party had built forty-one active locals in thirty states by 1981. It ran thirty-eight candidates for various offices in 1980, fifty-eight in 1981, and fifty-three in 1982, and its nominees won city council seats in Burlington, Vermont, and school board elections in Seattle and in Schenectady, New York.[27]

Commoner took 234,294 votes in 1980 in the twenty-nine states where his name made the ballot and the eight other jurisdictions where voters could write him in. He and his party shared in many of the adversities that other twentieth-century minor parties had experienced. Voters knew that ballots marked for Commoner could spoil the election for the major candidate the voter would have chosen if there had been no minor-party option. Commoner was excluded from the debate stage, overwhelmingly ignored by media, and additionally hamstrung by a rival, and more potent, challenge to the two major parties: John Anderson's 1980 independent campaign.

Lack of money was one of Commoner's most crushing problems. His two major-party foes received and spent, courtesy of the nation's taxpayers, Federal Election Campaign Act grants, each totaling $29,400,000. Commoner's privately collected campaign war chest was, by contrast, a pitiful $28,000, and only $5,429 of that went to media advertising. The Commoner campaign's media outreach was most remembered for its "bullshit." That was the word used in an October radio shock ad to portray the issue positions of Reagan, Carter, and Anderson.[28]

By 1984 the Citizens Party was clearly in decline. Many of its locals were in tatters, and the party was able to tap only a handful of candidates to run for office. Commoner himself left after seeking but failing to convince the party faithful to join him in working for Jesse Jackson's nomination through the 1984 Democratic primaries. The party Commoner had built died as a national movement when the November election was past.

Sonia Johnson, the 1984 Citizen Party nominee, did prove to be a better fundraiser than Commoner. The Johnson campaign raised more than $180,000, most of it collected in small donations qualifying her—the first minor-party candidate for which this was ever the case—for receipt of FECA matching funds.[29] The Socialist Party USA and California's Peace and Freedom Party joined the Citizens Party in endorsing and supporting her. But she made the ballots of just twenty states.

★ ★

The Political Odyssey of Lyndon LaRouche

For those in the movement built by Lyndon LaRouche, unswerving devotion to its bright, narcissistic leader and faith in his worldview are the paramount virtues. It is ironic that LaRouche's followers regard their leader's thoughts as virtually infallible, for his view of things has undergone substantial change over the years. But it has always featured enemies, dark conspiracies, and a reality that is very unlike what most people assume it to be. People old enough to remember late 1980s television spots may recall some remarkable LaRouche-sponsored ads alleging that Queen Elizabeth was involved with drugs, that Walter Mondale had links to the KGB, and that Henry Kissinger was leading a three-thousand-year-old global conspiracy.

LaRouche began his political odyssey in the late 1940s as a man of the Left. He joined the Socialist Workers Party, a Trotskyist communist group. Later he built ties to various 1960s New Left elements.

LaRouche's trek during the 1970s took him and the movement from far left to the radical right. By 1978 he was declaring that "it is not necessary to call oneself a fascist. It is simply necessary to be one." He and his staff also were garnering a reputation as effective spies—intelligence gatherers collecting information useful in neutralizing foes. They came into close contact with certain people in the Pentagon and National Security Council during the first Reagan term. A Pentagon official praised LaRouche's group for being "very supportive of the [Reagan] administration."

LaRouche declared for the presidency eight times, a record never equaled by anyone else. His first run, in 1976, was as the nominee of his own U.S. Labor Party. That campaign earned him 40,043 votes. An article carried in the *New York Times* in 1979 charged that the U.S. Labor Party had become an anti-Semitic Far Right cult.

After the 1970s LaRouche and his followers deserted the third-party approach. They found more potential and profit in becoming a third force, penetrating—infiltrating—a very reluctant Democratic Party through its accessible primary processes. LaRouche announced his quest for the Democratic nomination in every presidential round from 1980 through 2004. Over these years he qualified for and received nearly nineteen million dollars in federal matching funds as a nominal candidate for nomination by the Democrats.

During his 1992 race, LaRouche was a federal prison inmate in Minnesota serving the fourth year on a fifteen-year sentence for mail fraud and conspiracy to defraud the Internal Revenue Service. He won release on parole in 1994.

When in the 1986 Illinois Democratic primary two LaRouche followers defeated the party-endorsed "real Democrats" for lieutenant governor and secretary of state, Adlai Stevenson III, the Democratic gubernatorial nominee, felt compelled to withdraw from the ticket and to run as an independent. Stevenson lost, and the GOP reaped the benefit of the Democratic debacle. LaRouche and his movement were instrumental in convincing two million Californians to embrace an initiative proposition that, if it had passed, would have quarantined AIDS patients.

Followers of LaRouche were visible and active in the anti-Obama Tea Party rallies in the summer of 2009. The visual image they created and displayed depicted the new president as Adolf Hitler, complete with cutoff moustache.

Sources: Dennis King, *Lyndon LaRouche and the New American Fascism* (New York: Doubleday, 1988); David Corn, "Lyndon Who?" *Nation,* June 26, 1989, 248; Howard Blum, "U.S. Labor Party: Cult Surrounded by Controversy," *New York Times,* October 7, 1979, and Paul L. Montgomery, "One Man Leads U.S. Labor Party on Its Erratic Path," *New York Times,* October 8, 1979.

–––––––––––––––––––––––––––––– ★ ★ ––––––––––––––––––––––––––––––

Thus her tally in November 1984 was less than a third of what Commoner's numbers had been in 1980.

The New Alliance Party

The Bronx was the birthplace of the New Alliance Party in 1979. The party proclaimed itself to be a "black-led multi-racial coalition of progressive people."[30] For the first half decade of its existence, the New Alliance Party concentrated on politics in New York City, where it came to be known for its leftist positions on issues. It networked with the Reverend Al Sharpton and coalesced with various local grassroots groups opposed to Mayor Edward Koch and what the NAP described as Koch's antiblack, reactionary policies.

Venturing into national politics in 1984, the NAP nominated for the presidency Dennis Serrette, a Harlem-born African American who was an active trade unionist. By 1988 it was in a position to offer U.S. Senate nominees in four states as well as candidates for other offices. Lenora Fulani, a black New York psychologist and political activist, was the New Alliance presidential standard-bearer in 1988 and 1992. From the NAP's beginning until it was dissolved in 1994, Fulani was the party's most prominent and effective public face.

Fred Newman, a New York–based white psychologist, was by many accounts the party's real behind-the-scenes guiding light and a major source of its considerable wealth. Newman had founded Social Therapy, a radical, neo-Marxist strain of psychotherapy. Centers for Change was the name Newman chose for the health-care collective he set up to apply and advance his therapeutic regime.

New Alliance became a magnet, attracting a wide array of critics.[31] Rumors surfaced about life and events inside the NAP and Centers for Change, and exposés by people who had severed their connections with Newman and Fulani began to appear. One of the most damaging came from Dennis Serrette, who had carried the torch as NAP's first presidential nominee. In 1987 Serrette described New Alliance as a cult and wrote that it was not black-led and not even progressive.[32]

Newman had been associated in the past with LaRouche. Critics charged that Newman had learned stealth politics from him. There were even some who suspected that Newman and Fulani had followed LaRouche in his ideological trek from left to right and that NAP's real though secret purpose was to infiltrate, surveil, and disrupt genuinely leftist groups.

NAP leaders were also denounced for being anti-Semitic. The party denied it, but there were remarks on record that lent some support to the claim. In something she wrote in 1989, Fulani had declared that Jews "had to sell their souls to acquire Israel" and "to function as mass murderers" to stay there.[33]

"Two roads are better than one" was a prominent slogan within the NAP. What that meant in practice became clear in 1988. The NAP first announced its support for Jesse Jackson's 1988 presidential quest. With Jackson out of the race by the close of the Democratic primary season, New Alliance then ran its own candidate, Fulani, for president.

Fulani qualified for and took federal matching funds. She used them to seek ballot access and advertise her campaign. To the surprise of nearly everyone outside the NAP, she made the November ballot in all fifty states and the District of Columbia. It was the NAP's most substantial national achievement and a milestone in U.S. history. Fulani was both the first woman and the first black presidential nominee of any party whose name appeared in every jurisdiction with electoral votes to cast. Fulani took 225,934 votes nationwide.

Fulani ran again in 1992. Maria Elizabeth Munoz, her 1992 running mate, was a seasoned activist in the Chicano/a movement and in Peace and Freedom Party politics. The NAP's 1992 presidential vote was only a third what it had been in 1988. Over the years after the NAP died, Fulani and Newman gave their support to Perot's 1996 candidacy and then enlisted in the Independence Party, a rising star in New York partisan politics.[34]

The Natural Law Party

Travelers through rural Iowa are often surprised to find that Fairfield, the seat of Jefferson County, is a central U.S. venue of Transcendental Meditation. The TM movement swept America in the 1960s. More than a movement, in southeastern Iowa TM has become an important culture. It is the reason many of the area's inhabitants moved there. Since 1974 Fairfield has been home to Maharishi International University, now known as Maharishi University of Management. Nearby there is Maharishi Vedic City, a small community TM's devotees built as a demonstration plot for the ideal city.

Born in Fairfield in 1992, the Natural Law Party was the creation of local academics, businesspeople, and other citizens, who dedicated their new party to "bringing the light of science into politics." It eventually became a transnational party, with devotees and branches throughout the United States and in other nations.

Transcendental Meditation, with its related practices and assumptions, was the party's raison d'être—the reason it was born and what sustained it for over a decade. Its partisans believe in TM's power to improve the health and happiness of those who practice it and in its potential effect in fostering harmony and community in society at large.[35]

TM was indisputably its central theme, but Natural Law, like other parties, did interest itself in a range of issues. Its progressive platform called for a public health emphasis upon preventive medicine, sustainable agriculture, a reformed and fairer tax code, a moratorium on capital punishment, and a foreign policy respecting cultural diversity. The party demanded major revisions in ballot access and campaign finance laws to democratize elections and open the process to those who would challenge the duopoly.[36]

The party's appeal and electoral outreach peaked in 1996. That year Natural Law offered hundreds of candidates running for Congress and other offices across the United States. John Hagelin, the party's presidential nominee, won 113,670 votes in 1996.

That was the second of three consecutive runs Hagelin made as Natural Law presidential standard-bearer. He is a well-regarded physicist with a Harvard Ph.D. who was serving on the faculty of Maharishi University in Fairfield.[37] Hagelin is a devoted practitioner and advocate of Transcendental Meditation.

Hagelin decided in 2000 that he would also compete for the Reform Party presidential nomination. The party Perot had launched was by then deeply factionalized and in sharp decline. But its nomination remained a coveted prize because Perot's 1996 vote tally entitled the 2000 Reform nominee to a Federal Election Campaign Act grant of $12.5 million for the general election. One Reform Party faction nominated Hagelin. Another chose Pat Buchanan. The Federal Election Commission declared that Buchanan was the official nominee and awarded the FECA funds to Buchanan rather than Hagelin.

Although the national office of the Natural Law Party closed in 2004, the party clung to life in some locations. Ralph Nader's Michigan voters in 2008 found their candidate's name on a ballot line still belonging to Michigan's Natural Law Party.[38]

9

★ ★ ★

The New Independents

The Anderson and Perot Movements

> If someone blessed as I am is not willing to clean out the barn, who will?
>
> *Ross Perot*

Not since the election of Zachary Taylor, a Whig, in 1848 has presidential victory gone to anyone running without a *D* or an *R* by his name. The dominant pattern of contest between Republican and Democrat was already set by the time of the Civil War. In the years since 1930, the two parties have worked together to rig the election rules to institutionalize their duopolistic hold on power.

Three of the four most vigorous post-1930 challenges to the major parties' lock on the White House came as the twentieth century drew to a close. Leading them were John Anderson in 1980 and Ross Perot in 1992 and 1996.

Anderson in 1980 and challenger Perot in 1992 wore the mantle of independents, bypassing the ritual of birthing a new party and then running as its standard-bearer. Anderson did adopt a brand—the National Unity Campaign—for his candidacy, and Perot in 1992 used *United We Stand* as the title of his platform. But each made it crystal clear that he was offering voters something new, independent, and very unlike the partisan politics that were being practiced in the nation's capital.

Ballot-access rules presented Anderson and Perot with persuasive arguments for the independent track they took. Some of the states have over the years made it easier for an independent presidential candidate than for a new or unqualified party to qualify to appear on their ballots.[1]

Their decisions for independence also reflected the political temper of their times. Scholars for the last half century have observed and documented a tide of dealignment—the tendency of voters to move away from partisan devotion and to adopt an independent stance. Self-identified independents in annual Gallup surveys between 1988 and 2006 ranged from 31.2 percent to 39.1 percent of all the respondents, and in thirteen of these nineteen survey years, independents were larger in number than either Democrats or Republicans.[2]

Anderson and Perot both recognized the potential payoff value of their independent appeals. Exit polls revealed that independents were twice as likely as Democrats and three times as likely as Republicans to vote for Anderson.[3] Thirty percent of independents, compared to 17 percent of Republicans and 14 percent of Democrats, voted for Perot in 1992.[4]

Ralph Nader too eventually set out on the independent path charted by Anderson and Perot. Although Nader had run as the Green nominee in 1996 and 2000, for 2004 and 2008 he recast his campaigns as independent ones.

John Anderson and the National Unity Campaign, 1980

By American measures of such things, 1980 was a remarkable year for those who battered at the walls of duopoly. More than 8 percent of the general election voters selected presidential candidates other than Reagan and Carter. Ed Clark took the largest vote tally given so far for a Libertarian presidential nominee: 921,128, more than 1 percent of all votes cast. Barry Commoner received nearly a quarter of a million, and another 252,303 gave their ballots to sixteen other, much smaller campaigns.

By far the most lustrous of these bounties went that year to independent candidate John Anderson. Anderson's name (like Clark's) appeared on the ballots of all fifty states and of the nation's capital. Anderson received 5,719,850 votes (6.6 percent). Of all nonmajor-party candidates up to 1980, only the vote tally Wallace had received in 1968 exceeded in number that which went to Anderson in 1980.

The fifty-eight-year-old Anderson was white-haired, dignified, and intelligent. Many voters thought he "looked presidential." He was serving his tenth term in the U.S. House, with nearly twenty years of experience as the Republican representative of a district in northern Illinois. But like many of the 435 in the lower house, he entered 1980 mostly unknown to Americans living beyond the borders of his district and state.

Although his congressional voting record was moderately conservative, that was not conservative enough for the emerging New Right. Narrowly surviving a primary challenge in 1978, Anderson was expecting real trouble in 1980 as the GOP center of gravity shifted further to the right. Anderson may never have felt much real hope of winning the presidency. It is likely that, seeing defeat in his cards, he opted for the dignity of failing in a bid for the nation's highest office rather than the ignominy of a congressional reelection loss.

Anderson began the year by announcing his candidacy for the Republican nomination and entering GOP presidential primaries. He did well in the early races in Vermont and Massachusetts but later suffered the fatal wounds of a second-place showing in his home state and then a third-place finish in adjacent Wisconsin. By the end of April, Anderson already was making moves to launch an independent general election campaign against Carter and Reagan, the major parties' presumptive nominees. But it was not until June 8 that he formalized his candidacy as the National Unity Campaign.

The National Unity Campaign was to be Anderson's brand and theme, but the candidate made it clear that he had no intention of giving birth to a new political party. Anderson and his staff well understood the potential appeal of an "independent" candidate in a nation where millions already had divorced themselves from the duopoly's two brands. Also by June 8 the books were closing in many states for new parties seeking ballot access, while time remained to qualify as an independent.

Anderson staked out center-left ground for his presidential campaign. He made an appeal to his party's disaffected "Rockefeller Republicans" and set out to forge a makeshift coalition of independents, Democrats, and Republicans who could neither support the Reagan campaign nor abide embracing Carter's reelection.

Anderson came across as a courageous, no-nonsense campaigner willing to suffer the fury of those who, not liking the message, might (figuratively) slay the messenger. He let it be known that of all his decisions during twenty years of congressional service, he most regretted his 1964 vote for the war-authorizing Gulf of Tonkin Resolution. He laid out the essence of his gun control program—handgun registration, a waiting period for purchase, a ban on Saturday night specials, and mandatory prison for those using guns to commit crimes—amid the heckles and boos of an audience who had gathered for the convention of the New Hampshire Gun Owners Association.

As a measure for conservation and energy independence, Anderson called for a steep hike in gasoline taxes along with a compensatory cut in Social Security taxes. In the aftermath of Three Mile Island, he declared his opposition to all new nuclear power plant start-ups. Anderson demanded ratification of the Equal Rights Amendment, and he supported abortion choice. He called for Social Security for homemakers and federally funded child care. Anderson opposed Carter's resurrection of draft registration for eighteen-year-old men and big-ticket items such as the MX missile and B-1 bomber.

The pressing need of the National Unity Campaign to build its candidate's name recognition was compounded by its inability to persuade a figure of national renown to make the race with him. Former Wisconsin governor Patrick Lucey, who became Anderson's running mate in August, was almost as much an unknown to the nation at large as Anderson had been at the beginning of 1980.

Calculating that Anderson's campaign burdened Carter's and thus benefited theirs, Reagan and his staff found themselves in a position to play "nice guy" in dealing with Anderson. Carter's people strongly signaled that a vote for Anderson would be a vote for Reagan, one of the most conservative major candidates in anyone's memory, and they made Anderson's ballot-access quest as tough, expensive, and litigious as possible.

Anderson's poll standings were strong enough in September to earn him a League of Women Voters invitation to participate in the first 1980 nationally televised general election debate on September 21. Unwilling to validate Anderson's candidacy by appearing onstage with him, Carter withdrew his plans to participate, and Reagan and Anderson debated alone. Anderson's numbers were plummeting by mid-October, and he was not invited to join the two major-party candidates in the second (final) fall presidential debate on October 28.

Starting at nearly 25 percent in opinion polls, Anderson saw his popularity steadily drop as election day approached. His Republican support was what declined most precipitously. Anderson's election day tally drew far more votes away from Carter than Reagan, but Anderson did not cost Carter his reelection. Reagan's margin of victory over Carter was 2,703,265 votes larger than Anderson's total vote.

Reagan's triumph was even larger in electoral votes: 489 to Carter's 49. If, in the absence of Anderson's campaign, Carter had taken every single Anderson popular vote in the fifteen Reagan states where Anderson's tallies were larger than the difference between Reagan's and Carter's, Reagan still would have won in the electoral college by a margin of 104 votes.

As the election day exit poll data in table 8.1 reveals, Anderson's appeal was strongest among voters who were young, well-educated, prosperous, politically independent, liberal or moderate, and nonsouthern. Jewish voters were twice as likely to vote for Anderson as were Protestants and Catholics.

Table 9.1 Demographic Groups and Voting for John Anderson

Percentage of Group Respondents Reporting That They Voted for Anderson

Democrats	6	Blue collar	5
Republicans	4	Agriculture	3
Independents	12	Unemployed	7
Liberals	11	Less than high school	3
Moderates	8	High school graduates	4
Conservatives	4	Some college	8
African Americans	3	College graduates	11
Latinos/Hispanics	7	Union households	7
Whites	8	Nonunion households	8
Females	7	18–21 years old	11
Males	7	22–29 years old	11
Protestants	6	30–44 years old	7
White Protestants	6	45–59 years old	6
Catholics	7	60 and older	4
Jews	14	East	9
Family income		South	3
under $10,000	6	White South	3
$10,000–$14,999	8	Midwest	7
$15,000–$24,999	7	Far West	9
$25,000–$50,000	8	Cities with more	
Over $50,000	8	than 250,000 inhabitants	8
Professionals or managers	9	Suburbs/small cities	8
Clerical, sales, white collar	8	Rural/towns	5

SOURCE: CBS/*New York Times* exit interviews with 12,782 voters on November 4, 1980. Reported in the *New York Times,* November 9, 1980.

In influencing political events to come, the legacy of Anderson's 1980 candidacy was far smaller than what George Wallace had left in 1968. Even so, the National Unity Campaign was a notable milestone in the history of electoral challenges to the duopoly. Anderson won an extraordinary amount of free press—not, of course, nearly as much as what went to the Democratic and Republican campaigns—and much of it was friendly if condescending in its treatment of his "noble if hopeless" campaign. Garry Trudeau virtually endorsed him in his *Doonesbury* cartoon, and Anderson made a guest appearance on *Saturday Night Live*.[5]

Anderson continued the movement to liberalize ballot-access requirements that Wallace had undertaken in 1968 and McCarthy continued in 1976. Later third-party and independent campaigns have reaped the benefits, although in many states the ballot burdens remain insufferably severe.

Anderson was the first nonmajor-party presidential candidate ever invited to join in a televised debate with even one major-party nominee. He was also the first nonmajor-party candidate to qualify by virtue of at least 5 percent of the general election share, to receive postelection funds by provision of the Federal Election Campaign Act passed in the 1970s. Using loans and private donations, he had had to compete with the major candidates, each the recipient of a federal grant of $29,400,000. Anderson eventually collected $4.5 million based upon his 6.6 share of the November votes.

Ross Perot and the Movement He Launched

For third-party and independent challengers, significance and success are measured by a movement's election tallies and by its impact on policy and on the way politics is done. By these gauges two late-twentieth-century challenges to the nation's duopoly far outpaced all their national contemporaries. One was the American Independent Party and George Wallace, the man who had led it. The other was the 1990s movement Ross Perot and his associates launched, which captured the devotion of millions of American voters.

Their movements were substantially different in how they viewed the world, but Wallace and Perot were like each other in significant ways. Perot, like Wallace, grew up southern in a home that was distant from the privileges of aristocracy or wealth. Achievement, not patrimony, brought recognition to them both. Wallace and Perot each reached out to real and potential supporters using language that was engaging, passionate, unvarnished, and sometimes earthy. The messages they conveyed were unmistakably populist in tone. They spoke as antiestablishment outsiders, berating the inside and those who occupied it.

It was Wallace, not Perot, who had induced the Republican and Democratic parties to recast themselves along ideological and geographical lines. But Perot and his associates grasped, embraced, and acted upon a new party premise. As they saw things, the two major parties had been moving away from each other on ideology and policy, and the widening chasm was opening up opportunity for a centrist movement with an attitude. They believed they could find living space for their new electoral movement, one that would appeal nonideologically to voters across the spectrum who were turned off by politics as usual and by both major parties' willful neglect of some key policy issues.

Perot the Man and His 1992 Independent Campaign

Perot, the featured guest on the February 20, 1992, edition of CNN's *Larry King Live*, took a calculated risk. Though well recognized in many quarters of the business community, he realized that to most of the electorate he was an unknown. Speaking as if the voters were his suitor, he declared himself available but not easy to get. *If* the people wanted him to run, he said, and *if* they would secure his place on every state's ballot, he would enter the presidential race and give it his very best shot.[6]

There were scoffers aplenty, and they said that Perot was being arrogant and naive. The man who offered himself, with conditions, that night was sixty-one years old. He is five feet six inches tall, and through his high-pitched nasal voice he speaks with a Texas-accented southern drawl.

The naysayers found nothing charismatic and little that was appealing in candidate Perot. But millions of rank-and-file American voters would eventually say yes to the man and the movement. Building from that February 20 appearance on CNN, Perot, his associates, and a growing legion of volunteers countrywide put together a remarkable populist crusade.

To many Perot came to represent the American dream. Born middle class, he is a billionaire several times over. What got him there was hard work and good fortune but also Perot's exceptional endowment in the can-do entrepreneurial spirit. His life experience led him to believe, and to convey to others, that problems some see as intractable are really solvable, and solvable *now*.

An IBM salesman years ago, Perot became frustrated by his employer's indifference to his idea for custom-designed computer systems. In 1962 he left IBM and started Electronic Data Systems, which he built from the ground up. EDS went on to become a U.S. leader in information services.

A graduate of the U.S. Naval Academy and a U.S. Navy veteran, Perot has been known to apply his can-do optimism and take-charge approach to hostile situations abroad. During the Vietnam War he tried his best to execute the delivery by air of twenty-six tons of food to American POWs imprisoned in Hanoi. A decade later he engineered a daring rescue of two Electronic Data Systems employees held in Iran. That Iranian episode was the subject of *On Wings of Eagles,* a 1983 best seller written by Ken Follett.

From very early in his presidential campaign, Perot seemed to sense that television would be his vital friend. His campaign staff aggressively solicited invitations for him, and by election day Perot had appeared on thirty-three television talk shows.[7]

Though he promised a campaign of substance, not sound bites, Perot proved himself to be the master sound biter. Ingeniously synthesizing two bites from George H. W. Bush, Perot proclaimed that the nation's economy was "in deep voo-doo."[8] His vow to "clean out the barn" tapped into the widespread throw-out-the-rascals voter sentiment at the time. Sometimes he placed that populist aim into a more elegant frame: *taking back America.* Other clichés that Perot liked—"we can fix anything" and "when the rubber hits the road"—may not have been Perot origin-als, but they contributed to the candidate's image as a no-nonsense problem solver.

The effect of Perot's media outreach astounded nearly everyone. A Harris poll taken the second week in June showed Perot at 37 percent—four points ahead of Bush and seven ahead of Clinton. Other surveys produced similar results. Some media pundits began to speculate that 1992 could be remembered as the year when an outside challenger took from the major parties their lock and key on the White House.

By early summer things in the Perot camp seemed to sour. As he came to be seen as having a real shot at the presidency, he found himself the subject of intense media scrutiny. There were unfriendly opinion pieces, some describing paranoia and per-sonality quirks that could be presidential disqualifiers. Recast as a very public man, Perot must have felt discomfort in watching his privacy fade away.

To the surprise of nearly everyone outside his inner circle, Perot announced on July 16 that he was withdrawing from the presidential race. The cover of *Newsweek* the very next week carried his face with the caption "The Quitter!" Perot's critics declared that it was bizarre. Millions of those who had counted on him now came to see their former hero as a dilettante or worse. Though Perot eventually an-nounced that he was returning to the race, that did not occur until October 1. Many Perot loyalists forgave him and reenlisted, but many other erstwhile fans never returned to the fold.

What possessed him to withdraw is still far from clear. A *Vanity Fair* article charged that, driven by his paranoia, Perot had spied on the intimate lives of his daughter Nancy and a Jewish Vanderbilt University professor, and that he had with-drawn hoping to avoid media exposure of what he had done.[9] Nine days before the election, Perot insisted in a *60 Minutes* interview that he had withdrawn when he learned that because of his candidacy a Republican dirty tricks operation was harassing Carolyn—another Perot daughter—and threatening to disrupt her upcoming wedding. Perot may never really have withdrawn at all. During the days he was said to be out of the race, he spent a remarkable eleven million dollars on organization building and ballot petition drives.[10]

United We Stand: How We Can Take Back Our Country reached the bookstores in the third week in August. This, Perot's campaign platform, soon rose to the best sell-ers list, despite Perot having declared that his campaign was over. Long before the platform was published, he had declared his positions on some policy issues. Now, with his platform in print, the picture became clearer as to what a President Perot would support or seek. He adamantly opposed the pending free trade agreement with Mexico. He wanted fundamental changes to democratize American elections. He was for term limits, the line item veto, abortion choice, and gun control. The plainspoken Perot boldly promised that to bring the budget under control a Perot presidency would deliver both higher taxes—a rise in the maximum income tax rate, a phased-in increase in federal gasoline taxes, higher taxes on Social Security benefits—and substantial cuts in military spending and in expenditures for Medicare and other social programs.[11]

Announcing on October 1 that he was returning to the race, Perot acknowledged that his supporters wanted a world-class campaign and vowed that such a campaign is what he would give them. It was mainly television the independent candidate used as the 1992 contest neared its end: "In the last weeks of the race, Perot mounted the most expensive political advertising campaign in American history. In the first two weeks of October, he spent $24 million on commercials. In the next ten days he was to spend another $10 million. An hour-long infomercial, which aired . . . ten days before the national elections, cost close to an additional $1 million."[12]

In October, Perot joined Bush and Clinton in the three televised general election debates. James Stockdale, the retired U.S. Navy vice admiral and former POW Perot had chosen to run with him, participated with Dan Quayle and Al Gore in the one fall vice-presidential debate. That Perot and Stockdale were invited to debate was itself a milestone in the history of outsider challenges to duopoly. It was a hole that the duopoly would soon plug.[13]

Almost all media assessors awarded high marks to Perot for his debate performances. The same could not be said of Stockdale, whose opening remarks were two rhetorical questions: "Who am I? Why am I here?" Coming as they did from someone who, despite a distinguished military career and many decorations, still was unknown to the public, these may have been reasonable questions. But they led to a savagely clever parody on *Saturday Night Live*. Stockdale was typecast as someone unsure even of his own identity and doubtful of his qualifications for the vice presidency or presidency.

Perot-Stockdale appeared on the ballots of all fifty states and the nation's capital. That was thanks to Perot's organization and money but also to a small army of volunteers who had pounded the pavement collecting petition signatures. Perot's 19 percent share of all votes cast was the second biggest since the Civil War for a non-major-party ticket. It was bigger than any since the 1912 Progressive campaign of popular ex-president Teddy Roosevelt.

Perot's state-by-state popular tallies ranged from just under 9 percent in Mississippi to more than 30 percent in Maine and Alaska. Because his support was widely dispersed, he did not take electoral votes anywhere. The Perot-Stockdale ticket came in second in Maine and Utah, and it led the voting in sixteen counties (or equivalents) in Maine, Texas, Kansas, Alaska, Colorado, California, and Nevada.

Table 9.2 Demographic Groups and Voting for Ross Perot, 1992 and 1996
Percentage of Group Respondents Reporting That They Voted for Perot

	1992	1996
VOTE	19	8
Liberal Republicans	30	9
Moderate Republicans	21	7
Conservative Republicans	13	5
Liberal Independents	30	18
Moderate Independents	30	17
Conservative Independents	30	19
Liberal Democrats	11	4
Moderate Democrats	15	5
Conservative Democrats	16	7
Married men	21	10
Married women	19	7
Unmarried men	22	12
Unmarried women	15	7
Whites	20	9
African Americans	7	4
Latinos/Hispanics	14	6
Asians	15	8
White Protestants	21	10
Catholics	20	9
Jews	9	3
Born again/Religious Right	15	8
18–29 year olds	22	10
30–44 years old	21	9
45–59 years old	19	9
60 and older	12	7
Not a high school graduate	18	11
High school graduate	21	13
Some college education	21	10
College graduate	20	8
Postgraduate education	14	5
Household income under $15,000	19	11
$15,000–$29,999	20	9
$30,000–$49,999	21	10
$50,000–$74,999	17	7
$75,000–$99,999	16	7
More than $100,000	No data	6

	1992	1996
East	18	9
Midwest	21	10
South	16	7
West	23	8
Population over 500,000	13	6
Population 50,000–500,000	16	8
Suburbs	21	8
Rural areas, towns	20	10

SOURCE: Data from Voter Research and Surveys and Voter News
Service exit polls as reported in the *New York Times,* November 10, 1996.

For 1992 and also for Perot's second presidential run in 1996, the exit poll data in table 9.2 reveals the demographic groups friendliest and least friendly to candidate Perot. His strongest support came from independents, men, whites, young voters, and people in the West and Midwest. African Americans, Latinos, Jews, and city dwellers were among those least inclined to vote for him.

Clinton scored a decisive victory in 1992. He took nearly six million more votes than the incumbent president seeking reelection. He received 370 electoral votes—100 more than he had to have. But because of Perot, the victor's popular vote share—43 percent—was the second smallest in the twentieth century. Only Woodrow Wilson in 1912 finished with a smaller percentage.

There is still debate as to whether Perot spoiled the election for Bush and sent Clinton to the White House. In an election-day exit poll, Perot voters evenly split when asked whether, without Perot, they would have voted for Bush or for Clinton.[14] But polls also reveal that Republicans were more likely than Democrats to join with independents in voting for Perot. It is likely, though the evidence to confirm it is inconclusive, that it was Perot who tipped some of these states to Clinton in 1992: Maine, New Hampshire, West Virginia, Kentucky, Georgia, Louisiana, Montana, and Nevada.

The Reform Party

Regular Americans countrywide had taken up Perot's challenge and gotten his name placed on the ballot of every state. Millions more readied themselves to give him their votes. Perot understood that the popular movement that had arisen in support of his 1992 campaign was a significant, valuable thing. But by temperament and his long experience in the military and corporate worlds, he was a top-down leader uncomfortable with anything organized from the bottom up. Perot's popular movement was like a bird in a cage, fortunate to be well fed (for a while at least) by its wealthy master but yearning for freedom and for flight. Perot insisted on controlling the movement. His sharpest critics claim that he betrayed and emasculated it.

Ross Perot, a former navy
officer, speaking at "The
Time of Remembrance"
ceremony in Washington,
D.C., September 20, 2008.
Photograph by Jerry J.
Gilmore for the U.S.
Department of Defense.

The pattern of top-down control continued on after the 1992 election. United
We Stand America came to life early in 1993. Envisaged as a grassroots movement
to lobby against NAFTA and for policies dear to Perot and his followers, UWSA was
chartered in every state and directed by staffers paid by Perot.

In 1995 the movement assumed a new incarnation: the Reform Party of the USA.
Perot himself proclaimed the new party's birth, and he chose friendly turf on which
to do it. He made his announcement as a guest on the September 25 edition of *Larry
King Live*.

On July 9, 1996, former Colorado governor Richard Lamm declared that he was
a candidate for the Reform Party presidential nomination. The very next day Perot
appeared on *Larry King Live* to state that he too was joining the nomination race.[15]
To select a presidential candidate for 1996, the party mailed out ballots for supporters to mark and return.[16] Perot emerged the victor out of the bitter nomination
struggle. Lamm then declined to endorse the new nominee. His supporters insisted
that the selection had been rigged and corrupted by Perot loyalists.

On August 22, 1996, the Federal Election Commission certified Perot's eligibil-
ity, as Reform Party nominee, for FECA general election funds amounting to $29.1
million. It was the first time that a candidate not running as a major-party nominee

had ever received FECA general election funds before election day, and the money went to him because of the vote share he had taken in 1992.[17]

For Perot that was a leg up on Lamm or anyone else who might have been interested in the Reform Party nomination. Perot had run as an independent in 1992, and the funds could not have transferred to any Reform nominee other than him. He took the money, even though it was far less than the FECA funds that went to Bill Clinton and Bob Dole, the Democratic and Republican nominees. Legally he could have used private money to make up the gap. Perot had spent more than $68 million in private funds—mostly his own—on his 1992 campaign. But in 1996 he reportedly spent only $30.1 million, most of it FECA money. Dole and Clinton each spent more than twice that much.

Although television had been Perot's congenial ally in 1992, in 1996 it left him lost and forlorn. The networks were markedly unfriendly to his overtures to buy blocks of prime time for those signature Perot infomercials. More crucially the Commission on Presidential Debates denied him access to the fall debates.[18] That may have been the kiss of death for the 1996 Perot campaign—duopoly's signal to the electorate that it had taken him seriously in 1992 but that now he had become just another frivolous also-ran.

Perot and Pat Choate, the economist who ran with him, appeared on every November ballot in 1996. The 8.4 percent share they took was the fifth highest in the twentieth century for a nonmajor-party presidential ticket. But it was a disappointment to those who had hoped to confirm in 1996 that 1992 had marked the beginning of something big.

It was in Minnesota that the Reform Party achieved its most remarkable victory, and it came without any direction or financial support from Perot. Jesse Ventura, the party's gubernatorial candidate there in 1998, won a narrow victory with 37 percent of the votes.

Ventura's defeated opponents carried golden pedigrees in the establishment politics of Minnesota. They were Republican St. Paul mayor Norm Coleman and Democratic attorney general Hubert H. "Skip" Humphrey III. In a compelling case study, Micah Sifry points out vital factors that lifted Ventura up and set his path toward victory:[19]

- The flamboyant ex-wrestler (and former small-town mayor) carried loads of name recognition, even if most of it grew out of his involvement in a profession that is more theater than sport.
- The Ventura campaign understood that a victorious outcome rested upon the candidate's ability to enlist and mobilize the support of independents, blue-collar workers, and young voters.
- Ventura was included in the televised debates, and he shrewdly presented himself as the outsider, the regular guy who sent his kids to public schools. Viewers saw on stage "two 'suits' and one nonsuit—and most of them don't wear suits."[20]

- Due largely to Minnesota's generous and reasonably accessible campaign-funding policies, the Ventura campaign reached out effectively via television and radio.
- Minnesota allows election-day voter registration. Fifteen percent of those who voted on the day Ventura won registered as voters that day, and 78 percent of these new voters went for Ventura.

For third parties the alignment of moon and stars is seldom as perfect as it was for Jesse Ventura on November 3, 1998.

As promised during the campaign, Governor Ventura governed from the center. The chief executive blended mostly progressive social policies with fiscal conservatism. Many of his critics eventually conceded Ventura's gubernatorial accomplishments.

Already beset by internal fissures and other weaknesses by 1996, the national Reform Party went into a tailspin in 2000. That year rival Reform conventions separately nominated Pat Buchanan and John Hagelin. Buchanan was a well-known figure in conservative circles of the GOP. Hagelin was a leader and the standard-bearer of the Natural Law Party.

The Federal Election Commission declared Buchanan the Reform Party victor and gave him the $12.2 million in federal dollars to which the nominee was entitled

Minnesota governor Jesse Ventura meets with First Vice-Premier Li Lanqing on the occasion of a 2002 trade mission to China. Courtesy of Minnesota Historical Society.

because of Perot's votes in 1996. Hagelin's forces cried foul. Many Reform Party activists left the party because of Buchanan and the conservative influence he brought to their party. In the general election, Buchanan took 449,225 votes, less than 1 in every 200 cast.[21]

The Reform Party gave its 2004 endorsement to Ralph Nader, but the enfeebled party could contribute to Nader's independent candidacy only its few remaining ballot lines. A tiny party remnant that still lived on nominated Mississippian Ted Weill to run in 2008. Weill's vote tally was just 481 votes, all of them in Mississippi, the only state that listed his name.

Toward Reconfiguring the Movement: The Independence Party

Independent and *independence* were favored words to those who devoted themselves to the Reform Party. They brought to mind the American nation but also the pursuit of a course that was outside of—even subversive to—the rules and strictures of the partisan duopoly. Many would have dearly loved the name Independent Party for what they launched in 1995, but in many states that was a brand name either already taken or forbidden by state ballot rules.

Some of the state parties supporting Perot named themselves the Independence Party. One was in Minnesota. Minnesota's Independence Party adopted the Reform label in 1995 but returned to *Independence* five years later. New York's Independence Party never altered its name. Both the New York and Minnesota parties left the Reform Party orbit in 2000 as the influence of Buchanan and his conservatism took possession of the national party.

The New York and Minnesota Independence parties are vigorous and influential, though minor, participants in the politics of their states. One is a beneficiary of the practices—long established and widely accepted in New York—of cross-endorsement and fusion politics. The other operates as the third largest party in a state known for its rich third-party history. Minnesota's Independence Party has sometimes fielded well-known and experienced candidates. In three-way races for the U.S. Senate, its nominees took 15–16 percent of the votes in 2002 and 2008.

The Independence Party of America was born in 2007. It was launched from New York and is headquartered there. The New York and Minnesota parties stand as its nucleus, but in at least three other states, fledgling parties have now affiliated with the IPA. As an incipient movement, it has set out to reconfigure what Perot had set in motion—absent Perot himself—and to recast it into its original centrist or nonideological moorings.

10

★ ★ ★

Taking the Less-Traveled Road
Women, African Americans, Latinos

America never was America to me, And yet I swear this oath—America will be!"

Langston Hughes, "Let America Be America Again"

Right Is of No Sex—Truth Is of No Color.

Motto of the North Star, *the newspaper of black abolitionist Frederick Douglass*

We hold these truths to be self-evident: that all men and women are created equal.

Seneca Falls Declaration of Sentiments, 1848

May God write us down as asses if ever again we are found putting our trust in either the Democratic or Republican parties.

W. E. B. Du Bois, 1922

In building and then maintaining a political community that fully encompasses the nation's uncommon diversity, the United States continues to be, as always, a work in progress. One in eight U.S. citizens today is an African American. Some 16 percent of the population of the United States is Latino. Latinos, also known as Hispanics, are identified by ethnicity, not race.[1] Nearly two-thirds of the American people are non-Latino whites. Ancestors of many whites began their American journeys full of hope on Ellis Island in New York Harbor.

The American family histories of many contemporary African Americans began, by contrast, on Sullivan's Island, off Charleston Harbor, where people arriving as new slaves were quarantined before being put up for sale. Generations of their descendants endured slavery and then southern Jim Crow laws mandating segregation of the races. The Fifteenth Amendment (1870) forbade denial of voter rights "on account of race, color, or previous condition of servitude." Despite this constitutional change, disenfranchisement regimes grew up that, especially in the Deep South, purged African Americans from the voter rolls and kept many of them off well into the first years of the 1960s.

Though women are not numerically a minority group, discrimination—even in denial of the most fundamental right of true citizenship, the vote—has been a clear and undeniable factor in women's history. In the earliest years of America's independent nationhood, New Jersey alone gave the franchise to both male and female property owners. New Jersey women lost that right in 1807. Women in Wyoming Territory received the vote in 1869. By 1911 women had won the franchise in six states, all of them in the West. Eight more states gave women full voting rights between 1912 and 1918. The Nineteenth Amendment for women's suffrage nationwide won ratification and entered the Constitution in 1920. African American men's right to vote had gone into the Constitution a half century before that.[2]

American Latinos really are not one group but many. There are, among others, Chicanos—Mexican Americans—as well as Puerto Ricans and Cubans. Each U.S. Latino group holds its own historical narrative in relation to American history. Yankee (or "Anglo") hegemony has been a central theme in all of them. All American Hispanic groups have endured discrimination, though the patterns of that discrimination are as varied as the historical narratives themselves. Mexican Americans in particular are acutely aware of what many see as know-nothing calls for closing borders. After all, encompassed within U.S. territory there are some 850,000 square miles that once belonged to Mexico.

Hopelessly Devoted? Or Tempted to Stray?

What has possessed men and women who have been marginalized, or who belong to groups of people who have suffered years of discrimination, to enlist in minor parties—organizations that themselves reside at the margins of American politics? Most marginalized people do *not* join or support minor parties, and a decision to stick with the major parties should not be judged to be irrational. After all, the Republicans and Democrats hold the bulk of partisan power in making policy.

New African American citizens after the Civil War embraced the party of Lincoln. Most black Americans' loyalties to the GOP continued after Reconstruction passed away, and even after factions of white southern Republicans—the so-called Lily Whites—arose and then proceeded to divest the "Black and Tan Republicans" of their positions of party leadership and access to federal patronage.[3]

African American voters were at the center of a vast partisan realignment that clearly established the Democrats as the majority party in the 1930s. Although FDR had taken just 23 percent of their votes in 1932, 70 percent of African American voters voted for Democratic nominee Harry Truman in 1948.[4] Eighty-eight of every 100 blacks who voted in 2004 cast for Democrat John Kerry, and in the general election of 2008, Barack Obama took nearly 96 percent of the African American vote.

Like their male counterparts, most American women vote routinely for candidates of the major parties. For reasons that are still debated but that surely relate to the respective Democratic and Republican positions on social welfare, abortion, and war and peace, women since 1980 have been more disposed than men to voting Democrat for president. In both 2004 and 2008, the percentage of women voting for the Democratic presidential nominee was seven points higher than that of men.

The disposition of most Latinos who are politically active and motivated to vote—Latinos were just 8 percent of the voting electorate in 2004, 9 percent in 2008—tends toward the Democrats. Cuban Americans are an exception. Most American citizens of Cuban origin are conservative and Republican. Kerry won 53 percent of all Latino votes in 2004. Obama received 66 percent four years later.

Their stories are best recorded anecdotally, not statistically, but over the centuries thousands of women and minority people have moved away from the major parties and enlisted in third-party movements. Although their reasons for taking the less-traveled road have been as varied as the actors themselves, two overarching factors may have been at play, influencing many in their decision to go. First, minor parties embraced and pushed for—sometimes they even found their reason to exist in—issue positions that have been vital to the liberation of excluded or marginalized groups.[5] The Liberty Party of the 1840s took a forthright stand for the abolition of slavery. Liberty was followed in turn by the Free Soil Party and then by the early Republicans—third parties hostile to the expansion of slavery and seeking to bottle it up and contain it.

The national Democratic and Republican platforms did not bear provisions endorsing women's suffrage until 1916. The Prohibition, Equal Rights, Greenback, Socialist, National Woman's, and Bull Moose Progressive parties as well as some state affiliates of the People's Party (the Populists) all got to that position and set out to make it happen years or decades before either major party.

The second overarching factor is that some minor parties have for many years reached out to African Americans and women and welcomed their participation and leadership in party affairs. Even when most African Americans were slaves and most free blacks were disenfranchised, there were blacks in the ranks of Liberty Party leaders. In 1869 women took their seats as full voting delegates at the first national convention of the Prohibition Party.

African American voters were a vital constituency in the coalitions the Greenback and People's parties set out to build late in the nineteenth century, and black delegates were at these parties' national conventions. Female delegates took part in the national convention deliberations of the People's Party and of the Bull Moose Progressives.

When the times arrived for racial and gender barriers to be broken down, third parties have almost always arrived first—ahead of the Republicans and Democrats—as the agents to break them.

The Democrats in 1984 nominated Geraldine Ferraro for the vice presidency. It was the first time a major party had ever given its vice-presidential nod to a woman.

Sarah Palin, the first Republican woman nominated for the vice presidency, ran for that office in 2008. Nominated and elected in 2008, Barack Obama was the first African American ever chosen by a major party for the presidency. No major party has nominated a woman for president or a Latino for president or vice president.

In 1924—just four years after ratification of the Nineteenth Amendment— the Prohibition Party nominated a woman, Marie Brehm, for vice president. The Communist Party nominated James W. Ford, an African American man, for vice president in 1932, 1936, and 1940 and Charlene Mitchell, a black woman, for the presidency in 1968. Dozens of women, blacks, and Latinos have won the presidential and vice-presidential nominations of many third parties.

Alice Paul and the National Woman's Party

Although far from the first shot fired across the bow warning those who wanted to keep women voteless, the National Woman's Party may well have been pivotal.[6] Founded in 1913 by Alice Paul, age twenty-eight, and her closest friend Lucy Burns, the new association first took the cumbersome name Congressional Union for Woman Suffrage. It recast itself as the National Woman's Party three years later.[7]

Decades would pass before the dawn of the television era, but Paul and her party already realized the enormous publicity value of nonviolent direct action. Putting to full use picketing and demonstrations, the NWP came to be known as the militant wing of the suffrage movement. The party infused into that movement a radical vigor and strength that probably were decisive in the last years before adoption of the Nineteenth Amendment.

Paul and other NWP activists recognized that they stood on the shoulders of past suffrage giants. Out of the historic 1848 Seneca Falls Convention there had come the Declaration of Sentiments. Based upon the document by which the nation had declared its independence in 1776, the Declaration of Sentiments served as a manifesto for female suffrage as well as a call for independent, free lives for women.

There also were the legacies of nineteenth-century suffrage leaders Susan B. Anthony and Elizabeth Cady Stanton, and of Victoria Woodhull and Belva Lockwood, the first women ever nominated for the presidency. In 1914 the eighty-three-year-old Lockwood joined Paul and her followers in a demonstration on Capitol Hill. The young feminists who gathered that day must have sensed that the torch was being passed on to them by an earlier generation of their sisters in struggle.

Although it did not formally nominate candidates, the National Woman's Party took a strong interest in election outcomes. Republican Jeannette Rankin, the first woman ever elected to Congress, won one of Montana's two House seats in 1916. NWP enrollees or women closely allied with the party sometimes presented themselves as candidates. One was Anne Martin, who ran as an independent in 1918 for a vacant Nevada U.S. Senate seat. Martin finished third, with 4,603 votes, compared to the 12,197 for the Democrat who won.[8]

★ ★

Women, African Americans, and Latinos Prominent in Third Parties

Minor parties have set many of the nation's historic milestones in engaging women, African Americans, and Latinos—incorporating their interests and mobilizing their talents. Although the following lists are not complete, they illustrate the leading roles played by women and minorities in third-party and independent movements.

Historic Milestones
Pre–Civil War African American Party Leaders
Liberty Party (1840s): Samuel Ringgold Ward, Henry Highland Garnet, Frederick Douglass

First Woman Nominated for the Presidency
Equal Rights Party: Victoria C. Woodhull (1872)

Pre–Nineteenth Amendment Women Party Leaders
Prohibition Party: Frances E. Willard (late nineteenth century)
National Woman's Party: Alice S. Paul and Lucy Burns

First Woman to Cast Electoral Votes for President and Vice President
Bull Moose Progressive Party: Helen J. Scott, state of Washington (1912)

First Woman Nominated for Vice President after the Nineteenth Amendment
Prohibition Party: Marie C. Brehm (1924)

First African American Vice-Presidential Nominee of an Established Party
Communist Party: James W. Ford (1932, 1936, and 1940)

First African American Woman Nominated for Vice Presidency
Progressive Party: Charlotta A. S. Bass (1952)

First African American Presidential Nominee of an Established Party
Socialist Workers Party: Clifton DeBerry (1964)

First African American Woman Nominated for President
Communist Party: Charlene Mitchell (1968)

Early Minority-Only Tickets
People's Constitution Party: Ventura Chavez for president and Adelico Moya for vice president (1968)
Socialist Workers Party: Peter M. Camejo for president and Willie Mae Reid for vice president (1976)

First Woman Ever to Receive an Electoral Vote
Libertarian Party: Theodora B. "Tonie" Nathan, vice-presidential nominee (1972); vote cast by a Republican "faithless elector"

Early Women-Only Tickets

Equal Rights Party: Belva Ann Lockwood for president, Marietta L. B. Stow for vice president (1884)

Right to Life Party (New York): Mary Jane Tobin for governor, Ellen C. McCormack for lieutenant governor (1978)

Peace and Freedom Party: Maureen Smith for president, Elizabeth C. Barron for vice president (1980)

First Woman and First African American Whose Name Appeared on Ballots of All Fifty States and Washington, D.C.

New Alliance Party: Lenora B. Fulani, presidential nominee (1988)

African American Women Nominated Together for President, Vice President

Green Party: Cynthia A. McKinney for president and Rosa A. Clemente for vice president

Female and/or Minority Presidential Nominees

American Party: Diane B. Templin (1996)

America's Independent Party: Alan L. Keyes (2008)

Citizens Party: Sonia Johnson (1984)

Communist Party: Charlene Mitchell (1968)

Equal Rights Party: Victoria C. Woodhull (1872); Belva Ann Lockwood (1884 and 1888)

Freedom and Peace Party: Dick Gregory (1968)

Green Party: Cynthia A. McKinney (2008)

Looking Back Party: Isabell Masters (1992 and 1996)

New Alliance Party: Dennis L. Serrette (1984); Lenora B. Fulani (1988 and 1992)

Party for Socialism and Liberation: Gloria E. La Riva (2008)

Peace and Freedom Party: Eldridge Cleaver (1968); Maureen Smith (1980); Ronald Daniels (1992); Marsha Feinland (1996)

People's Party: Margaret Wright (1976)

Right to Life Party: Ellen C. McCormack (1980)

Socialist Party: Willa Kenoyer (1988); Mary Cal Hollis (1996)

Socialist Workers Party: Clifton DeBerry (1964); Linda Jenness (1972); Andrew Pulley (1980); James Warren (1988 and 1992); James Harris (1996 and 2000); Roger Calero (2004 and 2008)

Workers League: Edwin Winn (1984 and 1988); Helen Halyard (1992)

Workers World Party: Deirdre Griswold (1980); Larry Holmes (1984 and 1988); Gloria E. La Riva (1992); Monica G. Moorehead (1996 and 2000); John Parker (2004)

Women, African Americans, and Latinos Otherwise Prominent in Third Parties:

Women have run as vice-presidential nominees of the American Independent, Citizens, Communist, Consumer, Green, Libertarian, New Alliance, Peace and Freedom, Populist (1984), Progressive (1952), Prohibition, Reform, Right to

Life, Socialist, Socialist Equality, Socialist Labor, Socialist Workers, and Workers World parties.

African Americans and Latinos have run as vice-presidential nominees of the Communist, Green, New Alliance, People's (1972), Progressive (1952), Reform, Socialism and Liberation, Socialist, Socialist Equality, Socialist Workers, and Workers World parties, and of the 2004 and 2008 Nader independent campaigns.

Theresa A. Amato: campaign manager and in-house counsel for 2000 and 2004 Ralph Nader campaigns; author, *Grand Illusion: The Myth of Voter Choice in a Two-Party Tyranny* (2009)

Theodore M. Berry: Charter Party, first African American mayor of Cincinnati (1972–75)

Ella Boole and Leah Cobb Marion: Prohibition Party nominees for U.S. Senate, in New York and Pennsylvania, in 1920—year the Nineteenth Amendment was ratified

Elaine Brown: Chair, Black Panther Party, 1974–77

John L. Cashin: African American founder and gubernatorial candidate, National Democratic Party of Alabama, 1968

Benjamin J. Davis: Communist Party; elected to the New York City Council from Harlem, 1943, 1945; imprisoned during the McCarthy era

Elizabeth Gurley Flynn: Arrested during McCarthy era and imprisoned for two years; chair, Communist Party, 1961–64

Clara Fraser and Gloria Martin: Founding leaders of the Freedom Socialist Party

Matthew E. Gonzalez: Green Party nominee for governor of California three times; former elected member of San Francisco Board of Supervisors

Jose Angel Gutierrez, Rodolfo "Corky" Gonzales, and Mario Campean: Founders of La Raza Unida Party, 1970

Fannie Lou Hamer: Cofounder and leader of the Mississippi Freedom Democratic Party (1964)

John Roy Harper and James E. Clyburn: Early leaders of the United Citizens Party of South Carolina, founded in 1969; Clyburn later a prominent congressional Democrat

Helen Keller: Socialist Party activist and perennial campaigner for Eugene V. Debs; active in advocacy of rights of the disabled and in the movement for women's suffrage

Clennon Washington King Jr.: Early African American recipient of state-recorded popular votes; ran under the label Independent Afro-American Party (1960)

Erin McKee: Founder and state chair of South Carolina Working Families Party

Gayle McLaughlin: Active in Green Party; Richmond, California mayor, 2006–

Huey P. Newton and Robert George "Bobby" Seale: Founding leaders of the Black Panther Party

Kate Richards O'Hare: Socialist Party antiwar activist in World War I; imprisoned for violating the Espionage Act

Laureen Oliver: Cofounder and first state chair of the Independence Party of New York

Agnes L. Riddle: Progressive (Bull Moose) nominee for secretary of state, Colorado, 1914

Paul Leroy Robeson: Prominent friend of the Soviet Union and of the Communist Party USA; singer, actor, writer, athlete

Olga Rodriguez: Long-term leader in the Socialist Workers Party

Bayard Rustin and A. Philip Randolph: Socialist Party activists; later prominent figures in the civil rights movement

Mae A. Schunck: Lieutenant governor of Minnesota, 1999–2003; elected on the Reform Party ticket with Jesse Ventura

Cindy L. M. Sheehan: Independent candidate for U.S. House, 2008; antiwar activist

Louise Simmons: Scholar, political activist, a leader in People for Change, a significant Hartford, Connecticut, local party in the late 1980s and early 1990s

J. J. Spellman: African American nominee for Mississippi secretary of state on the 1881 Greenback-Republican fusion ticket

Bobbie L. Sterne: Charter Party, first female mayor of Cincinnati (1975–76, 1978–79)

Rose Pastor Stokes: Early activist in Socialist and then Communist parties

Alfredo Zamora: La Raza Unida Party, first Chicano mayor of Cotulla, Texas

————————————————— ★ ★ —————————————————

But to Martin and her NWP friends, that tasted like victory. Martin's campaign had moved many Nevada women, who had been empowered by the franchise only four years before, to turn out to vote for the first time in their lives.

The National Woman's Party worked to defeat Democratic men, even those who had proclaimed that they favored the vote for women. The Democrats, after all, held the White House from 1913 to 1921, and they enjoyed congressional majorities for most of those years. Paul and her followers believed that the governing party must be held to full account for not walking the walk even though some of its members already were talking the talk. The NWP sought Woodrow Wilson's reelection defeat in 1916 even after a speech the president made to the National American Woman Suffrage Association (NAWSA) in which he declared his support for women's suffrage.

NAWSA, the mainstream suffrage association at the time, claimed two million members. National Woman's Party tactics and militancy alienated NAWSA from the NWP. But they attracted to the party Mary Ritter Beard, Crystal Eastman, and other well-known movement radicals, and they brought stature to young Paul as one with real potential to lead the suffrage movement to accomplish its goal.

THE AWAKENING

Women's suffrage cartoon. In this cartoon the women of the states without the vote are reaching for the "Votes for Women" figure as she strides across the states where women have the vote. Cartoon by Hy Mayer. Originally in *Puck,* February 20, 1915. Courtesy of the U.S. Library of Congress Print and Photographs Division.

Born in New Jersey, near Philadelphia, Paul earned her B.A. at Swarthmore in 1905. Quaker by birth, she lived in American and British intentional communities—experiments in utopian social construction—during her first four years after Swarthmore. Paul was a brilliant student. In 1912 she completed a Ph.D. in political science at the elite ivy University of Pennsylvania. She earned two law degrees in the 1920s and was admitted to practice law by the District of Columbia bar.

Paul spent most of the years 1907–10 in England. There she met Lucy Burns. Contemporaries observed that the two women's personalities completed each other. Paul was the compulsive one, driven by devotion to principles and goals. Burns was the tactful, more likable pragmatist.[9]

They were in Great Britain as students, but Paul and Burns also became deeply involved in the British suffrage movement. Along with English friends, they more than once were arrested and jailed. England provided valuable training for what Paul led when she returned to the United States. It was there that she and Burns grasped the potential power of direct action. They also learned about mass-media interest in prisoners' hunger strikes, and that people would sympathize sometimes with their motives and goals.

Soon after returning to the United States, Paul and Burns joined the National American Woman Suffrage Association. By 1913 they found themselves in command of the Congressional Committee, the puny NAWSA arm for lobbying Congress. The new Congressional Committee regime immediately shifted the focus away from lobbying and toward publicity-grabbing demonstrations and pickets.

Beard gave the tactical shift its best theoretical formulation: large but powerless groups can develop their own power by becoming conscious of themselves and visible to others. It was a lesson that had been learned by Beard—and later by Paul and Burns—in British streets. It proved to be valuable instruction to other movements that arose in America in the second half of the twentieth century.

Paul's most memorable demonstration came at the beginning of her movement leadership. It was a march up Washington's Pennsylvania Avenue on March 3, 1913—the day before Wilson's first presidential inauguration. The number who walked—estimated at five to ten thousand—was remarkable, given transportation difficulties and the absence of instant communication at the time. Although it was authorized by a parade permit, the march was beset by hostile onlookers, who harassed, jeered, and even blocked the women who marched. The publicity from newspaper accounts was a priceless asset for the suffrage movement:

> Five thousand women marching . . . today practically fought their way foot by foot up Pennsylvania Avenue, through a surging throng that completely defied Washington police, swamped marchers, and broke their procession into little companies. The women, trudging stoutly along under great difficulties, were able to complete their march only when troops of cavalry from Fort Myers were rushed into Washington to take charge of Pennsylvania Avenue. No inauguration has ever produced such scenes, which in many instances amounted to nothing less than riots.[10]

> The women had to fight their way from the start and took more than one hour in making the first ten blocks. Many of the women were in tears under the jibes and insults of those who lined the route. At Fourth Street progress was impossible. Commissioner Johnson called upon some members of a Massachusetts National Guard regiment to help clear the way. Some laughed, and one assured the commissioner they had no orders to act as an escort. At Fifth Street the crowd again pressed in and progress was impossible. . . . Very effective assistance was rendered by the students of the Maryland Agricultural College. . . . It was where Sixth Street crosses the avenue that police protection gave way entirely and the two solid masses of spectators on either side came so close that three women could not march abreast. It was here that the Maryland boys formed in single file on each side of the [women] and became a protective wall. In front a squad of boys locked arms and formed a crowd-breaking vanguard. Several . . . were forced to use their fists in fighting back the crowd. . . . The parade itself . . . was a great success. Passing through two walls of antagonistic humanity, the marchers . . . kept their tempers. They suffered insult, and closed their ears to the jibes and jeers. Few faltered, though some of the older women were forced to drop out from time to time.[11]

In 1917 Paul, the National Woman's Party, and the direct action methods they had deployed endured their severest test. Beginning on January 10, the NWP took the step, radical and unprecedented in the history of the suffrage movement, of picketing the White House. The determined pickets kept their White House protest going over the ensuing months. The signs they made and carried mocked the notion that a country disenfranchising half its citizens was any fit model of democracy for the world. Some of the placards the pickets carried blasted the president as "Kaiser Wilson."

The women grew accustomed to occasional sneers or hostile remarks from passersby; but it was not until after the United States entered World War I that things turned dark for the determined pickets. In June and the months that followed, nearly five hundred suffragists were arrested, nominally for blocking traffic on the White House sidewalk. Both Paul and Burns were arrested at least twice in 1917.[12]

In October Paul and an ally on the picket line were tried and sent to prison under a seven-month sentence. Paul immediately announced that she was undertaking a hunger strike because her fellow suffrage inmates (including Burns) had not been accorded the status of political prisoners. Other incarcerated suffragists joined Paul in her hunger strike. She and the other strikers were repeatedly held down and force-fed. Paul was moved to the prison's psychiatric ward. After serving a month, she was released along with all the other imprisoned suffragists. Popular demand may well have been what freed them. On March 4, 1918, the D.C. Court of Appeals ruled that all arrests and convictions of the suffrage pickets had been illegal.[13]

By 1918 moral suasion and political pressure had apparently hit their mark. Wilson urged Congress on January 9, 1918, to pass the suffrage amendment as a "war measure." The House quickly approved it, the Senate passed it on June 26, 1919, and on August 18, 1920, Tennessee became the necessary thirty-sixth state to give its ratification. On August 26, 1920, women's suffrage entered the Constitution as the Nineteenth Amendment.

Their primary mission accomplished, Burns and others put political activism behind them as they got on with their lives. Not so Paul. Proclaiming that suffrage was just "a tiny step" toward the full liberation of women, she drafted a new provision of law and then set out to press Congress to propose to the states that it be ratified as a constitutional amendment: "Equality of rights under the law shall not be denied or abridged by the United States or by any state on account of sex. The Congress shall have the power to enforce, by appropriate legislation, the provisions of this article. This article shall take effect two years after the date of ratification."

The Equal Rights Amendment was first introduced in Congress in 1923. In 1972—just five years before Paul's death—Congress at last proposed its ratification to the states. Thirty-five states did pass it, but the campaign for ratification ended in failure in 1982, three states shy of the necessary thirty-eight.

The movement to ratify was mainly smothered by conservatives, who warned about the unisex restrooms and military barracks they said would inevitably result. But much of the initial opposition had come from the Left, from groups charging that the ERA would void legislation enacted for workplace protection of blue-collar women. Paul had given an acrid reply to her critics on the left. "Protective legislation," she said, is false "recognition of the inferiority of women."[14]

The National Woman's Party probably influenced the content of the Civil Rights Act of 1964. As drafted the bill prohibited discrimination based upon race, color, religion, or national origin. An NWP delegation—constituents of Democratic congressman Howard W. Smith of Virginia—went to the Capitol to urge their representative to broaden the bill's coverage to include sex. Smith readily complied and sponsored the change.

Although Smith was a stalwart supporter of the ERA, he was better known as an arch-segregationist. Many suspected that the reason he gave his support was to add baggage to the proposed civil rights legislation to burden the bill's supporters in getting it enacted. To the surprise of many, the act passed, "sex" and all.

The Sewall-Belmont House sits at 144 Constitution Avenue in Washington, D.C. Today it is an important museum of women's history and of the movements by women for suffrage and freedom. Sewall-Belmont has been the National Woman's Party headquarters for many years. This is the place where Paul lived in her middle and old age. It is close to the U.S. Capitol and just two miles from the White House sidewalk where young Alice Paul had taken her turns on the NWP picket lines.

Southern Black-Led Parties in the Civil Rights Era

Black-led biracial parties grew up in Mississippi, Alabama, and South Carolina in the 1960s. Most were satellites operating in the orbit of the national Democratic Party. Their goal was to purge the Democratic parties in their states of their devotion to white supremacy and to open them up to full African American participation.

In 1964 the Mississippi Freedom Democratic Party challenged that state's white anti–civil rights party establishment, demanding to become its replacement at the Democratic National Convention. Through the earthy eloquence of leader Fannie Lou Hamer, the MFDP spoke with moral authority as the voice for 850,000 voteless black Mississippians. The MFDP sent to the convention in Atlantic City a delegation of sixty-eight men and women. Although most were African Americans, the delegation also included four whites. The MFDP won praise in the media and the support of thousands of Americans. But the national party seated the full white regular Mississippi delegation and offered the MFDP just two seats "at large." A remarkably stingy offer, it was turned down. As Hamer put the matter, "we didn't come for no two seats when all of us is tired."[15]

With the encouragement and support of Stokely Carmichael and other young activists of the Student Nonviolent Coordinating Committee, the Lowndes County

Freedom Organization was born in 1965. Lowndes County, Alabama, was one of the poorest places in the nation. African Americans made up the vast majority of Lowndes people, but whites held all local power, and not a single black was registered to vote there at the beginning of 1965. Daily wages of black maids and farmhands ranged from three to six dollars. Lowndes was the place where in March 1965 a Ku Klux Klansman aimed his gun and murdered white civil rights worker Viola Liuzzo.[16]

Adopting the image of a black panther as its symbol, the Lowndes Freedom Organization came to be known as the Black Panther Party. Its seven candidates for county office carried guns throughout the campaign.[17]

Amid constant threats of economic reprisal, misleading newspaper ads placed by the local Democratic Party, censure of the Panther "extremists" by some in the local and national African American communities, and almost no support from President Johnson, the movement succeeded in registering 2,758 of Lowndes County's 13,000 voting-age African Americans in time for the November 1966 election. But through flagrant election fraud, the 2,823 registered whites (149 percent of the potential pool!) still outnumbered registered blacks. Despite all, the Freedom Organization candidates polled 42 percent of the county vote.[18]

John L. Cashin, a Huntsville dentist and civil rights activist, founded the National Democratic Party of Alabama in 1968. That year the state Democratic Party pledged its electors to former Alabama governor George C. Wallace. The NDPA served black and white Alabamians who were loyal to the national Democratic Party by providing the line for them to vote for nominee Hubert Humphrey. Running against Wallace in the 1970 gubernatorial race, Cashin took 125,491 (15 percent) of the votes. During its short life as a separate partisan force, the NDPA mobilized many newly enfranchised African Americans to elect black local candidates in Alabama's Black Belt.[19]

South Carolina's United Citizens Party, unlike the black-led parties in Mississippi and Alabama, continues on as a minor force in the politics of its state today. The UCP was born in 1969 to pressure a resistant state Democratic Party to nominate African American candidates. The party adopted a progressive platform and ran candidates of its own in 1970. None of them won, but by 1972 black South Carolinians already were winning nomination and election as Democrats. By 2009 African American legislators were holding nearly 20 percent of the seats in the South Carolina Senate and almost a quarter in the state house of representatives.[20]

The UCP history has been shaped by the fact that South Carolina, like New York, allows ballot-level fusion through cross-endorsement. The UCP cross-endorsed Democratic nominee George McGovern in 1972. By the late 1970s, the party had grown dormant, though it retained its place on the state ballot. Seeking ballot access everywhere in 1988, the New Alliance Party took possession of the UCP ballot position and used it to place New Alliance nominee Lenora Fulani before Palmetto State voters. The UCP cross-endorsed Reform Party nominee Ross Perot in 1996.[21]

The UCP provided its ballot line to the Nader campaign in 2000. The 2,124 South Carolina voters casting for Socialist Party nominee Walt Brown in 2004 found Brown's name on the UCP line. The party endorsed Barack Obama in 2008. Over the last decade, the UCP has cross-endorsed several Democratic nominees for the state legislature and the U.S. House.[22]

The Black Panther Party

The 1965–66 events in Lowndes County, Alabama, drew little attention from national media. But young black militants in faraway Oakland, California, were watching closely. There in 1966 Huey Newton and Bobby Seale set up the Black Panther Party. Borrowing "Black Panther," the popular second name of the Lowndes Freedom Organization, the Oakland-based Panthers also drew on its symbolism. Their banner showed a scowling panther ready for attack.[23]

Newton then was twenty-four years old, and Seale was just shy of thirty. They were friends. Both had been born in the segregated South but grew up in Oakland. Each had had his run-ins with the law and had served some jail time. Both were inspired by the life and philosophy of the slain Malcolm X.

The Black Panther Party became one of the most distinctive organizations in the New Left movement of the 1960s. Part of the reason lay in its symbolism, for example, the prescribed Panther uniform: blue shirt and black pants, leather jacket, and beret. Panther words and slogans—"All power to the people," "Off the pig," and others—found their way into New Left and counterculture rhetoric.

The disciplined life was a theme of Black Panther membership. Even the party rank and file were to be role models for young blacks in the liberation struggle. Panthers were supposed always to refrain from drugs, and they were not to use alcohol while on party duty.

Remembering Mao Zedong's axiom that "power grows out of the barrel of a gun," Panthers were to carry weapons, make them visible to all, and keep them loaded for use. Wherever they found police harassing people, Panthers were to confront them. Americans around the country first tuned into the Panthers when, toting guns, they muscled their way to the floor of the California assembly to protest a soon-to-be-passed 1967 bill that prohibited carrying loaded weapons in California's incorporated areas.

Black nationalism clearly influenced the party's ethos. The leadership positions the Panthers established bore labels like those in national regimes. Newton was his party's first chair, Seale the minister of defense. Eldridge Cleaver, whose autobiographical *Soul on Ice* brought the party valued publicity, was named minister of information. Stokely Carmichael, formerly of the Student Nonviolent Coordinating Committee, received the honorary title of Panther prime minister.

The Panthers saw African Americans as colonial subjects suffering injustices like those endured by third-world peoples of color. But the party rejected the emphasis black cultural nationalists were placing on African dress, language, and customs, and it dismissed the vision of some nationalists for an independent black nation as nothing more than an impossible dream. The Panthers' goal was to deliver to community residents full control over the police, schools, and other institutions operating within their community.

The Panthers' soul as a nonwhite party may have come right out of the pages of *The Wretched of the Earth,* the famed and powerful book by Frantz Fanon. A black psychiatrist from French Martinique, Fanon had worked in a French Algerian hospital while secretly giving aid and comfort to the Algerian revolutionaries. In his book he embraces violent struggle, not only for its efficacy in bringing liberation but also for what it does to the psyches of the oppressed. "At the level of individuals, violence is a cleansing force. It frees the native from his inferiority complex and from his self-despair and inaction; it makes him fearless and restores his self-respect."[24]

The Panthers never were ideological purists. They denounced the nationalist bias against whites in general—"black racism" the party called it—and embraced the Communist view that class was the key dividing line. The Panthers drew more inspiration from experience and practice in Mao's China and in Cuba and other developing socialist nations than from regimes in the Soviet Union and Eastern Europe. And they believed that their party was fulfilling the Leninist necessity of a vanguard party. That is why they were not concerned that even at their party's peak around 1970 membership never exceeded five to seven thousand. Their class analysis led them to seek white allies in the 1960s leftist movements.

Most white New Leftists were enraptured by the Black Panthers. White radicals were impressed by the militant style with which the Panthers confronted the power structure. As the New Left itself radicalized in the late 1960s, many young radicals looked to the Panthers as leaders in a revolutionary struggle.

Black Panther, the party newspaper, found an audience growing eventually to a quarter of a million. But the Panthers' most effective outreach work came in community organizing. They set up free clinics, ambulance services, legal aid, schools, and free clothing stores. From their Oakland base they built Panther chapters in forty cities across the nation. Prison inmates organized Panther units. Supporters turned out by the thousands for some Panther rallies. Public opinion polls revealed that at its popular peak the party had the strong respect of a quarter of all African Americans and of 43 percent of those under twenty-one years old.

Marlon Brando and other prominent white progressives contributed to the party. News that Leonard Bernstein gave a Panther fund-raiser at his New York penthouse outraged the nation's conservatives.[25]

Their rhetoric was revolutionary, their philosophy and style violent; but the Panthers did enter into electoral politics. Cleaver ran for the presidency in 1968 as the first Peace and Freedom Party nominee. Kathleen Cleaver, his Panther comrade and spouse, ran that year as a Peace and Freedom Party candidate for the California assembly. Seale came in second, with 43,710 votes (a 35 percent share) in his 1973 campaign to become Oakland's mayor. Panther support helped elect the first African American mayor of Oakland in 1977.[26]

Panther history is filled with stories of run-ins and scrapes with the law. Some of the cases contributed substantially to the party's revolutionary image among 1960s radicals.

In October 1967 Newton was arrested for killing a policeman. The police apparently knew that he was driving the car they stopped that day, and they stopped him just to make life difficult. Newton himself was seriously wounded in the shoot-out that followed. He was convicted of voluntary manslaughter in the death of the policeman, but the conviction was reversed because of errors the trial judge made. Two later trials brought hung juries, and Newton won release after three years in jail.[27] "Free Huey!" had arisen out of Newton's incarceration as a mantra for the Panthers and their leftist allies.

When Newton was imprisoned for killing the policeman, the Panther chair went to Seale. During the turbulent 1968 Democratic convention in Chicago, he flew to the Windy City to throw Panther support behind the huge antiwar, antiestablishment demonstrations there. There for just hours, he gave only two speeches. Seale's message was full of standard, violent Panther rhetoric: "Roast the pigs," "Barbecue some pork."

Seale's Chicago trip made him a defendant in the infamous Chicago Eight conspiracy trial. His seven codefendants had been leaders of the Chicago demonstrations. Among those standing trial were New Left activists Tom Hayden, David Dellinger, and Rennie Davis and counterculture leaders Abbie Hoffman and Jerry Rubin. Even though Seale had never met or talked with most of the seven, he was charged with them on the federal offense of "conspiring to travel interstate for the purpose of fomenting a public disturbance."

Seale in court demanded his constitutional right to a lawyer of his choosing and, because the lawyer he wanted was ill, a delay of trial. Judge Julius Hoffman denied both these demands as well as Seale's follow-up entreaty that he be allowed to defend himself. Thereupon Seale denounced the judge in his court as a "racist, fascist pig," and Hoffman ordered that Seale be gagged and chained hand-and-foot to his courtroom chair.

The ghastly spectacle of a black militant champion of liberation in chains made worldwide headlines. Judge Hoffman eventually dismissed Seale's conspiracy charge, and in a new trial Seale won release from serving the lengthy sentence Hoffman had imposed for contempt.[28]

The Panthers conveyed a macho image and style, and their party was slow in accepting the feminist movement. A Panther spokesman angered almost everyone else in attendance at the 1969 convention of Students for a Democratic Society when he referred to the movement for women's liberation as "pussy power." But there were women in the Panthers, and some of them eventually came to positions of party leadership. Angela Davis joined the Black Panthers in 1967, a year before she affiliated with the Communist Party. In 1970 Newton appointed women to the Black Panther central committee. Elaine Brown assumed the party chair in 1974, and over the next few years she and a Panther named Ericka Huggins held the party's top two leadership posts.

Brown and others who directed Panther affairs after 1970 were seeking to preserve a party that was in decline. Membership was dwindling, and there were bitter internal animosities. The public mood in the nation was trending conservative in the 1970s in reaction to the social upheavals of the decade before. It is likely that the Black Panther Party would have died out in the natural course of things.

But that is not the story of what killed the party. The Panther organization was destroyed by federal policy. It was stealth policy, discharged with very little scrutiny and reportage by media or push back from the public. Carried out by COINTEL-PRO—the FBI Counterintelligence Program—at the behest of longtime FBI director J. Edgar Hoover, it amounted to a systematic targeted assault, one that succeeded in eradicating the party.

In September 1968 Hoover declared that the Black Panther Party was the "greatest threat to the internal security of the country." By 1969 the Panthers had become the primary target of COINTELPRO.[29]

> Mark Albert, in . . . *The Sixties Papers,* explains how "the FBI special agents sought to divide the Panther organization by spreading false rumors and misinformation. They composed letters to party members implicating Panther leaders in stealing from the party treasury, taking money from the police, maintaining secret Swiss bank accounts, and having liaisons with white women."
>
> Standard COINTELPRO techniques included telephone interception, monitoring shipments of the *Black Panther,* and close surveillance of meetings, rallies, headquarters, and individuals. During 1969 alone, the FBI and police conducted thirty-one raids on Panther offices in eleven states. They also arranged assassinations. According to Frank Donner in *The Age of Surveillance,* twenty-eight Panthers were killed during an eighteen-month period in the late 1960s, "some direct victims of aggressive intelligence actions and others traceable to Bureau-assisted feuds."[30]

In their later lives, Newton and Seale, the party's founders, went out in divergent directions. Newton returned to Oakland in 1977 after three years of self-imposed exile in Cuba. He became burdened with drug and alcohol addictions, and in 1989 he was convicted of embezzlement. That was the year a drug dealer drew his gun on an Oakland street and took Newton's life. Newton was forty-seven years old.

Seale left Oakland and the Panthers in 1974. *Barbeque'n with Bobby,* a cookbook he wrote, was published in 1988. In his post-Panther life, Seale advertised for Ben & Jerry's, a progressive national ice cream chain. He also spent some years teaching African American studies at Temple University.

Latino Third Parties in the United States

In the commonwealth politics of Puerto Rico, the pattern of interparty competition resembles that of the American mainland. Two major parties prevail. The New Progressive Party seeks U.S. statehood for Puerto Rico. Two separate factions of the NPP are connected with the two national major parties. The Popular Democratic Party defends Puerto Rico's commonwealth status but calls for modifications, advantageous to Puerto Rico, in arrangements between Washington and San Juan. The PDP is affiliated with the national Democratic Party.

Partido Independentista Puertorriqueno

Third parties have been organized in Puerto Rico by the *independentistas*—people whose goal is Puerto Rican nationhood. El Partido Independentista Puertorriqueno—the Puerto Rican Independence Party—is the most prominent of the parties seeking an independent Puerto Rico. The PIP was founded in 1946. Advocating fundamental change, the PIP and other independence groups were closely surveilled by the FBI and subjected to many years of harassment and destabilization.[31]

The PIP is the only independence party possessing a position on the Puerto Rican ballot. It occasionally wins seats in the legislative assembly. The PIP is affiliated with Socialist International, the global association of socialist, social democratic, and labor parties.

Partido de la Raza Unida

Slates of Hispanic candidates won fifteen seats in April 1970 elections in Crystal City, Cotulla, and Carrizo Springs. Their victories in those Texas towns included two mayoralties and majority control of two town councils and two school boards.[32] The three towns had a lot in common. They were county seats in the far south of Texas. Well over three-quarters of their populations were Chicanos. Until April 1970 the Mexican Americans' share of local power had been far less than their numbers would have warranted.

What made the 1970 victories remarkable was what all local residents—Anglo as well as Latino—knew. Although these candidates won in elections that were officially nonpartisan, they had run as the nominees of a Chicano party that had come to life just three months earlier.

Their party, el Partido de la Raza Unida—the United People's Party (RUP for short)[33]—was born at a January 17, 1970, meeting attended in Crystal City by three hundred Mexican Americans. It was called by Jose Angel Gutierrez. Gutierrez was a

graduate student, still young but already a recognized leader of the Chicano movement in Texas.[34]

In Colorado too the RUP emerged in 1970. There Rodolfo "Corky" Gonzales, a
businessman and former professional boxer, was the movement's driving force.
During the course of the 1970s other Raza Unida chapters grew up in Arizona, New
Mexico, and California and even in Illinois, Wisconsin, and Washington, D.C.

The RUP was deeply rooted in the civil rights movement. There had been parties
organized along racial lines, but Raza Unida was the first national party in the
United States built on ethnic foundations. Anyone committed to the party's goals
was eligible for membership, but the shared commitment of its leaders and activists
was to mobilize and empower the impoverished and powerless Chicanos in the
U.S. countryside, towns, and urban barrios. They intended by their movement to
throw down the gauntlet electorally to what they saw as "two-party dictatorship":[35]
Republicans and Democrats, "one animal with two heads that ate from the same
trough."[36]

Achieving Texas ballot status in 1972, Raza Unida ran that year candidates
for governor and other statewide offices. Ramsey Muniz was its gubernatorial nominee. The RUP chose Alma Canales to run for lieutenant governor. Canales was, at
twenty-four, younger than the minimum constitutional age for the office she
sought. Her nomination helped cut through the party's *machismo* image, and it sent
a message of welcome to Chicanas.[37] The party competed in later Texas elections in
the 1970s, and in that decade it offered nominees in Colorado and other states. In
places where the RUP did not have ballot access, it sometimes fielded candidates as
independents.

The party held its first (and only) national convention in El Paso in 1972. The
demographic profiles of those who attended—estimates range from 1,500 to 3,000—
attested to the party's vigor. Participants came from eighteen states. About half were
women, and gathered in El Paso were large numbers of the middle aged and seniors
sitting alongside the many who made up the party's young activist core.[38]

The RUP ultimately failed to build a strong, durable national governing body.
This could be attributed in part to a sustained and bitter rivalry between Gutierrez
and Gonzales, the party's two *caudillos*. The personal ambition to lead was one
problem their party faced, but there also was strife growing out of the sharp ideological cleavages within Raza Unida.

The ideological perspectives its leaders and activists brought to the RUP were like
concourses in a transportation terminal. Although they frequently intersected, they
presented views, each in contrast to the other, about the direction in which Raza
Unida should go.[39]

Many brought to the RUP a populism that was devoted to the enactment of
redistributive policies set up to deliver direct benefits to poor and marginalized people. Gutierrez was a populist. Populism was particularly strong within the Texas

RUP, and the platform adopted by the national party at its 1972 El Paso convention was distinctively populist in flavor. *Yo Soy Joaquim* (I Am Joaquim) is a poignant epic poem—a paean to Chicano ethnicity convincing to many that the nationalist claim to an independent Chicano homeland in the Southwest is legitimate. Gonzales wrote it in the 1960s. The impact of *Yo Soy Joaquim* everywhere in the Mexican American community undergirded Gonzales's stature in Raza Unida and contributed to the substantial influence of Chicano nationalism within his party. Finally within the party there also were veterans of the Communist, Socialist Workers, and other old leftist parties who brought their ideologies with them and worked to influence RUP.

La Raza Unida as a national party came to an end just before the beginning of the Reagan era. Certainly the RUP had been weakened by the personal rivalries and ideological strife that were features of party life. But the party's fatal wounds may have been those that also have killed off so many other minor parties—the decision of potential supporters to vote strategically—to hold their noses and vote for the lesser of the (only) two evils with the power to win.

For the RUP there is no present, but there may be a future. Today La Raza Unida organizing committees cling to life in several southwestern cities. As the nation's policy agenda inevitably returns to the difficult and unfinished business of charting a fair, effective immigration policy, the party may arise again as a voice for Mexican Americans.

11

★ ★ ★

Doctrinal Parties 1
The Socialists and Communists

[While] there is a lower class, I am in it; while there is a criminal element, I am of it; and while there is a soul in prison, I am not free.

Eugene V. Debs, upon his conviction of sedition in 1918

Are you now, or have you ever been, a member of the Communist Party?

Congressional query during the McCarthy period

There are times—rare ones—when a provocative, even outrageous act by a very small group at the distant edge of the political periphery can impact constitutional development and public policy. On June 21, 1989, the United States Supreme Court invalidated a Texas law that had banned the desecration of the American or Texas flag. The high court also set aside both the conviction and sentence—one year in prison and a two-thousand-dollar fine—of one Gregory Lee "Joey" Johnson.

Back in the summer of 1984, Johnson and his comrades in the Youth Brigade of the Revolutionary Communist Party had stolen and besieged an American flag. Johnson doused the cloth in kerosene and set it ablaze. As the flag disintegrated, Johnson's group chanted "America, red, white, and blue, we spit on you." They planned their demonstration to capture media attention. The RCP and its Youth Brigade chose Dallas at the time that Texas city was hosting the Republican National Convention.

In 1989 the Supreme Court found flag burning to be a constitutionally protected First Amendment right of symbolic speech. In overruling the statute from the Lone Star State, it also invalidated in effect similar laws in many other states. Anthony Kennedy and Antonin Scalia, two Reagan appointees, joined liberals William Brennan, Thurgood Marshall, and Harry Blackmun to make up the slender 5–4 majority.[1]

The hostile reaction to the high court's flag-burning decision could not have surprised anyone inside the Revolutionary Communist Party. Much of the public, along with President George H. W. Bush, demanded action. Many in Congress said that what was needed was a flag-protection amendment inserted into the Constitution.

Instead Congress passed a flag-protection act much like the state statutes the Court invalidated in 1989. In 1990 the Supreme Court declared this congressional act to be unconstitutional too.[2]

The Other Red America: The Socialist and Communist Left

In today's political lexicon, blue states are reliably Democratic. Red states, by contrast, are safe Republican turf. What a curious irony. Red now is shorthand for America's major conservative party. To people on the Far Left, that may seem like theft.

For many years now, in America as abroad, red has been a proud emblematic color for just about everyone left of liberal except for the Greens. Socialist Party nominee Eugene V. Debs campaigned for the presidency through whistle stops made on his Red Special train. *Red Chicago* is a recent book on the Depression-era Communist movement in the Windy City.[3]

From 1844 until the death of Karl Marx in 1883, Friedrich Engels was Marx's friend, intellectual collaborator, and frequent patron. A letter of lament the elderly Engels sent in 1893 to a Communist comrade living in the United States has been published under the title "Why There Is No Large Socialist Party in America."[4] Engels's answers to the question may be subject to challenge, but the premise of his letter is not. Unlike almost every other Western democracy, in the United States no party labeling itself Labor, Socialist, or Social Democratic, much less Communist, has ever become a major national party.

The Socialist Labor Party

Many have tried. Although historically the most significant, the Socialist Party and Communist Party USA are far from being the only national parties in this red America. They are not even the oldest.

Having emerged in 1876–77, the Socialist Labor Party in 2008 ranked fourth—behind the Democratic, Republican, and Prohibition parties—in longevity among living American parties.[5] Although it rejected Leninism, the body of thought associated with the principal founder of the Soviet state, the SLP considered itself to be revolutionary Marxist.

Daniel De Leon (1852–1914), a brilliant but rigidly doctrinaire figure, joined the party in 1890. The distinguishing features of the SLP outlook over the nearly 120 years that followed were De Leonist. Heavily influenced by French syndicalism, De Leon was convinced that the agency for the workers' revolution to come lay in industrial unionism, and he insisted that his party devote energies and treasure to construction and nourishment of the revolutionary industrial union.

The SLP was electorally active for many years, though its campaigns produced meager fruit. The party ran candidates in every presidential race from 1892 through 1976. By 1981 it had given up all participation in electoral campaigns, but for years after that it continued to publish and disseminate the *People,* the SLP newspaper. In 2008 the party closed down its national office. That seemed a signal that for the nation's longest-lasting socialist party, the light had finally flickered out.[6]

The Socialist Party

The Socialist Party of America was born at a founding convention in Indianapolis in 1901.[7] In its prime, it enjoyed remarkable success in electing candidates to local office, to legislatures in a handful of states, and even an occasional nominee to the U.S. House. The party attracted into its rank and file distinguished and talented people from nearly every field—people such as Carl Sandburg, John Dewey, Jack London, Helen Keller, Upton Sinclair, Charles Beard, Margaret Sanger, Thorstein Veblen, Walter Lippmann, and Reinhold Niebuhr.

Leading in the party's birth were Morris Hillquit, Eugene V. Debs, and Victor L. Berger. A dissident faction of the Socialist Labor Party had followed Hillquit in leaving in 1899. In 1898 Debs and Berger had joined together to launch the Social Democratic Party—a precursor, as it turned out, of the Socialist Party—and Debs had stood as the SDP presidential nominee in 1900.

Hillquit and Berger were ethnic Jews who had been born in Eastern Europe. Debs was the fifth child of French-Alsatian immigrants who had arrived, penniless, in the States six years before his birth. The three men's ethnic backgrounds reflected those of the many foreign-born or second-generation Americans who provided a substantial share of the support America's Socialist and Communist parties received in their early years. Hillquit and Berger were to play prominent roles in the Socialist Party in its first generation.

But it was Debs who came to be remembered as the most important leader that American Socialists ever had. He is a towering figure in both labor and third-party history. People in Debs's native Terre Haute and others who came to know him said that his strength lay in his personality and a social consciousness rooted in his own life experience. Debs was "fierce in his convictions, kind and compassionate in his personal relations."[8]

When he was fourteen, Debs quit school to work on the railroad. His first job— a grimy, nasty one that earned him fifty cents a day—was to scrape grease from steam engines. He rose within eighteen months to become a locomotive fireman, and by the time of his twentieth birthday he was involved in union activity.

Debs became president of the new American Railway Union in 1893. The ARU was organized not as craft unions were but on the more militant lines of industrial unions. In 1894 the ARU gave its support to striking Pullman Palace Car Company workers by refusing to handle Pullman rolling stock. President Grover Cleveland, a Democrat, intervened on the corporate side, dispatching troops to the strike scene. A federal court in Chicago issued an antistrike injunction, and Debs found himself sentenced to half a year in prison.[9]

This, the first of two times Debs was imprisoned for his political activity, gave him the opportunity to read the works of Karl Marx. His incarceration also made his name known in blue-collar homes nationwide.

Upon release Debs briefly participated in the Populist movement but then landed for good at the center of the drive for democratic socialism. He joined "Big Bill" Haywood, "Mother" Mary Jones, and others in launching the radical syndicalist Industrial Workers of the World in 1905. Haywood and Debs were personal friends, and they remained so even after a damaging permanent break between IWW and the Socialist Party—a rift occasioned by Haywood's fiery speeches advocating direct action and even industrial sabotage.

The Socialist Party was at its zenith during the years 1912–14. Formally enrolled members in 1912 numbered 118,045. More than three hundred party-affiliated English- and foreign-language publications were reaching over 2 million readers. The *Appeal to Reason,* the party's most important newspaper, claimed a weekly circulation of three-quarters of a million.

Elected to the U.S. House in 1910, Berger was representing Milwaukee in Congress in 1912. Twenty Socialists sat in the legislatures of New York, Pennsylvania, Rhode Island, Oklahoma, Wisconsin, and California. Socialists held 79 mayoralties and 1,200 local offices in 340 cities in 1912.

In the fourth of five presidential campaigns he waged, Debs took 6 percent of the vote that year. That was remarkable considering that 1912 was when popular ex-president Teddy Roosevelt campaigned for the presidency on another third-party ticket. Debs took one vote in six in Nevada and Oklahoma and more than one in ten in five other states.

By 1914 the number of Socialist state legislators had increased to thirty-one. In Oklahoma alone there were twelve thousand dues-paying members and one hundred Socialist local officeholders.[10] In 1914 New York Socialist Meyer London won the first of two consecutive elections as representative of a congressional district on the Lower East Side.

Haywood, the IWW leader, was expelled from the SP national executive committee in 1913. It was a political act taken to reach voters alienated by IWW radicalism, but the practical effect of this break with the IWW was to separate the party from a substantial part of its base of support. Within a year the Socialist Party had lost a third of its members.

Other damaging wounds were about to arise to affect the party. Although not fatal, they enfeebled the Socialist Party, leaving it in a state from which it could never fully recover.

World War I and the First Red Scare

America's first Red Scare began with the nation's entry into World War I. The governmental sanctions arising from it would impact Socialists, Communists, and anarchists. The Socialist Party and its antiwar leaders were among their earliest targets.

Woodrow Wilson had won reelection in November 1916 on the reminder that "he kept us out of war." Millions of Americans were unconvinced that circumstances had changed so drastically that a declaration of war was justified just five months later. Among Socialists there were many who were pacifists, whose ancestry was rooted in nations now declared to be America's enemy, or who had come to believe that Lenin was right that the blood and lives of the working class were what the capitalists were using to fight their capitalist war.

For a vigorous antiwar speech he gave in Canton, Ohio, on June 16, 1918, Debs was convicted of violating the Espionage Act and the Sedition Act, two remarkably repressive measures passed during the war.[11] He served two years and eight months of a ten-year sentence, finally securing pardon and release by President Warren Harding. Undoubtedly a prisoner of conscience—in a nation that long denied that it took political prisoners—Debs ran for the presidency for the fifth and last time in 1920 as an inmate of the Atlanta Federal Penitentiary. Nearly a million Americans gave the voteless prisoner their votes.

About the circumstances of Debs's release, historian Howard Zinn wrote that

> Debs had won the hearts of his fellow prisoners. . . . He had fought for them in a hundred ways and refused any special privileges for himself. On the day of his release, the warden ignored prison regulations and opened every cell-block to allow more than 2,000 inmates to gather in front of the main jail building to say good-bye to Eugene V. Debs. As he started down the walk-way from the prison, a roar went up and he turned, tears streaming down his face, and stretched out his arms to the other prisoners.
>
> Sam Moore, a fellow inmate, remarked how he felt as Debs was about to be released on Christmas Day, 1921: "As miserable as I was, I would defy fate and all its cruelty as long as Debs held my hand, and I was the most miserably happiest man on Earth when I knew he was going home Christmas."[12]

Although the first Red Scare eventually ran its course, it left a culture changed in its wake. *Socialism* had become a toxic, poisonous word, connoting something that many Americans were led to believe was sinister, evil, and oppressive. And so it has remained to the present day. Events in faraway Russia also diminished the party. Inspired by the Bolshevik Revolution and the advent of the new Soviet era, many in the Socialist Party's left wing departed in 1919 to begin building the new American Communist movement. It was a substantial loss for the party.

After Debs

The Socialist picture was not without some bright spots even as the Socialist Party entered its post-Debs era. Both Socialist former congressmen returned to the House in the 1920s. London went back for one term. Twice denied his House seat due to

SOCIALIST PARTY
FOR PRESIDENT

EUGENE VICTOR D

Eugene V. Debs in prison uniform. Convicted for his antiwar and anti-draft advocacy, Debs was a federal prisoner when he ran his fifth (and last) campaign for the presidency in 1920. Courtesy of the Eugene V. Debs Museum, Karen Brown, director.

his antiwar agitation, Berger returned for six more years. Socialists in Reading, Pennsylvania, swept the mayoralty and the other elected municipal seats in 1927. Socialist Jasper McLevy served continuously as mayor of Bridgeport from 1933 to 1957.

Milwaukee was the party's largest and longest-lasting "pink" city. Socialists held the mayoralty in Milwaukee for thirty-eight of the fifty years from 1910 until 1960, and the party won many council elections over those years. Milwaukee Socialists came to be known as "sewer Socialists" because they downplayed ideology and focused upon the quality of services delivered to city residents.

The Socialists threw their support behind Robert La Follette and his Progressive campaign in 1924. Returning to its own, the Socialist Party then nominated Norman M. Thomas for the presidency in 1928. That was be the first of six consecutive elections (1928 through 1948) in which Thomas bore his party's presidential standard. Thomas's most substantial result—2.3 percent—came in 1932. His share of the votes in the other five was always under 1 percent.

Though he never possessed Debs's internal authority over party affairs, Thomas was for nearly thirty years the leading national voice of the Socialist Party. Ordained, like his father, as a Presbyterian cleric, he had come to Socialism by a path very different from that by which Debs had come. But Thomas was a pacifist, and his views on social justice were every bit as radical as Debs's.

The Great Depression substantially altered the nation's political climate, and despite the baggage his party shouldered because of its name, Thomas and the Socialist Party were able to serve as a kind of left-wing conscience for the Democratic Party and the administration of Franklin Roosevelt. Demands the Socialists had made in their platform planks—for social security, public works programs, union rights and collective bargaining, public housing, and public ownership of electric power—found their way into New Deal measures advanced by the administration.

There were Socialists who suspected that history was about to repeat. Less than forty years had passed since the Democrats, having gobbled up crucial issue positions of the Populist movement, went on to devour the People's Party itself. The dread now was of co-optation. Some Socialists feared that the fate of the Populists could be awaiting their own party. This, rather than serious electoral hope, may be what underlay their devotion to fielding their own presidential candidate in every election in which Roosevelt was involved.

A maelstrom of irreconcilable viewpoints came to beset this multitendency party in the 1930s. There were, among others, the social democrats, a group of Trotskyists, and a contingent of people pressuring the Socialists to embrace the Communist-led worldwide Popular Front against rising fascism.

A contentious 1934 Declaration of Principles—the product of SP radicals—dedicated the party to "organizing and maintaining a government under the workers' rule." Thereupon, charging that this new declaration was communistic, many nonradical social democrats withdrew from the Socialist Party. They took with them a substantial portion of the party's human talent and media resources. Those who withdrew reconstituted themselves as the Social Democratic Federation, and many of them thereafter cast their votes for Roosevelt rather than Thomas. The SP and the SDF reconciled and merged in 1968, thirty-four years after the damaging split occurred.[13]

As the state-level agents of duopoly set the qualifications for ballot access so high that many of them finally became impossible for the Socialist Party (like other minor parties) to surmount, the Socialists after 1956 withdrew from running presidential candidates. Socialist partisans from that point on engaged in serious debate as to whether even to maintain their old party.

For the majority the answer was no. What was needed, they said, was not a third party but a meaningful, ideologically altered second one—the Democrats. Also pointing out that organized labor had long ago aligned itself with the Democratic Party, they contended that democratic socialists should be where labor is.

The minority dubbed themselves the Debs Caucus. They resolved to preserve or reconstitute the Socialist Party as an electoral party and to devote themselves to its support.

Associations emerged out of this split. Two of them currently exist as devotees of socialism in the United States. The Democratic Socialists of America, a nonparty group with ten thousand dues-paying members, operates outside the Democratic Party but also within that party's liberal/progressive wing.[14]

The Socialist Party USA claims to be the direct lineal descendent of the electoral Socialist Party of America—the party of Debs. Frank Zeidler, the Socialist mayor of Milwaukee from 1948 to 1960, was the first SPUSA presidential candidate in 1976. The party endorsed Citizens Party nominee Sonia Johnson in 1984, but it has run its own presidential candidate in every other election since 1976.

The Communist Party USA

In the 1981 film *Reds*—a courageous work, given the memories in Hollywood of McCarthy-era blacklisting—there is an intense scene in which the left-wingers storm off the floor of the 1919 Socialist Party convention, loudly singing the "Internationale" as they go. The people that scene depicts were on their way to participate in the first wave of American involvement in the new international Communist movement. Their departure was technically an expulsion; but it was a moment forced by the party's Communist wing, which had determined either to seize control of the Socialist Party or to desert it.

American Communism in its infancy already was being torn by sectarian strife. Two parties arose, each claiming the exclusive right to organize the Communist movement in America. Inspired by revolutionary events in the country of their birth or ancestry, ethnic Russians organized and led the Communist Party of America, and many of the party's participants were émigrés with almost no fluency in English. The Communist Labor Party sought a more distinctly American identity capable of reaching the native born among the laboring masses.

John Reed, a prominent leader of the CLP, wrote *Ten Days That Shook the World*, a laudatory account of the Bolshevik Revolution, which he had observed firsthand. Reed died of typhus in Moscow in 1920 at age thirty-three. The Soviets honored him by burial in Red Square with a plaque on the wall of the Kremlin.

Deployed during the closing year and a half of the Wilson era, the anti-red Palmer Raids were a ferocious federal assault upon Communist and anarchist movements in the country. Ten thousand leftists were rounded up, and many who were foreign born were deported. For a while both Communist parties were forced to operate underground.

The two new American Communist parties merged in 1921. They apparently received instructions to do so by the Communist International, the new Soviet-directed association of Communist parties. Because of its third place in a historical line of international leftist associations dating from 1864, scholars often referred to this new international Communist organization as the Third International. Most people called it the Comintern.

America's newly united Communist party initially labeled itself the Workers Party for the purposes of the presidential campaigns it waged in 1924 and 1928. It finally settled in 1929 on Communist Party of the USA.[15]

Joseph Stalin emerged the victor by 1927–28 in a bitter struggle with Leon Trotsky to succeed the dead Lenin at the helm of Soviet power. Drawing their strength from the triumph of Stalin, the Stalinists in CPUSA purged the party of its Trotskyists.

For over six decades the CPUSA was franchised by Moscow as the U.S. representative in the world Communist movement. Existing as it did, in the belly of the beast—on the very turf of the capitalist superpower—the American party must have been highly valued by the Soviet regime and ruling party.

Documents available since the Soviet collapse confirm that the CPUSA became a beneficiary of Soviet largesse. The American party received a $2.5 million grant from Moscow in 1980. That was far and away the largest grant shelled out by the Soviets to any of their fraternal parties that year.[16] Despite its leaders' criticism and warnings about Mikhail Gorbachev–era *glasnost* and *perestroika,* the CPUSA as late as 1988 received a Soviet grant of two million dollars.[17]

1930–1948

Communists' impact on the national mainstream was strongest during the Depression years and World War II. From an enrollment of less than ten thousand in 1929, the CPUSA grew by 1944 to a record high of eighty thousand. Membership in the Young Communist League may have been even larger than that of the adult party then.

The party's highest presidential tally—103,307 votes—was achieved by William Z. Foster in 1932. The CPUSA even came to taste some electoral success. Under a proportional representation system used for a decade but abandoned in 1947, New York voters elected Communist candidates Peter V. Cacchione and Benjamin J. Davis to their city council. Cacchione won three elections to the council from Brooklyn. Davis, an African American Harlem resident, twice won one of the Manhattan seats.

The CPUSA influenced large sectors of the labor movement, especially unions affiliated with the Congress of Industrial Organizations. For years the party controlled unions of miners, electrical workers, longshoremen, and seamen. It worked to unionize southern textile workers, and it organized a union of black sharecroppers.

In its flush years, as in the lean ones, the CPUSA has had some success in building a base of support among African Americans. In the early 1930s, the party called for black self-determination in black-majority areas of the South. It broke new historical ground when in 1932 it nominated African American James W. Ford for the vice presidency. African Americans as distinguished as W. E. B. Du Bois and Paul Robeson became devotees; so, later on, did Angela Davis, the scholar and social activist who ran as the Communist candidate for vice president in 1980 and 1984.

Under the leadership of Earl Browder from 1934 to 1945, the CPUSA line paralleled that of Moscow. No longer agitating for worker revolution, the party embraced the antifascist Popular Front in 1935. Party leaders and the party press began to praise Roosevelt and the New Deal. "Communism is twentieth-century Americanism" became the party's public slogan, and it is said that in the late 1930s comrades attending party meetings recited the Pledge of Allegiance.[18]

The CPUSA sought to connect with, and often to dominate, other "progressive" or antifascist associations. Many young Communists and other leftists went to fight on the antifascist side in the Spanish Civil War in the late 1930s.

Communists worldwide deserted the Popular Front when, in 1939, the Soviet Union and Nazi Germany entered into a Non-Aggression Pact. They returned to it in 1941 as Germany launched its invasion of the Soviet Union. In deference to his wartime capitalist allies, Stalin formally terminated the Comintern in 1943.

American Communists strongly supported and influenced the 1948 Progressive Party campaign, and for years after they remembered it as the last, dying gasp of the Popular Front. But by 1948 Cold War hostilities had plainly replaced whatever wartime felicity had been felt in the allied relationship between Washington and Moscow. Already by 1946, General Secretary Browder had been accused by his CPUSA comrades of "deserting to the side of the class enemy" and purged from the party.[19]

After 1948

With the Cold War came the second Red Scare. A valued, even decisive, ally during World War II, the Soviet Union now was appearing in the American psyche as rival superpower, ideological foe, and nuclear threat. The CPUSA, the party known for its fidelity to the Soviet line, was sure to be singled out in the rising anticommunist panic. Red-baiting was political capital valuable to Sen. Joseph McCarthy, members of the House Committee on Un-American Activities, and others. It cannot be denied that defense of the nation's security was a part of what motivated those who fanned the flames. But it is also true that political careers soared from the demagoguery of some of the shrillest of the period's red-baiters.

Although the CPUSA was the identified target of the anticommunist reaction, the nation itself was severely damaged. The China experts at the State Department, Robert Oppenheimer (the "father of the atomic bomb"), and other vital public servants were fired or lost security clearance. Ubiquitous blacklisting remolded Hollywood films, radio, and television into dull, soft, gutless media and kept many of the most creative writers and performers out of their crafts for years. The labor movement was weakened. Professors, teachers, and union leaders lost their jobs because they were suspected of being "fellow travelers" or they simply refused (often on principle) to sign loyalty oaths. Freedom itself was in serious jeopardy.

Of the many official sanctions against the party itself, two may have pierced and wounded CPUSA most deeply: the arrest and long imprisonment of top and middle-level CPUSA leaders, paralyzing the party in the conduct of its business; and new sedition laws passed in many states that made mere membership in CPUSA a crime punishable by long terms in prison.

Government repression during the second Red Scare very nearly destroyed the Communist Party. Nearly a third of the five thousand who were still enrolled in the party in the mid-1950s may have been spies for the FBI. The Supreme Court invalidated most of the legal sanctions erected during this period, and CPUSA membership rose to what may have been as many as fifteen thousand by the late 1980s. But the party had fallen much too far ever to recover all it had lost. Its effort to do so had been stymied in part by the second-punch blows delivered by COINTELPRO.

After a long hiatus, the party did return to presidential politics in the late 1960s. Charlene Mitchell was the party's presidential candidate in 1968. General Secretary Gus Hall became his party's standard-bearer for the four presidential rounds between 1972 and 1984. No longer fielding a presidential candidate after 1984, CPUSA sometimes endorsed progressive Democrats. On rare occasions in recent years, candidates have run as Communists for local or state offices.

The CPUSA merged the *Daily World,* its New York–based newspaper, with the West Coast weekly *People's World* and launched the *People's Daily World* in 1986. Cost considerations forced the party to downgrade its paper to weekly status around 1990. The *People's World* ceased distribution in paper form in 2009, but it remains available online.

The CPUSA persists, though it was clearly demoralized by the 1991 collapse of its Soviet lodestar and patron. Events at a party convention in Cleveland in December 1991—the month the Soviet flag over the Kremlin came down—attested to the difficulties American Communists faced in the years to come.

In Cleveland the party bitterly divided between hard-line Leninists and liberal insurgents. Nearly a thousand of the rebels—maybe a third of the party—had signed a manifesto demanding both internal democracy and CPUSA support for building a movement for genuinely humane and democratic socialism. These liberals were given just one opportunity to speak: an impassioned call for reform and renewal delivered by historian and longtime comrade Herbert Aptheker.

Led by Gus Hall, the hard-liners then used their power to declare the party's articles of faith: Leninism, centralism, the revolutionary role of the proletariat, and the vanguard party. They denounced the liberals for "factionalism"—an ominous term in the Leninist vernacular—and purged them from positions of party leadership. Among those removed were Charlene Mitchell and Angela Davis.

The bloodletting in Cleveland may have helped prolong the life of the beleaguered party, but at the cost of distancing it even further from mainstream America. About the convention one dissident remarked that "Gus Hall and his group turned the CP into a sect. Some people might have thought it was a sect already; there were hundreds of us who didn't think so."[20]

The Socialist Workers Party

Lenin died in 1924, and Stalin and Trotsky emerged as the leading contenders to succeed him.[21] The two protagonists in this power struggle proclaimed their faithful devotion to Lenin and Marx. Trotsky and Stalin both insisted that workers' revolution was necessary, but there were strategic differences between them as to its character and course.

Trotsky was a brilliant intellectual and political theorist. Though he was living in the United States early in 1917, he returned to Russia and took part in the Bolshevik Revolution. Trotsky then built up the Red Army, enabling it to defeat the anti-Soviet White forces in the Russian Civil War.

Stalin had risen in prerevolution Bolshevik ranks robbing banks for party revenue. His penchant for boring his way through any barrier to the achievement of his goals was clearly revealed in his struggle with Trotsky. Expelled from the Soviet Union in 1929 and stripped of his Soviet citizenship three years later, Trotsky was murdered in Mexico by an agent of Stalin in 1940.

American Trotskyists founded the communistic Socialist Workers Party in 1938. Also born that year was the Fourth International, a world association of Trotkyist parties in which the SWP was the leading section in the early years.

The Socialist Workers Party managed to gain a toehold within the labor movement. It was particularly strong in the Teamsters union in the years leading up to the American entry into World War II.

SWP national chair James P. Cannon and twenty-two other SWP and Teamsters leaders were convicted in 1941 of plotting to overthrow the U.S. government. They were sentenced to prison terms of from twelve to sixteen months. This was the first trial in which defendants were charged with violating the 1940 Smith Act. Its outcome damaged the SWP. The CPUSA had actually called for the indictment of its Trotskyist rivals. Ironically this litigation turned out to be a precursor to the prosecution and conviction of the Communist Party leadership eight years later.

The SWP image of itself is that of the disciplined Leninist vanguard party; but recurrent splintering has been a pivotal theme in its history almost from the beginning. One source of the internal fracturing lay in the ambiguity inherent in a remark Trotsky himself made. In defeat he had declared the Soviet Union to be a "degenerate workers' state." Many of Trotsky's doctrinal descendants came to quarrel over what their attitude should be toward that degenerate workers' state.

People have come and gone through the Socialist Workers Party. Many who leave the party go on to build or nurture rival Trotskyist associations. Others join leftist non-Trotskyist groups, and some have gone on eventually to become neoconservatives, conservatives, or even (rarely) disciples of the radical Right.

The impact of the SWP was more substantial than that of other old left parties on the New Left and the great movements for change in the 1960s. Copies of the *Militant,* the party newspaper, circulated on university campuses. The Young

Socialist Alliance, the SWP youth wing, was active and deeply involved in antiwar demonstrations and protests. This may be why J. Edgar Hoover sought to make life difficult for the SWP and why the party became an important target of COINTEL-PRO.

There are those in the Socialist Workers Party who remember the 1970s as their party's golden years. Offering a candidate in every presidential round since 1948, the party tallied its best result in 1976. Nominee Peter Camejo took 90,986 votes that year. The party's formal membership may have stood then at 2,500, but several times that number were attached in spirit. Late 1970s national SWP meetings could bring out 2,000 people, most of them under thirty years old.

In a speech he made in 1982, SWP national secretary Jack Barnes challenged a pivotal doctrinal point Trotsky had made. Barnes also warned that inflated Trotsky veneration could impede solidarity with movements different in tradition but kindred in spirit to the SWP—notably Castro's Cuba and the Sandinista government then in power in Nicaragua.

Today the SWP carries on. Although leaner and poorer than in the 1970s, it maintains its Pathfinder Press and continues to publish the *Militant* online. Cuba is the object of frequent praise in the SWP press. Devotion to Trotsky persists, but the party's self-identification today is less defined in Trotskyist terms.

Splintering on the Far Left

Simon Gerson died in 2004, and Sophie, his wife, two years later. They had been married for seventy-three years and were Communist Party comrades all their adult lives.

I was invited years ago to visit and interview the Gersons in their Brooklyn home. One of the things we discussed was the strong disposition of Left radicals to split over issues irrelevant and incomprehensible to mainstream people. The Gersons readily concurred with my assertion that sometimes the Left is its own worst enemy. We likened the situation to a bit of Jonathan Swift satire featuring bitter warfare between Big Endians and Little Endians over which end of a boiled egg one should crack. Si Gerson thought there should be a book on the fractured American Left titled either *The Joy of Sects* or *Let Dogma Eat Dogma*.

Gerson apparently was not thinking of his own Communist Party, although it too had been the fruit of a schism within the Socialist Party. He would have included the Industrial Union Party and other groupuscules birthed by dissidents who had left or been expelled from the Socialist Labor Party. He was thinking as well about the relentless bleeding of the Socialist Workers Party, out of which many small Trotskyist spin-offs have come. And he had in mind the microparties claiming devotion to China's Mao Zedong and Maoist thought. There once was even a party, the Marxist-Leninist Party of the USA, which followed the line of tiny Albania's ultra-Stalinist dictator, Enver Hoxha.

Current Trotskyist Spin-offs

Workers World Party

Founded in 1959, the Workers World Party is one of the oldest of the existing formations arising out of the Socialist Workers Party. Stephen Schwartz, an unsympathetic observer of U.S. Communist organizations, has described the ideological perspective of WWP as "a bizarre mixture of Trotskyism and Maoism."[22]

Workers World, the party newspaper, is published online. The WWP has frequently run candidates for public office. The party's largest presidential vote return to date—29,083 votes—went in 1996 to nominee Monica Moorehead, an African American woman. In 2008 the WWP endorsed Green Party nominee Cynthia McKinney.

Party for Socialism and Liberation

The Party for Socialism and Liberation grew out of the Workers World Party in 2004. It is one of the few minor parties still producing a print version of its party paper, *Liberation.*

Socialist Equality Party

The Socialist Equality Party is one of several Trotkyist parties sharing that name in countries around the world. The name dates only from the mid-1990s. The party itself is older than that. It was founded as the Workers League in 1966.

Maoist and Maoist-Originated Parties

Maoist parties emerged in the 1960s and the early to mid-1970s. That was a period when powerful forces were pushing for change in the United States and China was flaming bright red from its Cultural Revolution. Maoist groups in America praised China under Mao. Many of them became embittered foes of the pragmatic Chinese leadership that emerged after Mao's death in 1976.

Progressive Labor Party

The Progressive Labor Party first appeared on the ultra left between 1962 and 1965. Directing its birth were Milton Rosen and Mort Scheer, two longtime Communists who had been kicked out of CPUSA. Rosen and Scheer had had the audacity to say that revisionism and reform had replaced true Communist thinking within CPUSA. They believed that capitalism, far from being improvable, would inevitably descend into fascism; the only remedy, as they saw it, was violent revolution.

Rosen, Scheer, and their new party looked to China under Mao's leadership. The PLP claimed for awhile a fraternal relationship with the Chinese Communist Party, one comparable to CPUSA ties with the Soviet party. The PLP revered Mao, but it took pains to say that it never worshipped him. The party was critical both of the cult of personality in Mao's China and the nationalist features of Mao's thought.

The domestic influence of the PLP, such as it was, peaked in the late 1960s. This was largely due to the success of the party and of its youth wing—the May 2 Movement—in forging ties with radical elements of the New Left.[23]

I once sat and talked with Scheer, the party's cofounder, in a New York coffee shop. He told me that as the 1960s came to an end the only real challenger to PLP for control of Students for a Democratic Society had been the extreme Left formation known at the time as the Weathermen. Scheer thought that his party's internal discipline and its self-image as a vanguard party had been valuable to PLP in positioning itself within a New Left that was weak in discipline and structure.

The Progressive Labor Party lives on, now nearly a half century after its birth. *Challenge/Desafío,* the party's bilingual newspaper, appears online every two weeks.

Revolutionary Communist Party

In 1975 Berkeley radical Bob Avakian and his circle of San Francisco Bay area leftists founded the Revolutionary Communist Party.[24] For a bright shining moment the RCP would claim—and relish—the official blessing of China's Maoist leadership.

That was not to last. Mao's death, the denunciation and purge of the Gang of Four, and the rise of Deng Xiaoping as China's top leader brought distressing confirmation that China had fallen into the hands of leaders for whom developing the nation was far more important than being red.

The RCP broke apart in 1978. Comrades whose devotion remained with the Chinese Communist leadership even in the post-Mao era left or were purged from the party. To Chairman Avakian and the other hardcore Maoists who remained, Deng was a "posturing boot-licking sawed-off pimp."

Leaner and smaller because of the departures, the RCP did outrageous things to demonstrate its fidelity to Mao. In 1979 four hundred RCP partisans protesting Deng's visit to Washington battled police in Lafayette Park. There were fifty injuries, sixty-nine arrests, and felony charges against Avakian and sixteen others.

In 1980 three RCP members hauled down the Texas flag flying at the Alamo and hoisted a red banner in its place. Two others threw red paint on Soviet and American diplomats at UN headquarters in New York. It was in 1984 that party members torched an American flag in Dallas—a sign of contempt that eventually resulted in Supreme Court decisions that flag burning is a constitutionally protected form of expression.

To avoid prosecution following the bloody 1979 battle in Lafayette Park, Avakian skipped the country and fled to France. Cloaking its leader's travels and locations since then in a veil of secrecy, the RCP has fostered for Avakian the epic image of liberation fighter, underground and on the run. Critics insist that within the party a

Chairman Avakian personality cult has developed that replicates in miniature the cult of personality once prevailing in Mao's China.[25]

Today there are RCP bookstores in several cities. *Revolution,* the party's biweekly paper, appears online. The RCP maintains fraternal ties with the Sendero Luminoso (Shining Path) movement of Peru and with the powerful Maoist party in Nepal.

★ ★ ★

12

Doctrinal Parties 2
The Neo-Nazis

This Time the World
Autobiography of
George Lincoln Rockwell

Although history never repeats in every detail, what happened one Saturday morning in an African American neighborhood in Greensboro, North Carolina, resembled the pitched battles between Nazis and Communists in German streets during the years leading up to Hitler's Third Reich. Soon after 11:20 A.M. on November 3, 1979, Ku Klux Klansmen and Nazis shot up a "Death to the Klan" rally just commencing at the poor and black Morningside Homes housing project.[1] The rally had attracted some fifty demonstrators, along with curious spectators from the neighborhood. Planning the rally and directing as it got under way were activists of the Communist Workers Party, a tiny group with a Maoist outlook.

Greensboro officials had given a permit authorizing the rally. That permit stipulated no guns. The demonstrators used their fists and placard sticks to pelt arriving Klan and Nazi cars. The two sides then began stick fighting before the first shots rang out. All of the lethal fire came from the raiders' guns. There were a few weapons secreted away by some demonstrators, and they managed to get off a few shots in return.

The raiders did not shoot randomly. No ordinary bystander was slain. It was more like a carefully preplanned surgical strike. The raiders spent their deadly force on the leading demonstrators and CWP people at the scene. Eight lay injured, one of them paralyzed from a head wound. Five others died in the gunfire. They were a well-known Durham pediatrician, another physician who had left his practice to do union organizing, an African American nurse who had done advocacy work for cotton-mill workers who suffered from brown lung disease, a union activist with a Harvard divinity degree, and a Duke honor graduate.

Some of the forty or so raiders were local people, but most had come in from the North Carolina textile belt an hour's drive southwest of Greensboro. They were truck drivers, longtime workers in the region's cotton mills, and other blue-collar people. Along with the Klansmen in this raiding force, there were members of the

Tarheel branch of the National Socialist Party of America. The NSPA already was known for its neo-Nazi rabble-rousing in the Chicago area, where the party had its national headquarters.

This was not the first trouble between the CWP and the raiding groups. In July CWP activists invading a Klan rally at tiny China Grove, North Carolina, had burned a Confederate flag. In a public letter it sent in October, the Communist Workers Party denounced the Klan as "one of the most treacherous scum elements produced by the dying system of capitalism." That letter dared the Klansmen to show up for the Greensboro "Death to the Klan" event.

The Greensboro police had a paid informant, Edward Dawson, planted inside the raiders. Dawson worked both sides of the street. He told the police that Klansmen and Nazis would show up, armed to the teeth. Dawson assured the raiders that the anti-Klan demonstrators were supposed to come unarmed. The Klansmen and Nazis knew exactly where the rally would begin. Weeks before the Greensboro massacre, photographs of the intended human targets had been passed among the raiders.

Dawson arrived in the vehicle at the head of the nine-car raiding caravan. The police arrived too late to provide security for the demonstrators, even though an unmarked cruiser had followed the Klan-Nazi procession into the demonstration neighborhood. Greensboro police arrested sixteen of the raiders.

Four Klansmen and two Nazis were brought to trial. Although videotape evidence positively identified five of the six as having fired shots at demonstrators that day, the all-white jury in one of the lengthiest trials in North Carolina history accepted the defendants' claim of self-defense and exonerated them all. A follow-up federal case on civil rights charges brought a six-month sentence, to be served on work release, for just one Klansman and acquittals for the other defendants. Nearly seven years after the massacre occurred, a case in civil court did yield a $350,000 judgment against the city of Greensboro and the raiding Klan and neo-Nazi groups.

The White Supremacist and Neo-Nazi Far Right

Individuals and organizations of the American Far Right regard themselves as bitter adversaries of those of the Left.[2] Even so there is a curious symmetry in the situations faced by the radical Left and radical Right in confronting the political mainstream.

Like its leftist counterpart, the Right is too dispersed and divided to be seen as a single coherent movement. Yet shared ideas and descent in a common tradition define and, to an extent, bond the elements of the Far Right, just as people and organizations of the Far Left share in a very different tradition and hold certain beliefs in common.

The lineage of the contemporary radical Right extends as far back as the first Ku Klux Klan, born after the Civil War. This tradition carried on in the substantial revival of the Klan after World War I and in the pro-Nazi, anti-Semitic Silver Shirts and the German-American Bund of the 1930s.

Federal taxes perceived to be overbearing or confiscatory, statutes deemed to intrude on cherished gun rights, and official actions seen as assaults on the liberty simply to be left alone all have produced deep-seated animosities on the Far Right toward the federal government. The so-called Ruby Ridge Massacre in 1992 and the 1993 federal siege and lethal assault on the Waco compound of the apocalyptic Branch Davidians both were perceived on the Right to be abhorrent, atrocious provocations for the bombing and mass slaughter that was to come at the Murrah Federal Building in Oklahoma City in 1995.

The radical Right holds antiblack, white supremacist views. By the 1990s *mud people* was becoming a part of the linguistic currency used by many extreme Right people in communicating with each other; according to this line, people with "blood in the face"—"Aryans," whose racial hue and purity enable them to blush—can confidently await an earth purged someday of its nonwhite "inferior, pre-Adamic mud people."[3] That idea originated as a quasi-theological prophecy of Christian Identity, one of the central components of the contemporary ultra Right. Just about every radical Right activist has read *The Turner Diaries*, William Pierce's 1978 novel about a band of white racists who launch a full-scale race war resulting in a system of white supremacy.

The American radical Right speaks with special clarity in its condemnation of Israel. Beyond this shared anti-Zionism, many of the disparate extreme Right elements also are overtly, even crudely anti-Semitic. *ZOG* is another of those terms in the Far Right lexicon. An acronym for Zionist Occupation Government, ZOG is what many ultraright people call the government of the United States. Like some of their leftist counterparts, people on the Far Right are fond of spinning conspiracy theories. The rightist formulations often feature "crafty, scheming Jews," who, it is said, have come to control mass media, the Federal Reserve Board, and other positions of clout and influence.

The Far Right, like its radical Left counterpart, for many years endured harsh repression from lawmakers and through administrative actions. Government suppression of the pro-Nazi Right during World War II was comparable in ferocity to the assault on antiwar and pro-Bolshevik activity during and just after World War I. Although the primary targets of the FBI COINTELPRO operations in the late 1950s and the 1960s were organizations of the Left, COINTELPRO agents also infiltrated and sometimes set out to manipulate, weaken, or destroy Klan and neo-Nazi organizations.

Apart from the FBI and related intelligence agencies, no one has more carefully and systematically studied the groups of the Far Right than the nongovernmental Southern Poverty Law Center. According to the SPLC, "hate groups" in America—most of them resting clearly on the Far Right side—numbered 926 in 2008. That was up from 888 in 2007. Antipathy toward Latino immigrants and a deep-seated aversion to the rise of African American Barack Obama were what fed this increase. There were Klan chapters and racist skinhead groups. Many of the 186 Klan groups were locals of two national KKK associations. And there were the avowedly Nazi parties, mostly descendants of the party-building activities of George Lincoln Rockwell.[4]

Online publications, numerous Web sites and blogs, and even some scheduled programs on cable television serve radical Right groups in their internal communication and outreach to people in the mainstream.

The National States' Rights Party

The National States' Rights Party was one of those Far Right groups that stopped just short of expressly avowing Nazism. The NSRP adopted its name to appeal to southern racial traditionalists. Orval E. Faubus, the arch-segregationist Arkansas governor, took 44,984 votes as the NSRP presidential nominee in 1960.

The party's de facto connection to the neo-Nazi movement was indicated by its selection of the thunderbolt, a symbol familiar in Nazi Germany, as party emblem. The NSRP drew up its platform in 1958 and adhered to it without revision for the nearly three decades of its active life. That statement of party principles demanded a "White Folk Community," whites-only government, complete racial separation, laws banning interracial marriage, and the voluntary repatriation of African Americans to Africa.

At its peak the NSRP claimed 12,000 members. Its leaders boasted that theirs was the largest party on the radical Right. Outside observers estimated the party's membership at closer to 1,500.[5]

J. B. Stoner, the NSRP chair, achieved notoriety for the crude and corrosive racial rhetoric used in his many unsuccessful Georgia electoral campaigns. Stoner served as the attorney for James Earl Ray, the assassin of Martin Luther King. A veteran Klan activist, Stoner was convicted in 1980 for the 1958 bombing of a Birmingham black church.[6]

The *Thunderbolt,* the monthly NSRP paper, was edited for years by Edward R. Fields, a Georgia chiropractor. The paper's coverage included NSRP gatherings attended by white South African neo-Nazis or anti-Semitic refugees from Communist Eastern Europe.

Rockwell's Neo-Nazi Children: America's Avowed Nazi Parties

George Lincoln Rockwell, the "fabled founder of the American Nazi Party,"[7] was the father of the post–World War II avowed Nazi movement in the United States. In his careful study of the American Far Right, James Ridgeway refers to Rockwell as Hitler's Lenin. Radical Right activists—non-Nazis and avowed Nazis alike—today remember Rockwell as "a seminal figure in the Aryan movement."[8] Rockwell's larger-than-life aura is due in part to his assassination in 1967.

Rockwell, the son of two vaudeville comedians, attended Hebron Academy and later Brown University. The United States entered World War II just as he was about to undertake a career as an advertising illustrator. He enlisted in the U.S. Navy and became a pilot so that he could (as he would later say, with considerable irony) "go fight Hitler." Rockwell was recalled to service during the Korean War. A supporter of early 1950s McCarthyite red-baiting, he moved on to the hard racist Right after reading Hitler's *Mein Kampf* and hearing a veteran leader of the 1930s Silver Shirts speak.

American Nazi Party

In 1959 Rockwell set up the American Nazi Party and installed its headquarters in Arlington, Virginia. Years later an activist in Rockwell's party romanticized this act of creation: "Commander Rockwell," he said, had chosen Arlington because it was just a heartbeat—"striking distance"—from the center of national power. Rockwell knew that National Socialism's enemies used *nazi* as a pejorative, comparable to the term *commie* used by the foes of Communism. Rockwell dubbed his new party *Nazi* because he knew it would assure torrents of free publicity.[9]

The World Union of National Socialists, an international body with affiliated national groups, had its American headquarters at the Arlington home of the American Nazi Party. Its European office was in Denmark.

The American Nazi Party never had, even by the most generous estimates, more than a few thousand members;[10] but under Rockwell's flamboyant leadership, it was showered with mass-media attention. Millions of *Playboy* readers learned of Rockwell and his party when the magazine ran an interview in which African American writer Alex Haley questioned the Nazi leader. Publicly forecasting their imminent rise to power by election, these American Nazis adopted a disquieting slogan: "The Jews Are Through in '72." Rockwell at least once suggested a tactical alliance between his party and the Black Muslims against the Jews, their common foe.

Adopting the principle that even hostile publicity is good, Rockwell and his followers traveled the South in an improvised "hate bus"—a VW van provocatively adorned with Nazi signs. American Nazi Party pickets outside a Boston theater showing the film *Exodus* were pelted with eggs and rocks. Seeking to proselytize other "Aryan people," Rockwell was denied entry into Australia and was expelled from Britain.[11]

National Socialist White People's Party

Seeking some support from whites who were deeply opposed to African American gains through the movement for civil rights, Rockwell and his group early in 1967 reconstituted themselves as the National Socialist White People's Party.

On August 25, 1967, Rockwell was shot dead outside a Laundromat in Arlington. Rockwell's assassin, John Patsalos, had adopted the name Patler because it sounded

OFFICIAL
PROGRAM

NATIONAL SOCIALIST
WHITE PEOPLE'S PARTY

Cover of program booklet of the former National Socialist White People's Party.

more like Hitler. Patler had been closely associated with the American Nazi leader; but three times Rockwell had purged the mentally unstable Patler from his party, the last time permanently.[12]

Assuming the position of NSWPP commander upon Rockwell's death, Matt Koehl laid credible claim as second-generation leader of the partisan house built by Rockwell. According to the NSWPP line, the task of the first generation had been to grab and exploit free publicity to build public awareness of the Nazi movement. Now it was time to develop a small, disciplined core of racial idealists dedicated to constructing the Aryan New Order. A number of people who went on to become hard-right luminaries (some would say rogues), William Pierce and David Duke among them, had cut their teeth on Rockwell's party in the first or second generation.

The NSWPP nurtured local units, particularly in midwestern cities. The party ran mayoralty, city council, and school board candidates in Baltimore, Milwaukee, San Francisco, and St. Louis. Local elections often are officially nonpartisan, but NSWPP candidates wore swastikas and revealed their affiliation in other ways while campaigning. They frequently took 5 to 10 percent, sometimes as much as 20 percent, of the votes.[13]

———————————————————————— ★ ★ ————————————————————————

An Interview with Martin Kerr

Conducted years ago, this interview still attests to the values and hopes of many of the neo-Nazi ideological descendants of George Lincoln Rockwell.

I was in Washington interviewing leaders of various minor parties when the time came to travel to the Arlington headquarters of the National Socialist White People's Party for a prearranged interview with Martin Kerr. Not knowing the way, I mustered the nerve to summon a taxi and ask the African American driver to take me to National Socialist White People's Party headquarters. The cabbie glanced at me with the scornful look of someone overcome by the aroma of rotten fish, but he agreed to take me there. On the way he made a point of telling me that he had been one of the American GIs who had gone in to liberate the notorious Dachau concentration camp in 1945. He shared every gory detail of this experience and told me how much he hated Nazis. I kept repeating to him that my mission that day was scholarship, not solidarity with the Nazis in Arlington.

The German swastika banner flew alongside the American flag at the entrance of the two-story headquarters building. After paying (and generously tipping) the cabbie, I was greeted by three young men who wore brown shirts and swastika armbands. They showed me inside to a tiny bookstore, where *Mein Kampf, The Eternal Jew,* and a few other selections were on display.

Kerr struck me as unexceptional in appearance. He wore a mustache—a big, bushy one, not the Hitler cutoff kind. He directed me to a second-floor conference room, and we seated ourselves across from each other at a table. A large Hitler portrait and a swastika banner adorned the wall. For the next hour and a half, I questioned and he answered. Everything was taped on a portable recorder sitting atop the table. You will be reading only a few of the exchanges between us.

One caveat: Narratives, like Mr. Kerr's, that minimize and trivialize the Holocaust may be a greater transgression upon truth than the blanket claims of those who categorically deny that it ever happened. That is because the uninformed are more likely to believe the former than the latter.

JDG: Please state your name, your position with the party, and tell me about your background and what brought you to the party.

MK: I am Martin Kerr. I am the party's national organizer and head of the editorial department, which produces *White Power* [the NSWPP paper] and other materials.

I am twenty-nine years old. I grew up in the state of New Jersey, in suburbs of New York City. My father was in business with a Jew. My parents were moderate moderates. They were aghast when I became a National Socialist. Maybe it was not too surprising; that was in the 1960s, when kids were breaking away from what the old folks believed.

I owe my conversion to Hugh Hefner, and to Alex Haley's *Playboy* interview with George Lincoln Rockwell. I had started reading and thinking early. Everywhere I turned, there were platitudes: equality, peace, love. "Red and yellow, black and white, they are precious in his sight." I saw the same theme, with just a little different packaging, in Christianity, in Socialism, and in Communism.

Obviously it was untrue. People were machine-gunning each other, blacks were being hosed, dogs being unleashed on them.

One day I picked up my dad's *Playboy*. I came to the Rockwell interview and thought "this will be good for a few laughs." But I was amazed. For the first time I actually read someone who didn't skirt the issue—blacks and whites are not equal, for example. I wrote his party, got information, studied it, and eventually joined up.

I went to Hofstra University. It was the publicity-grabbing days of the party, and I was good at it. I worked in organizing and other party activities.

The Jewish Defense League marked me for death. The JDL blew up my father's home and also the home of a party supporter, because it thought I was in one of those places. It nearly killed my parents. It also fundamentally changed their attitudes toward Jews. My parents and I later reconciled.

JDG: What makes you think that America now is fertile ground for a movement like yours?

MK: Actually, I would have to agree with the implication of your question. America is not fertile ground for a National Socialist mass movement right now. Here's the thing— we're a revolutionary movement in stable, prerevolutionary times. So we're biding our time for now, preparatory to building a National Socialist mass movement.

There are many Jews in America and they are extremely wealthy, powerful, and well organized. Because they control the media, Americans have been brainwashed against National Socialism. In most people's minds, *nazi* is synonymous with evil. The educational establishment and media nurture this.

But as Adolf Hitler said, just because a movement is out of sync with public opinion doesn't mean it is doomed. It just means that when victory comes, it will be more of a triumph!

As long as the situation remains moderate, people will turn to moderate leaders. But when the situation becomes extreme—an economic collapse, with massive social upheaval—they will turn to extreme leaders. The country is in decline right now, and already we are seeing growing polarization. The traditional minority groups will gravitate toward Left organizations that have upheld their special needs and interests. Whites, on the other hand, will gravitate toward Right groups and eventually to extreme groups—Klan outfits and the National Socialist White People's Party—which truly uphold their racial interests. We are going to see a radicalization of the white masses in America!

One of our worst problems right now is our media image. All that the white masses know is what National Socialism's enemies have told them. They're told that National Socialists are murderers, haters who kill babies and put people in ovens.

Because people believe this, individuals with personality defects—sadists, jerks, losers—are attracted to the party in numbers disproportionate to their percentage in the population. A large percent of the people who show up downstairs say, "I'm here. I want to be a Nazi. I want to kill niggers. I want to gas Jews!"

We don't want them in NSWPP. It's as simple as that. They have only a Hollywood image of Nazis. In the past, unfortunately, our party (and some National Socialist splinter groups continue to do this today) let these people in, thinking they could be used, then thrown out later. That doesn't work. If you let them in, then when the rare decent person comes by who's psychologically balanced, he encounters these cretins talking about torturing Jews and blowing up places—and it drives the decent person away.

One thing that has hurt the National Socialist movement tremendously is that many would-be National Socialists think that the goal of the party should be to establish [an exact] copy of the Third Reich here on American soil—the uniforms, the symbols, the salute, and all. But that's inorganic. It won't work.

Adolf Hitler had only six years to build a new society before war was forced upon him. The Third Reich, then, should not be equated with the Aryan "New Order," National Socialists' perfect vision. The National Socialist worldview is a totalitarian one; therefore any state built on National Socialist principles would be totalitarian in scope. But we know that the power of the National Socialist state would be benevolent. We confidently predict that freedoms like those in the First Amendment (speech, press, and others like that) would be preserved in a National Socialist state.

It is on the precept of race that we base our vision of the future. Our immediate goal is the creation of a white people's republic on the North American continent. Never in history has there been a successful multiracial society. Either one race has subjugated and enslaved the other, or the state and society have been broken down into chaos and race war.

Here we will see the same. The federal system will break up. Mexicans will colonize the southwestern part of the United States, and Mexico will eventually take it over. Some parts of North America, probably in the Southeast, will be taken over by blacks. When this collapse comes, we want a significant place for the North American white republic; not necessarily the whole continent, but a goodly section—probably toward the U.S. and Canadian Midwest.

Many people ask: "What will you do to the blacks and the Jews?" We'll not do anything to them. Simply put, we'll separate ourselves from them. The repatriation of blacks to Africa may or may not be workable. A black people's republic may be a more likely possibility.

Our bottom line, though, will be a white people's state. Jews will not be a part of it. As for the Jews, we're not fortune-tellers. We do know that we won't gas or otherwise kill people. Our party has no projection about the Jews. But I personally think that if the Jews see National Socialists about to take power, many will emigrate, they will choose to pack and leave. They will not stay around to find out if these are "nice Nazis" or not.

We are not out to hurt other races. But just as Communists believe that history progresses through class struggle, we believe changes come through race struggle.

JDG: A recent issue of your *White Power* newspaper carried an article headlined "There Was No Holocaust!" Given the abundance of pictorial and documentary evidence affirming the authenticity of the Holocaust, would you please comment? Was there a Holocaust or not?

MK: As it has been presented to the American people, the Holocaust story is so inaccurate, with so many distortions, that it bears no relation to actual events.

Certainly the Jews were put in camps, and they were not handled with kid gloves. SS guards were not pro-Jewish! I've heard some people say that no one was killed, that they served ice cream to the Jews, and that sort of thing. Well, that isn't true either. These were concentration camps, and it was pretty bad, in all of them.

But there was no program to systematically exterminate the Jews. I think that probably what happened was that, especially near the war's end, certain camp commanders, without sufficient food or medical supplies, undertook to exterminate or murder a certain percentage of the camps' populations. And I think there were some organized exterminations early on, on the eastern front, especially of Jews who were in partisan groups.

The total number of Jews killed in the war, including those killed by Allied bombs, was around a million, not the six million you usually hear about. Auschwitz was bombed by the Allies!

I'd say Hitler did not know about the Holocaust. When Himmler learned about it, he ordered it stopped. An SS attorney named Karl Morgan was commissioned to wipe out corruption in the SS. Based on his investigations, some SS guards, even some camp commanders, were transferred to penal battalions or executed for mistreating prisoners. Killing prisoners went against SS policy and the policy of National Socialist Germany.

So it is a question of degree, not one of whether there was or wasn't a Holocaust. If you mean a deliberate, systematic attempt to exterminate all of Europe's Jews, the answer is no, there was no Holocaust. But if you mean were there Jews killed and mistreated, the answer is yes, there was a Holocaust.

These things must be seen in the light of Allied war crimes as well. The greatest single war crime in human history was the Allied bombing of Dresden, Germany, in which four hundred thousand people died in a twenty-four-hour period. People were never brought to justice for this or for Hiroshima, Nagasaki, or Hamburg. In comparison to Dresden, the largest number ever killed by German bombs at a single time during the Battle of Britain was eight hundred.

In war, no one is truly a civilian—everyone is a combatant. Bad things happen. People are killed. The fact that many Vietnamese civilians died at My Lai by official action of the U.S. Army does not mean that mass extermination was U.S. policy. It means only that low-level field commanders undertook to do this. This is what happened in Europe, both in the camps and on the eastern front.

There were no extermination camps in wartime Europe. There were concentration camps. The United States also had concentration camps, which it used for Japanese people in America.

Source: Author's interview with Martin Kerr, June 30, 1981, National Socialist White People's Party Headquarters, Arlington, Virginia.

★ ★

The New Order

A spokesman for the National Socialist White People's Party announced late in 1982 that the party would be leaving Arlington for a location in the Midwest. By 1987 the party—renamed the New Order—had established new quarters, ironically enough, in New Berlin, a Milwaukee suburb. Attesting to their place in the Rockwell legacy, Matt Koehl and his followers had taken the assassinated leader's ashes with them after pulling up stakes in Arlington. But it no longer seemed credible to claim an unbroken line as "the party of Rockwell."

National Socialist Party of America

Rockwell's movement had shown signs of splintering even in its second generation. In 1974 a group led by William Pierce left Koehl's Arlington fold to establish the National Alliance. Four years before that, Frank Collin, a former member of the NSWPP, had established the National Socialist Party of America with headquarters in Chicago. The Nazis who took part, alongside Klansmen, in the 1979 Greensboro massacre were members of Collin's neo-Nazi outfit.

The tiny NSPA band was, if anything, even more extreme and provocative than Koehl's NSWPP. Collin was fond of making crude public jokes about knowing "what God's 'chosen people' have been chosen for" and about his party being "the final solution." Ironically Chicago columnist Mike Royko alleged and went a long way toward confirming that Collin was half-Jewish and that his father had survived imprisonment in Dachau concentration camp.[14] Collin may have provided one of the purest examples of what scholars observe as the self-hate often associated with a prejudiced personality.[15]

Collin lost his position as NSPA leader following a 1980 conviction for child sexual abuse.[16] But he still was firmly at the party's helm at the time of the Skokie controversy.

Most of the inhabitants of Skokie, a large Chicago suburb, are Jewish. In the 1970s a large number of Skokie's citizens were Holocaust survivors. That was the reason Collin and his NSPA wanted to demonstrate there. In state and federal cases decided in 1978, the party won the right to march even in that hostile community. David Goldberger, an attorney for the Illinois ACLU, represented Collin and his Nazi group in court. For Goldberger, a Jew, the issue was freedom of speech.[17]

NSPA bluster going into the cases was supplanted by seeming timidity coming out. Faced with the promise of hostile, even violent, response—from the Jewish Defense League in particular—the NSPA shelved its Skokie plans and marched instead, under heavy police protection, in nearby Chicago.

Current Neo-Nazi Parties

The largest neo-Nazi party in America today is the National Socialist Movement. The American National Socialist Workers Party, with thirty-five chapters in twenty-eight states, ranks second. The National Socialist Movement is deeply engaged in demonstrations and propaganda against illegal immigration.[18] In Missouri the Springfield NSM chapter successfully pushed its associational right to participate in the Adopt-a-Highway program. Missouri responded by naming the highway for Rabbi Abraham Joshua Heschel, a prominent theologian and refugee from Nazi Europe.[19]

13

★ ★ ★

State/Local Significant Others

> The People's Republic of Burlington
> *caption on a Vermont bumper sticker*

Over nearly two centuries now there have been parties that established themselves as influential participants in the electoral and policy-making processes of their communities or states. For some the accomplishment has come as a single event: for example Walter Hickel's 1990 gubernatorial election on the Alaskan Independence Party line.

The benchmarks of significance are more often a good bit deeper than that. Some of these parties have even managed to become major actors within their limited territorial scope. But as electoral agents with clout and impact, parties of this type are confined (or virtually confined)—or they limit themselves by choice—to their own communities or states. It would be a mistake to discount the importance of these nonnational partisan actors. As politicians and political scientists often point out, in America *all* politics really is local politics.

It is not that the leaders of these parties have no interest in national affairs. They are likely to grasp the impact of federal policy on their localities and states. Many of their parties nominate or endorse candidates for president. Some have offered and even elected congressional candidates.

There have even been those parties that visualized their movements in national terms but did not develop organizations commensurate with their visions. Today ballot-certified state Working Families parties operate in New York and in Connecticut, South Carolina, Delaware, Oregon, and Vermont. Though they are linked in spirit and cooperate with each other, these state Working Families parties have never convened a general meeting to select national officers and or taken any other step requisite to creating a national party organization.[1]

Local and State Parties in the Nineteenth Century

Many nonnational parties arose and ran their course in the nineteenth century. That is not surprising given nineteenth-century Americans' preoccupation with local issues and events and the absence of true national news media at the time.

Labor, Farmer, and Related Class-Based Parties

Parties of workers and the poor grew up in the Northeast: first, near the end of the 1820s, the Working Men's Party in Philadelphia and in New York the State Guardianship Party. The ephemeral Locofoco Party appeared in New York City in 1835 and after that the Anti-Rent Party around 1839.[2] The Locofocos had split away from their city's Tammany Democratic machine. At a demonstration they held at Tammany Hall they underscored their departure by lighting candles known at the time as locofocos. It was outsiders who gave the Locofocos their informal name.[3]

Local Labor parties grew up in post–Civil War Virginia, Wisconsin, and Arkansas. Radicalized farmers set up antimonopoly parties in California, Oregon, and most of the states in the Midwest in the 1870s. These nineteenth-century agrarian and labor parties were important precursors of the coalitions of workers and farmers that came to be organized as the national Greenback and People's parties as well as of the Socialist parties that emerged in time.

Henry George, whose radical "single tax" plan had won him fame and a nationwide following of hundreds of thousands but also the undying enmity of many conservatives, ran for mayor of New York in 1886.[4] Campaigning as the nominee of the local United Labor Party, George took on the entrenched, corrupt Tammany machine. According to the official count (said to have been grossly manipulated by Tammany), he won 31 percent, second only to Tammany's Abram S. Hewitt with 41 percent. Young Theodore Roosevelt, the Republican nominee, came in third at 28 percent.

The earliest of the labor parties had pressed for suffrage expansion to encompass working-class white men. The general histories of the nineteenth-century state and local labor parties document their legitimate, inevitable, and necessary push for labor rights, limits on working hours, and the regulation of workplace conditions.

But racism and nativism also affected nineteenth-century labor movements. Born in 1877, the California Workingmen's Party found in nativism and race its reason to exist. Under Denis Kearney's leadership, the party became notorious for agitation around the slogan "The Chinese must go!" Its appeal spread like wildfire through the Golden State. Just two years after its birth, the Workingmen's Party won the San Francisco mayoralty and took possession of city government there. The party was implicated in mob assaults on Chinese businesses and threats to burn down Chinatown. The party's leaders took credit, and they had earned it, for passage of the federal Chinese Exclusion Act.

Notable State-Level Parties in the Nineteenth Century

Parties that grew up in the South bore commitments to the interests of their region and states as these were perceived through the lens of party leaders and supporters. Prodded by interregional disputes over tariff policy, the Nullifier Party was devoted to John C. Calhoun. It embraced his views on national and regional "concurrent

Table 13.1 Notable State-Level Parties in the Nineteenth Century

Party and State	Time	Party Program/ Objectives	Relations with Other Parties	Gubernatorial Representation	Congressional Representation
Nullifier Party (mainly South Carolina; 1 Nullifier elected to U.S. House from Alabama, 1833, 1835)	1830–39	States' rights; support for John C. Calhoun and right of states to nullify federal acts	Split from Democrats	States' Rights Democrats sympathetic to Nullifiers were selected by South Carolina legislature	Senate: 2 (1831–37); House: 4 (1831–33), 9 (1833–35), 8 (1835–37), 6 (1837–39)
Suffrage Party (Rhode Island)	1841–42	Dorr Rebellion; demand for expansion of suffrage and democratic constitution	Bitterly opposed by Law and Order Party	Thomas Dorr (extralegal), elected 1842	
Law and Order Party (Rhode Island)	1842–46	Landowner opposition to democratic Dorr Rebellion	Adversary of Suffrage Party	James Fenner, elected 1843, 1844; Byron Dimon, selected by the legislature, 1846	House: 2 (1843–45); Senate: 1 (1844–45)
Conservative Party (North Carolina)	1865–68	Restoration of statehood, opposition to radical Reconstruction	De facto coalition of North Carolina Democrats, former Whigs	Jonathan Worth, elected 1865, 1866; served until 1868	
Conservative Party (Virginia)	1869– mid-1870s	Opposition to GOP "radicals" and radical Reconstruction	Linked to Liberal Republican movement; eventually co-opted by Democrats		House: 6 (1869–71)

Party and State	Time	Party Program/ Objectives	Relations with Other Parties	Gubernatorial Representation	Congressional Representation
Readjuster Party (Virginia)	1877–80s; dominant party in Virginia in early 1880s	Populist, antielitist, reformist, biracial; advocated (downward) adjustment of prewar Virginia debt, abolition of poll tax, and strengthening of public education	Participation by (former) Democrats and white and black Republicans; some links to Greenbackers and early Populists; eventually merged with GOP	William E. Cameron, elected 1881 and served 1882–86	House: 2 (1881–83), 4 (1883–85); Senate: 1 (1881–83) 2 (1883–87), 1 (1887–89)
Silver Party (Nevada)	1892 into first decade of twentieth century	Bimetallism, free coinage of silver, and other issues in common with People's Party	Links to national People's Party and to Silver Republicans of other states; various factions eventually absorbed by Democrats and GOP	Silverites John E. Jones and Reinhold E. Sadler elected in 1894 and 1898, respectively; Democratic-Silver fusion candidate elected, 1902, 1906	House: 1 (1893–1901); Senate: 1 (1893–95), 2 (1895–1901)

SOURCES: Kenneth C. Martis, *The Historical Atlas of Political Parties in the United States Congress, 1789–1989* (New York: Macmillan, 1989); Joseph E. Kallenbach and Jessamine S. Kallenbach, *American State Governors, 1776–1976* (Dobbs Ferry, N.Y.: Oceana, 1977); and Biographical Directory of the United States Congress, 1774–Present, http://bioguide.congress.gov/biosearch/biosearch.asp (accessed August 5, 2011).

majorities" and the right Calhoun claimed for states to nullify federal acts. The Nullifiers dominated government and politics in South Carolina through most of the 1830s.

As America entered the 1840s, Rhode Island still was governing itself under its 1663 royal charter, a document the landowner qualification of which effectively disenfranchised even most Rhode Island white men. Rebellion resulted, and a bitter struggle broke out between the state's Suffrage and Law and Order parties. By 1842 Rhode Island had two competing elected governors. Thomas Dorr, the Suffrage leader, was imprisoned on a state charge of treason. But the movement he led had made its mark. In 1843 Rhode Island replaced its charter with a much more liberal new state constitution.

In North Carolina and Virginia, post–Civil War Conservative parties were briefly influential. They stood in opposition to national policies of "radical" Reconstruction in the South.

Pre–Civil War Virginia had encumbered itself and its tax-paying citizens with enormous debt to pay for infrastructure. The war then damaged or destroyed substantial portions of what Virginia had built with the borrowed money. Much of what was left intact was in the section that became West Virginia during the war.

Many postwar Virginia conservatives insisted their state should repay its debt in full. But a new partisan movement championed the populist sentiments of small farmers and others who were burdened by taxes and had nothing to gain from debt repayment. This Readjuster Party demanded debt adjustments and that West Virginia shoulder its share of responsibility for repayment. Issues of the debt finally were settled through federal litigation, but the resolution did not come until years after the Readjuster movement had ceased to be.

Dominant in Virginia politics in the early 1880s, the Readjusters coalesced with African American and white Republicans and became a force for progress, especially in public education. Their party eventually succumbed to the same force that for years neutralized the power of southern Republicans: the disenfranchisement of southern blacks and the rise of the one-party Democratic Solid South.

The Silver Party ruled Nevada—the Silver State—in the 1890s. Sparsely settled Nevada was the home of fewer than fifty thousand people at the time. Silver mining was the crucial core of the economy and had been for more than thirty years before the birth of the Silver Party. The party pushed for bimetallism and the free coinage of silver. It also shared other policy interests of the national People's Party and its Populist supporters.

Parties and Electoral Movements in the Upper Midwest, 1915–1945

Parts of the upper Midwest were fertile ground for leftist third parties and other reformist electoral movements during and between the two world wars. Contributing to this was the ax that millions of the region's underprivileged inhabitants were determined to grind about conditions of their lives and what had to be done to improve them. Farmers in a corridor of states from Wisconsin through the Dakotas recognized themselves as have-nots victimized by grain elevator operators, railroads, and other interests. Workers in Milwaukee, St. Paul and Minneapolis, and other cities harbored similar grievances against corporate foes, and the overlapping concerns sometimes called out for united farmer and worker political action.

Also in play were the region's cultural values. Daniel Elazar, a political scientist with an interest in the relationship between geography and value systems, identified three distinct political cultures, each influencing politics in sections of the United States. Elazar labeled them individualism, moralism, and traditionalism.

Elazar observed that over many years moralism has pervaded political values and practice in Minnesota and in other states of the upper Midwest. Moralism incorporates participation as the central obligation of virtuous citizenship. Midwesterners were among the first to adopt the open primary, initiative and referendum, recall, and other participatory processes. Voters in many parts of the upper Midwest regularly cast their ballots at some of the highest turnout rates in the country. The most visionary of Elazar's culture types, moralism imagines active government—government at work as the instrument of the commonweal, the agent of the public good.[5] Moralist culture has cradled numerous reform movements in the region.

The Nonpartisan League

Not all of the movements, or all the electoral ones, organized themselves as third parties. The leftist Farmers' Nonpartisan Political League was born in North Dakota in 1915. Although its influence soon reached eight other states and even crossed into Canada, the league was strongest in the state of its birth. North Dakota's party primaries were open to all voters, and registration was not required for voting. Arthur Townley, the Socialist Party organizer who played the principal role in bringing the Nonpartisan League to life, realized that the league could use its voter appeal and those accessible rules to penetrate and take control of the state Republican Party—the dominant party in North Dakota.

Although its enemies red-baited it during World War I, the league successfully commanded the GOP and, through it, North Dakota state government from 1917 to 1921. Popular governor Lynn J. Frazier and the league-dominated state legislature passed a glittering array of radical measures—branded by many as socialist—mostly for the benefit of their farmer constituency.[6] The Bank of North Dakota, one of their enactments, still stands today as the only state-owned bank in the United States.

In 1921 conservatives turned out Frazier, a Nonpartisan Leaguer, in the first successful gubernatorial recall election in American history. Frazier won a seat in the U.S. Senate just one year later.[7] Though it has never regained its vigor of the

Table 13.2 Minnesota and Wisconsin Third-Party Governors and Members of Congress, 1919–1947

Party	Governor and Term	Percent of Popular Votes	U.S. Senator and Dates of Service[a]	U.S. House Member and Dates of Service[a]
Minnesota				
Union Labor[b]				William L. Carss (1919–21)
Minnesota	Floyd B. Olson (1931–33)	59.30	Magnus Johnson (1923–25)	Knud Wefald (1923–27)
Farmer-Labor	Floyd B. Olson (1933–35)	50.57	Henrik Shipstead (1923–41)	Ole J. Kvale (1923–29)
	Floyd B. Olson (1935–36)	44.61	Elmer A. Benson (appointed) (1935–36)	William L. Carss (1925–29)
	Hjalmar Petersen (1936–37)	Lt. governor; succeeded the deceased Olson	Ernest Lundeen (1937–40)	Paul J. Kvale (1929–33, 1935–39)
	Elmer A. Benson (1937–39)	60.74		Henry M. Arens (1933–35)
				Magnus Johnson (1933–35)
				Ernest Lundeen (1933–37)
				Francis H. Shoemaker (1933–35)
				Richard T. Buckler (1935–43)
				Dewey W. Johnson (1937–39)
				Henry G. Teigan (1937–39)
				John T. Bernard (1937–39)
				Harold C. Hagen (1943–45)

Party	Governor and Term	Percent of Popular Votes	U.S. Senator and Dates of Service[a]	U.S. House Member and Dates of Service[a]
Wisconsin				
Socialist				Victor L. Berger[c] (1919–21, 1923–29)
Wisconsin Progressive	Philip F. La Follette (1935–37)	39.12	Robert M. La Follette Jr. (1935–47)	Thomas R. Amlie (1935–39)
	Philip F. La Follette (1937–39)	46.38		Gerald J. Boileau (1935–39)
	Orland S. Loomis[d]	49.67		George J. Schneider (1935–39)
				Gardner R. Withrow (1935–39)
				Bernard J. Gehrmann (1935–43)
				Harry E. Sauthoff (1935–39, 1941–45)
				Merlin Hull (1935–47)

a. Some senators and representatives served other years as elected nominees of a major party. The dates in the table show only those years in which the senator or representative served as the elected nominee of a third party.

b. Union Labor was a short-lived local party in Duluth.

c. Berger also had served in the House from 1911 to 1913. Although he was elected in 1918 and won again in a 1920 special election, the House declined to seat him, and his Milwaukee seat remained vacant from 1919 to 1921. Berger had been convicted of violating the Espionage Act.

d. Loomis was elected in 1942 but never took office. He died of a heart attack before inauguration day, and the Republican elected as lieutenant governor served Loomis's full gubernatorial term.

SOURCES: Kenneth C. Martis, *The Historical Atlas of Political Parties in the United States Congress, 1789–1989* (New York: Macmillan, 1989); Joseph E. Kallenbach and Jessamine S. Kallenbach, *American State Governors, 1776–1976* (Dobbs Ferry, N.Y.: Oceana, 1977); and Biographical Directory of the United States Congress, 1774–Present, http://bioguide.congress.gov/biosearch/biosearch.asp (accessed August 5, 2011).

1917–21 years, the Nonpartisan League lives on. It realigned in 1956 with the North Dakota Democratic Party.

Minnesota Farmer-Labor Party

Instrumental in launching the Nonpartisan League, Arthur Townley also took some part in founding the movement that began to take shape in Minnesota in 1918.[8] In a state with both a large urban working class and a substantial agrarian base, the Minnesota movement took a form very different from that which had grown up in its rural North Dakota neighbor. Minnesota's was the first of several twentieth-century state farmer-labor parties. From the beginning farmers' support for this new party was as important as workers'. But it was *St. Paul Union Advocate* editor William Maloney and other labor leaders who persuaded their counterparts on the farmer side to accept for their state the third-party approach.

Minnesota Farmer-Laborites were among those who took part in an initiative, active from 1919 through 1924 though it was doomed to fail, to build and sustain a national farmer-labor party. Of those state-level parties that outlived this national movement, the Minnesota Farmer-Labor Party was the longest lasting and most successful by far.

Farmer-Labor solicited the votes and support of its natural constituents in Minnesota working and farming families, but it also reached beyond its base. Recognizing that the interests of local merchants and small-business people often collided with the power and positions of big business, Farmer-Labor positioned itself as champion of local mercantile interests.

The Farmer-Labor demographic additionally featured an ethnic component. The party commanded the devotion of scores of Minnesotans with ancestry in Scandinavia. Farmer-Labor was weakest in the fertile Anglo lands of southern Minnesota, much stronger in western and northern areas settled by Swedes, Norwegians, Danes, and Finns. Many of the party's officeholders were the children or grandchildren of Scandinavian émigrés. Some had themselves come to America from native lands in northern Europe.[9]

Borrowing from the mass membership model used by European social democratic parties, the Minnesota party builders made Farmer-Labor membership formal but accessible. Members of unions, cooperatives, and farm groups affiliated with the party were automatically party members, their dues paid by the associated organization. Other Minnesotans joined through enlisting in a ward or township club and paying annual party dues.

The achievements of Farmer-Labor during the quarter century of its existence as a freestanding party were remarkable. By 1923 it had entirely displaced Minnesota's feeble Democratic Party as the real electoral alternative to the long-dominant GOP. It then went on to achieve at least parity with the Republicans, and it sustained it through the Depression era 1930s. Over the years Minnesotans elected three Farmer-Laborites to the U.S. Senate, thirteen to the federal House, and two to the mayoralty of Minneapolis.

Floyd B. Olson, Farmer-Labor's thirty-nine-year-old candidate for governor, swept the state in a 1930 landslide victory. Twice reelected, Olson died of cancer in 1936 as his third term neared its end.

Historians who have written about Minnesota rank Olson high among the state's ablest and most accomplished governors. He managed to persuade a legislature controlled by conservatives who were not his dispositional allies to institute a progressive state income tax, to enact far-reaching measures for social security and unemployment compensation, and to pass minimum wage and environmental measures. The governor's various interventions secured employer recognition of the union rights of striking truckers and, for desperate farmers, a moratorium on mortgage foreclosures.

Olson's contemporaries found in the governor a complex blend of pragmatism, populism, and socialism. Through an All-Party Group he set up, the pragmatic Olson solicited campaign support from Republicans and Democrats. He appointed to his administration some of these Minnesotans who supported him but not his party. While there were Farmer-Laborites seeking to renew the movement for a national third party, Olson was positioning his state party within the orbit of the national Democrats.[10]

But in his public voice Olson spoke with the passion and fire of a populist leader whose people were miserable and forced to suffer for the transgressions of others. To angry demonstrators assembled in 1933 he proclaimed that if the system could not remedy the conditions in which the people found themselves or prevent their recurrence, "I hope the present system of government goes right to hell, where it belongs."[11] Speaking at the 1934 Farmer-Labor convention, the governor declared that "when the final clash comes between Americanism and Fascism, we will find the so-called Red as the defender of democracy and the super-patriot and captain of industry on the side of mass slavery." About himself, he said in his speech, "I am not a liberal. I am what I want to be—I am a radical."[12]

The "Cooperative Commonwealth" platform that Olson's party drafted, adopted, and featured in 1934 may well have been the most radical ever offered by any American governing party. This Farmer-Labor document declared "that capitalism has failed and that immediate steps must be taken by the people to abolish capitalism in a peaceful and lawful manner and that a new, sane, and just society must be established." The platform called for federal policies that would underwrite land tenure for American farmers, provide a government monopoly on banking and lending, encourage cooperative enterprise, and nationalize factories, mines, public utilities, and transportation and communication. For Minnesota itself one of the platform's most ambitious prescriptions was for a state insurance monopoly offering Minnesotans cradle-to-grave financial security.[13]

Farmer-Labor's cooperative commonwealth vision, as conveyed through its 1934 platform, had little if any policy effect either in Washington or St. Paul. For Olson and his party, it was a serious political misstep, one that produced red-baiting howls from Farmer-Labor's conservative foes. Although Olson managed to win a plurality and reelection in 1934, most voters' ballots went for the two candidates running against him.

Elected with Olson as lieutenant governor in 1934, Hjalmar Petersen closed out the last 132 days of the deceased Olson's third term. Then, following the 1936 election, Elmer A. Benson was installed as the third Farmer-Labor governor on January 4, 1937.

Petersen and Benson were the leading rivals for their party's leadership in the immediate post-Olson years. Benson was devoted to Olson's vision and policy goals but lacked his tempering pragmatism. Benson's rhetoric matched Olson's at its most radical. Petersen held liberal but anticommunist views, and he positioned himself on his party's right flank.

Farmer-Laborites must have become hardened over the years to their adversaries' red-baiting—politically motivated charges, many of which were hyperbolic or plainly false. But though no consensus has developed about just how much, historians do concur that Communists came to influence Farmer-Labor affairs in the late 1930s and into the war years.[14]

The parties of the Comintern adopted their antifascist Popular Front strategy in 1935, and American Communists began reaching out to potential allies among liberals, progressives, and socialists. In Minnesota itself the initiation of the Popular Front coincided with Benson's landslide gubernatorial victory in 1936.

Governor Benson did not hesitate to work with Communists in what he considered to be a common and just cause. James M. Shields, Benson's adulatory biographer, wrote that "the term 'red' when applied to anyone fighting on his side aroused . . . [Benson's] soul to deep and bitter indignation. . . . Nor did he think it improper to accept support of so-called 'reds' or to use their talents to advantage in government jobs."[15] Nine years after his gubernatorial term ended, Benson became national chair of the Progressive Party. That was the party of nominee Henry Wallace, the party that, with strong Communist involvement, ran a campaign to end the Cold War.

By 1938 Farmer-Labor was beginning that downward spiral so often featured in third-party narratives. That was the election year when the Minnesota GOP started reclaiming much of the ground it had lost. Minnesota's Democratic Party continued to be, as it had been, little more than a state dispenser for national Democratic patronage.

Although the Farmer-Labor slide was clear by the 1940s, the party's vote share remained many times larger than the Democrats'. In Farmer-Labor's last gubernatorial contest as a freestanding party, nominee Hjalmar Petersen took 300,000 votes against 410,000 for the popular Republican incumbent and just 75,000 for the Democrat.

Minnesota's Democratic and Farmer-Labor parties merged in 1944. The Farmer-Labor name survived the demise of its designee. To this day the Democratic lines on

Governor Elmer Benson speaking at the 1938 Farmer-Labor state convention, Duluth, Minnesota. Courtesy of Minnesota Historical Society.

Minnesota ballots carry the label Democratic-Farmer-Labor. Candidates elected on those lines are known as DFLers.

The Wisconsin Progressive Party

Just a dozen years elapsed between the birth of the Wisconsin Progressive Party in 1934 and its leaders' decision to declare its end.[16] Short lived it was, but nonetheless it was a power to be reckoned with. The WPP was the dominant partisan force in Wisconsin during its first four years. By 1935 the party held the governor's office, a seat in the U.S. Senate, and seven of Wisconsin's ten seats in the House. The WPP swept all statewide offices and won control of the state senate and assembly in the 1936 elections.

The La Follette brothers—Robert M. Jr. and Philip F.—were the principals in founding the party. The birth of the WPP commemorated the earlier labors of "Fighting Bob" La Follette—"Mr. Progressive," their late father. It also served his sons' political outlook and goals.

Running as a Republican to fill out his deceased father's last Senate term, Robert La Follette Jr. won the office in 1925. He was reelected three times, the last two, in 1934 and 1940, on the Progressive line. Philip La Follette won his first Wisconsin gubernatorial race as a Republican in 1930 but then lost his bid for reelection in the Depression-driven 1932 national and state Democratic sweep. Running as the Progressive nominee, he reclaimed the governor's office in 1934 and again in 1936.

Leading the powerful progressive wing of the state GOP in the early 1930s, the La Follette brothers understood that the progressive torch had been dropped by national Republicans but that it had been retrieved and was being carried by the other side—by Franklin Roosevelt and the New Deal Democrats. Given the circumstances, the solution they chose made good intuitive sense: a freestanding state party without formal attachment to either national major party. Wisconsin Progressives did support a broad range of Democratic domestic policy initiatives, and FDR came to regard the La Follette brothers as devoted New Dealers.

The impact of the La Follettes and their liberalism was strong, but a crucial second factor also contributed to the birth and identity of the Wisconsin Progressive Party. Present and working alongside La Follette forces at the party's 1934 founding convention were influential leaders and activists of organizations representing workers and farmers. Insofar as they held sway in defining the new party, the WPP was the Wisconsin incarnation of a radical agrarian-and-labor partisanship that had previously taken shape in adjacent Minnesota.

Ties naturally developed between the WPP and Minnesota Farmer-Laborites. Governor Philip La Follette gave the oration at the public funeral of Floyd B. Olson in 1936. Assuming that FDR would not break precedent to seek a third presidential term, Wisconsin Progressives joined Farmer-Laborites and others in talks about rekindling the initiative to build a progressive national third party. Despite ideological differences the WPP also forged friendly, beneficial relations with the Milwaukee Socialists.

Progressive policy makers achieved a lot in 1930s Wisconsin, both before and during the life of the Progressive Party. Their programs of public works and unemployment insurance served as important models for federal policy development during the New Deal. The lawmakers in Madison set up a public agency for electric power and enacted protections for Wisconsin farmers, workers, and consumers. In Washington Sen. Robert La Follette helped draft and push through legislation assisting drought-stricken farmers and the unemployed. Investigations he led exposed the corporate use of spies to infiltrate labor unions.[17]

Fully conscious of their common stock in stopping the Progressives, Wisconsin's Republicans and Democrats worked as de facto coalition partners in 1938. The WPP suffered grievous losses in the 1938 election round. Governor La Follette was one of many Progressives who went down to defeat. The party lost five of the seven seats it had held in the U.S. House.

Painful they were, but the 1938 setbacks were not the death knell of the Wisconsin Progressive Party. In 1940 voters renewed the Senate tenure of Robert La Follette for six more years. Progressive nominee Orland Loomis won the governorship in

1942. It was his party's misfortune (and of course his own) that Loomis died before inauguration day.

In 1946 Robert La Follette declared that the party was over. He ran as a Republican for the Senate seat that his father and then he had held for more than forty years. La Follette lost in the Republican primary to Joseph R. McCarthy. McCarthy's red-baiting during his tenure in the Senate earned him notoriety and an image in history as a reckless demagogue.

The irony of McCarthy's acquisition of the "progressive La Follette seat" was enlarged by another fact: the Communist Party reportedly backed McCarthy's conservative campaign in 1946. Inveighing against Soviet expansionism as the Cold War began, Senator La Follette had picked up the animus of domestic Communists.[18]

Progressive Parties in American Cities

In Berkeley, a university city known for radical politics, the leftist coalition Citizens Action held the mayoralty for the fifteen years from 1979 until 1994. Progressive parties also arose in a handful of other twentieth-century U.S. cities. Aiming to clean up corruption in local politics, they appeared as partisan voices of dissent or reform. Most of them grew up in communities with values to the left of the political cultures of their states.

Cincinnati: The Charter Party

Founded in 1924 and now well into its ninth decade of life, the Charter Party today is a minor player in Cincinnati politics. Charter arose to challenge and fight Cincinnati's corrupt Republican Cox machine, which had dominated that city since the 1880s. The Charter Party has been an advocate for reform and clean government, local services, and community and environmental values.

At Charter's peak in the 1950s, it was the allied partner of local Democrats in Cincinnati's governing coalition. The Charter Party drew strength from the local proportional representation system used in Cincinnati city council elections from 1924 until it was abandoned in 1957.

Theodore M. Berry, the first African American mayor of Cincinnati, was affiliated with the Charter Party. So was Reginald "Reggie" Williams, a well-known linebacker for the Cincinnati Bengals, who served two years on city council.

Madison: Progressive Dane

Dane County was the birthplace of Robert La Follette Sr.—"Mr. Progressive" in the state that was long known as the heartland of progressivism—and the home of the La Follette family. Madison is Wisconsin's capital, the Dane county seat, and also the home of the flagship campus of the University of Wisconsin. Madison is where the senior La Follette launched his *La Follette's Weekly Magazine* in 1909. Renamed the *Progressive* twenty years later, the magazine is published still in its Madison home.

In all of America, there could not be more suitable turf than Madison and Dane County for a progressive local party to sprout and grow.

A party did grow up in that fertile ground, beginning in 1992. Known as Progressive Dane, it began as a part of the national New Party movement. The New Party did not last, but Progressive Dane continues on as a significant factor in local Madison and Dane County politics. Its dues-paying members set and determine its policy agenda. The city and county platforms of Progressive Dane embrace affordable housing, transparency in government, and growth commensurate with the maintenance of community and environmental values.

Operating in local election systems that are officially nonpartisan, Progressive Dane in 2010 was claiming three of the twenty members of the Madison common council, four of thirty-seven on the Dane County board, and four of seven—a majority—of the Madison school board members.

The Vermont Story

Given the conservatism associated with the public mood in the "Reagan 1980s," the Vermont and Burlington story is remarkable. Tucked away in the northwest corner of the state, Burlington, with its forty-two thousand inhabitants, is the largest city in America's most rural state. Burlington's mayor during eight years of the 1980s was Bernard "Bernie" Sanders.

Sanders's rise contradicted stereotypes about Vermont parochialism. Jewish and Brooklyn born, he also holds ideological proclivities one may not expect to find in rural places such as Vermont. The tag he proudly and publicly wears is socialist. Sanders had affiliated in 1971 with Liberty Union, a small Vermont party that proclaimed—and still proclaims—its devotion to finding a nonviolent path to socialism. During Sanders's mayoral tenure, the wall of the chief executive's office bore the weight of a large portrait of Eugene V. Debs, the patron saint of American Socialists.

A new local lexicon reflected Burlingtonians' sense of their mayor's uniqueness. Friends and enemies alike adorned their car bumpers with stickers proclaiming the People's Republic of Burlington. Municipal employees often greeted each other as comrade.[19] Local people sometimes dubbed Sanders's supporters on city council the Sandernistas.[20]

Expressions such as those usually came with a lot of tongue in cheek. Sanders believed in a democratic form of socialism, and in any case the limited place of local government in the constitutional scheme of things denied him the authority, even if he had had the will, to create a socialist utopia in northwest Vermont.

Sanders ran as an independent in his first successful bid for the mayoralty in March 1981. He then joined with other Burlingtonians who initiated the Progressive Coalition, a new local political party. The Progressive Coalition garnered some support from students and faculty of the University of Vermont and other local colleges and from local good-government advocates. Many of its votes came from the elderly, tenants, and the working people of the city. The Progressives' successful intrusion into the community mainstream bought for Burlington a status unique in the 1980s and since: the city with the only true three-party system in America.[21]

The Progressives on council and in the mayor's office sometimes called their opponents Republicrats or referred to them as the Regressive Coalition. On key votes Republican and Democratic local legislators often combined against the Progressive agenda. An anti-Sanders candidate jointly endorsed by Republicans and Democrats won 45 percent of the votes in the March 1987 mayoralty election.[22]

Traditional local power holders—Democratic and Republican politicians, businesspeople, the utilities, some of the administrators at the university and at Medical Center Hospital, and others—bitterly resented Sanders's resort to what they saw as the rhetoric of class warfare. For a polemical opinion piece he composed for the *New York Times,* Sanders wrote that

> the United States has the lowest turnout of any industrialized nation. . . . The main reason is that Democratic and Republican candidates have little or nothing to say to tens of millions—mostly the poor, working people, and youth. Both major parties, dominated by wealthy individuals and corporate interests, are deeply out of touch with these citizens.
>
> The two major parties not only fail to provide serious solutions to the problems of society but, in many cases, don't even discuss the issues. Given the level of the current debate, the interesting thing is not why half of the people don't vote, but why half of the people do.
>
> The richest 1 percent . . . now owns more than half of the nation's wealth. While we had a doubling of billionaires [recently], close to three million Americans now sleep out on the streets.[23]

Sanders and the Progressives managed to tilt local policy in directions friendlier to low- and moderate-income Burlingtonians. Sanders's city accomplished progressive tax reform. It won federal grants for two hundred housing units and also established a municipal land trust to sell houses but retain public ownership of lots. Two emergency shelters with eighty beds for homeless people attracted the favorable attention of national media. Major steps came in areas ranging from environmental protection, downtown beautification, and enhanced police protection to women's rights and child care.

Burlington infused new life into its neighborhood planning groups, encouraging wider citizen participation in local decision making. The size of the voting electorate doubled in the 1980s, testimony perhaps to the excitement generated by the Sanders factor. In 1987 *U.S. News & World Report* recognized Sanders as one of the nation's twenty best mayors.[24]

Sanders left the mayor's office in April 1989. He had decided against seeking a fifth mayoral term, opting instead to run for Congress in 1988. Sanders lost that first bid for Vermont's only seat in the House; but two years later he won, taking 56

The Vermont Secession Movement

An organized movement originating around 2003 calls for the peaceful secession of the Green Mountain State from the American union. Present at its founding and one of its leading exponents, Thomas Naylor has described this movement as "left-libertarian, anti-big government, anti-empire, antiwar, with 'small is beautiful' as our guiding philosophy." Movement leaders denounce federal policies of imperial warfare, corporate welfare, and intrusion into the private lives of citizens. They sharply criticize Sanders and the other members of the Washington congressional delegation. The secessionists publish the newspaper *Vermont Commons*. Poll results indicate that they may have the support of more than one in every eight Vermonters.

The Second Vermont Republic is one of the Vermont secessionists' principal organizations. Its Web site carries links to the Alaskan Independence Party and to a secessionist movement in Texas.

In January 2010 the secessionists launched the Vermont Independence Day Party and announced that they would be fielding a slate of candidates for governor, lieutenant governor, and seven seats in the state senate. Dennis Steele, the party's gubernatorial candidate, owns Radio Free Vermont, an Internet station. He vowed that if elected he would bring home to Vermont all of that state's National Guard troops deployed overseas.

Sources: Christopher Ketcham, "The Secessionist Campaign for the Republic of Vermont," Time.com, January 31, 2010, http://www.time.com/time/nation/article/0,8599,1957743,00.html; and Mitch Pittman, "Vermont Independence Day Party Announces Candidates," FOX 44 Now.com, January 15, 2010, http://www.fox44now.com/story/11832270/vermont-independence-day-party-announces-candidates.

---

percent of the votes statewide. His 1990 win was the first of eight consecutive victories in contests for the House. Congressman Sanders then racked up nearly two-thirds of the votes in his successful 2006 quest for a six-year term in the Senate.

Although running as an independent in all his congressional campaigns, Sanders has maintained his close connections with the Progressives in Burlington and throughout Vermont. Studies show that the statewide circle of Sanders voters does include liberals and progressives but also thousands of moderates, single-issue voters, and even conservatives. A Vermont editorialist attributed Sanders's enormous electoral appeal to "charisma and bold convictions." Many Vermonters apparently admire his fidelity to principle even when they disagree with his perspective on things.[25]

The Progressives in Burlington carried on following the departure for Washington of their first local leader. Progressive Peter Clavelle won the mayoralty in 1989, and he was reelected in 1991.

Vermont's progressives began in 1990 to take the needed steps to transform the Progressive Coalition into a party that would be statewide in scope. By 1999 they were ready to designate what they had been building over the 1990s: the Vermont Progressive Party.

As of 2011 Progressive Bob Kiss was serving as Burlington's mayor. Two other elected Progressives sat on the Burlington council, and the party held seven seats in the Vermont legislature: two in the senate, five in the house. Four of these Progressive state legislators were women. Notably five of the seven had won election in Vermont communities other than Burlington.

Fusion Politics and Third Parties in New York

Minor parties often find advantage in interparty fusion: often, but not always. The danger of co-optation—the big fish swallowing the little fish—does lurk sometimes, and there are also occasions when the two major parties fuse, transforming duopoly into a temporary monopoly. In 1946, for example, California governor Earl Warren commanded the general election lines of both the Republican and Democratic parties in his hugely successful reelection bid.

New York is where third parties, mainly state-level ones, have cultivated and refined cross-endorsement, drawing the most substantial benefits available from ballot-level fusion. Scholars refer to the New York party system as "modified two-party" or even "multiparty" in essence.[26]

New York state law has long allowed more than one ballot-qualified party to run the same candidate for office,[27] and a party retains its ballot certification as long as its gubernatorial nominee receives fifty thousand votes on the party's general election line. In a state the size of New York, that typically is little more than 1 percent of the votes cast for governor.

Cross-endorsement is the method New York third parties use most often. Cross-endorsement can empower the voter to support a minor party while evading the problem of "wasted votes." Sometimes the cross-endorsing party is able to show that the margin of victory came on its third-party line. Third parties also sit out some elections. And they can wield a powerful "spoiler" club by threatening to run a candidate on their own.

American Labor Party

David Dubinsky, Sidney Hillman, and other New York labor leaders launched the American Labor Party in 1936. The ALP quickly rose to wield the balance of power between the Democrats and Republicans in New York politics.

The ALP gave its presidential lines to Roosevelt in 1936, 1940, and 1944. Its cross-endorsement of Democratic governor Herbert H. Lehman may have been crucial to Lehman's reelection in 1938. Lehman returned the favor, appointing American Laborites to positions in government.

In New York City, the ALP coalesced with the Republicans and other anti-Tammany forces. Successfully seeking a second term in 1937, reform mayor Fiorello H. La Guardia received 482,790 of his votes on the ALP line.

Two American Laborites served New York constituencies in the U.S. House. Vito Marcantonio first won his congressional race as a Republican in 1934. Losing in 1936, he then ran successfully in the sequence of elections from 1938 through 1948. Although clearly and publicly identified with the ALP, Marcantonio drew some cross-endorsement votes in elections from 1938 through 1946. Marcantonio's 1948 victory—his last—came as the candidate ran only on the ALP line. ALP nominee Leo Isacson, a special-election victor, served eleven months in the U.S. House in 1948.

Forty-four percent of the votes Henry Wallace received nationwide as the 1948 Progressive Party presidential nominee came in New York on the ALP line.[28] As McCarthyism descended, foes and critics of the ALP paraded the party's connection with the 1948 Progressives as a smoking gun. It confirmed, they said, what they had long been charging: that the ALP, a willing participant in the Popular Front, was intimately connected with and eventually dominated by the Communist Party.

Losing its ballot status in 1954, the ALP disbanded two years later. The Cold War and McCarthyism were factors in play contributing to the party's demise.

Liberal Party

Allegations about Communist influence were what led David Dubinsky, Alex Rose, and other labor leaders to desert the ALP and establish the Liberal Party in 1944. Theologian Reinhold Niebuhr and other notables joined them in this partisan venture.

The Liberal Party gave its 1948 line to Harry Truman. This new party developed some affinity for the Democrats as their "natural" major coalition partners. But in a state with a tradition of progressive "Rockefeller Republicanism," the Liberals also cross-endorsed Republicans: Jacob Javits, for example, and Rudy Giuliani.

The Liberals' most stunning electoral achievement involved John Lindsay, a liberal Republican. Lindsay had won the mayoralty of New York City in 1965. Although cross-endorsed by the Liberal Party, he had taken most of his votes on the Republican line. Seeking reelection in 1969, he lost to a conservative in the Republican primary. Lindsay retained his office for four more years due to the votes he received on the Liberal line.

The Liberal Party has been inactive since losing ballot position in 2002. Working Families, a new party born in 1998, appropriated union support that had belonged to the Liberal Party. Long before that there were some signs that the Liberal Party might be losing its way. Outsiders observed that patronage goals seemed to be trumping ideological devotion in driving decisions made by the party.

Conservative Party

Conceived as the Liberal Party's ideological opposite bookend, New York's Conservative Party was born in 1962. These Conservatives came armed with both carrots and sticks in their campaign to wean New York Republicans (and Democrats) away from the liberalism that long prevailed in Empire State politics. They have been in a position to choose, case by case, whether to cross-endorse, to sit out an election, or to offer a candidate of their own.

The Buckley brothers—James L. and William F. "Bill"—brought positive media attention to the Conservative Party. The Buckleys substantially influenced the party's course. Nationally known as a public intellectual, Bill Buckley was revered by American conservatives for what he had won for the conservative movement in the marketplace of ideas. He stood in 1965 as the Conservative nominee for mayor of New York City. In 1970 James Buckley won a six-year term in the U.S. Senate. Remarkably his victory came on the Conservative line. Buckley defeated both the liberal Republican incumbent and his Democratic challenger.

New York conservatives have devoted themselves to bringing ideological purity to the state GOP by purging its nonconservative aspirants and officeholders. This resolve was fully displayed in a 2009 special election to fill a vacant seat in New York's Twenty-third Congressional District. The district has been New York's most Republican. But conservatives reproached the 2009 Republican nominee, who had supported abortion choice and legalizing gay marriage. She was, they said, a "RINO": a Republican in name only. The election came down to a choice between the Conservative and Democratic nominees. Winning a plurality—48.7 percent, against the Conservative's 46 percent—the Democrats took the seat.[29] Democrats celebrated. But so did many Conservatives and conservative Republicans. As they saw it, they had driven another nail into the coffin of liberal Rockefeller Republicanism.

Right to Life Party

The Right to Life Party was born three years prior to *Roe v. Wade* (1973) in a state that had already developed a liberal policy on abortion. The RTLP won ballot status in 1978 and kept it until 2002. The party was initiated by a circle of homemakers living in Merrick, on Long Island, forty miles from New York City. Ellen McCormack, its principal founder, was a dedicated political novice. McCormack was a suburban wife and mother.

The RTLP looked for and sometimes found pro-lifers—usually conservative Republicans or Conservatives—to cross-endorse. But often it made its way alone. McCormack ran a token Right to Life presidential campaign in 1980. Making the ballot in New Jersey and Kentucky as well as New York, she received 32,327 votes.

Robert Spitzer, an authority on the Right to Life Party, surveyed RTLP leaders and identifiers. He found that the majority were married and under forty years old. Most labeled themselves as conservatives or moderates. Eighty-four percent of the surveyed leaders and 71 percent of the identifiers were Roman Catholics. Nearly three-quarters of the identifiers said that they would deny an abortion under any circumstance or that they would allow it only to save the mother's life.[30]

The public image that developed of the RTLP was that its partisans were rigid and narrow in focus. RTLP candidates normally managed to attract only a third of all New York voters who identified themselves as pro-life.[31]

Independence Party

Dating from 1991, the Independence Party of New York is the largest third party in the Empire State today. State records released in October 2008 showed that 399,478 voters were registered as IPNY members. By comparison Conservative Party registrants numbered 151,063.[32] Two IPNY enrollees, Timothy P. Gordon and Fred W. Thiele Jr., were serving in the state legislature in 2010.

The founders of IPNY were a trio of Rochester citizens: Thomas Golisano, Laureen Oliver, and Gordon Black. Oliver became her party's first state chair and twice its candidate for statewide offices. Black, a political scientist, went on to work as a pollster for Ross Perot. Golisano, a wealthy businessman, ran in 1994, 1998, and 2002 as the IPNY gubernatorial nominee. His campaigns cost him nearly as much as Perot spent in his two presidential bids. In 2002 one in every seven New York votes went to the IPNY line and Golisano.

Under the leadership of Frank MacKay, its longtime state chair, the IPNY cultivates its image and place as a welcoming home for independents and ideological centrists. Unlike New York Democrats and Republicans, it opens its primaries to unaffiliated voters. In the 1990s the party was identified and connected with Perot's movement of the "angry middle"[33] and with the national Reform Party. MacKay has been at the heart of an initiative since 2007 to build a national Independence Party.

An internal power struggle has afflicted the IPNY since 2005. The antagonists on one side, psychotherapists Fred Newman (who died in 2011) and Lenora Fulani, have been in control of the party's local New York City organization. Frank MacKay is the leading voice on the other side. *Charlatan* is just one of the insulting terms used in their war of words. Ideological differences fuel the conflict, but personal and material factors also are clearly in play.

The pattern of IPNY cross-endorsements may be less predictable than those of other New York minor parties. Democratic gubernatorial nominee Eliot Spitzer took almost 191,000 general election votes on the IPNY line in 2006. The party has endorsed Michael Bloomberg in all of his New York City mayoralty campaigns. In 2009 over a fourth of Bloomberg's votes—far more than his margin of victory—were cast on the Independence Party line. The IPNY cross-endorsed Republican presidential nominee John McCain in 2008.

Some of the IPNY's critics in the New York media contend that the objectives of money and influence figure too strongly into the party's cross-endorsement decisions. IPNY ballot lines, they say, are sometimes available for rent.[34] These are unproven charges, and they may be false or grossly inflated. But it is undoubtedly true that the IPNY has reaped material benefit from its relationships with Bloom-berg and others it has endorsed at election time.[35]

Working Families Party

Though smaller than either the IPNY or the Conservatives,[36] the leftist Working Families Party is soaring. Losing five consecutive New York City mayoralty elections from 1993 through 2009, the Democrats have been cut off from the arsenal of patronage incentives available to the mayor to get out the vote. For voter mobiliza-tion Democrats have become dependent upon the remarkably effective field opera-tion deployed by the Working Families Party. WFP candidates for the second- and third-highest elective posts in New York City—public advocate (Bill de Blasio) and comptroller (John Liu)—won Democratic primary endorsements and then the general election in 2009.

The reach of the WFP extends far beyond New York City. Outside observers now see Working Families as "the most potent new political force in the city and state."[37] The WFP line produced for Eliot Spitzer, the Democrats' 2006 gubernatorial nom-inee, almost as many votes as Spitzer took on the Independence Party line. Demo-cratic congressional and legislative candidates throughout the state actively seek WFP cross-endorsements. The party's presidential line went to Obama in 2008. Witnessing the third party's growing clout in fusion with the Democrats, Jay Jacobs, the state Democratic chair, admitted in 2009 that the WFP has become "the tail that wags the dog."[38]

The Working Families Party dates from 1998. It ascended from the ashes of the New Party; from that party the WFP drew its general ideological disposition, its electoral fusion strategy, and its intimate connections with labor unions and com-munity organizations. According to Daniel Cantor, the party's executive director, the WFP was the creation of three associations joined in coalition: the United Auto Workers, the Communication Workers of America, and the Association of Commu-nity Organizations for Reform Now (ACORN).[39] Unions of teachers and of hospi-tal workers are also pivotal actors within the WFP.

Instead of a lengthy platform, the WFP carries on its Web site a listing of the party's "issues and vision." Besides its stands on education, taxes, equal rights, pub-lic transportation, and veterans, the WFP calls for

- paid sick days for all New Yorkers,
- affordable housing,
- green jobs and green homes,
- clean elections,[40]
- good jobs and living wages,
- health care for all, and
- paid family leaves.

Working Families Parties in Other States

Ballot-certified Working Families parties currently operate in Connecticut and South Carolina, and in Delaware, Oregon, and Vermont—all of which, like New York, allow fusion through cross-endorsement. The New York party calls them "sister parties," but it is clear that the alpha sister resides in the Empire State. New York's WFP provides financial and human resources support. Founded in 2002, the party in neighboring Connecticut is the oldest and most active of the WFPs outside New York.

Source: Edward-Isaac Dovere, "All in the Family Part 5," *City Hall News,* December 4, 2009, http://www.cityhallnews.com/2009/12/all-in-the-family-part-5/.

The WFP was instrumental in the passage of a state minimum wage that is a good bit higher than the national statutory requirement.

Conclusion

Territorially circumscribed and with aims not as lofty as competing for the presidency, state minor parties and independent candidates in Minnesota, Wisconsin, New York, Vermont, Maine, Connecticut, and elsewhere over the past century have emerged the occasional victors in local, congressional, and gubernatorial campaigns. New York state parties draw strength from fusion, and third parties in other states where cross-endorsement is allowed carry the potential for achieving a status like that of their Empire State counterparts.

Advocates of more democratic processes must be careful shoppers, rejecting the siren songs of new state-adopted reform projects that falsely proclaim that democratization will be their legacy. Particularly worrisome is the top two primary, a procedure approved by voters in Washington State and California and in 2008 sustained by the U.S. Supreme Court. Top two virtually assures that no third-party candidate will appear on a state's general election ballot in elections in which top two is used.[41]

But some other electoral reforms have provided openings for third parties as alternative choices available to voters. Local proportional representation systems (later abandoned) transformed minor parties into local power holders in Cincinnati and New York City. Now instant runoff voting can assist in shelving the notion that third-party votes in partisan local and state elections are election-spoiling "wasted" votes.

14

★ ★ ★

Looking Back, Looking Ahead
The Third-Party Legacy and the Future

> As they say in electoral politics, two's company, three's a problem that must be undermined through legislative obstacles. . . .
>
> *Jon Stewart,* America (the Book)

> America's seemingly perfect two-party duopoly has produced a politics of near-total paralysis.
>
> *Micah Sifry*

> It's not easy bein' [G]reen.
>
> *Kermit the Frog*

> It's tough to make predictions, especially about the future.
>
> *attributed to Yogi Berra*

Minor parties they are, minor parties they have been, but their collective footprint in American history has been far from minor. Individual third parties have broken down the barriers of gender, race, ethnicity, and sexual orientation in nomination for high office. Victories of Latinos in elections for state governor date from 1917, of women from 1925, and of African Americans from 1990. All of these earliest gubernatorial trailblazers ran on major-party lines. But insofar as third parties themselves were not shut out from the mainstream, their experience helped illuminate the victory path. President Obama too may owe a debt to the groundbreaking of third parties; likewise Hillary Clinton, Geraldine Ferraro, and Sarah Palin.

Insofar as freedom exists in the American marketplace of ideas, many third parties also have made valuable, even vital contributions in the evolution of the political community and the development of policy.

The Tea Party Movement: A New Wild Card

A new specter arose in 2009. In its reach and potential, it has come to haunt both major parties. It is the national Tea Party movement. Public outrage over the TARP (Troubled Asset Relief Program) bailouts of financial institutions and over the stimulus program fostered it. The Tea Party movement picked up strength following the news of extravagant bonuses paid to executives at AIG and other corporations.

————————————————— ★ ★ —————————————————

Third Parties and the Marketplace of Ideas

In the public discourse about direction, policy, and process in the United States, third parties have long contributed ideas. They continue to offer them today. Not all of these ideas originated with minor parties, but minor parties characteristically adopted and pushed them before either major party arrived on the scene. Many of the ideas they offered proved to be useful, important, even necessary; many, but not all: some were ill considered and unworkable, dangerous or mean spirited. Some of their ideas have been reformist, progressive, or radical. Others were presented by conservatives in reaction to changes already made or proposed.

Many have been passed as policy. Many have not. Some are pending today. Pressure groups sometimes have stood as the crucial agents pushing ideas that are also important to minor parties. The relationship between third-party sponsorship and policy enactment is seldom linear or fully transparent. Hamstrung by their relative powerlessness, third parties usually are not able to provide the policy makers with authority to take ideas and pass them. Actions that decision makers take do sometimes manifestly follow or succeed from the incorporation of popular third-party ideas into major-party platforms or campaigns.

These are among the values and goals that American third parties have embraced and have worked to insert into the nation's public agenda:

- transparency in public life,
- national party conventions,
- party program presented as a written platform,
- international free trade,
- nullification of federal enactments,
- nativism and restrictive immigration policies,
- opposition to the territorial expansion of slavery,
- abolition of slavery, emancipation of slaves,
- defense of slavery,
- preservation of the Union,
- federal merit-based civil service,
- women's suffrage,
- single tax plan,
- farmer-worker coalitions,
- racial equality as public policy,
- currency expansion,
- free coinage of silver,
- progressive/graduated income tax,
- wages and hours legislation,
- election of U.S. senators,
- prohibition (beverage alcohol),
- public land trusts,

- equal pay for equal work,
- initiative and referendum,
- recall elections,
- nationalization of railroads,
- universal health care,
- antitrust legislation,
- Equal Rights Amendment,
- legislation forbidding child labor,
- collective bargaining as a protected right,
- pacifism, antiwar, antidraft,
- government ownership of power plants,
- public works programs for jobs and infrastructure development,
- Social Security,
- government ownership of banks, controlling access to investment capital,
- ending the Cold War, its unsustainable costs, and its frightful dangers,
- racial or ethnic autonomy/self-determination,
- defense of "the southern way of life,"
- southern strategy,
- "law and order"/toughness on crime,
- abortion choice,
- pro-life policy,
- legalization of marijuana,
- abolition of capital punishment,
- marriage as a private contract,
- green economy and sustainability,
- legalization of gay marriage,
- noninterventionism/opposition to military alliances and economic unions,
- antiglobalization,
- virtually open borders,
- privatization of public education,
- radical reductions in military spending,
- repeal of the income tax,
- substantial reforms of the tax system (various proposals),
- elimination of the Federal Reserve,
- radical shifts in energy policy,
- green jobs,
- public health emphasis upon preventive medicine,
- elimination of ballot-access restrictions,
- nondiscriminatory public campaign funding,
- instant runoff voting,
- term limits,
- a federal balanced budget amendment or requirement,
- citizen nomination of candidates through online conventions.

★ ★

It has mobilized scores of people, turning out thousands for some of its demonstrations and rallies. The largest to date occurred in Washington, D.C., on September 12, 2009. Credible estimates of participants that day ranged from seventy-five thousand up to ten times that number.

Antigovernmental in essence, the movement has been distinctly unfriendly to President Obama and to the nation's direction under the Obama administration. Opposition to "Obamacare" and to "cap and trade" legislation has galvanized tea partiers. Some of the movement's shriller voices portray Obama as a totalitarian, and there are those who persist in the fiction that the president was not born on American soil. But as columnist Frank Rich points out, the movement's rank and file may be nearly as hostile to Republicans in power as to Democrats: "tea partiers hate the GOP establishment and its Wall Street allies, starting with the Bushies who created TARP, almost as much as they do Obama and his Wall Street pals."[1]

David Brooks, a Republican columnist for the *New York Times,* sees the Tea Party movement as "a large, fractious confederation of Americans who are defined by what they are against. They are against the concentrated power of the educated class. They

Tea Party protest, Pennsylvania Avenue, September 12, 2009. Photograph by Freedom Fan. Courtesy of Wikipedia, "Tea Party Movement."

believe big government, big business, big media, and the affluent professionals are merging to form self-serving oligarchy—with bloated government, unsustainable deficits, high taxes, and intrusive regulation."[2]

Tea Party activism clearly influenced many outcomes in the 2010 round of congressional elections—elections that returned the Republicans to power in the House and cut deeply into Democratic control of the Senate. A new congressional "Tea Party caucus," chaired by Michele Bachmann, a Minnesotan serving her third term in the House, was a crucial factor in the summer 2011 debt-limit brinksmanship that led to the federal government nearly defaulting for the first time in U.S. history. And despite evidence that its popular appeal was beginning to wane, the Tea Party remained a pivotal power in the selection of a GOP challenger in the campaign to defeat Obama in 2012.

Traditional Republican leaders may be as perplexed about the Tea Party as are their Democratic counterparts, who simply want it to fade away. The GOP is at work to harness the movement, draw upon its energy, and appropriate as much of its voter support as possible. Within the movement the Tea Party Express and Tea Party Nation have moved toward the Republican orbit. Palin was the keynote speaker at the national Tea Party Convention that Tea Party Nation hosted early in February 2010.[3] Among mainstream Republicans there are some who fear that if their party succeeds in co-opting the movement, the result could be "the ruin of the party, pulling it in an angry direction that suburban voters will not tolerate."[4]

But for Republicans the graver threat may lie in the movement's standing as an independent force and its potential to institutionalize as a third party, splitting conservatives and producing Democratic victories. On a three-choice generic ballot featured in a March 2010 Quinnipiac poll, voters elected the Democrat, with 36 percent of their votes. The Republican took 25 percent, the Tea Party candidate 15 percent. In a two-choice matchup in the same Quinnipiac poll, 44 percent voted Republican and just 39 percent Democratic.[5]

The Tea Party Patriots and some other Tea Party groups seek to assist their movement in steering an independent course and resisting the Republicans' gravitational pull.[6] In Florida and some other states, election officials have already certified the Tea Party as a ballot-qualified political party.

The Very Best Candidate Money Can Buy

On January 21, 2010, justices Anthony Kennedy, John Roberts, Samuel Alito, Antonin Scalia, and Clarence Thomas announced their opinion in the landmark *Citizens United v. Federal Election Commission*. The five in the *Citizens United* majority had produced a decision laced with controversy and lacking in the restraint for which in previous cases they had presented themselves as the protective bulwark. Their decision "overruled established precedents and declared dozens of national and state statutes unconstitutional, including the McCain-Feingold Act, which forbade corporate or union television advertising that endorses or opposes a particular candidate."[7]

Writing for the *New York Review of Books,* Ronald Dworkin blasted the majority opinion, which, he said, "announces and perpetuates a shallow, simplistic understanding of the First Amendment, one that actually undermines one of the most basic purposes of free speech, which is to protect democracy." Its "argument—that corporations must be treated like real people under the First Amendment—is . . . preposterous. Corporations are legal fictions. They have no opinions of their own to contribute and no rights to participate with equal voice or vote in politics."[8]

Criticized by public figures ranging from Obama to John McCain, the *Citizens United* decision has received the particular censure of many on the third-party periphery. It is unimaginable that its outcome could be other than a burdensome disincentive to those who might dare to challenge the duopoly. Corporate support goes to those positioned to win. That is why business PACs over the years have given so much more to the campaigns of incumbents than to those seeking to unseat them.

The Future: What You Make It

For a press release issued on the day it was announced, Ralph Nader wrote that the *Citizens United* decision "shreds the fabric of our already weakened democracy by allowing corporations to more completely dominate our corrupted electoral process."[9]

As well positioned as anyone in the United States for the role he has come to assume, Nader is a vital critic of the nation's political process and a prophetic voice for reform. It may take more than a glance to see it, but embedded in his somber post–*Citizens United* statement there is the glimmer of hope and resolve.

Democracy, Nader is saying, endures in America. It is democracy weakened— shredded—by powerful interests. Hyperpartisanship may be choking its policy processes. The major parties curtail access to the election contest for potential challengers, and they limit the voters' freedom to choose. The American system falls short of some of the democratic standards to which the nation has given its commitment.[10] But it is democracy still.

Though it may seem a vacuous cliché, it is true: in democracy people retain some power and responsibility to assess and to change. The future may be tough to predict, but in America you can steer its course.

Appendix 1

Web Sites of Nonmajor Parties and Related Information Sources

Information Sources

Ballot Access News	ballot-access.org
D.C.'s Political Report	dcpoliticalreport.com
Dave Leip's Atlas of U.S. Presidential Elections	uselectionatlas.org
Free and Equal	freeandequal.org
Independent Political Report	independentpoliticalreport.com
Intelligence Report	splcenter.org/intel/intelreport/intrep.jsp
Irregular Times	irregulartimes.org
Poli-Tea: Third Party and Independent Opposition to the Two-Party State	politeaparty.blogspot.com
Third Party and Independent Daily	thirdpartydaily.blogspot.com
ThirdPartyPolitics.us	thirdpartypolitics.us/blog

Leading Current Third Parties

Constitution Party	constitution-party.net
State affiliates of the Constitution Party in many states maintain active Web sites.	
Green Party of the United States	gp.org
State affiliates of the Green Party in many states and in the District of Columbia maintain active Web sites.	
Libertarian Party	lp.org
State affiliates of the Libertarian Party in many states maintain active Web sites.	
Conservative Party of New York State	cpnys.org
Independence Party of Minnesota	mnip.org
Independence Party of New York State	independencepartyny.com
Vermont Progressive Party	progressiveparty.org
Working Families Party (New York)	workingfamiliesparty.org

Other Third/Minor Parties

Alaskan Independence Party	akip.org
All-African People's Revolutionary Party	panafricanperspective.com/aaprp
Aloha Aina Party (Hawaii)	no listed Web site
America First Party	americafirstparty.org
American Centrist Party	americancentristparty.net
American Conservative Party	theamericanconservatives.org
American Independent Party (California)	aipca.org
American Moderate Party	americanmoderateparty.org
American Nazi Party	americannaziparty.com
American Party	theamericanparty.org
American Patriot Party	americanpatriotparty.cc
American Reform Party	americanreform.org
American 3rd Party	3rdparty.org
Americans Elect	americanselect.org
America's Independent Party	selfgovernment.us
Boston Tea Party	bostontea.us
British Reformed Sectarian Party (Florida)	brsparty.com
Center Party	centerparty.us
Centrist Party	uscentrist.org
Charter Party (Cincinnati)	chartercommittee.org
Christian Liberty Party	christianlibertyparty.org
Christian Phalange	phalange.com
Christian Socialist Party	christiansocialistparty.usa
Citizens Party	votecitizens.org
Committee for a Unified Independent Party	independentvoting.org
Communist Party USA	cpusa.org
Connecticut for Lieberman Party	ctforlieberman.blogspot.com
Conservative Party USA	conservativepartyusa.com
DC Statehood Green Party	dcstatehoodgreen.org
Ecology Party (Florida)	ecologyparty.org
Expansionist Party USA	expansionistparty.tripod.org
Freedom Road Socialist Organization	freedomroad.org
Freedom Socialist Party	socialism.com
Greens/Green Party USA	greenparty.org
Independence Party (New York City)	ipnyc.org
Independence Party of America	independenceamerica.com
Independent Green Party (Virginia)	votejoinrun.us
Independent Party of Delaware	independentpartyofdelaware.org
Jefferson Republican Party	jeffersonrepublicanparty.blogspot.com
Labor Party (South Carolina)	thelaborparty.org
LaRouche Political Action Committee	larouchepac.com
Liberal Party of New York (inactive)	liberalparty.org

Libertarian National Socialist Green Party	nazi.org
Liberty Union Party (Vermont)	libertyunionparty.org
Marijuana Reform Party	See norml.org
Moderate Party of Rhode Island	moderate-ri.org
Modern Whig Party	modernwhig.info
Mountain Party (West Virginia)	mtparty.org
National Independent American Party	independentamericanparty.org
National Socialist Movement	nsm88.org
National Woman's Party (historic)	sewallbelmont.org
Natural Law Party (disbanded nationally)	natural-law.org
New American Independent Party	newamericanindependent.com
New Black Panther Party	See dayofactionmovement.org
Objectivist Party	objectivistparty.us
Party for Socialism and Liberation	pslweb.org
Peace and Freedom Party (California)	peaceandfreedom.org
Personal Choice Party (Utah)	thepersonalchoicecommunity.com
Populist Party of America	populistamerica.com
PR Party (New York)	prparty.org
Progressive Dane (Dane County, Wisconsin)	prodane.org
Progressive Labor Party	plp.org
Prohibition Party	prohibitionparty.org and prohibitionists.org
Puerto Rican Independence Party	independencia.net
La Raza Unida Party	larazaunida.tripod.com
Reform Party	reformparty.org
Revolutionary Communist Party	revcom.us or rwor.org
Socialist Equality Party	socialequality.com
Socialist Labor Party	slp.org
Socialist Party USA	sp-usa.org
Socialist Workers Party	See themilitant.com
Southern Party (disbanded)	southernparty.org
United Citizens Party (South Carolina)	theunitedcitizensparty.org
Unity Party of America	unityparty.us
Unity08 (dormant)	unity08.com
U.S. Marijuana Party	usmjparty.com
U.S. Pacifist Party	uspacifistparty.org
U.S. Pirate Party	us.pirate.is
Vermont Independence Day Party	vermontindependence.net
Veterans Party of America	veteransparty.us
Whig Party (Florida)	floridawhig.com
Workers Party	workersparty.org
Workers World Party	workers.org
Working Families Party (Connecticut)	ct-workingfamilies.org

Working Families Party (Delaware)   delworkingfamilies.org
Working Families Party (Oregon)   oregonwfp.org
Working Families Party (South Carolina)   scwfp.org
Working Families Party (Vermont)   vtworkingfamilies.org
World Socialist Party (U.S.)   wspus.org

Appendix 2

Minor-Party and Independent Candidates Receiving More Than 1 Percent of Popular Vote for President

Election	Candidate and Party	Popular Votes and Percent		Electoral Votes and Percent	
1832	William Wirt, Anti-Masonic	100,715	7.78%	7	2.43%
1844	James G. Birney, Liberty	62,103	2.30%	0	
1848	Martin Van Buren, Free Soil	291,501	10.12%	0	
1852	John P. Hale, Free Soil	155,210	4.91%	0	
1856[a]	Millard Fillmore, Know Nothing with Whig endorsement	873,053	21.53%	8	2.70%
1860	John C. Breckinridge, Southern Democratic	848,019	18.09%	72	23.76%
1860	John Bell, Constitutional Union	590,901	12.61%	39	12.87%
1872[b]					
1880	James B. Weaver, Greenback	305,997	3.32%	0	
1884	Benjamin F. Butler, Greenback/Anti-Monopoly	175,096	1.74%	0	
1884	John P. St. John, Prohibition	147,482	1.47%	0	
1888	Clinton B. Fisk, Prohibition	249,813	2.19%	0	
1888	Alson J. Streeter, Union Labor	146,602	1.29%	0	
1892	James B. Weaver, Populist	1,026,595	8.51%	22	4.95%
1892	John Bidwell, Prohibition	270,889	2.24%	0	
1896[c]					
1900	John C. Wooley, Prohibition	210,867	1.51%	0	
1904	Eugene V. Debs, Socialist	402,810	2.98%	0	
1904	Silas C. Swallow, Prohibition	259,103	1.92%	0	
1908	Eugene V. Debs, Socialist	420,852	2.83%	0	
1908	Eugene W. Chafin, Prohibition	254,087	1.71%	0	
1912	Theodore Roosevelt, Progressive (Bull Moose)	4,122,721	27.40%	88	16.57%
1912	Eugene V. Debs, Socialist	901,551	5.99%	0	

Appendix 2 continued

Election	Candidate and Party	Popular Votes and Percent		Electoral Votes and Percent	
1912	Eugene W. Chafin, Prohibition	208,156	1.38%	0	
1916	Allan L. Benson, Socialist	590,524	3.19%	0	
1916	J. Frank Hanley, Prohibition	221,302	1.19%	0	
1920	Eugene V. Debs, Socialist	913,693	3.41%	0	
1924	Robert M. La Follette, Progressive (and Socialist, Farmer-Labor)	4,831,706	16.61%	13	2.45%
1932	Norman M. Thomas, Socialist	884,885	2.23%	0	
1936	William Lemke, Union	892,378	1.95%	0	
1948	J. Strom Thurmond, Dixiecrat	1,175,930	2.41%	39	7.34%
1948	Henry A. Wallace, Progressive and NY American Labor	1,157,328	2.37%	0	
1968	George C. Wallace, American Independent	9,901,118	13.53%	46	8.55%
1972	John G. Schmitz, American	1,100,868	1.42%	0	
1980	John B. Anderson, National Unity (Independent)	5,719,850	6.61%	0	
1980	Edward E. Clark, Libertarian	921,128	1.06%	0	
1992	H. Ross Perot, Independent	19,743,821	18.91%	0	
1996	H. Ross Perot, Reform	8,085,402	8.40%	0	
2000	Ralph Nader, Green	2,883,105	2.73%	0	

NOTES

a. Fillmore of the Know Nothing or American Party finished in third place. Republican John C. Fremont was second, behind James Buchanan, the victorious Democrat. Fremont won 1,342,345 popular votes (33.11 percent) and 114 electoral votes (38.51 percent). The two-year-old Republican Party was not yet firmly installed as a major party, but clearly it was establishing itself as such by 1856.

b. In a fusion campaign, the Democrats in 1872 nominated Liberal Republican nominee Horace Greeley and adopted the LRP platform verbatim. Greeley won 2,834,761 votes (43.83 percent). Greeley died before the meeting of the Electoral College, but electors to whose votes he would have been entitled cast 66 votes. Congress declined to count three of these because they were cast for the deceased nominee.

c. Populists nominated Democratic nominee William Jennings Bryan, who had two vice-presidential running mates, one Democratic, the other Populist. Bryan won 6,511,495 popular votes (46.73 percent) and 176 electoral votes (39.37 percent). Thomas Watson, Bryan's Populist running mate, received twenty-seven electoral votes, even though some Populist electors voted instead for the Democratic vice-presidential nominee.

SOURCES: *Presidential Elections since 1789* (Washington, D.C.: Congressional Quarterly, 1975); *History of U.S. Political Parties,* ed. Arthur Schlesinger Jr. (New York: Chelsea House, 1975); various election reports from the Federal Election Commission; and Dave Leip, *Atlas of U.S. Presidential Elections,* available online at http://uselectionatlas.org (accessed September 5, 2011).

Appendix 3

Candidates and Votes for President, 2008

Candidate	Party Designation[a]	Ballot Positions (Number of States + D.C.)	Votes[b]
Barack Obama	Democrat	51	69,498,516
John McCain	Republican	51	59,948,323
Ralph Nader	Independent, Peace and Freedom	46	739,034
Bob Barr	Libertarian	45	523,715
Chuck Baldwin	Constitution, Reform, U.S. Taxpayers	39	199,750
Cynthia McKinney	Green, Independent, WV Mountain	32	161,797
Reported Write-in	(Miscellaneous)		112,597
Alan Keyes	America's Independent	3	47,746
Ron Paul	MT Constitution,[c] LA Taxpayers	2	42,426
Roger Calero/ James Harris[d]	Socialist Workers	10	7,575
Gloria La Riva	Socialism and Liberation	12	6,818
Brian Moore	Socialist, Liberty Union	8	6,538
None of these candidates		Nevada	6,267
Richard Duncan	Independent	1	3,905
Charles Jay	Boston Tea, Independent	3	2,422
John Joseph Polachek	New	1	1,149
Frank Edward McEulty	Unaffiliated	1	829
Jeffrey Wamboldt	We the People, Independent	1	764
Thomas Robert Stevens	Objectivist	2	755
Gene C. Amondson	Prohibition	3	653
Jeffrey Boss	Vote Here	1	639
George Phillies	Libertarian	1	531

Appendix 3 continued

Candidate	Party Designation[a]	Ballot Positions (Number of States + D.C.)	Votes[b]
Ted Weill	Reform	1	481
Jonathan E. Allen	Heartquake '08	1	480
Bradford Lyttle	U.S. Pacifist	1	110

NOTES

a. Because of the intricacies and diversity of state ballot access laws, third-party and independent candidates often appear under different labels in different states.

b. The results include returns in states where candidates had ballot access as well as reported write-in votes in other states.

c. Although Paul declined all overtures to run as a third-party candidate after losing the Republican nomination, his supporters secured for him places on the Louisiana and Montana ballots, and he received some write-in votes elsewhere. In Montana Paul's name appeared instead of Chuck Baldwin's on the line of the state affiliate of the Constitution Party.

d. Calero is not a U.S. citizen and is thus constitutionally ineligible for the presidency. Harris stood in for Calero on the ballots of those states that certified the Socialist Workers Party but excluded Calero because of his noncitizen status.

SOURCES: *Federal Elections 2008* (Washington, D.C.: Federal Election Commission, 2009); and "2008 Presidential Vote," *Ballot Access News,* December 1, 2008, http://www.ballot-access.org/2008/120108.html#10 (accessed September 5, 2011)

Appendix 4

Third-Party and Independent Gubernatorial Popular Elections

The table includes campaigns in which the candidate won on a single ballot or ballot line and also fusion campaigns in which a third party played a major or crucial role. It excludes fusion campaigns in which the participating third party had little or no impact.

Election Year(s)	State	Successful Candidate	Party/Parties
1831, 1832, 1833, 1834	Vermont	William A. Palmer	Anti-Masonic
1835	Pennsylvania	Joseph Ritner	Anti-Masonic
1842	Rhode Island	Thomas Dorr (extralegal)	RI Suffrage (Dorr Rebellion)
1843, 1844	Rhode Island	James Fenner	RI Law and Order
1845	Alabama	Joshua L. Martin	Independent
1845	Rhode Island	Charles Jackson	Liberation (fusion)
1846	Rhode Island	Byron Diman[a]	RI Law and Order
1853, 1855	Texas	Elisha M. Pease	Unionist
1854	Delaware	Peter F. Causey	Know Nothing
1854	Maine	Anson P. Morrill	Know Nothing–Republican[b]
1854, 1855, 1856	Massachusetts	Henry J. Gardner	Know Nothing
1854	Rhode Island	William W. Hoppin	Know Nothing–Whig
1855	California	J. Neely Johnson	Know Nothing
1855, 1856	Connecticut	William T. Minor	Know Nothing–Temperance
1855	Kentucky	Charles S. Morehead	Know Nothing
1855, 1856	New Hampshire	Ralph Metcalf	Know Nothing
1855	Ohio	Salmon P. Chase	Republican
1855	Vermont	Stephen Royce	Republican
1855	Wisconsin	Coles Bashford	Republican
1856	New Jersey	William A. Newell	Know Nothing–Republican

1856[c]

Appendix 4 continued

Election Year(s)	State	Successful Candidate	Party/Parties
1857	Maryland	Thomas H. Hicks	Know Nothing
1859	Texas	Sam Houston	Independent–Know Nothing
1865, 1866	North Carolina	Jonathan Worth	N.C. Conservative
1870	Missouri	B. Gratz Brown	Liberal Republican
1872[d]	Louisiana	John McEnery	Democratic–Liberal Republican
1880	Maine	Harry S. Plaisted	Greenback-Democratic
1881	Virginia	William E. Cameron	Virginia Readjuster
1882	Massachusetts	Benjamin F. Butler	Democratic-Greenback
1882	Michigan	Josiah Begole	Greenback-Democratic
1890	Oregon	Sylvester Pennoyer	Democratic-Populist
1890	Tennessee	John P. Buchanan	Democratic–Farmers' Alliance
1892	Colorado	Davis H. Waite	Populist–Silver Democratic
1892	Kansas	L. D. Lewelling	Populist
1892	North Dakota	Eli C. D. Shortridge	Populist-Democratic–Farmers' Alliance
1894, 1896	Nebraska	Silas A. Holcomb	Populist–Silver Democratic
1894	Nevada	John E. Jones	Nevada Silver
1896	Idaho	Frank Steunenberg	Democratic-Populist
1896	Kansas	John H. Leedy	Populist
1896	Montana	Robert B. Smith	Democratic-Populist
1896, 1898	South Dakota	Andrew E. Lee	Populist
1896, 1898	Washington	John R. Rogers	Populist-Democratic
1898	Colorado	Charles S. Thomas	Democratic-Populist
1898	Nebraska	William A. Poynter	Populist–Silver Democratic
1898	Nevada	Reinhold Sadler	Nevada Silver
1898	Minnesota	John Lind	Democratic-Populist–Silver Republican
1900	Colorado	James Bradley Orman	Democratic-Populist–Silver Republican
1902, 1906	Nevada	John Sparks	Nevada Silver–Democratic
1914	California	Hiram W. Johnson	Progressive (Bull Moose)
1916	Florida	Sidney J. Catts	Prohibition
1916, 1918, 1920	North Dakota	Lynn J. Frazier[e]	Nonpartisan League–Republican

Election Year(s)	State	Successful Candidate	Party/Parties
1921	North Dakota	Ragnvold A. Nestos[e]	Independent Voters Association–Republican
1930, 1932, 1934	Minnesota	Floyd B. Olson	Minnesota Farmer-Labor
1930	Oregon	Julius L. Meier	Independent
1934, 1936	Wisconsin	Philip F. La Follette	Wisconsin Progressive
1936	Minnesota	Elmer A. Benson	Minnesota Farmer-Labor
1936	North Dakota	William Langer	Independent
1942	Wisconsin	Orland S. Loomis[f]	Wisconsin Progressive
1974	Maine	John B. Longley	Independent
1990	Alaska	Walter J. Hickel	Alaskan Independence
1990	Connecticut	Lowell P. Weicker	A Connecticut
1994, 1998	Maine	Angus S. King Jr.	Independent
1998	Minnesota	Jesse Ventura	Reform; later Minnesota Independence
2010	Rhode Island	Lincoln Chafee	Independent

Notes

a. Diman, who won a popular plurality but not a majority, was elected by the Rhode Island General Assembly.

b. Morrill was elected by the Maine legislature following the 1854 popular election.

c. By 1856 the Republican Party was far along in its transition to major-party status. Republican gubernatorial candidates won election in Illinois, Maine, New York, and Vermont in 1856.

d. McEnery's election was overturned by the Grant administration and by pro-Grant Republican forces in Louisiana.

e. Although winning election in 1916 and reelection in 1918 and 1920 on the Republican ballot line, Frazier was the candidate put forward by the powerful leftist Nonpartisan League. Nestos, representing the more conservative Independent Voters Association, won on the Republican line in 1921 in an election recalling Frazier. Frazier was the first of only two U.S. governors ever removed in a recall election.

f. Loomis died before inauguration day. The governorship went to the Republican lieutenant governor–elect.

Sources: Joseph E. Kallenbach and Jessamine S. Kallenbach, *American State Governors, 1776–1976* (Dobbs Ferry, N.Y.: Oceana, 1977); historical records from secretaries of state in various states; and *Ballot Access News.*

Appendix 5

Third-Party Presence (Excluding Independents) at Opening Sessions of the U.S. Congress

Congress and Year of Opening Session	U.S. Senate: Party and Seats	U.S. House: Party and Seats
21st, 1829	—	Anti-Masonic 5
22nd, 1831	SC Nullifier 2	Anti-Masonic 17; South Carolina Nullifier 4
23rd, 1833	South Carolina Nullifier 2	Anti-Masonic 25; Nullifier (South Carolina, Alabama) 9
24th, 1835	South Carolina Nullifier 2	Anti-Masonic 16; Nullifier (South Carolina, Alabama) 8
25th, 1837	—	Anti-Masonic 7; South Carolina Nullifier 6
26th 1839	—	Anti-Masonic 6; Virginia Conservative 2
28th, 1843	—	Rhode Island Law and Order 2
29th, 1845	—	Know Nothing 6
30th, 1847	—	Know Nothing 1
31st, 1849	Free Soil 2	Free Soil 9; Know Nothing 1
32nd, 1851	Free Soil 3	Unionist 10; Free Soil 4; States Rights 3
33rd, 1853	Free Soil 2	Free Soil 4
34th, 1855	Know Nothing 1	Know Nothing 51
35th, 1857[a]	Know Nothing 5	Know Nothing 14
36th, 1859	Know Nothing 2	Opposition 19; Know Nothing 5
37th, 1861	—	Constitutional Union 2; Rhode Island Union 2
41st, 1869	—	Virginia Conservative 5
42nd, 1871	Liberal Republican 1	Liberal Republican 2
43rd, 1873	Liberal Republican 7	Liberal Republican 4
46th, 1879	—	Greenback 13
47th, 1881	Virginia Readjuster 1	Greenback 10; Virginia Readjuster 2

Appendix 5 continued

Congress and Year of Opening Session	U.S. Senate: Party and Seats	U.S. House: Party and Seats
48th, 1883	Virginia Readjuster 2	Virginia Readjuster 4; Greenback 2
49th, 1885	Virginia Readjuster 2	Greenback 1
50th, 1887	Virginia Readjuster 1	Labor/fusion 3; Greenback 1
51st, 1889	—	Labor 1
52nd, 1891	Populist 2	Populist 8
53rd, 1893	Populist 3; Nevada Silver 1	Populist 11; Nevada Silver 1
54th, 1895	Populist 4; Nevada Silver 2	Populist 9; Nevada Silver 1
55th, 1897	Populist 8; Silver Republican 5; Nevada Silver 2	Populist 22; Silver Republican 3; Nevada Silver 1
56th, 1899	Populist 5; Silver Republican 3; Nevada Silver 2	Populist 6; Silver Republican 2; Nevada Silver 1
57th, 1901	Populist 2	Populist 5; Nevada Silver 1; Anti-Machine 1
58th, 1903	Silver Republican 3	Silver Republican 1
62nd, 1911	—	Socialist 1
63rd, 1913	Progressive 1	Progressive 9
64th, 1915	—	Progressive 6; Prohibition 1; Socialist 1
65th, 1917	—	Progressive 3; Prohibition 1; Socialist 1
66th, 1919	—	Minnesota Union Labor 1; Prohibition 1; Socialist 1[b]
67th, 1921	—	Socialist 1
68th 1923	Minnesota Farmer-Labor 1	Minnesota Farmer-Labor 2; Socialist 1
69th, 1925	Minnesota Farmer-Labor 1	Minnesota Farmer-Labor 3; Socialist/Liberty Bell 1; Socialist 1
70th, 1927	Minnesota Farmer-Labor 1	Minnesota Farmer-Labor 2; Socialist 1
71st, 1929	Minnesota Farmer-Labor 1	Minnesota Farmer-Labor 1
72nd, 1931	Minnesota Farmer-Labor 1	Minnesota Farmer-Labor 1
73rd, 1933	Minnesota Farmer-Labor 1	Minnesota Farmer-Labor 5
74th, 1935	Minnesota Farmer-Labor 1; Wisconsin Progressive 1	Wisconsin Progressive 7; Minnesota Farmer-Labor 3

Congress and Year of Opening Session	U.S. Senate: Party and Seats	U.S. House: Party and Seats
75th, 1937	Minnesota Farmer-Labor 2; Wisconsin Progressive 1;	Wisconsin Progressive 7 Minnesota Farmer-Labor 5; Progressive 1
76th, 1939	Minnesota Farmer-Labor 2; Wisconsin Progressive 1;	Wisconsin Progressive 2 Minnesota Farmer-Labor 1; New York American Labor 1
77th, 1941	Wisconsin Progressive 1	Wisconsin Progressive 3; Minnesota Farmer-Labor 1; New York American Labor 1
78th, 1943	Wisconsin Progressive 1	Wisconsin Progressive 2; Minnesota Farmer-Labor 1; New York American Labor 1
79th, 1945	Wisconsin Progressive 1	New York American Labor 1; Wisconsin Progressive 1
80th, 1947	—	New York American Labor 1
81st, 1949	—	New York American Labor 1; New York Liberal[c]
92nd, 1971	New York Conservative 1	—
93rd, 1973	New York Conservative 1	—
94th, 1975	New York Conservative 1	—

NOTES

a. By 1856 the two-year-old Republican Party was well in transition to major-party status. Twenty Republicans served in the Senate and ninety in the House in the Thirty-fifth Congress.

b. The one Socialist was Victor Berger of Wisconsin. Included in the table because he was duly elected. The House declined to seat him in the Sixty-sixth Congress.

c. Franklin D. Roosevelt Jr., installed on May 17, 1949, following election in a special election on the Liberal line. Included because he served all but 4 $\frac{1}{2}$ months of the Eighty-first Congress.

SOURCES: Kenneth C. Martis, *The Historical Atlas of Political Parties in the United States Congress, 1789–1989* (New York: Macmillan, 1989); *Biographical Directory of the United States Congress, 1774–Present,* http://bioguide.congress.gov/biosearch/biosearch.asp (accessed September 5, 2011); and "Candidates Elected to the House, 1902–2000, Who Weren't Nominees of the Democratic or Republican Parties" and "Minor Party Members Elected to the House, 1902–2000, Who Were Nominated by Their Own Minor Party, Plus a Major Party," *Ballot Access News,* June 1, 2001, http://web.archive.org/web/20030417 164754/http://www.ballot-access.org/2001/0601.html#17 and http://web.archive.org/ web/20030417164754/http://www.ballot-access.org/2001/0601.html#18, respectively (both accessed September 5, 2011).

Appendix 6

Post–World War II Third-Party and Independent Members of Congress

Member	Service under Third-Party or Independent Designation	Inclusive Dates of All Congressional Service
Sen. Robert La Follette Jr.	1934–47 Wisconsin Progressive	Senate, 1925–47
Rep. Merlin Hull	1935–47 Wisconsin Progressive	House, 1929–31, 1935–53
Rep. Vito Marcantonio	1939–51 New York American Labor	House, 1935–37, 1939–51
Rep. Leo Isacson	1948–49 New York American Labor	House, 1948–49
Rep. Franklin D. Roosevelt Jr.	1949–51 New York Liberal	House, 1949–55
Rep. Frazier Reams	1951–55 Independent, Ohio	House, 1951–55
Sen. Wayne L. Morse	1952–55 Independent, Oregon	Senate, 1945–69
Sen. J. Strom Thurmond[a]	1955–57 Independent, South Carolina	Senate, 1955–2003
Rep. Quentin N. Burdick	1959–60 North Dakota Nonpartisan League	House, 1959–60; Senate, 1960–92
Sen. Harry F. Byrd Jr.	1970–83 Independent, Virginia	Senate, 1965–83
Sen. James L. Buckley	1971–77 New York Conservative	Senate, 1971–77
Rep./Sen. Bernard Sanders	1991– Independent, Vermont	House, 1991–2007; Senate, 2007–
Rep. Virgil H. Goode Jr.	2000–2002 Independent, Virginia	House, 1997–2009
Sen. James M. Jeffords	2001–7 Independent, Vermont	House, 1975–89; Senate, 1989–2007
Sen. Dean M. Barkley[b]	2002–3 Minnesota Independence	Senate, 2002–3
Sen. Joseph I. Lieberman	2007– Independent, Connecticut	Senate, 1989–
Sen. Lisa A. Murkowski[a]	2011– Independent Republican, Alaska	House, 1998–2000; Senate, 2002–

NOTES

a. Strom Thurmond in 1954 and Lisa Murkowski in 2010 won U.S. Senate elections as write-in candidates.

b. Dean Barkley was appointed by Minnesota governor Jesse Ventura to a short interim.

SOURCE: Biographical Directory of the United States Congress, 1774–Present, http://bioguide.congress.gov/biosearch/biosearch.asp (accessed August 5, 2011).

Notes

1. Duopoly and Its Challengers

1. Richard Winger's daily blog, Ballot-access.org, June 30, 2008, http://www.ballot
-access.org/2008/06/30/maine-democrats-sue-secretary-of-state-to-get-independent
-senate-candidate-off-the-ballot/.

2. Copenhagen Document of the Human Dimension of the CSCE (1990), available
online at http://idw.csfederalismo.it/attachments/349_Copenhagen%20Document%20
-%20human%20dimension.pdf2 (accessed September 2, 2011).

3. See Richard Winger, "Ballot Access: A Formidable Barrier to Fair Participation,"
Ballot Access News (1999), also available online at http://www.ballot-access.org/winger/fb
fp.html (accessed August 5, 2011).

4. Tim Rutten, "The Winter of America's Discontent," *Los Angeles Times,* February 5,
2010.

5. Eight percent of respondents in a late September 2008 *Washington Post*/ABC News
poll selected the "Other" label, rather than "Democrat," "Republican," or even "Independent," to identify their party affiliation.

6. John F. Bibby and L. Sandy Maisel, *Two Parties—or More? The American Party System,* 2nd ed. (Boulder, Colo.: Westview, 2003), 21.

7. Poll commissioned by Unity 08. See "Group Seeks Cross-Party Ticket for 2008,"
Online Newshour, May 31, 2006, transcript available online at http://www.pbs.org/
newshour/bb/politics/jan-june06/unity_05-31.html (accessed September 2, 2011).

8. Grace, "Top Question Tuesday Results: Two Parties or More?" IBOPE Zogby International, August 5, 2009, http://www.zogby.com/blog/2009/08/05/top-question-tuesday
-results-two-parties-or-more/.

9. See Mark Leibowitz, "The Socialist Senator," *New York Times,* January 21, 2007.

10. Data from an unpublished study by Richard Winger.

11. Micah L. Sifry, *Spoiling for a Fight: Third-Party Politics in America* (New York:
Routledge, 2002), 63–141.

12. Ibid., 66–68.

13. Jeremy D. Mayer and Clyde Wilcox, "Understanding Perot's Plummet," in *Ross for
Boss: The Perot Phenomenon and Beyond,* ed. Ted G. Jelen (Albany: SUNY Press, 2001),
143.

14. Ibid., 144.

15. Steven A. Holmes, "The 1992 Elections," *New York Times,* November 5, 1992.

16. Jacob Lentz, *Electing Jesse Ventura: A Third-Party Success Story* (Boulder, Colo.: Lynne Rienner, 2002), 43–44.

17. See Sifry, *Spoiling for a Fight,* 175.

18. *Bush v. Gore,* 531 U.S. 98 (2000).

19. David J. Rosenbaum, "The 2004 Campaign; Relax, Nader Advises Alarmed Democrats, but the 2000 Math Counsels Otherwise," *New York Times,* February 24, 2004.

20. J. David Gillespie, "Third-Party 'Spoilers' Don't Deserve Punishment," *Atlanta Journal-Constitution,* November 12, 2000, op. ed. sect.

21. For example, see Tim Russert's February 26, 2008, interview of Nader on NBC's *Meet the Press.*

22. See Tony Norman, "Nader Deserves More Respect Than He Gets," *Pittsburgh Post-Gazette,* October 23, 2009.

23. "Connecticut for Lieberman Party Nominates Anti-Lieberman Activist for U.S. Senate in 2010," Ballot-access.org, January 14, 2010, http://www.ballot-access.org/2010/01/14/connecticut-for-lieberman-party-nominates-anti-lieberman-activist-for-u-s-senate-in-2010/.

24. For example Lou Dobbs, one of the nation's sharpest media critics of corporate power and globalization, of free trade agreements and illegal immigration. Dobbs, *Independents Day: Awakening the American Spirit* (New York: Viking, 2007). Also political consultant Douglas E. Schoen, *Declaring Independence: The Beginning of the End of the Two-Party System* (New York: Random House, 2008).

25. Ron Paul, *The Revolution: A Manifesto* (New York: Grand Central, 2008).

26. "Ron Paul's Appeal," *Washington Post,* editorial, January 11, 2008.

27. "Ron Paul, a Republican Outsider, Sets Fund-raising Record," *International Herald Tribune,* December 18, 2007.

28. Aaron Gould Sheinin, "Barr Asks Paul to Be His Running Mate," *Atlanta Journal-Constitution,* September 10, 2008.

29. "2008 Ballot Status for President," *Ballot Access News,* November 1, 2008, also available online at http://www.ballot-access.org/2008/110108.html#6 (accessed September 2, 2011).

30. Miller had the strong backing of Sarah Palin. A write-in candidate also won a sheriff's race in Sublette County, Wyoming. Other victories included four county-level partisan races won by the Nevada branch of the Constitution Party and various successful (mainly) nonpartisan races by Greens and Libertarians at scattered locations nationwide.

31. For a (critical) commentary on No Labels, see Frank Rich, "The Bipartisanship Racket," *New York Times,* December 18, 2010, op. ed. sect.

32. See Thomas L. Friedman, "Third Party Rising," *New York Times,* October 2, 2010, op. ed. sect.; also Matt Miller, "Why We Need a Third Party of (Radical) Centrists," *Washington Post,* November 10, 2010, op. ed. sect.

2. Protecting Major-Party Turf

1. Micah L. Sifry, *Spoiling for a Fight: Third-Party Politics in America* (New York: Routledge, 2002), 4.

2. William Safire, *Safire's Political Dictionary* (Oxford: Oxford University Press, 2008), 46.

3. These party primaries should not to be confused with the Top Two primary, a procedure adopted through popular referenda in Washington state in 2004 and in California in 2010. Top Two is virtually nonpartisan, except that candidates may indicate their party preference on the primary ballot. The primary winnows the general election choices to the two leading vote getters, who may be of different parties or the same party. Although third parties are particularly disadvantaged by Top Two, major- and minor-party leaders share a dislike of Top Two because it largely factors out a party role in nominating candidates.

4. Louis Hartz put forth these ideas in his classic treatise on American thought and practice, *The Liberal Tradition in America* (New York: Harcourt, Brace and World, 1955), esp. 5–14.

5. Daniel A. Mazmanian, *Third Parties in Presidential Elections* (Washington, D.C.: Brookings Institution, 1974), 1–2.

6. John F. Kirch, "Third-Party Blind Spot," *Baltimore Sun,* November 20, 2008, op. ed. sect.

7. Steven J. Rosenstone, Roy L. Behr, and Edward H. Lazarus, *Third Parties in America: Citizen Response to Major Party Failure,* 2nd ed. (Princeton, N.J.: Princeton University Press, 1996), 33.

8. Jonathan Laurence, "Ross Perot's Outsider Challenge: New and Old Media in American Presidential Campaigns," in *The Media and Neo-Populism: A Contemporary Comparative Analysis,* ed. Gianpetro Mazzolini et al. (Westport, Conn.: Praeger, 2002), 175.

9. Ibid., 176.

10. Maurice Duverger, *Political Parties: Their Organization and Activity in the Modern State,* trans. Barbara and Robert North (New York: Wiley, 1954).

11. Ibid. Also see Bernard Grofman, *Duverger's Law of Plurality Voting* (New York: Springer, 2009).

12. These include the open party list, closed party list, and single-transferable forms.

13. Rob Richie and Steven Hill, "The Case for Proportional Representation," *Social Policy* 26, no. 4 (1996): 25–37; also available online at Third World Traveler, http://www.third worldtraveler.com/Political/CaseForPropRep.html (accessed August 17, 2011).

14. Simon W. Gerson, *Pete: The Story of Peter V. Cacchione, New York's First Communist Councilman* (New York: International Publishers, 1976), esp. 186–91.

15. Fair Vote is one of the leading groups advocating IRV. See http://www.fairvote.org.

16. James Wiseman, "Antiquated Runoff System Does Not Reflect Voters' Views," *Atlanta Journal-Constitution,* November 17, 2008, op. ed. sect.

17. For a general critical assessment of the Electoral College, see "Flunking the Electoral College," *New York Times,* November 19, 2008.

18. It also bears noting that it takes an electoral vote majority to win the presidency. A third-party candidate someday may be in a king-making position, able to make policy or appointment demands in return for the promise to deliver the needed electoral votes. This apparently was an unfulfilled goal of George Wallace's 1968 third-party quest.

19. Rosenstone, Behr, and Lazarus, *Third Parties,* 24–25.

20. Richard Winger, "How Many Parties Ought to Be on the Ballot? An Analysis of *Nader v. Keith*," *Election Law Journal* 5, no. 2 (2006): 172–76.

21. Ibid., 176–77. Some of these were later rescinded or were overturned by judicial decree.

22. *Williams v. Rhodes,* 393 U.S. 23 (1968). Three years after *Williams v. Rhodes,* the high court unanimously sustained a high Georgia statutory threshold for challengers seeking to attain and retain ballot access. *Jenness v. Fortson,* 403 U.S. 431 (1971).

23. Winger, "How Many Parties," 175.

24. *Burdick v. Tukushi,* 504 U.S. 428 (1992).

25. "2008 Ballot Status for President," *Ballot Access News,* November 1, 2008, also available online at http://www.ballot-access.org/2008/110108.html#6 (accessed September 2, 2011).

26. Rosenstone, Behr, and Lazarus, *Third Parties,* 24.

27. The author's November 1, 1988, telephone interview with Annie Roboff, New Alliance Party press secretary.

28. Troy K. Schneider, "Can't Win for Losing," *New York Times,* July 16, 2006, op. ed. sect.

29. *Storer v. Brown,* 414 U.S. 737 (1974).

30. See Marc Gallagher, "Ron Paul Third Party Bid Impossible—GOP Forbade It," November 5, 2008, http://libertymaven.com/2008/11/05/ron-paul-third-party-run-impossible-gop-forbade-it/3048/.

31. "Do 'Sore Loser' Laws Apply to Presidential Candidates?" *Ballot Access News,* July 20, 2007, also available online at http://www.ballot-access.org/2007/07/20/do-sore-loser-laws-apply-to-presidential-candidates/.

32. The other two states are Massachusetts and New Hampshire. Pennsylvania allows fusion in school board elections but in not much else.

33. Micah L. Sifry, "Obama, the New Party, and Stanley Kurtz's Horror," *Huffington Post,* October 20, 2008, http://www.huffingtonpost.com/micah-sifry/obama-the-new-party-and-s_b_136330.html.

34. *Timmons v. Twin Cities Area New Party,* 520 U.S. 351 (1997).

35. Ibid. See Lisa J. Disch, *The Tyranny of the Two-Party System* (New York: Columbia University Press, 2002).

36. "League Refuses to 'Help Perpetuate a Fraud': Withdraws from Final Presidential Debate," press release, League of Women Voters, October 3, 1988, http://www.lwv.org/AM/Template.cfm?Section=Home&template=/CM/HTMLDisplay.cfm&ContentID=7777 (accessed August 17, 2011).

37. Rosenstone, Behr, and Lazarus, *Third Parties,* 26.

38. Obama, the beneficiary of the most successful fund-raising operation in the history of presidential campaigns, was the first major-party nominee since public funding went into effect in 1976 to turn down the general election funds and thus the spending cap that his acceptance would have imposed. McCain did accept the federal money, and he attempted to make a campaign issue of Obama's refusing it.

39. Jeremy D. Mayer and Clyde Wilcox, "Understanding Perot's Plummet," in *Ross for Boss: The Perot Phenomenon and Beyond,* ed. Ted G. Jelen (Albany: SUNY Press, 2001), 144.

40. "Presidential Public Funding," *Ballot Access News,* November 1, 2008, also available online at http://www.ballot-access.org/2008/110108.html#8 (accessed August 17, 2011).

41. *Buckley v. Valeo,* 424 U.S. 1 (1976). In 1982 the Supreme Court specifically upheld a Socialist Workers Party claim for exemption from requirements, set forth in an Ohio law, for disclosure of donors and also of expenditures. *Brown v. Socialist Workers '74 Campaign Committee,* 459 U.S. 87 (1982).

42. In 2009 U.S. District Court judge Stefan Underhill declared the Connecticut public funding statute to be unconstitutional because it severely discriminated against minor parties and independent candidates. Unfortunately in a remarkably broad July 13, 2010, ruling, the U.S. Second Circuit Court of Appeals overturned Judge Underhill's decision, 2–1, thus sustaining these discriminatory elements of the Connecticut law. The U.S. Supreme Court later declined to hear the case on appeal.

43. Debs served more than thirty-two months before securing release by President Warren G. Harding.

44. See *Schenck v. United States,* 249 U.S. 47 (1919); and *Gitlow v. New York,* 268 U.S. 652 (1925).

45. Harvey Klehr, John Earl Haynes, and Fridrikh I. Firsov, *The Secret World of American Communism* (New Haven: Yale University Press, 1995), 6.

46. *Dennis v. the United States,* 341 U.S. 494 (1951). See Hugo Black's dissent.

47. See *Yates v. the United States,* 354 U.S. 298 (1957); and *Watkins v. the United States,* 354 U.S. 178 (1957).

48. The literature on COINTELPRO is extensive. See especially the Senate Select Committee on Intelligence Activities' two-volume report titled *COINTELPRO and Other Intelligence Activities Targeting Americans, 1940–1975* (Ipswich, Mass.: Mary Ferrell Foundation Press, 2010).

49. "Schwarzenegger Vetoes Bill That Eliminated Some Discrimination against Communist Party Members," *Ballot Access News,* September 30, 2008, also available online at http://www.ballot-access.org/2008/09/30/schwarzenegger-vetoes-bill-that-eliminated -some-discrimination-against-communist-party-members/ (accessed August 17, 2011).

3. On the Outside, Looking In

1. Omar H. Ali, *In the Balance of Power: Independent Black Politics and Third-Party Movements in the United States* (Athens: Ohio University Press, 2008).

2. Kari Lydersen, "David v. Goliath," *In These Times* 24, no. 10 (2000), available online at http://www.inthesetimes.com/issue/24/10/lyderson2410.html (accessed September 2, 2011).

3. See no. 51 of *The Federalist,* written by Madison.

4. Factions, known as the Federalists and Antifederalists, had in fact been created in response to the Constitution and whether it should be ratified.

5. Former president Theodore Roosevelt, the 1912 Progressive nominee, actually supplanted William Howard Taft, the Republican incumbent seeking reelection, as the leading opponent of victorious Democratic nominee Woodrow Wilson. Roosevelt won more than 27 percent of the popular vote. Three other twentieth-century nonmajor-party candidates received popular tallies ranging from 13.5 percent to 19 percent.

6. Realignment theory as it is conventionally presented does have its challengers. See David R. Mayhew, *Electoral Realignments: A Critique of an American Genre* (New Haven: Yale University Press, 2002).

7. For example Timothy Egan, "This American Moment—the Surprises," *New York Times,* November 5, 2008; Jay Cost, "Is 2008 a Realignment?" Real Clear Politics, November 11, 2008, http://www.realclearpolitics.com/horseraceblog/2008/11/is_2008_a _realignment.html; Nate Silver, "Was 2008 a Realigning Election? Ask Me in Eight Years," November 12, 2008, http://www.fivethirtyeight.com/2008/11/was-2008-realigning -election-ask-me-in.html; and Peter Beinart, "The New Liberal Order," *Time,* November 13, 2008, http://www.time.com/time/magazine/article/0,9171,1858873,00.html.

8. See V. O. Key Jr., *Politics, Parties, and Pressure Groups,* 5th ed. (New York: Crowell, 1964), 255.

9. Ibid.

10. See Leon Epstein, *Political Parties in the American Mold* (Madison: University of Wisconsin Press, 1986), esp. 343–46.

11. I was invited to observe gavel-to-gavel the 1979 Prohibition National Convention.

12. See James Hedges, "Architect of Oblivion," Prohibitionists.org, http://www .prohibitionists.org/History/Bios/dodge/body_dodge.html (accessed July 17, 2011).

13. Convened by Prohibitionists.org Web editor James Hedges, this Memphis meeting brought together participants from Alabama, Florida, Michigan, Mississippi, Pennsylvania, Tennessee, Virginia, and Washington state.

14. Roger C. Storms, *Partisan Prophets: A History of the Prohibition Party* (Denver: National Prohibition Foundation, 1972).

15. C. L. Gammon, *America's Other Party: A Brief History of the Prohibition Party* (N.p.: FEP International, 2007), vi–vii.

16. See Wayne Flynt, *Cracker Messiah: Governor Sidney J. Catts of Florida* (Baton Rouge: Louisiana State University Press, 1977).

17. In 1914 Randall took 31 percent of the vote, defeating the incumbent and two other candidates. The Prohibition nominee benefited from interparty fusion in all three of his successful congressional campaigns.

18. Jack S. Blocker, *Retreat from Reform: The Prohibition Movement in the United States, 1890–1913* (Westport, Conn.: Greenwood, 1976).

19. Elizabeth Purdy, "Prohibition Party, 1869– ," in *The Encyclopedia of Third Parties in America,* 3 vols., ed. Immanuel Ness and James Ciment (Armonk, N.Y.: Sharpe Reference, 2000), 2:475–81.

20. "Statistics of the Congressional and Presidential Election of November 2, 1920," available online at http://clerk.house.gov/member_info/electionInfo/1920election.pdf (accessed August 17, 2011).

21. Stephen R. Duncombe, "The American Beat Party, 1959–1960s," in Ness and Ciment, *Encyclopedia of Third Parties,* 1:120–22.

22. "British Reformed Sectarian Party Polls 33% in Two-Way Florida Race," *Ballot Access News,* November 18, 2008, also available online at http://www.ballot-access.org/2008/11/18/british-reformed-sectarian-party-polls-33-in-two-way-florida-legislative-race/ (accessed September 2, 2011).

23. Steven J. Rosenstone, Roy L. Behr, and Edward H. Lazarus, *Third Parties in America: Citizen Response to Major Party Failure,* 2nd ed. (Princeton, N.J.: Princeton University Press, 1996).

24. The Revolutionary Communist Party should not be confused with the Communist Party USA.

25. For an account of the Alabama Sharecroppers Union, see Theodore Rosengarten, *All God's Children: The Life of Nate Shaw* (Chicago: University of Chicago Press, 1974).

26. The 1932 William Z. Foster–James W. Ford ticket won 103,307 votes. That was the largest vote ever received by a Communist presidential ticket.

4. Constitutionalists, Greens, and Libertarians

1. Christian Collett, "U.S. Taxpayers Party, 1992– ," in *The Encyclopedia of Third Parties in America,* 3 vols., ed. Immanuel Ness and James Ciment (Armonk, N.Y.: Sharpe Reference, 2000), 3:578–79.

2. Although the Constitution provides a procedure for calling a constitutional convention, the Constitution Party opposes all initiatives to do so. This arises from the fear that wide-ranging and undesirable constitutional revisions might result from such a meeting.

3. "Three Constitution Party Members Elected to Utah City Office in Non-Partisan Elections," Ballot-access.org, November 4, 2009, http://www.ballot-access.org/2008/11/18/british-reformed-sectarian-party-polls-33-in-two-way-florida-legislative-race/.

4. The Southern Poverty Law Center gathers and publishes information about many right-wing groups. The SPLC places various Constitution Party state organizations in its "patriot groups" classification. That is the same classification given by the SPLC to many of America's militia groups.

5. Paul's name also appeared in Louisiana, but not as the Constitution Party nominee. Although Paul had run in 1988 as the nominee of the pro-choice Libertarian Party, his congressional record and pronouncements have been distinctly and consistently pro-life.

6. See Chuck Baldwin, "More on the New World Order," NewsWithViews.com, January 30, 2009, http://www.newswithviews.com/baldwin/baldwin488.htm (accessed August 17, 2011). Baldwin addressed this and related themes in his October 3, 2008, keynote speech at the fiftieth anniversary celebration of the John Birch Society. See Brian Farmer, "Chuck Baldwin Addresses John Birch Society," *New American,* October 7, 2008, http://www.thenewamerican.com/usnews/election/408 (accessed August 17, 2011).

7. Harry Siegel and Fred Siegel, "New York's Two-Party System," *City Journal,* October 7, 2009, http://www.city-journal.org/2009/eon1007fshs.html (accessed September 2, 2011).

8. David Reynolds, "The Greens, 1980s– ," in Ness and Ciment, *Encyclopedia of Third Parties,* 2:276.

9. See Suzanne Herel, "It's Easy to Be Green for This Activist," *San Francisco Chronicle,* October 2, 2002.

10. Cris Moore, a twenty-five-year-old Green, won a seat on the Santa Fe city council in 1994. In a three-candidate 1997 special election for a seat in the U.S. House, Carol Miller, the Green nominee, took a remarkable 17 percent share of the vote. See Micah L. Sifry, *Spoiling for a Fight: Third-Party Politics in America* (New York: Routledge, 2002), 152–62.

11. See Associated Press, "Cynthia McKinney on Board Gaza Aid Boat Intercepted by Israeli Navy," *Huffington Post,* June 30, 2009, http://www.huffingtonpost.com/2009/06/30/cynthia-mckinney-on-board_n_223284.html.

12. This compares with a figure of 240,328 registered Libertarians as of October 2008. "2008 October Registration Totals," *Ballot Access News,* December 1, 2008, also available online at http://www.ballot-access.org/2008/120108.html#9 (accessed September 2, 2011).

13. "Current Green Party Members Holding Elected Office in the United States," a spreadsheet produced by Green Party of the United States and available at http://www.gp.org/elections/officeholders/index.php (accessed August 1, 2011). McLaughlin was re-elected as Richmond's mayor in 2010.

14. See William S. Maddox and Stuart A. Lilie, *Beyond Liberal and Conservative: Reassessing the Political Spectrum* (Washington, D.C.: Cato Institute, 1984).

15. The Nolan chart, a two-dimensional figure illustrating libertarianism's dedication to both economic and personal freedom, is available on many Internet sites.

16. Quotations from the 2008 platform of the Libertarian Party were accessed in March 2009 from the party Web site (http://www. lp.org). They have since been replaced by later platforms.

17. In this survey 86 percent chose the word *libertarian.* A small scattering selected *conservative* or *progressive* or another term. This Libertarian Lists survey is referenced on the KC Libertarian blogspot, July 24, 2007, http://kclibertarian.blogspot.com/2007/07/libertarian-lists-survey-results.html (accessed September 2, 2011).

18. Anne Groer, "Libertarian Lark," *New Republic,* October 3, 1983, 15–17.

19. By comparison, the Greens ran 58 candidates for the House and 67 for state legislative seats. The Constitution Party ran 41 for the House and 113 in state legislative elections. "U.S. House of Representatives Nominee on the Ballot," and "State Legislative Nominees on the Ballot," *Ballot Access News,* November 1, 2008, also available online at http://www.ballot-access.org/2008/110108.html#4 and http://www.ballot-access.org/2008/110108.html#5, respectively (accessed September 2, 2011).

20. See Operation ELECT-US (http://www.lp.org/operation-elect-us) and FAQ (http://www.lp.org/faq), both available on the Libertarian Party Web site. Bill Masters has served as sheriff of San Miguel County since he was first elected in 1980.

5. The Early Years

1. Darcy C. Richardson, *Others,* vol. 1: *Third-Party Politics from the Nation's Founding to the Rise and Fall of the Greenback-Labor Party* (New York: iUniverse, 2004), 68.

2. Inferring from the precipitous decline of the Whigs and the meteoric rise of the Republicans within the same narrow frame of time, party historian William Hesseltine declares that "the Republicans were never a third party." Hesseltine was not alone in drawing that conclusion, though his has been the minority position among historians. William B. Hesseltine, *Third-Party Movements in the United States* (Princeton, N.J.: Van Nostrand, 1962), 47.

3. "Live Fast, Love Hard, Die Young," sung by Faron Young (1955).

4. Many of these ran solely on the ticket of their short-lived party. The others ran fusion campaigns in which their transient party was recognized as the more or most influential of the fusion partners.

5. Hesseltine, *Third-Party Movements*, 15–16.

6. This maxim is attributed to *Pogo* cartoonist Walt Kelly.

7. Hesseltine, *Third-Party Movements*, 15–16; and Michael F. Holt, "The Anti-Masonic and Know Nothing Parties," in *History of U.S. Political Parties*, 4 vols., ed. Arthur M. Schlesinger (New York: Chelsea House, 1973), 1:576–77.

8. See Kenneth C. Martis, *The Historical Atlas of Political Parties in the United States Congress, 1789–1989* (New York: Macmillan, 1989).

9. Holt, "Anti-Masonic," 592.

10. It was a single-issue platform and program, devoted entirely to the party's war on Freemasonry.

11. This change was largely attributable to the initiative and temporary power of the California Workingmen's Party, a short-lived party in the 1870s that inveighed against Chinese and Chinese labor.

12. Steven J. Rosenstone, Roy L. Behr, and Edward H. Lazarus, *Third Parties in America: Citizen Response to Major Party Failure*, 2nd ed. (Princeton, N.J.: Princeton University Press, 1996), 56–59.

13. Ray Allen Billington, *The Protestant Crusade, 1800–1860* (New York: Macmillan, 1938), 411.

14. See, for example, Hesseltine, *Third-Party Movements*, 27–28.

15. The Kansas-Nebraska Act was an important topic in the famed 1858 debates between Democrat Stephen Douglas and Republican Abraham Lincoln.

16. *Dred Scott v. Sandford*, 60 U.S. (19 How.) 393 (1857).

17. Four years earlier, in 1852, Jacob Broom of Pennsylvania had won some two thousand votes on a Native American Party presidential ticket. Broom was elected as a Know Nothing to the U.S. House in 1854.

18. Rosenstone, Behr, and Lazarus, *Third Parties*, 58.

19. Glyndon G. Van Deusen, "The Whig Party," in Schlesinger, *History of U.S. Political Parties*, 1:362.

20. The African nation of Liberia is the legacy of this movement.

21. This dying Liberty Party nominated party leader Gerrit Smith in 1848. Smith took only 2,545 votes, all of them in New York.

22. Omar H. Ali, *In the Balance of Power: Independent Black Politics and Third-Party Movements in the United States* (Athens: Ohio University Press, 2008), 32–44.

23. Richard H. Sewell, *Ballots for Freedom* (New York: Norton, 1975); and Frederick J. Blue, *The Free Soilers: Third Party Politics, 1848–54* (Urbana: University of Illinois Press, 1973). Also see Jonathan H. Earle, *Jacksonian Antislavery and the Politics of Free Soil, 1824–1854* (Chapel Hill: University of North Carolina Press, 2004).

24. Chase would later be appointed by President Lincoln as chief justice of the United States.

6. Union, Reform, and Class

1. Michael F. Holt, "The Democratic Party, 1828–1860," in *History of U.S. Political Parties*, 4 vols., ed. Arthur M. Schlesinger (New York: Chelsea House, 1973), 1:532–33. Kansas was admitted to the Union as a free state on January 29, 1861.

2. Howard P. Nash Jr., *Third Parties in American Politics* (Washington, D.C.: Public Affairs Press, 1959), 89.

3. David M. Potter, *The Impending Crisis, 1848–1861* (New York: Harper and Row, 1976), 443–45.

4. Steven J. Rosenstone, Roy L. Behr, and Edward H. Lazarus, *Third Parties in America: Citizen Response to Major Party Failure,* 2nd ed. (Princeton, N.J.: Princeton University Press, 1996), 60–61.

5. Holt, "Democratic Party," 533–35.

6. Donald E. Greco, "Liberal Republican Party, 1872," in *The Encyclopedia of Third Parties in America,* 3 vols., ed. Immanuel Ness and James Ciment (Armonk, N.Y.: Sharpe Reference, 2000), 2:335.

7. Leon Friedman, "The Democratic Party, 1860–1884," in Schlesinger, *History of U.S. Political Parties,* 2:900.

8. Darcy C. Richardson, *Others,* vol. 1, *Third-Party Politics from the Nation's Founding to the Rise and Fall of the Greenback-Labor Party* (New York: iUniverse, 2004), 446–48.

9. The ending of Reconstruction was apparently a part of a quid pro quo understanding between Democrats and Republicans in which the Democrats acquiesced in Hayes's assumption of the presidency following the much-disputed outcome of the election of 1876.

10. Henry George was the nominee of the United Labor Party. His radical "single tax" plan had many supporters around the country.

11. Peter H. Argersinger, "Greenback Party, 1873–1886," in Ness and Ciment, *Encyclopedia of Third Parties,* 2:272.

12. Ibid., 2:273; and Leonard Dinnerstein, "Election of 1880," in *History of American Presidential Elections,* 4 vols., ed. Arthur M. Schlesinger and Fred L. Israel (New York: McGraw-Hill, 1971), 2:1505.

13. Jack W. Gunn, "Greenback Party," *Handbook of Texas Online,* http://www.tshaonline.org/handbook/online/articles/wag01 (accessed August 1, 2011).

14. Omar H. Ali, *In the Balance of Power: Independent Black Politics and Third-Party Movements in the United States* (Athens: Ohio University Press, 2008), 70–71.

15. George B. Tindall, "The People's Party," in Schlesinger, *History of U.S. Political Parties,* 2:1701.

16. See Lawrence Goodwyn, *Democratic Promise: The Populist Movement in America* (New York: Oxford University Press, 1976), esp. 351–86.

17. Some historical accounts declare an earlier birth, at a convention of Populists in Cincinnati in May 1891.

18. WCTU president Frances Willard, the vice-chair of the convention in St. Louis, had worked unsuccessfully to merge the Prohibition and emerging Populist movements. See Robert C. McMath Jr., *American Populism: A Social History, 1877–1898* (New York: Hill and Wang, 1993), 160.

19. Quoted by Tindall, "People's Party," 2:1714.

20. Planks in several state People's Party platforms demanded women's suffrage, but neither the 1892 nor 1896 national platform carried a explicit call for the enfranchisement of women.

21. The Web site of the Kansas Historical Society lists 182 Kansas Populist newspapers in its collection. Also see Donna A. Barnes, "People's Party," *Handbook of Texas Online*, http://www.tshaonline.org/handbook/online/articles/wap01 (accessed August 1, 2011).

22. See V. O. Key, *Southern Politics in State and Nation* (New York: Vintage, 1949), esp. 7–9.

23. Bryan is remembered for the anti-Darwinist position he took in the 1925 trial of schoolteacher John Scopes in Tennessee. Some revisionist scholars argue that Bryan's quarrel was far less with Charles Darwin and his work than with social Darwinism, the extrapolation by political conservatives. See Matthew J. Tontonoz, "The Scopes Trial Revisited: Social Darwinism versus Social Gospel," *Science as Culture* 17, no. 2 (2008): 121–43.

24. C. Vann Woodward, *Tom Watson: Agrarian Rebel* (New York: Macmillan, 1938), 293.

25. See Betty Glad, *Key Pittman: The Tragedy of a Senate Insider* (New York: Columbia University Press, 1986), 9.

26. Bryan received 6,511,495 votes. According to historian C. Vann Woodward, Populist vice-presidential nominee Tom Watson took 217,000 votes in the seventeen states where it was possible to designate votes specifically for a vice-presidential candidate. Watson also received twenty-seven vice-presidential electoral votes. Woodward, *Tom Watson*, 329.

27. Key, *Southern Politics*, 118.

28. Elliott Shore, *Talkin' Socialism* (Lawrence: University Press of Kansas, 1988), esp. 75–93.

29. Goodwyn, *Democratic Promise*, 558–59.

30. Richard Hofstadter, *The Age of Reform: From Bryan to F.D.R.* (New York: Knopf, 1955), 61. But Hofstadter is remembered as a critic both of 1890s Populism and of twentieth-century "populist" politicians and movements, for their irrational resentments, their designation of ogres—for conveying a paranoid style of politics. For those embracing Hofstadter's perspective, a list of twentieth-century "populists" would have to include some well-known race-baiters, red-baiters, anti-Semites, and conspiracy theory propagators. See Hofstadter's *The Paranoid Style in American Politics and Other Essays* (New York: Knopf, 1965).

7. Thunder Left and Right

1. Arthur M. Schlesinger Jr., *The Cycles of American History* (Boston: Houghton Mifflin, 1986).

2. Charles McCarthy, *The Wisconsin Idea* (New York: Macmillan, 1912).

3. William B. Hesseltine, *Third-Party Movements in the United States* (Princeton, N.J.: Van Nostrand, 1962), 68–71.

4. Lewis F. Gould, ed., *The Progressive Era* (Syracuse, N.Y.: Syracuse University Press, 1974).

5. He was clearly within his rights to do so. The Twenty-second Amendment that limited presidential terms of office did not become part of the Constitution until 1951.

6. See "Theodore Roosevelt and the National Park System," available online at http://www.nps.gov/history/history/hisnps/npshistory/teddy.htm (accessed September 2, 2011).

7. Paul F. Boller Jr., *Presidential Campaigns* (New York: Oxford University Press, 1985), 192.

8. Omar H. Ali, *In the Balance of Power: Independent Black Politics and Third-Party Movements in the United States* (Athens: Ohio University Press, 2008), 111–13. There is evidence that Roosevelt attributed his failure to win the GOP nomination in 1912 to African American influence in some pivotal GOP party establishments. See the letter from Theodore Roosevelt to William H. Maxwell, July 30, 1912, marked "Private, Not for Publication," in John A. Gable, *The Bull Moose Years: Theodore Roosevelt and the Progressive Party* (Port Washington, N.Y.: Kennikat, 1978), 63–64.

9. John A. Gable, "The Bull Moose Years," available on Theodore Roosevelt Association Web site, http://www.theodoreroosevelt.org/life/bullmoose.htm (accessed September 2, 2011).

10. Boller, *Presidential Campaigns,* 195.

11. Gable,"The Bull Moose Years."

12. La Follette's perspective as presented by Hesseltine, *Third-Party Movements,* 83.

13. Nancy C. Unger, *Fighting Bob La Follette: The Righteous Reformer* (Madison: Wisconsin Historical Society Press, 2008), 282–84.

14. Darcy C. Richardson, *Others,* vol. 4: *"Fighting Bob" La Follette and the Progressive Movement: Third-Party Politics in the 1920s* (New York: iUniverse, 2008), 200–203. In most of these states, La Follette appeared under one or more other labels as well.

15. Ibid., 201.

16. William E. Leuchtenburg, "Election of 1936," in *History of American Presidential Elections, 1789–1968,* 4 vols., ed. Arthur M. Schlesinger and Fred L. Israel (New York: McGraw-Hill, 1971), 3:2822–23.

17. "Charles Coughlin, '30s 'Radio Priest' Dies," *New York Times,* October 28, 1979.

18. Ibid. Joseph P. Kennedy Sr., the patriarch of the Massachusetts Kennedy clan, was one of the most persistent and influential Catholic critics of Father Coughlin.

19. Steven J. Rosenstone, Roy L. Behr, and Edward H. Lazarus, *Third Parties in America: Citizen Response to Major Party Failure,* 2nd ed. (Princeton, N.J.: Princeton University Press, 1996), 106.

20. V. O. Key, *Southern Politics in State and Nation* (New York: Random House, 1949), 342.

21. In deference to his capitalist allies, Soviet leader Joseph Stalin terminated the Comintern as an organization during World War II.

22. For a critical and incisive account of the links of some American progressives to the world Communist movement and the Communist Party USA in the 1940s and 1950s, see William L. O'Neill, *A Better World: The Great Schism; Stalinism and the American Intellectuals* (New York: Simon and Schuster, 1982).

23. "Progressive Party Platform," text in Hesseltine, *Third-Party Movements,* 180–85.

24. Alberta Lachicotte, *Rebel Senator: Strom Thurmond of South Carolina* (New York: Devon-Adair, 1966), 101–2.

25. See Jack Bass and Marilyn W. Thompson, *Strom: The Complicated Personal and Political Life of Strom Thurmond* (New York: Public Affairs, 2005).

26. Key, *Southern Politics,* 335.

27. See William D. Bernard, *Dixiecrats and Democrats* (Tuscaloosa: University of Alabama Press, 1974), 115; and Lachicotte, *Rebel Senator,* 43.

28. "States' Rights Platform of 1948," text in *History of U.S. Political Parties,* 4 vols., ed. Arthur M. Schlesinger (New York: Chelsea House, 1973), 4:3422–25.

29. Just as in 1948, Alabamians in 1964 did not have the option to vote for the incumbent Democratic president (in this case Lyndon Johnson) seeking election. There was a slate of uncommitted Alabama electors that year. In 1968 American Independent nominee Wallace appeared on the Alabama ballot as the Democratic Party nominee, but Alabamians were able to vote for national Democratic nominee Hubert Humphrey as the candidate of the National Democratic Party of Alabama.

8. George Wallace and Beyond

1. See Jonathan Darman, "1968: The Year That Changed Everything," *Newsweek,* November 19, 2007, available online at http://www.prnewswire.com/news-releases/newsweek-cover-1968-the-year-that-made-us-who-we-are-58630047.html (accessed September 3, 2011).

2. Daniel Walker, *Rights in Conflict: The Violent Confrontation of Police and Protestors in the Parks and Streets of Chicago during the Week of the Democratic National Convention of 1968* (New York: New American Library, 1968).

3. Marshall Frady, "The American Independent Party," in *History of U.S. Political Parties,* 4 vols., ed. Arthur M. Schlesinger (New York: Chelsea House, 1973), 4:3436.

4. *Williams v. Rhodes,* 393 U.S. 23 (1968).

5. Lewis Chester, Godfrey Hodgson, and Bruce Page, *An American Melodrama: The Presidential Campaign of 1968* (New York: Viking, 1969), 284–85.

6. This at any rate is the interpretation or insight of ballot-access expert Richard Winger; in conversation with the author.

7. American Institute of Public Opinion surveys 771 and 772, Center for Political Studies (University of Michigan), 1968 National Election Study, available online at http://www.icpsr.umich.edu/icpsrweb/ICPSR/studies/7281 (accessed September 3, 2011).

8. Rick Perlstein, "The Southern Strategist," *New York Times Magazine,* December 30, 2007, E30–E31; also available online at http://www.nytimes.com/2007/12/30/magazine/30DENT-t.html.

9. "American Independent Party Platform of 1968," in Schlesinger, *History of U.S. Political Parties,* 4:3447–48.

10. Ibid., 4:3447–74.

11. Only in those jurisdictions where absolute majorities voted for Nixon or Humphrey does it appear certain that the Wallace factor had no impact on the electoral outcome. Majorities voted for Nixon in fifteen states. Humphrey took majorities in five states and Washington, D.C. These twenty-one jurisdictions possessed a total of only 118 of the nation's 538 votes.

12. Thomas Byrne Edsall and Mary D. Edsall, "Race," *Atlantic Monthly,* May 1991, 62–63.

13. Ibid., 62. Also see Thomas Byrne Edsall and Mary D. Edsall, *Chain Reaction: The Impact of Race, Rights, and Taxes on American Politics* (New York: Norton, 1992), esp. 74–98.

14. The Democratic Party, of course, did not lose all traction in the South, because millions of African Americans were mobilized and empowered to support it. Both in ideology and practice, southern Democratic parties moved much closer to the orbit of the national Democratic Party.

15. Years later the John Birch Society, charging that Schmitz was an "extremist," revoked his society membership.

16. Lawrence Lader, *Power on the Left: American Radical Movements since 1946* (New York: Norton, 1979), 246–47.

17. After the election Cleaver jumped bail and left the country to avoid prosecution.

18. Gregory may not have intended his general election role to be as stand-in for Cleaver. Repositioning words in the name of the party that had selected Cleaver, Gregory proclaimed himself to be the candidate of the Freedom and Peace Party. He actually won more votes than Cleaver.

19. "2008 Ballot Status for President," *Ballot Access News,* November 1, 2008, also available online at http://www.ballot-access.org/2008/110108.html#6 (accessed September 3, 2011).

20. Ted Vaden, "New Congress Faces Familiar Faces," *Congressional Quarterly Weekly Report,* January 1, 1977, 17.

21. Steven J. Rosenstone, Roy L. Behr, and Edward H. Lazarus, *Third Parties in America: Citizen Response to Major Party Failure,* 2nd ed. (Princeton, N.J.: Princeton University Press, 1996), 115–16.

22. Allan J. Mayer, Frank Maier, and William D. Marbach, "Dr. Ecology for President," *Newsweek,* April 21, 1980, 48.

23. Vernon Mogensen, "Citizens Party, 1979–1984," in *The Encyclopedia of Third Parties in America,* 3 vols., ed. Immanuel Ness and James Ciment (Armonk, N.Y.: Sharpe Reference, 2000), 1:201.

24. Fred Harris, LaDonna Harris's spouse, had served as a U.S. senator from Oklahoma (1964–73) and as chair of the Democratic National Committee (1969–70). Harris actively supported the Citizens Party national ticket in 1980.

25. Mogensen, "Citizens Party," 202.

26. Ibid., 202, 204.

27. Ibid., 204.

28. Ibid., 203–4; and Richard J. Walton, "Citizens Party," *Nation,* May 16, 1981, 589.

29. Mogensen, 204–5.

30. November 1, 1988, telephone interview with NAP press secretary Annie Roboff and various printed NAP campaign materials.

31. For example, Bruce Shapiro, "The New Alliance Party: Dr. Fulani's Snake Oil Show," *Nation,* May 4, 1992, 585–94, and Vanessa Tait, "California Elections Depress Progressives," *Guardian,* June 27, 1990.

32. Dennis L. Serrette, "Inside the New Alliance Party," *Radical America* 21 (1987): 17–21; also available online at http://www.publiceye.org/newman/critics/Serrette.html (accessed September 3, 2011).

33. Sewell Chan, "City Plan to Aid Group Draws Fire from Four Officials," *New York Times,* September 12, 2006.

34. Newman (who died in 2011) and Fulani have controlled the IPNY organization in New York City, but their relationship with Frank MacKay and other state party leaders has been stormy. Fulani was expelled from the state executive committee in 2005.

35. Many people outside the Natural Law Party stringently denied that TM bore any connection either to natural law or scientific method. Referencing TM's claim or practice of "floating," some joked that levitation must be the focal point of party meetings.

36. Although the party Web site is no longer updated, the party platform was still accessible there (http://natural-law.org/platform/index.html) as of August 17, 2011.

37. As of this writing, Hagelin continues to occupy his position at Maharishi University of Management.

38. "Ballot Status for President 2008," *Ballot Access News,* November 1, 2008, also available online at http://www.ballot-access.org/2008/110108.html#6 (accessed September 3, 2011).

9. The New Independents

1. See, for example, "1992 Petitioning," *Ballot Access News,* January 2, 1992, also available online at http://www.ballot-access.org/1992/1-2-92.pdf; and "2008 Petitioning for President," *Ballot Access News,* April 1, 2008, also available online at http://www.ballot-access.org/2008/040108.html#10 (both accessed September 3, 2011).

2. Jeffrey M. Jones,"Democratic Edge in Partisanship in 2006 Evident at National, State Levels," Gallup.com, January 30, 2007, http://www.gallup.com/poll/26308/democratic-edge-partisanship-2006-evident-national-state-levels.aspx.

3. CBS/*New York Times* exit interviews with 12,782 voters, reported in *New York Times,* November 9, 1980.

4. Data from Voter Research and Surveys, 1992; available online to members of the Inter-University Consortium for Political and Social Research (ICPSR).

5. Steven J. Rosenstone, Roy L. Behr, and Edward H. Lazarus, *Third Parties in America: Citizen Response to Major Party Failure,* 2nd ed. (Princeton, N.J.: Princeton University Press, 1996), 118.

6. Tony Chiu, *Ross Perot: In His Own Words* (New York: Warner, 1992), x.

7. W. Lance Bennett, *News: The Politics of Illusion,* 3rd ed. (White Plains, N.Y.: Longman, 1996), 176.

8. See James Rowley, "Perot: 'We're in Deep Voodoo,'" Associated Press, October 7, 1992.

9. Marie Brenner, "Perot's Final Days," *Vanity Fair,* October 1992, 74ff.

10. See Gerald L. Posner, *Citizen Perot: His Life and Times* (New York: Random House, 1996), 286–306.

11. Ross Perot, *United We Stand* (New York: Hyperion, 1992).

12. Kenneth D. Norton, "The Television Candidate," in *Ross for Boss: The Perot Phenomenon and Beyond,* ed. Ted G. Jelen (Albany: SUNY Press, 2001), 24.

13. In 2000 the bipartisan Commission on Presidential Debates set new rules virtually assuring that only major-party nominees have access to the fall debates under CPD regulation.

14. Thirty-eight percent said Bush and 38 percent Clinton if it had not been for Perot. See Steven A. Holmes, "The 1992 Elections," *New York Times,* November 5, 1992.

15. Norton, "Television Candidate," 27.

16. Nearly one million ballots were sent out, but only 4.9 percent of them were returned. "Reform Party," *Ballot Access News,* August 12, 1996, also available online at http://web.archive.org/web/200101212346/http://ballot-access.org/1996/0812.html#19 (accessed September 3, 2011).

17. Federal Election Commission Annual Report, 1996, available at http://www.fec .gov/info/arfrm.htm (accessed September 3, 2011).

18. Norton, "Television Candidate," 28–29.

19. Micah L. Sifry, *Spoiling for a Fight: Third-Party Politics in America* (New York: Routledge, 2002), 19–42.

20. Attributed by Sifry to Ed Gross, one of the pivotal members of the Ventura campaign; ibid, 36.

21. Dave Leip, Atlas of U.S. Presidential Elections, http://uselectionatlas.org (accessed August 5, 2011).

10. Taking the Less-Traveled Road

1. In addition Asian Americans make up about 5 percent of the population, and Native Americans some 1 percent. Native Americans and Asian Americans have, like African Americans and Latinos, suffered discrimination, some of it egregious, in the history of the United States.

2. Mary Ruthsdotter, "Chronology of Woman Suffrage Movement Events," National Women's History Project, available online at http://www2.scholastic.com/browse/ article.jsp?id=4929 (accessed September 3, 2011).

3. See Hanes Walton, *Black Republicans: The Politics of the Black and Tans* (Metuchen, N.J.: Scarecrow, 1975).

4. David Greenberg, "The Party of Lincoln," *Slate,* August 10, 2000, http://www.slate.com/id/87868/; and Nancy J. Weiss, *Farewell to the Party of Lincoln: Black Politics in the Age of FDR* (Princeton, N.J.: Princeton University Press, 1983).

5. Not all third parties, of course. There are, and have been, some minor parties that are antiblack, antiminority, or anti-immigrant. One even named itself the National Socialist White People's Party.

6. This account of the National Woman's Party is indebted to Eleanor Flexner, *Century of Struggle: The Woman's Rights Movement in the United States,* rev. ed. (Cambridge, Mass.: Belknap, 1975); Dale Spender, *Women of Ideas* (London: Routledge and Kegan Paul, 1982); and Sara M. Evans, *Born for Liberty: A History of Women in America* (New York: Free Press, 1989).

7. In *Iron Jawed Angels,* a film about the National Woman's Party released by HBO in 2004, Alice Paul is played by Hilary Swank. Frances O'Connor plays Lucy Burns.

8. Betty Glad, *Key Pittman: The Tragedy of a Senate Insider* (New York: Columbia University Press, 1986), 53–54.

9. Eleanor Clift, *Founding Sisters and the Nineteenth Amendment* (Hoboken, N.J.: Wiley, 2003), 152.

10. *Baltimore American,* March 4, 1913, cited in Flexner, *Century of Struggle,* 273.

11. *Baltimore Sun,* March 4, 1913, cited in ibid.

12. Kathryn Cullen-Dupont, "The Trials of Alice Paul and Other National Woman's Party Members: Suggestions for Further Reading," Law Library—American Law and Legal Information, http://law.jrank.org/pages/2806/Trials-Alice-Paul-Other-National-Woman -s-Party-Members-1917.html (accessed July 28, 2011).

13. Ibid.

14. This was not the only time on record that Alice Paul gave a reply that was criticized as cavalier and off-putting. Her answer to an entreaty from African American women for a National Woman's Party campaign against the continued disenfranchisement of black women (along with black men) in the Jim Crow South was that this was "a race issue, not a woman's issue." See Paula Giddings, *When and Where I Enter: The Impact of Black Women on Race and Sex in America* (New York: Morrow, 1984), 166–69.

15. Quoted by Christopher Myers Asch, *The Senator and the Sharecropper* (Chapel Hill: University of North Carolina Press, 2011), 213.

16. Lawrence Lader, *Power on the Left: American Radical Movements since 1946* (New York: Norton, 1979), 187, 191.

17. Milton Viorst, *Fire in the Streets* (New York: Simon and Schuster, 1979), esp. 367–69 and 486.

18. Lader, *Power on the Left,* 193.

19. "John Cashin Jr. Dies at 82; Campaigned for Civil Rights," *New York Times,* March 26, 2011. Cashin's daughter has written a memoir of her father's remarkable life: Sheryll Cashin, *The Agitator's Daughter: A Memoir of Four Generations of One Extraordinary African-American Family* (New York: Public Affairs, 2008).

20. Brett Bursey, "Is South Carolina Ready for a Progressive Third Party?" *The Point: South Carolina's Independent Newsmonthly,* Summer 2000, http://www.scpronet.com/point/0006/p04.html (accessed July 29, 2011).

21. During the period of the party's connection to Fulani and then Perot, UCP's name was changed to the Patriot Party. It reverted to the United Citizens Party in the late 1990s.

22. Bursey, "Is South Carolina Ready?"

23. Early in its existence, the party was known as the Black Panther Party for Self-Defense.

24. Frantz Fanon, *The Wretched of the Earth,* trans. Constance Farrington (New York: Grove, 1963), 73. The insight about the Panthers as the embodiment of Fanon's "revolutionary native" comes from Tom Hayden, *Reunion: A Memoir* (New York: Random House, 1988), 308; also see 164.

25. Lader, *Power on the Left,* 268–69.

26. Ibid., 335.

27. Todd Gitlin, *The Sixties: Years of Hope, Days of Rage* (New York: Bantam, 1989), 348

28. See Hayden, *Reunion,* 339–412.

29. Michael Stohl, ed., *The Politics of Terrorism* (New York: Dekker, 1983), 249. Hoover's racial attitudes, his attacks even on Martin Luther King Jr., and his hostility to all left-wing things are fully documented. See, for example, David J. Garrow, *The FBI and Martin Luther King, Jr.* (New York: Norton, 1981).

30. Alexander Cockburn, "The Fate of the Panthers," *Nation,* July 2, 1990, 6.

31. Mireya Navarro, "Decades of FBI Surveillance of Puerto Rican Groups," *New York Times,* November 28, 2003; and the Web site FBI Files on Puerto Ricans, http://www.pr-secretfiles.net/ (accessed July 30, 2011).

32. Teresa Palomo Acosta, "Raza Unida Party," *Handbook of Texas Online,* http://www.tshaonline.org/handbook/online/articles/war01 (accessed July 30, 2011).

33. The literal translation of *raza* is race; but the consensus of most scholars is that *people* is the most faithful translation of the term as used by those who chose La Raza Unida as their party's name.

34. Armando Navarro, "La Raza Unida Party, 1970–1981," in *The Encyclopedia of Third Parties in America,* 3 vols., ed. Immanuel Ness and James Ciment (Armonk, N.Y.: Sharpe Reference, 2000), 2:323.

35. See Armando Navarro, *La Raza Unida Party: A Chicano Challenge to the Two-Party Dictatorship* (Philadelphia: Temple University Press, 2000).

36. Navarro, "Raza Unida Party," 323.

37. Palomo Acosta, "Raza Unida Party."

38. Ibid.

39. Navarro, "Raza Unida Party," 325.

11. Doctrinal Parties 1

1. *Texas v. Johnson,* 491 U.S. 397 (1989).

2. *United States v. Eichman,* 496 U.S. 310 (1990).

3. Randi Storch, *Red Chicago: American Communism at Its Grassroots, 1928–1935* (Urbana: University of Illinois Press, 2007).

4. Engels's letter, addressed to Friedrich A. Sorge, was dated December 2, 1893, and sent from London; "Why There Is No Large Socialist Party in America," in *Marx and Engels: Basic Writings on Politics and Philosophy,* ed. Lewis S. Feuer (Garden City, N.Y.: Anchor, 1959), 457–58. For a more general discussion of the matter, see Seymour Martin Lipset and Gary Marks, *It Didn't Happen Here: Why Socialism Failed in the United States* (New York: W. W. Norton, 2000).

5. See Harry W. Laidler, *History of Socialism* (New York: Crowell, 1968).

6. "Socialist Labor Party Closes Office," Ballot-access.org, December 31, 2008, http://www.ballot-access.org/2008/12/.

7. This section is indebted to Laidler, *History of Socialism;* Nick Salvatore, *Eugene V. Debs: Citizen and Socialist* (Urbana: University of Illinois Press, 1982); James C. Duram, "Norman Thomas as Presidential Conscience," *Presidential Studies Quarterly* 20, no. 3 (1990): 581–89; Michael Bassett, "The Socialist Party Dilemma, 1912–1914," in *Political Parties in American History,* ed. Paul L. Murphy (New York: Putnam, 1974), 1021–34; and James Weinstein, *The Decline of Socialism in America* (New York: Monthly Review, 1967), 27, 84–85, 93, 103, 115.

8. Howard Zinn, "Eugene V. Debs and the Idea of Socialism," *Progressive,* January 1999, http://www.marxists.org/archive/debs/bio/zinn.htm (accessed August 1, 2011).

9. The Pullman strike and Debs's involvement in it resulted in an important commerce clause case settled by the Supreme Court. *In re Debs,* 158 U.S. 564 (1895).

10. Zinn, "Eugene V. Debs."

11. The Supreme Court sustained the Espionage Act and Debs's conviction under it in *Debs v. the United States,* 249 U.S. 211 (1919).

12. Zinn, "Eugene V. Debs."

13. Bridgeport mayor Jasper McLevy was one of the most prominent leaders who left the Socialist Party and enlisted in the Social Democratic Federation.

14. Michael Harrington, a longtime Socialist Party leader, led in the establishment of the Democratic Socialists of America. Harrington's *The Other America* (1962) is considered to have provided the spark for the Johnson administration's War on Poverty.

15. Much has been written about the Communist Party USA; for example, *Highlights of a Fighting History: Sixty Years of the Communist Party, USA,* ed. Phillip Bart (New York: International Publishers, 1979); Simon W. Gerson, *Pete: The Story of Peter V. Cacchione, New York's First Communist Councilman* (New York: International Publishers, 1976); Joseph R. Starobin, *American Communism in Crisis, 1943 to 1957* (Berkeley: University of California Press, 1975); Robin D. Kelley, *Hammer and Hoe: Alabama Communists during the Great Depression* (Chapel Hill: University of North Carolina Press, 1990); Storch, *Red Chicago;* and Harvey Klehr, John Earl Haynes, and Fridrikh I. Firsov, *The Secret World of American Communism* (New Haven: Yale University Press, 1995). This account is indebted to some of these sources.

16. Robert Service, *Comrades: A World History of Communism* (London: Macmillan, 2007), 326.

17. Harvey Klehr, John Earl Haynes, and Kyrill M. Anderson, *The Soviet World of American Communism* (New Haven: Yale University Press, 1998), 158–59.

18. The words "under God" were not added to the pledge until 1954.

19. Charles Hobday, *Communist and Marxist Parties of the World* (Santa Barbara, Calif.: ABC-CLIO, 1986), 307.

20. Statement of "Geoffrey," quoted by Max Elbaum, "Death or Rebirth at Communist Convention?" *Guardian,* December 18, 1991. Also see Carl Bloice, "I Would Call What Happened a Quasi-Purge," *Guardian,* December 18, 1991.

21. This section is indebted to *The Founding of the Socialist Workers Party,* ed. George Breitman (New York: Anchor Foundation, 1982); James P. Cannon, *History of American Trotskyism* (New York: Pathfinder, 1972); Constance A. Myers, *The Prophet's Army: Trotskyism in America, 1928–1941* (Westport, Conn.: Greenwood, 1977); and *The FBI on Trial: Victory of the Socialist Workers Party against Spying,* ed. Margaret Jayko (New York: Pathfinder, 1988).

22. See Stephen Schwartz, "United States of America," in *Yearbook on International Communist Affairs,* ed. Richard Staar (Stanford, Calif.: Hoover Institution Press, 1990).

23. The PLP youth wing took its name from a major early demonstration against the Vietnam War that took place on May 2, 1964. The party laid credible claim to having planned and fostered the demonstration.

24. This account of the Revolutionary Communist Party draws information from various annual editions of *Yearbook on International Communist Affairs* and from Hobday, *Communist and Marxist Parties.*

25. See, for example, Mark Oppenheimer, "Free Bob Avakian! Oh, He's Already Free? Never Mind," *Boston Globe,* January 27, 2008.

12. Doctrinal Parties 2

1. This account of the Greensboro massacre and follow-up events is based upon Wyn Craig Wade, *The Fiery Cross: The Ku Klux Klan in America* (New York: Simon and Schuster, 1987), esp. 379–82 and 398–99; and Elizabeth Wheaton, *Codename GREENKIL: The 1979 Greensboro Killings* (Athens: University of Georgia Press, 1987).

2. This section is indebted to Elinor Langer, "The American Neo-Nazi Movement Today," *Nation,* July 16–23, 1990, 82–107; and James Ridgeway, *Blood in the Face: The Ku Klux Klan, Aryan Nations, Nazi Skinheads, and the Rise of a New White Culture* (New York: Thunder's Mouth, 1990).

3. Langer, "The American Neo-Nazi Movement Today," 83; also Ridgeway, *Blood in the Face,* 17.

4. David Holthouse, "The Year in Hate, 2008: Number of Hate Groups Tops 900," *Intelligence Report* (Southern Poverty Law Center), Spring 2009, http://www.splcenter.org/get-informed/intelligence-report/browse-all-issues/2009/spring/the-year-in-hate (accessed August 18, 2011). Paul Schlesselman and Daniel Cowart faced charges under federal law for alleged conspiracy in 2008 to kill presidential candidate Barack Obama and dozens of other African Americans. Schlesselman entered a guilty plea in January 2010. Law enforcement authorities identified Schlesselman and Cowart as young white supremacist skinheads.

5. Claran O. Maolain, *The Radical Right: A World Dictionary* (Santa Barbara, Calif.: ABC-CLIO, 1987), 388.

6. Wade, *Fiery Cross,* 325.

7. Donald Alexander Downs, *Nazis in Skokie: Freedom, Community, and the First Amendment* (Notre Dame, Ind.: Notre Dame University Press, 1985), 31.

8. Ridgeway, *Blood in the Face,* 66.

9. Author's June 30, 1981, interview with Martin Kerr, Arlington, Virginia.

10. Ridgeway, *Blood in the Face,* 66.

11. Dennis King, *Lyndon LaRouche and the New American Fascism* (New York: Doubleday, 1989). 37.

12. Kerr interview.

13. Ibid.

14. See Mike Royko, "'Ol' Daddy o' Mine' Isn't a Nazi Favorite," *Chicago Daily News,* June 23, 1977.

15. See Gordon Allport, *The Nature of Prejudice* (Reading, Mass.: Addison-Wesley, 1954).

16. Maolain, *Radical Right,* 386.

17. *Village of Skokie v. NSPA,* 51 Ill. App. 3d. 279; 366 N.E. 2d. 347 (1977); and *Collin v. Smith,* 447 F. Supp. 676 (1978). See Downs, *Nazis in Skokie.*

18. Holthouse, "Year in Hate."

19. See Michael Cooper, "In Missouri, a Fight over a Highway Adoption," *New York Times,* June 20, 2009.

13. State/Local Significant Others

1. See a comment Richard Winger posted December 18, 2009, 3:49 P.M. to "Reform Party Calls Teleconference National Committee Meeting," *Ballot Access News,* December 18, 2009, available online at http://www.ballot-access.org/2009/12/18/reform-party-calls -teleconference-national-committee-meeting/ (accessed September 24, 2011).

2. See Charles C. McCurdy, *The Anti-Rent Era in New York Law and Politics, 1839–1865* (Chapel Hill: University of North Carolina Press, 2001).

3. Hans Sperber and Travis Trittschuh, *American Political Terms* (Detroit: Wayne State University Press, 1962), 245–47.

4. The single-tax plan envisaged public ownership of land, with all governmental revenues derived from rents imposed on landholders based upon the value of land minus buildings and other improvements.

5. Daniel J. Elazar, *American Federalism: A View from the States,* 2nd ed. (New York: Crowell, 1972), esp. 84–126.

6. Robert P. Wilkins and Winona H. Wilkins, *North Dakota* (New York: Norton, 1977), 142–43.

7. Frazier's service in the Senate continued until 1941.

8. This section is indebted to Millard L. Gieske, *Minnesota Farmer-Laborism: The Third-Party Alternative* (Minneapolis: University of Minnesota Press, 1979), and John E. Haynes, *Dubious Alliance* (Minneapolis: University of Minnesota Press, 1984).

9. Sen. Magnus Johnson was born in Sweden, Congressman Knud Wefald in Norway, and Governor Hjalmar Petersen in Denmark. The parents of Floyd Olson and Elmer Benson, the party's two other governors, were born in Scandinavia.

10. William B. Hesseltine, *Third Parties in the United States* (Princeton, N.J.: Van Nostrand, 1962), 98–99.

11. "Proposal to Use Troops if Necessary for Needy Applauded by Nation," *Farmer-Labor Leader,* April 30, 1933.

12. Quoted by Robert S. McElvaine, *The Great Depression: America, 1929–1941* (New York: Three Rivers Press, 1993), 232.

13. "1934 Farmer-Labor Platform," *Congressional Record,* 79 (August 17, 1935), 13525–26.

14. Among others, John Earl Haynes and Harvey Klehr, "Researching Minnesota History in Moscow," *Minnesota History Magazine,* Spring 1994, 3–15; James M. Youngdale, *Populism in a New Perspective* (Ph.D. dissertation, University of Minnesota, 1972), esp. 211–16; Arthur Naftalin, *A History of the Farmer-Labor Party of Minnesota* (Ph.D. dissertation, University of Minnesota, 1948); and Elmer A. Benson and Robert Claiborne, reply by Hal Draper, "American Communism: An Exchange," *New York Review of Books,* December 6, 1984, 49; accessed online at http://www.nybooks.com/articles/archives/1984/dec/06/american-communism-an-exchange/?page=2 (accessed September 4, 2011).

15. James M. Shields, *Mr. Progressive: A Biography of Elmer A. Benson* (Minneapolis: Denison, 1971), 161.

16. This section is indebted to Robert T. Johnson, *Robert M. La Follette, Jr., and the Decline of the Progressive Party in Wisconsin* (New York: Anchor, 1970), and Jonathan Kasparek, *Fighting Son: A Biography of Philip F. La Follette* (Madison: Wisconsin Historical Society Press, 2006).

17. Richard N. Current, *Wisconsin* (New York: Norton, 1977), 206–7.

18. Ibid., 211.

19. Nancy Shulins, "Socialist Mayor of Burlington," Associated Press, July 3, 1988.

20. Allan R. Gold, "Exit a Socialist, to Let History Judge," *New York Times,* March 6, 1989.

21. See Shulins, "Socialist Mayor."

22. George Thabault, Bernard Sanders's administrative assistant, interview with the author, October 1, 1988.

23. Bernard Sanders, "This Country Needs a Third Political Party," *New York Times,* January 3, 1989, op. ed. sect.

24. Gold, "Exit a Socialist"; Shulins, "Socialist Mayor."

25. Debbie Bookchin, "Mayor's Showing Makes History," *Rutland Herald,* November 10, 1988. See James W. Endersby and W. David Thomason, "Spotlight on Vermont: Third-Party Success in the 1990 Congressional Election," *Social Science Journal* 31 (July 1994): 251–62.

26. For example, Daniel A. Mazmanian, *Third Parties in Presidential Elections* (Washington, D.C.: Brookings Institution, 1974), 115–35; and Robert J. Spitzer, "Multi-Party Politics in New York: A Cure for the Political System?" in *State Government,* ed. Thad L. Beyle (Washington, D.C.: CQ Press, 1989), 46–51.

27. The only significant limit on cross-endorsement in New York is a 1947 law that requires a candidate enrolled in one party to secure permission to run for another party's nomination from that party's committee.

28. Moreover 46 percent of the votes Progressive Vincent Hallinan received in 1952 came on the New York ALP line.

29. Some prominent national Republicans stuck with the Republican nominee. Others, including Sarah Palin and Minnesota governor Tim Pawlenty, endorsed the Conservative Party candidate.

30. Robert J. Spitzer, *The Right to Life Movement and Third-Party Politics* (Westport, Conn.: Greenwood, 1987), 84–87.

31. Spitzer, "Multi-Party Politics in New York," 49.

32. "2008 October Registration Totals," *Ballot Access News,* December 1, 2008, http://www.ballot-access.org/2008/120108.html#9 (accessed September 24, 2011).

33. See Micah L. Sifry, *Spoiling for a Fight: Third-Party Politics in America* (New York: Routledge, 2002), 63–141.

34. See, for example, Harry Siegel and Fred Siegel, "New York's Two-Party System," *City Journal,* October 7, 2009, http://www.city-journal.org/2009/eon1007fshs.html (accessed September 4, 2011).

35. Both the city party organization controlled by Newman and Fulani and the MacKay-led state IPNY have been in receipt of Bloomberg money. In 2009 the state IPNY received $1.2 million, ostensibly for election-day services on behalf of Bloomberg's reelection campaign. See Elizabeth Benjamin, "Bloomberg's Independence (Pay) Day," *New York Daily News,* January 25, 2010; and David Seifman, "Independence Party Big Promises Change after 'Secret Deal' with Mike," *New York Post,* February 7, 2010.

36. State records in October 2008 showed 40,560 registered members of the Working Families Party; "2008 October Registration Totals," http://www.ballot-access.org/2008/120 108.html#9 (accessed September 24, 2011).

37. Edward-Isaac Dovere, "All in the Family Part 5," *City Hall News,* December 4, 2009, http://www.cityhallnews.com/2009/12/all-in-the-family-part-5/(accessed September 24, 2011).

38. Quoted by Siegel and Siegel, "New York's Two-Party System."

39. Ibid.

40. Ironically a 2009 media investigation reported that the WFP had evaded New York City campaign contribution limits through a for-profit firm established by the party. Edward-Isaac Dovere, "City Hall Special Investigative Report," *City Hall News,* August 10, 2009, http://www.cityhallnews.com/2009/08/city-hall-special-investigative-report/ (accessed September 24, 2011).

41. Washington state voters approved top two in 2004, and California voters in 2010. Because the procedure virtually eliminates a party role in nominating candidates, leaders of party organizations—major and minor—in these two Pacific states had forged a united front in seeking defeat of top two. In *Washington State Grange v. Washington State Republican Party et al.* (2008), seven of the nine Supreme Court justices sustained top two, rejecting the concerted claims of Washington's Republican, Democratic, and Libertarian parties that it impermissibly denies associational rights.

Top two is a wide-open primary in which all candidates seeking the office compete and any registered voter may participate. Candidates may indicate a party preference or that they are independent or declare nothing at all. The top two vote-getters then compete in a runoff. The runoff nominees may be a Democrat and a Republican, two Democrats, or two Republicans, but it is extremely unlikely that either competitor in what is in effect the general election will be the candidate of a third party.

14. Looking Back, Looking Ahead

1. Frank Rich, "The Great Tea-Party Rip-off," *New York Times,* January 16, 2010.

2. David Brooks, "The Tea Party Teens," *New York Times,* January 10, 2010.

3. See Zachary Roth, "Tea Party Dilemma: To GOP or Not to GOP?" Talking Points Memo, January 28, 2010, http://tpmmuckraker.talkingpointsmemo.com/2010/01/tea _party_dilemma_to_gop_or_not_to_gop.php. The Tea Party Nation was disparaged both inside and outside the movement for levying the hefty fee of $549 for credentialing as a convention delegate. The group and Palin also were criticized for arranging for Palin to receive a reported $100,000 for appearing and delivering her convention speech.

4. Brooks, "Tea Party Teens."

5. Alex Koppelman, "Poll: Tea Parties Could Spell Trouble for GOP," *Salon,* March 24, 2010, http://www.salon.com/news/politics/war_room/2010/03/24/tea_party_poll.

6. Roth, "Tea Party Dilemma."

7. Ronald Dworkin, "The 'Devastating' Decision," *New York Review of Books,* February 25, 2010, 39; also available online at http://www.nybooks.com/articles/archives/2010/ feb/25/the-devastating-decision/ (accessed September 4, 2011).

8. Ibid.

9. "Statement of Ralph Nader on Supreme Court Decision in *Citizens United v. Federal Election Commission*," PR Newswire, January 21, 2010, http://www.prnewswire.com/ news-releases/statement-of-ralph-nader-on-supreme-court-decision-in-citizens-united -v-federal-election-commission-82256182.html.

10. See the Copenhagen Document of the Human Dimension of the CSCE (1990), available online at http://idw.csfederalismo.it/attachments/349_Copenhagen%20Docu ment%20-%20human%20dimension.pdf (accessed September 4, 2011).

Suggestions for Further Reading

Works on Third Parties in General

Ali, Omar H. *In the Balance of Power: Independent Black Politics and Third-Party Movements in the United States.* Athens: Ohio University Press, 2008.

Amato, Theresa A. *Grand Illusion: The Myth of Voter Choice in a Two-Party Tyranny.* New York: New Press, 2009.

Bennett, James D. *Not Invited to the Party: How the Demopublicans Have Rigged the System and Left Independents Out in the Cold.* New York: Springer, 2009.

Bibby, John F., and L. Sandy Maisel. *Two Parties—or More? The American Party System.* 2nd ed. Boulder, Colo.: Westview, 2003.

Black, Gordon S., and Benjamin D. Black. *The Politics of American Discontent: How a New Party Can Make Democracy Work Again.* New York: Wiley, 1994.

Caiazzo, Thomas A., and Robert L. Marsh. *Third-Party Presidential Politics in America: The Institutional Obstacles Such Candidates Face.* Lewiston, N.Y.: Edwin Mellen Press, 2011.

Cox, Vicki. *The History of Third Parties.* New York: Chelsea House, 2007 (juvenile literature).

Disch, Lisa J. *The Tyranny of the Two-Party System.* New York: Columbia University Press, 2002.

Gerring, John. "Minor Parties in Plurality Electoral Systems." *Party Politics* 11, no. 1 (2005): 79–107.

Gilbert, Christopher P., et. al. *Religious Institutions and Minor Parties in the United States.* Westport, Conn.: Praeger/Greenwood, 1999.

Green, Donald J. *Third Party Matters: Politics, Presidents, and Third Parties in American History.* Santa Barbara, Calif.: Praeger, 2010.

Hazlett, Joseph M. *The Libertarian Party and Other Minor Political Parties in the United States.* Jefferson City, N.C.: McFarland and Co., 1992.

Herrnson, Paul S., and John Clifford Green, eds. *Multiparty Politics in America.* 2nd ed. Lanham, Md.: Rowman and Littlefield, 2002.

Hesseltine, William B. *Third-Party Movements in the United States.* Princeton, N.J.: Van Nostrand, 1962.

Hill, Steven. *Fixing Elections: The Failure of America's Winner Take All Politics.* New York: Routledge, 2002.

Hirano, Shigeo, and James M. Snyder Jr. "The Decline of Third-Party Voting in the United States." *Journal of Politics* 69, no. 1 (2007): 1–16.

Klobuchar, Lisa. *Third Parties: Influential Political Alternatives.* Minneapolis: Compass Point Books, 2008.

Lowi, Theodore J., and Joseph Romance. *A Republic of Parties? Debating the Two-Party System.* Lanham, Md.: Rowman and Littlefield, 1998.

Mazmanian, Daniel A. *Third Parties in Presidential Elections.* Washington, D.C.: Brookings Institution, 1974.

Ness, Immanuel, and James Ciment, eds. *The Encyclopedia of Third Parties in America.* 3 vols. Armonk, N.Y.: Sharpe Reference, 2000.

Peterson, Geoff, and J. Mark Wrighton. "Expressions of Distrust: Third-Party Voting and Cynicism in Government." *Political Behavior* 20, no. 1 (1998): 17–34.

Rapoport, Ronald B., and Walter J. Stone. *Three's a Crowd: The Dynamic of Third Parties, Ross Perot, and Republican Resurgence.* Ann Arbor: University of Michigan Press, 2005.

Richardson, Darcy G. *Others.* Vol. 1, *Third Parties from the Nation's Founding to the Rise and Fall of the Greenback-Labor Party* (2004); vol. 2, *Third Parties during the Populist Period* (2007); vol. 3, *Third Parties from Teddy Roosevelt's Bull Moose Party to the Decline of Socialism in America* (2007); vol. 4, *"Fighting Bob" LaFollete and the Progressive Movement* (2008); vol. 5, *Third Parties during the Great Depression* (2010). New York: iUniverse, 2004–.

Rosenstone, Steven J., Roy L. Behr, and Edward H. Lazarus. *Third Parties in America: Citizen Response to Major Party Failure.* 2nd ed. Princeton: Princeton University Press, 1996.

Schoen, Douglas E. *Declaring Independence: The Beginning of the End of the Two-Party System.* New York: Random House, 2008.

Shock, David R. "Securing a Line on the Ballot: Measuring and Explaining the Restrictiveness of Ballot Access Laws for Non-Major Party Candidates in the United States." *Social Science Journal* 45, no. 1 (2008): 45–60.

Sifry, Micah L. *Spoiling for a Fight: Third-Party Politics in America.* New York: Routledge, 2002.

Smallwood, Frank. *The Other Candidates: Third Parties in Presidential Elections.* Hanover, N.H.: University Press of New England, 1983.

Stratmann, Thomas. "Ballot Access Restrictions and Candidate Entry in Elections." *European Journal of Political Economy* 21, no. 1 (2005): 59–71.

"Third Parties in American Politics: Rich History, Many Roles." U.S. State Department Interview with J. David Gillespie by Thomas Mann, August 30, 2004, available online at http://www.america.gov/st/washfile-English/2004/August/20040830165442frlle hctim0.307461.html (accessed August 16, 2011).

Winger, Richard. "How Many Parties Ought to Be On the Ballot? An Analysis of *Nader v. Keith.*" *Election Law Journal* 5, no. 2 (2006): 170–200.

Other Works Relevant to the Study of Third Parties

Aldrich, John H. *Why Parties? The Origin and Transformation of Political Parties in America.* Chicago: University of Chicago Press, 1995.

Amy, Douglas J. *Real Choices / New Voices: How Proportional Representation Elections Could Revitalize American Democracy.* 2nd ed. New York: Columbia University Press, 2002.

Bibby, John F., and Brian F. Schaffner. *Politics, Parties. and Elections in America.* 6th ed. Boston: Thomson/Wadworth, 2008.

Binning, William C., Larry E. Esterly, and Paul A. Sracic. *Encyclopedia of American Parties, Campaigns, and Elections.* Westport, Conn.: Greenwood, 1999.

Brancati, Dawn. "Winning Alone: The Electoral Fate of Independent Candidates Worldwide." *Journal of Politics* 70, no. 3 (2008): 648–62.

Carroll, Susan J., ed. *Women and American Politics: New Questions, New Directions.* New York: Oxford University Press, 2003.

Cohen, Jeffrey E., Richard Fleisher, and Paul Kantor, eds. *American Political Parties: Decline or Resurgence?* Washington, D.C.: CQ Press, 2001.

Colomer, Josep M. *Political Institutions: Democracy and Social Choice.* New York: Oxford University Press, 2001.

Craig, Stephen C., ed. *Broken Contract? Changing Relationships between Americans and Their Government.* Boulder, Colo.: Westview, 1996.

Dobbs, Lou. *Independents Day: Awakening the American Spirit.* New York: Viking, 2007.

Duverger, Maurice. *Political Parties: Their Organization and Activity in the Modern State.* Translated by Barbara and Robert North. New York: John Wiley, 1954.

Eldersveld, Samuel J., and Hanes Walton Jr. *Political Parties in American Society.* 2nd ed. New York: Bedford / St. Martin's, 2000.

"Fair and Free Elections." Special issue, *Issues of Democracy* 1, no. 13 (1996). Also available online at http://www.4uth.gov.ua/usa/English/politics/ijde0996/ijde0996.htm (accessed August 16, 2011).

Finkelman, Paul, and Peter Wallenstein, eds. *The Encyclopedia of American Political History.* Washington, D.C.: CQ Press, 2001.

Green, John C., and Daniel J. Coffey, eds. *The State of the Parties: The Changing Role of Contemporary American Politics.* 5th ed. Lanham, Md.: Rowman and Littlefield, 2007.

Herbst, Susan. *Politics at the Margin: Historical Studies of Public Expression outside the Mainstream.* New York: Cambridge University Press, 1994.

Hershey, Marjorie Randon. *Party Politics in America.* 14th ed. Upper Saddle River, N.J.: Pearson / Prentice Hall, 2011.

Hofstadter, Richard. *The Age of Reform: From Bryan to F.D.R.* New York: Knopf, 1955.

———. *The Paranoid Style in American Politics, and Other Essays.* New York: Knopf, 1965.

Katz, Richard S., and William J. Crotty, eds. *Handbook of Party Politics.* London: Sage, 2006.

Kraus, Jeffrey. "Bloomberg Triumphant: The Collapse of Democratic Hegemony in New York City." *Forum* 5, iss. 2, article 1 (2007), http://www.bepress.com/forum/vol5/iss2/art1 (accessed August 16, 2011).

———. "Rudy and Mike: Will Either of the Mayors Who Saved New York Get to Save America?" *Forum* 5, iss. 2, article 11 (2007), http://bepress.com/forum/vol5/iss2/art11/ (accessed August 16, 2011).

Lofland, John. *Social Movement Organizations: Guide to Research on Insurgent Realities.* Piscataway, N.J.: Transaction, 1996.

Magarian, Gregory P. "Regulating Political Parties under a 'Public Rights' First Amendment." *William and Mary Law Review* 44, iss. 5 (2003), http://scholarship.law.wm.edu/wmlr/vol44/iss5/2 (accessed August 15, 2011).

Paul, Ron. *The Revolution: A Manifesto.* New York: Grand Central Publishing, 2008.

Works Treating Particular Third Party and Independent Movements and Leaders

Adams, Katherine H., and Michael L. Keene. *Alice Paul and the American Suffrage Campaign.* Urbana: University of Illinois Press, 2008.

Alkebulan, Paul. *Survival Pending Revolution: The History of the Black Panther Party.* Tuscaloosa: University of Alabama Press, 2007.

Allen, Neal, and Brian J. Brox. "The Roots of Third Party Voting: The 2000 Nader Campaign in Historical Perspective." *Party Politics* 11, no. 5 (2005): 623–37.

Anbinder, Tyler. *Nativism and Slavery: The Northern Know Nothings and the Politics of the 1850s.* New York: Oxford University Press, 1992.

Bart, Philip, ed. *Highlights of a Fighting History: 60 Years of the Communist Party, USA.* New York: International Publishers, 1979.

Bass, Jack, and Marilyn W. Thompson. *Ol' Strom: An Unauthorized Biography of Strom Thurmond.* Atlanta: Longstreet, 1998.

———. *Strom: The Complicated Personal and Political Life of Strom Thurmond.* New York: Public Affairs, 2005.

Berggren, D. Jason. "Ralph Nader and the Green Party: The Double-Edged Sword of a Candidate, Campaign-Centered Strategy." *Forum* 3, iss. 1, article 4 (2005), http://www.bepress.com/forum/vol3/iss1/art4 (accessed August 16, 2011).

Bisnow, Mark. *Diary of a Dark Horse: The 1980 Anderson Presidential Campaign.* Carbondale: Southern Illinois University Press, 1983.

Blue, Frederick J. *The Free Soilers: Third Party Politics, 1848–54.* Urbana: University of Illinois Press, 1973.

Burns, Jennifer. "O Libertarian, Where Is Thy Sting?" *Journal of Policy History* 19, no. 4 (2007): 452–71.

Carter, Dan T. *The Politics of Rage: George Wallace, the Origins of the New Conservatism, and the Transformation of American Politics.* 2nd ed. Baton Rouge: Louisiana State University Press, 2000.

Chamberlain, Adam. "An Inside-Outsider or an Outside-Insider? The Republican Primary Campaign of Ron Paul from a Third-Party Perspective." *Politics and Policy* 38, no. 1 (2010): 97–116.

Cleaver, Kathleen, and George H. Katsiaficus, eds. *Liberation, Imagination, and the Black Panther Party: A New Look at the Panthers and Their Legacy.* New York: Routledge, 2001.

Clift, Eleanor. *Founding Sisters and the Nineteenth Amendment.* Hoboken, N.J.: John Wiley, 2003.

"Crashing the Parties." *Intelligence Report* 115 (Fall 2004): 26–28.

Davis, Angela. *Angela Davis—an Autobiography.* New York: Random House, 1974.

Doherty, Brian. *Radicals for Capitalism: A Freewheeling History of the Modern American Libertarian Movement.* New York: Public Affairs, 2007.

Duram, James C. *Norman Thomas.* New York: Twayne Publishers, 1974.

Earle, Jonathan H. *Jacksonian Antislavery and the Politics of Free Soil, 1824–1854.* Chapel Hill: University of North Carolina Press, 2004.

Flynt, Wayne. *Cracker Messiah: Governor Sidney J. Catts of Florida.* Baton Rouge: Louisiana State University Press, 1977.

Ford, Linda G. *Iron-Jawed Angels: The Suffrage Militancy of the National Woman's Party, 1912–1920.* Lanham, Md.: University Press of America, 1991.

Frederickson, Kari A. *The Dixiecrat Revolt and the End of the Solid South, 1932–1968.* Chapel Hill: University of North Carolina Press, 2001.

Gable, John Allen. *The Bull Moose Years.* Port Washington, N.Y.: Kennikat Press, 1978.

Gammon, C. L. *America's Other Party: A Brief History of the Prohibition Party.* N.p.: FEP International, 2007.

Gerson, Simon. *Pete: The Story of Peter V. Cacchione, New York's First Communist Councilman.* New York: International Publishers, 1976.

Gieske, Millard L. *Minnesota Farmer-Laborism: The Third-Party Alternative.* Minneapolis: University of Minnesota Press, 1979.

Gilmore, Glenda Elizabeth. *Defying Dixie: The Radical Roots of Civil Rights, 1919–1950.* New York: W. W. Norton, 2008.

Girard, Frank, and Ben Perry. *The Socialist Labor Party, 1876–1991: A Short History.* Philadelphia: Livra Books, 1991.

Gold, Howard J. "Explaining Third-Party Success in Gubernatorial Elections: The Cases of Alaska, Connecticut, Maine and Minnesota." *Social Science Journal* 42, no. 4 (2005): 523–40.

———. "Third Party Voting in Presidential Elections: A Study of Perot, Anderson, and Wallace." *Political Research Quarterly* 48, no. 4 (1995): 751–73.

Hawkins, Howie, ed. *Independent Politics: The Green Party Debate.* Chicago: Haymarket, 2006.

Jelen, Ted G., ed. *Ross for Boss: The Perot Phenomenon and Beyond.* Albany: SUNY Press, 2001.

Kazin, Michael. *A Godly Hero: The Life of William Jennings Bryan.* New York: Random House, 2006.

Klehr, Harvey, John Earl Haynes, and Fridrikh I. Firsov. *The Secret World of American Communism.* New Haven: Yale University Press, 1995.

Klehr, Harvey, John Earl Haynes, and Kyrill M. Anderson. *The Soviet World of American Communism.* New Haven: Yale University Press, 1998.

Leibowitz, Mark. "The Socialist Senator" [Bernard Sanders]. *New York Times,* January 21, 2007.

Lentz, Jacob. *Electing Jesse Ventura: A Third-Party Success Story.* Boulder, Colo.: Lynne Rienner, 2002.

Lesher, Stephan. *George Wallace: American Populist.* Reading, Mass.: Addison-Wesley, 1994.

Lipset, Seymour Martin, and Gary Marks. *It Didn't Happen Here: Why Socialism Failed in the United States.* New York: W. W. Norton, 2000.

Lunardini, Christine A. *From Equal Suffrage to Equal Rights: Alice Paul and the National Woman's Party, 1910–1928.* New York: New York University Press, 1986.

Mason, Jim. *No Holding Back: The 1980 John B. Anderson Presidential Campaign.* Lanham, Md.: University Press of America, 2011.

McCann, James A., Ronald B. Rapoport, and Walter J. Stone. "Heeding the Call: An Assessment of Mobilization into H. Ross Perot's 1992 Presidential Campaign." *American Journal of Political Science* 43, no. 1 (1999): 1–28.

McGaughey, William. *The Independence Party and the Future of Third-Party Politics.* Minneapolis: Thistlerose, 2003.

McMath, Robert C., Jr. *American Populism: A Social History, 1877–1898.* New York: Hill and Wang, 1993.

Meyer, Gerald. *Vito Marcantonio: Radical Politician, 1902–1954.* Albany: SUNY Press, 1989.

Nader, Ralph. *Crashing the Party: Taking on the Corporate Government in an Age of Surrender.* New York: Thomas Dunne / St. Martin's, 2002.

Navarro, Armando. *La Raza Unida Party: A Chicano Challenge to the U.S. Two-Party Dictatorship.* Philadelphia: Temple University Press, 2000.

Noble, Flower, and David Wagner. "Running as a Radical." *Journal of Progressive Human Resources* 15, no. 1 (2004): 1–24.

Pinchot, Amos R. E. *History of the Progressive Party, 1912–1916.* 2nd ed. Edited by Helene M. Hooker. Westport, Conn.: Greenwood Press, 1978.

Schmaltz, William H. *Hate: George Lincoln Rockwell and the American Nazi Party.* Washington, D.C.: Brassy's, 1999.

Simmons, Solon J., and James R. Simmons. "If Weren't for Those ?*!&*@! Nader Voters, We Wouldn't be in This Mess: The Social Determinants of the Nader Vote and the Constraints on Political Choice." *New Political Science* 28, no. 2 (2006): 229–44.

Spitzer, Robert J. *The Right to Life Movement and Third Party Politics.* New York: Greenwood Press, 1987.

Stock, Catherine McNicol. *Rural Radicals: Righteous Rage in the American Grain.* Ithaca, N.Y.: Cornell University Press, 1996.

Stone, Walter J., and Ronald B. Rapoport. "It's Perot Stupid! The Legacy of the 1992 Perot Movement in the Major-Party System, 1994–2000." *PS: Political Science and Politics* 34, no. 1 (2001): 49–58.

Storch, Randi. *Red Chicago: American Communism at Its Grassroots, 1928–35.* Urbana: University of Illinois Press, 2007.

Storms, Roger C. *Partisan Prophets: A History of the Prohibition Party, 1854–1972.* Denver: National Prohibition Foundation, 1972.

Tichenor, Daniel, and Daniel Fuerstman. "Insurgency Campaigns and the Quest for Popular Democracy: Theodore Roosevelt, Eugene McCarthy, and Party Monopolies." *Polity* 40, no. 1 (2008): 49–69.

Unger, Nancy C. *Fighting Bob La Follette: The Righteous Reformer.* Madison: Wisconsin Historical Society Press, 2008.

Vaughn, William P. *The Antimasonic Party in the United States, 1826–1843.* Lexington: University Press of Kentucky, 1983.

Ventura, Jesse, with Dick Russell. *Don't Start the Revolution without Me!: From the Minnesota Governor's Mansion to the Baja Outback: Reflections and Revisionings.* New York: Skyhorse, 2008.

White, Graham, and John Maze. *Henry A. Wallace: His Search for a New World Order.* Chapel Hill: University of North Carolina Press, 1995.

Woodward, C. Vann. *Tom Watson: Agrarian Radical.* New York: Oxford University Press, 1963.

Young, Marguerite. *Harp Song for a Radical: The Life and Times of Eugene Victor Debs.* New York: Knopf, 1999.

Index of Parties, Associations, and People

.

CPSIA information can be obtained at www.ICGtesting.com
Printed in the USA
LVOW080839160113

315633LV00007B/14/P

9 781611 170146